Nietzsche
on Morality

"This is a very impressive book, offering a distinctive and highly intelligent reading of Nietzsche's moral philosophy.... A real achievement."

Aaron Ridley, *University of Southampton*

"This work is simply the best, most sustained, book length exposition of Nietzsche's *Genealogy of Morality*. As such it will be the reference point for all further scholarly work on the subject."

Ken Gemes, *Birkbeck College, University of London*

Nietzsche is one of the most important and controversial thinkers in the history of philosophy. His writings on moral philosophy are amongst his most widely read works, both by philosophers and non-philosophers. Many of the ideas raised are both startling and disturbing and have been the source of great contention.

On the Genealogy of Morality is Nietzsche's most sustained and important contribution to moral philosophy, featuring many of the ideas for which he is best known: the slave revolt in morals, will to power, genealogy, perspectivism. The Routledge Philosophy GuideBook to *Nietzsche on Morality* introduces the reader to these and other important Nietzschean themes patiently and clearly. It is the first book to examine the work in such a way and will be a vital point of reference for any Nietzsche scholar.

The Routledge Philosophy GuideBook to *Nietzsche on Morality* will be vital for all students coming to Nietzsche for the first time.

Brian Leiter is Charles I. Francis Professor of Law and Philosophy at the University of Texas at Austin. He is the editor of *Objectivity in Law and Morals* (2001).

Routledge Philosophy GuideBooks

Edited by Tim Crane and Jonathan Wolff
University College London

Hegel and the Philosophy of Right   *Dudley Knowles*

Descartes and the Meditations   *Gary Hatfield*

Nietzsche on Morality   *Brian Leiter*

Hegel and the Phenomenology of Spirit   *Robert Stern*

Berkeley and the Principles of Human Knowledge
Robert J. Fogelin

Aristotle on Ethics   *Gerard J. Hughes*

Hume on Religion   *David O'Connor*

Leibniz and the Monadology   *Anthony Savile*

The Later Heidegger   *George Pattison*

Hegel on History   *Joseph McCarney*

Hume on Morality   *James Baillie*

Hume on Knowledge   *Harold Noonan*

Kant and the Critique of Pure Reason   *Sebastian Gardner*

Mill on Liberty   *Jonathan Riley*

Mill on Utilitarianism   *Roger Crisp*

Wittgenstein and the Philosophical Investigations
Marie McGinn

Spinoza and the Ethics   *Genevieve Lloyd*

Heidegger on Being and Time   *Stephen Mulhall*

Locke on Government   *D. A. Lloyd Thomas*

Locke on Human Understanding   *E. J. Lowe*

Plato and the Republic   *Nickolas Pappas*

LONDON AND NEW YORK

Routledge Philosophy GuideBook to

Nietzsche
on Morality

■ Brian Leiter

First published 2002
by Routledge
11 New Fetter Lane,
London EC4P 4EE

Simultaneously published in
the USA and Canada
by Routledge
29 West 35th Street,
New York, NY 10001

*Routledge is an imprint of
the Taylor & Francis Group*

© 2002 Brian Leiter

Typeset in Times by Florence
Production Ltd, Stoodleigh, Devon
Printed and bound in Great Britain
by Biddles Ltd, Guildford and
King's Lynn

*British Library Cataloguing in
Publication Data*
A catalogue record for this book is
available from the British Library

*Library of Congress Cataloging
in Publication Data*
A catalog record for this book has been
requested

ISBN 0–415–15284–4 (hbk)
ISBN 0–415–15285–2 (pbk)

*For Sheila and our beautiful children,
Sam, William, and Celia*

Contents

Preface and acknowledgments   xi
Abbreviations   xxi

1   Introduction: Nietzsche, naturalist or postmodernist?   1

What is naturalism?   3
What kind of naturalist is Nietzsche?   6
How *could* Nietzsche be a naturalist?   11
Nietzsche's project: the revaluation of values   26

2   Intellectual history and background   31

Classical philology   35
The Presocratics and the Sophists   39
Schopenhauer   53
German Materialism   63
Summary   71

3 Nietzsche's critique of morality I: the scope of the critique and the critique of moral agency   73

The scope problem   74
"Morality" as the object of Nietzsche's critique:
   a formal account   78
The Descriptive Component of MPS   80
The critique of the Descriptive Component: fatalism
   and agency   81
The critique of free will   87
Transparency of the self   101
Universality and similarity   104

4 Nietzsche's critique of morality II: the critique of moral norms   113

"Higher men"   115
Higher men and the critique of MPS: objections   125
The normative content of MPS and the causal mechanism
   of harm   127
Metaethics: realism about value?   136
Metaethics: anti-realism about value   146
Two final puzzles   156
Conclusion   161

5 What is "genealogy" and what is the *Genealogy*?   165

The principles and method of "genealogy"   166
"Genealogy" and critique   173
What is the *Genealogy*?   180
The unity of the *Genealogy*   181

6   A commentary on the First Essay   193

Explaining historical blindness	195
Ressentiment	202
Beyond good and evil	206
The triumph of slave morality	217

7   A commentary on the Second Essay   223

The morality of custom and the origin of conscience (1–3)	226
Bad conscience: debt and guilt (4–8)	229
Bad conscience: internalized cruelty (16–18)	232
The moralization of conscience through religion (19–22)	235
Bad conscience and the ascetic ideal (23–5)	242

8   A commentary on the Third Essay   245

Artists, philosophers, and the will to power	248
Priests, humanity, *ressentiment*, and the ascetic ideal	254
Truth, science, and perspectivism	264
Two final puzzles about the Third Essay	279
Unifying the three essays	283

9   Nietzsche since 1900: critical questions   289

Bibliography	305
Index	315

Preface and acknowledgments

Studies of Nietzsche proliferate. How can one justify yet another? What does this one add to the voluminous literature on Nietzsche? I offer the reader three rationales for the text that follows.

1 While there are now several English-language books that are devoted, in whole or in part, to Nietzsche's *On the Genealogy of Morality*, none are entirely satisfactory, from either a pedagogical or scholarly point of view.[1] I hope this book will fill the role of a student-friendly companion to the *Genealogy* that is, at the same time, attentive to the arguments and problems that interest serious philosophers. To that end, one

---

[1] I have found Ridley (1998) and May (1999) the most useful, and engage at various points with their interpretations. Stegmaier (1994) is the major German commentary on the book, though like much of the German secondary literature it does not probe deeply into philosophical and interpretive difficulties; it is more useful on various philological points, many of which have also now been addressed in English by Thatcher (1989) and the Clark and Swensen edition of the *Genealogy*.

premise of this volume is that it is impossible to read the *Genealogy* in isolation from Nietzsche's other works, which provide both the context for and development of the *Genealogy*'s main themes. Thus, this study is not only about the *Genealogy*, but also Nietzsche's *moral philosophy* as a whole – in particular, the project he calls the 'revaluation of all values.' The *Genealogy* stands, in turn, as one of the most important texts in the mature Nietzsche's revaluative project.

Now there are, of course, many books about his ethics, boasting titles like "Nietzsche's Moral Philosophy" or "The Ethics of an Immoralist." Yet the existing studies of Nietzsche's ethics are largely unsound – usually in their philosophy, often in their scholarship. While important book-length contributions have been made on specialized issues within Nietzsche's ethics (e.g., Hunt 1991), my aim here is to provide what has heretofore been unavailable: namely, a book-length overview of Nietzsche's ethics that will be of use not only to Nietzsche students and scholars, but also to moral philosophers, who have shown increasing levels of interest in Nietzsche in recent years (see Leiter 1997).

2   The Nietzsche literature may be voluminous, but as students of philosophy know, most of it has not been very good – certainly not when compared to the best recent work on the other major German figures like Kant or Marx. Commentators, it seems, do not hesitate to write on Nietzsche's "philosophy of science" without any understanding of philosophy of science or Nietzsche's "moral philosophy" without any understanding of philosophical ethics. Many seem to regard clarity and coherent argument as vices. The situation has begun to improve, happily, in the last decade. Philosophically substantial and textually scrupulous studies by scholars like Maudemarie Clark (1990) and John Richardson (1996) set new standards in Nietzsche studies – for scholarship, philosophical argumentation, and (importantly) clarity. Another goal of this book, then, is to synthesize, utilize and, in some cases, criticize selected major themes of the best recent literature on Nietzsche. In this sense, the study aims to give the reader a sense of the "state of the art" of Nietzsche scholarship. I also hope it will encourage more interchange between the competing views of Nietzsche scholars than has been typical in the secondary literature.

3   A final rationale for this study – though surely the least important of
the three – is that while many books have been published on Nietzsche
in recent years, relatively few have appeared that bring to bear the
tools of so-called "analytic" philosophy (though there are some; e.g.,
Clark 1990, Hunt 1991, Poellner 1995, Richardson 1996). Unfortunately, the most famous work of this genre (Danto 1965) also gave the
genre a bad name, both because of the author's condescending attitude
towards his subject and because of the sloppy scholarship that Walter
Kaufmann and others have long since exposed.

Yet the vices of Danto's particular book should not obscure the
virtues of the general approach. The Nietzsche presented here does,
indeed, aspire to speak clear, precise, "analytical" philosophical
English. This is neither because I think Nietzsche is really a "closet"
analytic philosopher – happily, he is not – nor because analytic philosophy is more "advanced" than Nietzsche (which, in several respects,
it plainly is, but which is beside the point here). Rather, the virtues of
good analytic philosophy – clarity, precision, concern for evidence,
dialectical rigor – are simply the *ideal* scholarly virtues, virtues that
any commentary must exhibit. (To the extent anything defines analytic
philosophy today, it is nothing more than these stylistic characteristics.) If we are to *understand* Nietzsche, then we must be able to
articulate his views in terms that amount to more than *paraphrase* (the
bane of the Nietzsche literature). Analytic philosophy, as it developed
during the twentieth century, gave us an enormous repertoire of finely
tuned philosophical categories and arguments for thinking about ethics,
epistemology, metaphysics – in short, all the issues that engaged
Nietzsche. It is simply irresponsible for commentary not to avail itself
of the philosophical resources that enable Nietzsche *to speak to us*.
Those who find that Nietzsche speaks to them already obviously have
no need for commentary.

Nietzsche – certainly more than many of his self-styled succes-
sors – would have well-appreciated the scholarly practice outlined
above. "School," says Nietzsche, "has no more important task than to
teach rigorous thinking, cautious judgment and consistent reasoning,"
and he cautions us against losing "the scientific sense which [is] owed
to the Greeks" (HAH: 265). Recall, too, that Nietzsche, for all his
hostility to Platonism and Plato, still speaks admiringly of the "Platonic

dialogue" in which "souls were filled with drunkenness at the rigorous and sober game of concept, generalisation, refutation, limitation" and contrasts it, derisively, with "how philosophy is done today" in which philosophers "want to be 'artistic natures'" and enjoy "the divine privilege of being incomprehensible" (D: 544). And while no one has written more perceptively than Nietzsche on the limitations of the professional scholar – of "his zeal, his seriousness, his fury, his over-estimation of the nook in which he sits and spins, his hunched back" (GS: 366, cf. U III: 6, BGE: 45, EH II: 8) – it is still Nietzsche who says:

> my scholarly friends, I bless you even for your hunched backs. And for despising, as I do, the "men of letters" and culture para-sites. . . . And for having opinions that cannot be translated into financial values. . . . And because your sole aim is to become masters of your craft, with reverence for every kind of mastery and competence, and with uncompromising opposition to every-thing that is semblance, half-genuine, dressed up, virtuosolike, demagogical, or histrionic in *litteris et artibus* – to everything that cannot prove to you its unconditional *probity* in discipline and prior training.
>
> (GS: 366)

The Nietzsche who was trained in the "*science*" of classical philology (see Chapter 2) and who had himself praised and *practiced* disciplined and rigorous textual scholarship (cf. Barnes 1986) would surely have been appalled at much that has been written about him. Certainly the many scholars who take their philosophical and interpretive cues from Derrida and Heidegger would do well to recall Nietzsche's pertinent quip: "Those who know that they are profound strive for clarity. Those who would like to seem profound strive for obscurity" (GS: 173). I do not know that what this book has to say about Nietzsche will prove profound, but I do hope it will be clear.

It has, of course, become fashionable lately to emphasize that Nietzsche's "style" is inseparable from his content and to claim that this "truism" (as I shall call it) somehow dictates against the "ana-lytical" – I would say simply "philosophical" – style of exposition employed here. Now while Nietzsche is arguably the greatest German prose stylist of the nineteenth century, it is not readily apparent what moral is to be drawn from this fact about how *commentary* on his work should be written. (Scholars writing on Yeats do not write poetry, after all; they write scholarly commentary in prose.) Obviously, any interpretation that ignored the truism would be a poor interpretation. Yet there is no principled reason why one cannot, as a commentator, state with excruciating clarity and precision what an author means, even as one determines that meaning by considering both *what* he says and *how* he says it. This may include stating clearly that what the author means is not always reducible to discursive form. But the "ineffable" element in Nietzsche has been greatly exaggerated, while the intelligible, if sometimes unfamiliar, philosophical content has been too often ignored. I will have a number of things to say about Nietzsche's *style* in the *Genealogy*, but none of them have any bearing on the style in which this commentary is written.

Thus my rationales for this volume: to provide the student a "companion" to one of Nietzsche's most important mature texts; to provide the student, the scholar and the moral philosopher with a serviceable overview of Nietzsche's moral philosophy as a whole; to give some sense of the accomplishments and claims of recent, high-quality secondary literature; and to contribute to the development of argumentatively rigorous Nietzsche studies.

Because this text is first and foremost a companion for the English-speaking student reading Nietzsche, it seemed important to settle on a single, competent, and widely available translation of the main text. Three good editions, with different virtues, are currently in wide use: one by Kaufmann (from Viking); one by Diethe (from Cambridge); and one by Clark and Swensen (from Hackett). The translations by Diethe and Clark and Swensen are more literal (and often more philosophically sensitive) than that by Kaufmann (including, importantly, in their rendering of the title, to which I return in Chapter 5), though Kaufmann often has a brilliant ear for how to capture Nietzsche's German in English. The Clark and Swensen translation is also notable for bringing sound philosophical judgment to bear on questions of translation, and thus is probably to be preferred over the others. Their edition also has invaluable critical apparatus for the scholar. I particularly commend it to students for its detailed explanations of Nietzsche's many historical and literary allusions. (Indeed, in my own commentaries on the three essays, in Chapters 6, 7 and 8, I do *not* discuss every specific historical and literary allusion Nietzsche makes; I refer the student to the Clark and Swensen or Diethe editions (with useful, if less elaborate notes by Raymond Geuss) for help with these references.)

Unfortunately, a purely practical consideration intervened in the final decision about which edition to work from. For the fact is that the Cambridge edition is more widely and reliably available throughout the English-speaking world. In addition, it does contain some useful notes and supplementary texts, though the volume's introduction cannot be recommended. Because of its wide availability, I generally start with the Diethe translation (with some emendations), though where issues of translation seem especially important, I address them in the text or footnotes.

For Nietzsche's other texts, I begin, where possible, with the widely available editions by Kaufmann (sometimes Kaufmann *and* Hollingdale), except for *Daybreak* and *Human, All-too-Human*, where I start with the Hollingdale editions. Where necessary, I make emendations to these translations relying on the standard Colli and Montinari edition of the collected works. Translations from all other material are my own, unless otherwise noted. A guide to citation format is contained in the abbreviations and the relevant bibliographical information can be found in the bibliography at the end of this book.

A special word about the text known as *The Will to Power*, and the *Nachlass* more generally, is required. At the time of his mental collapse in early 1889, Nietzsche left behind several volumes worth of unpublished notes. Some of these were compiled by others in to a book first published in 1906 as *The Will to Power*; many more notes (the *Nachlass*) only appeared in the various later editions of Nietzsche's collected works, though few of these have been translated into English at the date of this writing. Some secondary works – both good ones (like Schacht 1983, Poellner 1995, Richardson 1996) and more problematic ones (like Heidegger 1961, Nehamas 1985) – rely extensively (at points exclusively) on this material. Serious doubts have been raised about such an interpretive methodology, doubts which are worth reviewing briefly at the beginning of this study.[2]

For one thing, it has been conclusively established that Nietzsche had abandoned the project of writing a book called *The Will to Power*, so that by compiling such a book after his collapse, the editors were clearly contravening "Nietzsche's literary intentions" (Montinari 1982: p. 104). Moreover, we also now know that Nietzsche wanted his notebooks destroyed after his death, and that it was only the intervention of others (again, against Nietzsche's wishes) that saved this material for posterity (Hollingdale 1985: 166–72, 182–6). Finally, it is a striking fact about the *Nachlass* material (including much of that incorporated into *The Will to Power*) that it contains some of Nietzsche's *philosophically weakest* and sometimes *silliest* claims – for example, his attempts to provide a "scientific" proof for the doctrine of eternal recurrence (WP: 1066); to construct a "physiological" theory of value (WP: 392, 462); and to "prove" that power is the ultimate criterion of value (WP: 674, 710; cf. Leiter 2000) – which find no analogue in the published works. Given that, in general, Nietzsche culled the books he chose to publish from his notebooks; given that he clearly chose *not* to publish much of the material that now survives in *The Will to Power* and the *Nachlass*; and given that he wanted the remaining notebook material destroyed – surely a plausible explanation for all these facts is precisely that Nietzsche recognized that a lot this material was of dubious merit. Presumably, then, he would have been surprised to find it at the center of so much contemporary scholarship.

Yet notwithstanding the foregoing, it still remains undeniable that there are striking continuities between *some* themes and arguments in the published works and those in the *Nachlass*. It does not seem advisable, then, to *completely* ignore the notebook material (as, e.g., Clark 1990 does), given that it sometimes serves to deepen our understanding of the works Nietzsche chose to publish, including the

---

[2]   For an overview, see Magnus (1988). Magnus, however, appears to misunderstand the philosophical impact of eliminating the *Nachlass*. Without the *Nachlass*, it seems to me quite impossible to support the postmodernist and deconstructionist readings of Nietzsche, to which Magnus is sympathetic.

Genealogy. No interpretive claim is advanced in this work that cannot be sustained on the basis of the works Nietzsche published. But some of these claims receive further support or clarification from *Nachlass* material, which I draw on accordingly.

To students reading this book in conjunction with the *Genealogy*, I recommend you use it as follows. Start by reading the first four chapters, and then read the fifth chapter in conjunction with the Preface to the *Genealogy*. The first four chapters of this book will give you crucial orientation for what is to come in the *Genealogy*, while the fifth chapter discusses some of the general methodological issues about what Nietzsche is up to in the *Genealogy*. After you read each essay of the *Genealogy*, I suggest you read the corresponding chapter of this book commenting on it. You may also read Chapters 6–8 independently of 1–5, though some cross-references to ideas from the earlier chapters may prove difficult; I have tried to create an index that would permit the student pressed for time to simply turn to the core chapters on the *Genealogy* and yet still find necessary references from earlier chapters. When you are all done, you may read the final chapter of this book.

I have incorporated, usually in substantially reworked form, portions of a number of my earlier articles, as follows. I am grateful to the publishers for permission to reuse the material:

    Portions of "Beyond Good and Evil," *History of Philosophy Quarterly* 10 (1993): 261–70, are incorporated into Chapter 6. Reproduced by kind permission of the University of Illinois Press.

    Portions of "Perspectivism in Nietzsche's *Genealogy of Morals*," in Richard Schacht (ed.), *Nietzsche, Genealogy, Morality* (Berkeley: University of California Press, 1994) are incorporated into Chapter 8.

    Much of "Morality in the Pejorative Sense: On the Logic of Nietzsche's Critique of Morality," *British Journal for the History of Philosophy* 3 (1995): 113–45, is incorporated into Chapters 3 and 4. © Routledge.

    Portions of "Nietzsche and the Morality Critics," *Ethics* 107 (1997): 250–85, are incorporated into Chapters 4 and 9.

"One Health, One Earth, One Sun: Nietzsche's Respect for Natural Science," *Times Literary Supplement* (October 2, 1998): 30–1, is incorporated into Chapter 1.

Much of "The Paradox of Fatalism and Self-Creation in Nietzsche," in Christopher Janaway (ed.), *Willing and Nothingness: Schopenhauer as Nietzsche's Educator* (Oxford: Clarendon Press, 1998) is incorporated into Chapters 2 and 3.

Portions of "Nietzsche's Metaethics: Against the Privilege Readings," *European Journal of Philosophy* 8 (2000): 277–97 are incorporated into Chapter 4. © Blackwell Publishing.

Some of the ideas and arguments in this book were first broached in my doctoral thesis. For his invaluable and constructive guidance on that project, I am most grateful to Peter Railton. My Deans and colleagues in the School of Law at the University of Texas at Austin have been wonderfully supportive of my philosophical work; I am especially appreciative of Dean William Powers' generous support of my work and of philosophy in the Law School. I have learned much from the many talented graduate students in the Department of Philosophy that we have been fortunate to attract to Austin with interests in Nietzsche. I am especially grateful to the group that read through and discussed almost the entire manuscript with me during 2000–1: Jessica Berry, John Bowin, Jeffrey W. Davis, Matt Evans, Joel Mann, Iain Morrison, and Ariela Tubert; I learned from them all, though I would be remiss if I did not single out two quite advanced students, Jessica and Matt, who saved me from many errors. The book improved as a result of the opportunity to teach a seminar on Nietzsche and Freud with Ken Gemes at Yale in the Spring of 1999, as well as from the opportunity to try out my interpretation in several seminars in Austin.

For comments on some or all of the manuscript, or helpful discussion, I am grateful to Ken Gemes, Christopher Janaway, Joshua Knobe, Maurice Leiter, Richard Posner, John Richardson, Mathias Risse, Neil Sinhababu, James Q. Whitman, Allen Wood, and Paul Woodruff. Maurice Leiter, in particular, greatly improved the clarity and readability of the manuscript. Thanks also to Thomas Brobjer for sharing with me the fruits of his exhaustive work in Nietzsche's library, and for correcting a number of factual errors in the early chapters.

My friend and occasional co-author, the distinguished philosopher of language Alex Miller, kindly organized a conference on the book manuscript at Cardiff University in Wales in November 2000. I am very grateful to Alex for this opportunity and to my commentators on that occasion – Maudemarie Clark, Sebastian Gardner, Peter Poellner, Peter Sedgwick, and Alessandra Tannesini – for making it so worthwhile.

Comments by the Routledge referees on the penultimate draft enabled me to make many valuable final edits to the manuscript. Since these referees all generously disclosed their identity, I am pleased to be able to acknowledge them by name: Maudemarie Clark, Ken Gemes, Peter Poellner, and Aaron Ridley. I am especially indebted to Clark not only for the stimulus of her work and collegiality over the last decade, but also for her detailed comments on Chapters 6–8.

I received useful research assistance on certain points in Chapter 1 from Chad McCracken. Jonathan Pratter of the Tarlton Law Library provided, as always, excellent research support throughout.

I have been occupied with Nietzsche almost continually since first reading him (ironically enough) on Easter Sunday in 1982. I hope this book will help the reader relatively new to Nietzsche share the delight in his genius that has sustained my own interest for the last two decades.

B. L.
Austin
December 17, 2001

Abbreviations

The following abbreviations are used for references to works by Nietzsche. For full details of works cited, and methods of citation, see the bibliography at the end of the volume.

Nietzsche's works are cited as follows: roman numerals refer to major parts or chapters in Nietzsche's works; arabic numerals refer to sections, not pages. The exceptions to this are KSA, PN, and PT where the page numbers are given. *Ecce Homo* contains chapters dealing with some of the other works. Where these are cited, the abbreviation for the work under discussion is given after the colon, e.g., EH III: Z-1.

A	*The Antichrist*, in *The Portable Nietzsche*
BGE	*Beyond Good and Evil*
BT	*The Birth of Tragedy*
CW	*The Case of Wagner*
D	*Daybreak: Thoughts on the Prejudices of Morality*
EH	*Ecce Homo*

GM	*On the Genealogy of Morality*
GS	*The Gay Science*
HAH	*Human, All-too-Human*
KSA	*Sämtliche Werke: Kritische Studienausgabe in 15 Bänden*
NCW	*Nietzsche contra Wagner*, in *The Portable Nietzsche*
PN	*The Portable Nietzsche*
PT	*Philosophy and Truth: Selections from Nietzsche's Notebooks of the Early 1870s*
PTAG	*Philosophy in the Tragic Age of the Greeks*
TI	*Twilight of the Idols*, in *The Portable Nietzsche*
U	*Untimely Meditations*
WP	*The Will to Power*
Z	*Thus Spoke Zarathustra*, in *The Portable Nietzsche*

Chapter 1

Introduction

Nietzsche, naturalist
or postmodernist?

A familiar, yet still curious, feature of Nietzsche's reception over the last century is that figures with radically divergent views and methodologies all claim the mantle of his influence. Thinkers on the political "right" find him attractive for his elitism and anti-egalitarianism; those on the "left" embrace him for his hatred of all the pillars of bourgeois civilization: religion, industrial capitalism, the state. Intellectual movements as diverse as literary modernism, deconstruction in literary theory, psychoanalysis, existentialism, relativism, late nineteenth- and early twentieth-century evolutionary naturalism, and pragmatism have all claimed Nietzsche as their own. Writers as different as the German sociologist Max Weber, the French deconstructionist Jacques Derrida, the British moral philosopher Bernard Williams, and the American pragmatist Richard Rorty have all felt the need to situate their thought with respect to its debt to Nietzsche.

Perhaps the most oddly matched pair of professed Nietzschean "disciples" are the founder of

psychoanalysis, Sigmund Freud (1856–1939), and the "postmodern" philosopher and historian Michel Foucault (1926–84). Freud famously remarked that Nietzsche "had a more penetrating knowledge of himself than any man who ever lived or was ever likely to live" (Jones 1955: 344) and claimed to have stopped reading Nietzsche's work for fear that Nietzsche had anticipated too many of his own ideas about human nature and the role of unconscious forces (Freud 1957, vol. 14: 15–16; Gay 1988: 46).[1] Foucault proclaims that, "Nietzsche marks the threshold beyond which contemporary philosophy can begin thinking again; and he will no doubt continue for a long while to dominate its advance" (1966: 342). He situates his own "genealogies" of psychiatry, the prison, and sexuality in a Nietzschean tradition, a tradition which allegedly teaches that "behind things" there is "not a timeless secret, but the secret that they have no essence or that their essence was fabricated in a piecemeal fashion from alien forms" (Foucault 1971: 78). In doing genealogy, "one finds not the fixed meaning of a text, or of the world, but only other interpretations ... inherent[ly] arbitrar[y]" interpretations (Dreyfus and Rabinow 1983: 107). While for Freud, Nietzsche is the philosopher who anticipates psychoanalysis by trying to discover the *deep, hidden* facts about human nature which explain who we are and what we believe, for Foucault, Nietzsche is precisely the philosopher who denies that there are any "deep facts" about human nature and who recognizes that all such putative facts are *mere* interpretations, mere contingent constructs.

So who can justifiably claim to be heir to Nietzsche's philosophy, Freud "the naturalist" or Foucault "the postmodernist"? Since the 1960s, the "postmodern" reading of Nietzsche has been dominant, helped along by both its "French" proponents, and even certain Anglophone commentators.[2] This book joins cause with some recent literature[3] in arguing that, rightly understood, Nietzsche belongs not in the company of postmodernists like Foucault and Derrida, but rather in the company of naturalists like Hume and Freud – that is, among,

[1]   See Anderson (1980) for documentation of Freud's familiarity with Nietzsche, especially pp. 16–18.

[2]   See, e.g., Danto (1965), Nehamas (1985), and Rorty (1989).

[3]   See, e.g., Schacht (1983), Gemes (1992), Leiter (1992, 1994, 1998a), Beam (1996), Clark and Leiter (1997), and Clark (1998a, b).

broadly speaking, *philosophers of human nature*. The *Genealogy*, in turn, is Nietzsche's most systematic attempt to give a *naturalized* account of the phenomenon of morality. Such an account is not, ultimately, presented by Nietzsche as an end-in-itself. Rather, Nietzsche develops a naturalistic account of morality in the service of a very particular *normative* goal, namely, to force us to reconsider the *value* of morality: naturalism is enlisted in the service of what Nietzsche calls his "revaluation of all values."

What is naturalism?

What does it mean for a philosopher to be a "naturalist"?[4] We may start by distinguishing between two basic naturalistic doctrines: *methodological* (or M-Naturalism) and *substantive* (S-Naturalism).[5] Naturalism in philosophy is, typically, in the first instance, a *methodological* view about how one should do philosophy: philosophical inquiry, on this view, should be continuous with empirical inquiry in the sciences.[6] Some M-Naturalists (especially contemporary ones) want "continuity with" only the *hard* or *physical* sciences (Hard M-Naturalists); others seek "continuity with" any successful science, natural or social (Soft M-Naturalists). Soft M-Naturalism, as we shall see, is the dominant strand in philosophy.

What does "continuity with" the sciences mean? One view it certainly encompasses is the repudiation (associated, most famously, with Quine (1961, 1969)) of a "first philosophy," a philosophical solution to problems that proceeds entirely a priori, that is, prior to any experience or empirical evidence. But M-Naturalism requires continuity with the sciences in a more precise sense than this. We may introduce a further distinction, then, between "Results Continuity" and "Methods Continuity."

---

4   For a detailed discussion, see Leiter (1998b).
5   Cf. Railton (1990) for one version of this distinction.
6   Although philosophers have never solved the so-called "demarcation problem" – the problem of what precisely demarcates genuine science from pseudo-science – this fact does not undermine M-Naturalism, as long as there are enough *clear* cases of science on which to draw for methodological guidance.

The Results Continuity branch of M-Naturalism requires that philosophical theories – e.g., theories of morality or of knowledge – be supported or justified by the results of the sciences: philosophical theories that do not enjoy the support of our best science are simply *bad* theories. "Methods Continuity," by contrast, demands only that philosophical theories emulate the "methods" of inquiry of successful sciences. "Methods" should be construed broadly here to encompass not only, say, the experimental method (e.g., the method of testing progressively refined claims against experience), but also the styles of explanation and understanding employed in the sciences.[7]

Historically, M-Naturalism has constituted the most important type of naturalism in philosophy. Spinoza – whom Nietzsche greatly admired – gives expression to both types of M-Naturalism when he writes in the Preface to Part III of the *Ethics* as follows:

> [N]ature is always the same, and its virtue and power of acting are everywhere the same, i.e., the laws and rules of nature, according to which all things happen, and change from one form to another, are always and everywhere the same. So the way of understanding the nature of anything, of whatever kind, must also be the same, viz. through the universal laws and rules of nature.

Philosophical understanding, in short, must be the same as scientific understanding: it must employ the same methods of understanding that the sciences deploy with good effect elsewhere, and it must heed the *result* of the sciences that nature is "everywhere the same."

Unlike the M-Naturalists who draw on the actual *results* of established sciences, many M-Naturalists drawn to Methods Continuity simply try to *emulate* a scientific way of understanding the world in developing their philosophical theories. We might call these M-Naturalists, accordingly, "Speculative M-Naturalists." Hume, for example, constructs a "speculative" theory of human nature – modeled on the most influential scientific paradigm of the day (Newtonian

---

[7] Note that such a view does not presuppose the methodological *unity* of the various sciences – i.e., that all sciences employ the same methods – only that successful sciences have some methodological *uniqueness*, i.e., there are distinctive scientific methods, even if those methods differ across the sciences.

mechanics) – in order to *explain* various human phenomena, like morality. The speculative theories of M-Naturalists are "modeled" on the sciences most importantly in that they take over from science the idea that natural phenomena have deterministic causes. One commentator has aptly observed that Hume, like Freud and Marx (and, one might have added, Nietzsche), puts "forward a general theory of human nature" in order to "provide a basis for explaining *everything* in human affairs. And the theories they advance are all, roughly, deterministic" (Stroud 1977: 4). Just as we often understand events in the inanimate world by identifying the natural causes that determined them, so, too, we understand human beliefs, values, and actions by locating their causal determinants in various features of human nature.

M-Naturalists, then, construct philosophical theories that are continuous with the sciences either in virtue of their dependence upon the actual results of scientific method in different domains or in virtue of their employment and emulation of distinctively scientific ways of looking at and explaining things.[8]

Many naturalists go beyond methodological naturalism, however, and embrace a *substantive* doctrine. S-Naturalism in philosophy is either the (ontological) view that the only things that exist are *natural* (or perhaps simply *physical*) things; or the (semantic) view that a suitable philosophical analysis of any concept must show it to be amenable to empirical inquiry. In the ontological sense, S-Naturalism historically involved opposition to "supernaturalism," to "the invocation of an agent or force which somehow stands outside the familiar natural world and so whose doings cannot be understood as part of it" (Stroud 1996: 44). Historical S-Naturalists (including both Hume and Nietzsche) reject, in particular, any explanatory role for God in an account of the world. Contemporary S-Naturalists, however, go well beyond opposition to supernaturalism and advance the more radical view

---

[8] One possibility, then, is that Foucault himself is an M-Naturalist, just the kind of M-Naturalist who thinks that "human nature" does no useful explanatory work; Nietzsche, by contrast, is just the M-Naturalist who thinks facts about "human nature" do explain things. It is not clear to me that this is how Foucault understood himself, but it is a possible interpretation of what was earlier called his postmodern skepticism about human nature. (I am indebted to instructive comments from Huw Price on this point.)

known as physicalism, the doctrine that only those properties picked out by the laws of the physical sciences are real.[9] There is no evidence that Nietzsche is at all sympathetic to this latter kind of S-Naturalism.

Many philosophers are drawn to some type of S-Naturalism in virtue of their M-Naturalism: being a philosophical naturalist in the methodological sense sometimes leads a philosopher to think that the best philosophical account of some concept or domain will be in terms that are substantively naturalistic (see Railton 1990). But it is important to notice that a commitment to M-Naturalism does *not* entail this conclusion: methodologically, it is an open question whether the best philosophical account of morality or mind or knowledge must be in substantively naturalistic terms.

What kind of naturalist is Nietzsche?

Like most of the great philosophical naturalists, Nietzsche's naturalism is fundamentally *methodological*.[10] Its central themes are sounded in a famous passage from *Beyond Good and Evil*, the major work preceding the *Genealogy*:

> To translate man back into nature; to become master over the many vain and overly enthusiastic interpretations and connotations that have so far been scrawled and painted over the eternal basic text [*ewigen Grundtext*] of *homo natura*; to see to it that man henceforth stands before man as even today, hardened in the discipline of science, he stands before the *rest* of nature, with

---

9   In the semantic sense, by contrast, S-Naturalism is just the view that predicates like "morally good" can be analyzed in terms of characteristics (e.g.,"maximizing human well-being") that admit of empirical inquiry (e.g., by psychology and physiology, assuming that well-being is a complex psycho-physical state).

10   The point here concerns Nietzsche's actual philosophical practice, i.e., what he spends most of his time doing in his books. But it is worth keeping in mind that Nietzsche himself actually reserves the label "philosopher" ("genuine philosophers" he calls them in BGE: 211) for those who discharge a different kind of task than that of the naturalist: namely, those who create or legislate values. In this particular usage, "philosopher" is something of an honorific for Nietzsche. We shall return to some of these issues in the following chapters.

intrepid Oedipus eyes and sealed Odysseus ears, deaf to the siren songs of old metaphysical bird catchers who have been piping at him all too long, "you are more, you are higher, you are of a different origin!" – that may be a strange and insane task, but it is a *task* – who would deny that? Why did we choose this insane task? Or, putting it differently: "why have knowledge at all?"

(BGE: 230, cf. GS: 109)

Several things about this passage are striking. First, notice that Nietzsche here calls for man to stand "hardened in the discipline [*Zucht*] of science," rather than, say, "schooled in particular substantive scientific doctrines." This is in keeping with a recurring (M-Naturalist) theme in his mature work, namely that what is important about science is scientific *method*, rather than particular scientific theories: "[S]cientific *methods* . . . one must say it ten times, *are* what is essential, also what is most difficult, also what is for the longest time opposed by habits and laziness" (A: 59). "[T]he most valuable insights are the *methods*," he says (A: 13), adding in a note of 1888 that, "It is not the victory of science that distinguishes our nineteenth century, but the victory of scientific method over science" (WP: 466).

At the same time, Nietzsche's clarion call for a methodological continuity with science also involves a certain type of Results Continuity, namely, continuity with the "result" foremost in the mind of mid-nineteenth-century Germans: that man is not of a "higher . . . [or] of a different origin" than the rest of nature. This is a view shared not only by Nietzsche, Spinoza, and Freud – as well as by contemporary naturalists like Daniel Dennett and Ruth Garrett Millikan (see Dennett 1984) – but by many of Nietzsche's contemporaries (see Chapter 2). For example, the famous nineteenth-century German Materialist, Ludwig Büchner, wrote that "the researches and discoveries of modern times can no longer allow us to doubt that man, with all he has and possesses, be it mental or corporeal, is a *natural product* like all other organic beings" (1870: lxxviii); or similarly: "Man is a product of nature in body and mind. Hence not merely what he is, but also what he does, wills, feels, and thinks, depends upon the same natural necessity as the whole structure of the world" (1870: 239).

So Nietzsche, the philosophical naturalist, aims to offer theories that explain various important human phenomena (especially the phenomenon of morality), and that do so in ways that both draw on actual scientific results, particularly in physiology (see Chapter 2), but are also *modeled* on science in the sense that they seek to reveal the causal determinants of these phenomena, typically in various physiological and psychological facts about persons. More elaborately, we will see that Nietzsche embraces a view that we may call the "Doctrine of Types" (Leiter 1998a), according to which:

Each person has a fixed psycho-physical constitution, which defines him as a particular *type* of person.

We may call the relevant psycho-physical facts "type-facts." It is type-facts, in turn, that figure in the explanation of human actions and beliefs (including beliefs about morality). One of Nietzsche's central undertakings, then, is to specify the type-facts – the psychological and physiological facts – that explain how and why an essentially ascetic or "life-denying" morality should have taken hold among so many people over the past two millennia.

One particularly famous type-fact is of central importance for Nietzsche: what he calls "will to power." Its central explanatory role is articulated in the *Genealogy* as follows:

Every animal . . . instinctively [*instinktiv*] strives for an optimum of favourable conditions in which fully to release his power [or strength; *Kraft*] and achieve his maximum feeling of power; every animal abhors equally instinctively, with an acute sense of smell "higher than all reason," any kind of disturbance and hindrance which blocks or could block his path to the optimum.
(GM III: 7)

If it is a natural fact about creatures like us that we "instinctively" maximize our strength or power, then this fact, together with other type-facts and facts about circumstances, must figure in any explanation of what we do and believe. So, for example, those who are essentially weak or impotent (e.g., the slaves of GM I) express their will to power by *creating* values that are favorable to their interests; those who are *strong*, by contrast, express their power through physical action. (We shall return to the notion of "will to power" in greater detail in Chapter 8.)

Although the language of "type-facts" is not Nietzsche's, the concept figures centrally in all his mature writings (a point that will not prove surprising, once we appreciate the intellectual milieu in which Nietzsche was writing; see Chapter 2). A typical Nietzschean form of argument, for example, runs as follows: a person's theoretical beliefs are best explained in terms of his moral beliefs; and his moral beliefs are best explained in terms of natural facts about the type of person he is (i.e., in terms of type-facts). So Nietzsche says, "every great philosophy so far has been . . . the personal confession of its author and a kind of involuntary and unconscious memoir"; thus, to really grasp this philosophy, one must ask "at what morality does all this (does *he*) aim" (BGE: 6)? But the "morality" that a philosopher embraces simply bears "decisive witness to *who he is*" – i.e., who he *essentially* is – that is, to the "innermost drives of his nature" (BGE: 6). This explanation of a person's moral beliefs in terms of psychophysical facts about the person is a recurring theme in Nietzsche. "[M]oralities are . . . merely a sign language of the affects" he says (BGE: 187). Accepting the Golden Rule is significant because "it betrays a *type of man*" (WP: 925). "Answers to the questions about the *value* of existence . . . may always be considered first of all as the symptoms of certain bodies" (GS Pref: 2). "Moral judgments," he says are, "symptoms and sign languages which betray the process of physiological prosperity or failure" (WP: 258). "[O]ur moral judgments and evaluations . . . are only images and fantasies based on a physiological process unknown to us" (D: 119), so that "it is always necessary to draw forth . . . the *physiological* phenomenon behind the moral predispositions and prejudices" (D: 542). A "morality of sympathy," he claims, is "just another expression of . . . physiological over-excitability" (TI IX: 37). *Ressentiment* – and the morality that grows out of it – he attributes to an "actual physiological cause [*Ursache*]" (GM I: 15).

The general Nietzschean view is aptly captured in a preface of 1886: "assuming that one is a person, one *necessarily* [*nothwendig*] has the philosophy that belongs to that person" (GS Pref: 2). Or as he put it the following year, in his preface to the *Genealogy*: "our thoughts, values, every 'yes,' 'no,' 'if' and 'but' grow from us with the same inevitability as fruits borne on the tree – all related and each with an affinity to each, and evidence of one will, one health, one earth, one sun" (GM Pref: 2) (cf. Schopenhauer 1844: 239). Nietzsche seeks to understand in naturalistic terms the *type* of "person" who would necessarily bear such ideas and values, just as one might come to understand things about a type of *tree* by knowing its fruits. And just as natural facts about the tree explain the fruit it bears, so too type-facts about a person will explain the ideas and values he comes to bear.

Nietzsche's naturalism bears a striking *structural* similarity to Hume's, even though the two philosophers have rather different views about the operative facts in human nature (cf. Beam 1996). For each thinker is driven to construct a quasi-speculative theory of human nature to explain certain features of human belief systems (philo-sophical, common-sensical, evaluative) precisely because he finds that these features do *not* admit of rational vindication. We must look beyond human reason – to certain natural facts and dispositions about human beings – to explain why they hold these beliefs nonetheless. Thus, Hume argues that our belief in "causation" cannot be rationally justified, i.e., justified on the basis of experience; to explain why humans nonetheless believe in causation, Hume posits a certain natural tendency or disposition to view instances of constant conjunction as instances of something much stronger: namely, the operation of a *necessary* causal relationship.[11]

Similarly, Nietzsche famously views morality as being without rational foundation. He commends the Sophists for having "the first *insight* into morality," namely that "every morality can be dialectically justified ... [so that] all attempts to give reasons for morality are necessarily *sophistical*" (WP: 428). He remarks that the attempt of all philosophers "to supply a *rational* foundation for morality ... inspires laughter" (BGE: 186), and dismisses the Kantian notion of "practical reason" – the type of "reason" that is supposed to guide us in moral matters – as "a special kind of reason for cases in which one need not

---

[11] For a detailed comparison of Hume and Nietzsche on this issue, see Poellner (1995): 36–43.

bother about reason – that is, when morality, when the sublime 'thou shalt,' raises its voice" (A: 12). But like Hume, Nietzsche clearly recognizes that, notwithstanding the lack of rational justification, morality – in particular, the "ascetic" morality with which he is concerned in the *Genealogy* – continues to have a firm grip on the human mind. How are we to explain this fact? The *Genealogy*, and Nietzsche's mature philosophy generally, proposes a *naturalistic* explanation, i.e., an explanation that is continuous with both the results and methods of the sciences.

If the bulk of his philosophical activity is devoted to variations on this naturalistic project, it is also worth keeping in mind that Nietzsche often uses "philosopher" as a kind of term of art, to mean, essentially, the one who "creates" values (BGE: 211). *That* project is *not* part of the naturalistic project of explaining how creatures like us came to take certain values so seriously, but is an independent undertaking (though it may, as Nietzsche suggests in the Note at the end of GM I, benefit from information produced by the naturalistic project). Of course, this should not be surprising, given that Nietzsche is *not*, as already noted, an S-Naturalist except in the sense of repudiating supernaturalism. As a Nietzschean term of art, the "philosopher" is an honorific for the one who creates values. But most of Nietzsche's books are devoted, in fact, to the M-Naturalistic project.

How *could* Nietzsche be a naturalist?

Any interpretation of Nietzsche as naturalist engenders five objections, objections that seem all the more powerful to readers whose picture of Nietzsche has been shaped by the dominant postmodern reading of the past several decades. First, all forms of philosophical naturalism demand some type of continuity with the sciences; but is not Nietzsche a critic of science, a Rortyesque debunker of the epistemic pretences of science for the late nineteenth-century? Second, M-Naturalists like Hume, Nietzsche and Freud purportedly seek causal explanations for human actions and beliefs; but is not Nietzsche an avowed skeptic about notions like causation? Third, how can Nietzsche's alleged naturalism be reconciled with his apparent hostility to "materialism" in the *Genealogy* and elsewhere? Fourth, the naturalistic tradition which includes figures like Hume, Nietzsche, and Freud supposes that there is some "essence" to human nature; but has not Nietzsche rid us of "metaphysical" notions such as that "human nature" has an "essence?" Fifth, the naturalistic Nietzsche characterized in the prior section seems to suppose that he *knows* certain *truths* that his opponents (Christians, moralists) do not; but does not Nietzsche's famous "perspectivism" signal his profound skepticism about all claims to knowledge and truth?

All five objections involve significant misreadings of Nietzsche, misreadings that make an understanding of the *Genealogy* impossible. Thus, before embarking upon our commentary, it will help to spend some time demonstrating briefly how each is mistaken.[12] We may start with the last objection, since in many ways it informs all the others.

---

[12] A rather different kind of objection to reading Nietzsche as a naturalist has been raised more recently in Gardner (1999), who is particularly concerned with the Freud–Nietzsche–Schopenhauer connections. Gardner treats Nietzsche's naturalism as a matter of his advancing "certain [true] motivational claims about human psychology" (p. 399), which is, to be sure, part of Nietzsche's naturalism even on my account. But since Nietzsche did not employ "the systematic clinical methods on which Freud relied" his "'anticipations' of Freud amount to nothing more than inspired guesses – correct guesses, perhaps, but not ones for which Nietzsche had sufficient justification to warrant the enormous philosophical weight he put on them" (p. 400). This is both unfair to "inspired guesses" and unfair to Nietzsche's actual methods. On the one hand, "inspired" seems to understate the remarkable quality of the putative guesses about human psychology given the extent to which the same psychological hypotheses reappear in the work of Freud, who "confirmed" so many of them based on "systematic clinical methods." (And we know, as noted earlier, that Freud had read Nietzsche's "guesses," making the case for a link even stronger.) On the other hand, there is a long continuum between clinical work on the one hand, and pure guesses on the other, and Nietzsche's methods – primarily his readings in contemporary science, and his acute observations of his contemporaries complemented by a rich knowledge of history, and of psychologically astute writers, like Thucydides and La Rochefoucauld – are surely somewhere on the middle of that spectrum. Gardner's point, in any case, impugns Nietzsche's credentials as a philosophical naturalist as little as it impugns Hume's.

This, however, brings us to what is perhaps the core of Gardner's worry. For the naturalistic reading of Nietzsche "leaves him in the position of a dogmatic naturalist [in Kant's terms] – one who poses no more of a threat to

Truth and knowledge

Nietzsche's famous doctrine of "perspectivism" is sometimes thought to undermine *both* the idea that there is any such thing as "objective truth" and the idea that we could have "objective knowledge" of this truth (call this "the Skeptical Reading"). The Skeptical Reading, which for many years constituted something like the "received view" of Nietzsche (Leiter 1994: 334), has come under attack more recently.[13] The most important published discussion of perspectivism appears in the *Genealogy* (GM III: 12), which we will consider in detail in Chapter 8. Here we may just summarize some of the significant conclusions of the recent literature on Nietzsche's "epistemology."

The Skeptical Reading of Nietzsche has always been in profound tension with Nietzsche's actual philosophical practice, in which he repeatedly and regularly employs the *epistemic value* terms in attacking competing views and promoting his own. By "epistemic value terms" we mean that whole family of related concepts that presuppose the possibility of objective truth and our knowledge of it: e.g., "true," "false," "real," "unreal," "justified," "unjustified," and the like. Remarks like, "In Christianity neither morality nor religion has even a single point of contact with reality [*Wirklichkeit*]" so that the Christian, in

reason than Hume, whose challenge the Kantian system had already successfully assimilated" (pp. 400–1). This presupposes that the Kantian response to Hume was a success – a question-begging assumption, obviously, for naturalists. As Nietzsche himself notes, Kant's answer to the question, "How are synthetic judgments a priori possible?" is "By virtue of a faculty." "But is that – an answer? An explanation? Or is it not rather merely a repetition of the question?" (BGE: 11). So "the naturalistic reading of Nietzsche appears to make his critique of traditional philosophy much less powerful than it is widely regarded as being" (Gardner 1999: 400) only on the dubious assumption – one Nietzsche plainly rejects – that Kant has decisively deflected naturalistic objections. Of course, Gardner also worries how insights into the motivation "of metaphysical and moral belief" can be "converted into philosophical critique" and "deliver the categorical negative claims which Nietzsche is generally taken to be making" (p. 400). This worry, however, depends on a mistaken picture of the structure of Nietzsche's critique, a topic to which we will turn at length in Chapters 3 and 4.

13 See Wilcox (1974), Schacht (1983), Westphal (1984a, 1984b), Clark (1990), and Leiter (1994).

effect, must "lie his way out [*wegzulügen*] of reality" (A: 15); or "The more abstract the truth [*Wahrheit*] is that you would teach, the more you have to seduce the senses to it" (BGE: 128); or "Today we possess science precisely to the extent to which we have decided to *accept* the testimony of the senses. ... The rest is miscarriage ... [in which] reality is not encountered at all." (TI III: 3); or the whole treatment of the "Four Great Errors [*Irrthümer*]" (TI VI) and the related claim that, "Moral judgments agree with religious ones in believing in realities [*Realitäten*] which are no realities" (TI VII: 1); or Nietzsche's claim "to stand in opposition to the mendaciousness [*Verlogenheit*] of millennia," to be "the first to *discover* [*entdeckt*] the truth [*Wahrheit*] by being the first to experience lies as lies [*Lüge*] (EH IV: 1); all these claims presuppose that Nietzsche *knows* certain *truths* that others – Christians, most philosophers, moralists – fail to comprehend.

More generally, Nietzsche's explicit *empiricism* – his view that "all evidence of truth comes only from the senses" (BGE: 134) – is impossible to reconcile with the Skeptical Reading (Leiter 1994: 336–8). For any *empiricist* critique necessarily presupposes that there exists some epistemically privileged class of claims about the world – those based on, or inferable from, sense experience. But a class of claims can only be *epistemically* privileged if it is possible for there to be *objective* truths about them and for us to have *objective* knowledge of those truths. Yet it is this possibility that the Skeptical Reading rules out.

We move a considerable distance towards resolving the tension between the Skeptical Reading and Nietzsche's actual philosophical practice by appreciating, as the postmodern writers do not, that Nietzsche's epistemological views *evolved* quite dramatically during his philosophical career. The early (1873) essay "On Truth and Lie in an Extra-Moral Sense" – one which Nietzsche never published – has exerted a strong influence on "postmodern" and deconstructionist readings of Nietzsche (e.g., DeMan 1979). Yet Clark (1990, Chapter 3) demonstrates both that the deconstructionists misunderstand what Nietzsche says about *language* in this essay *and*, more importantly, that Nietzsche's views on truth and knowledge evolved beyond this essay in any case (1990: 77–125). Elaborating upon an idea first broached by Wilcox (1974: 123–4), Clark argues that the famous 1888 section on "How the 'True World' Finally Became a Fable" (TI IV) is actually a veiled description of Nietzsche's own epistemological evolution, an evolution which proceeds roughly as follows.

Under the influence of Schopenhauer's Kantian idealism and Friedrich Lange's NeoKantianism (see Chapter 2), the early Nietzsche thinks that genuinely objective "truth" must involve correspondence to the way the world really is in-itself, i.e., the way things *really* are quite apart from how they may happen to *appear* to human beings. Following Schopenhauer, Nietzsche concludes we cannot have such knowledge: our merely "human" knowledge necessarily falsifies the world as it is in-itself, since it is couched in terms of concepts and categories of *our* making, not the world's. By the early 1880s at the latest, Nietzsche begins to have doubts about the intelligibility of the Kantian idea of a noumenal world, of a way things are in-themselves quite apart from how human beings represent them to be.[14] But it is only in his last six works, beginning with the *Genealogy*, that Nietzsche realizes that if the *only* world is the world as it appears to us humans, then truth and knowledge are none the worse for being *human* truth and *human* knowledge. Only when contrasted with the unintelligible notion of a way things are quite apart from how human beings take them to be does the Kantian point that the human mind helps constitute the world we come to know, count against claims to objectivity.[15]

It is precisely this epistemological story, according to Clark, that Nietzsche tells in the aforementioned section of *Twilight of the Idols* (IV). The section concerns the six stages constituting "the history of an error," the error being that of "the true world" [*Die Wahre Welt*]. By the "true world" Nietzsche plainly means the metaphysical doctrine commonly attributed to Plato and Kant[16] – what we now call *realism*

---

[14] I am here summarizing Clark's interpretation; others are explored in Chapter 8.

[15] Kant, of course, takes his transcendental deduction of the categories to vindicate the objectivity of our judgments – at least regarding the phenomenal world – against empiricist skepticism. The worry is that truly *objective* knowledge must be knowledge of the world as it really is, not simply of how it appears to us.

[16] It also has analogues in the view of some of the Presocratics, notably the Eleatics, who held that beneath the flux of change and "becoming" that characterizes our experience of the world there lies an unchanging and timeless reality, that is unavailable to the senses. For further discussion, see Chapter 2.

– according to which reality (*noumenal* reality, for Kant) has a nature and character wholly *independent* of what humans think or even *could* think about it: even under epistemically ideal conditions, we could still be wrong about what this reality is like. (Plato and Kant differ, of course, over whether we can attain *knowledge* of this reality.) The "error" is traced through its various Christian, Kantian, and positivist manifestations until, in stages 4 and 5 of the history, we arrive at Nietzsche's own earlier views (in HAH [stage 4] and GS and (in part) BGE [stage 5]). These views culminate a few years later in *Beyond Good and Evil* with the realization that this "true world" – which is "unattainable," "indemonstrable" and "unknown" – is "no longer good for anything," is "useless and superfluous – *consequently* [*folglich*] a refuted idea." But it is the mature Nietzsche of stage 6 who finally recognizes that the repudiation of the noumenal world does not leave us with a world of *mere* appearances, for "*With the true world we have also abolished the apparent one*." "Denying the 'true' world destroys all basis for characterizing the remaining world as merely apparent or illusory" (Clark 1990: 113). Thus, in his earlier works (through BGE),

> Nietzsche's characterization of truths as illusions or fictions amounts to calling the empirical world, the world accessible through common sense and science, illusory or fictitious. His history of the "true" world [in TI IV] indicates that he gives up ascribing reality to any world other than the empirical world (stage 5), *and* that he recognizes that this requires him to relinquish his claim that the empirical world is illusory (stage 6). That he puts the logical consequences of stage 5 in a separate stage [i.e., stage 6] gives strong evidence that Nietzsche later recognized his initial failure to appreciate the consequences of denying the thing-in-itself [as he first does in BGE], which means that he himself went through a period in which he denied the thing-in-itself, but continued to characterize the empirical world as mere appearance or illusion.
>
> (Clark 1990: 114)[17]

---

[17] In an important recent article, Clark (1998b) revises in some significant ways her account of Nietzsche's development. Her new claim is that beginning with

If this correctly describes the trajectory of Nietzsche's epistemology, the argument in support of it is not always very clear. In particular, we must ask why exactly Kant's idea of a *noumenal* world is supposed to be unintelligible and hence "refuted"?[18]

As Clark notes (1990: 99–100), Nietzsche claims that "'absolute knowledge' and the 'thing in itself' . . . involve a *contradictio in*

Human, All-too-Human in 1878, and its Schopenhauer-inspired empiricism and naturalism, Nietzsche's skepticism about truth and knowledge ends, though the reasons change over the course of his subsequent career. In *Human, All-too-Human*, the view is that even if we do not have access to truth (understood as correspondence to the way things are in-themselves), "we are deprived only of a truth that is of absolutely no use" (p. 48); "the metaphysical world . . . [is] cognitively superfluous" (p. 49), while "science gives us our only access to truth (apart from perception, on which it is based), the only truth that could be of any real concern to us" (p. 51). In later work, this pragmatic position (only accessible truths matter) is supplemented by skepticism about the intelligibility of the very idea of the thing-in-itself (pp. 62 ff.). For a related account of Nietzsche's view, but that also takes issue with parts of Clark (1990), see Poellner (2001).

[18] Anderson (1996) is the most sustained attack on Clark's reading, and thus merits some comment given the importance being laid upon Clark (1990).

We should note, first, that even Anderson concedes that Clark's Neo-Kantian reading of Nietzsche "is broadly accurate to Nietzsche's later writings" (p. 311) and that it is historically plausible that Nietzsche held such views since he "wrote in the midst of a major 'back to Kant' movement in German philosophy" (ibid.). What Anderson disputes is Clark's claim that Nietzsche "abandoned the falsification thesis [the thesis that our human knowledge necessarily falsifies the way the world is in-itself] starting with the *Genealogy*" (p. 317). Part of his argument depends on taking two remarks out of context from GM III and pasting them together to support the conclusion that, "According to the *Genealogy*, then, all our theoretical beliefs are infected by endemic falsification" (ibid.) In fact, the first remark (GM III: 12) pertains to Nietzsche's doctrine of perspectivism, while the second (GM III: 24) is a parenthetical in the midst of a polemic against a naive positivist's commitment to the ideal of a "naked" or "brute" fact. The discussion in neither context supports the falsification thesis, as shall become clear from the discussion in Chapter 8.

Anderson also appeals to remarks from the "'Reason' in Philosophy" section of *Twilight of the Idols* in which Nietzsche charges "reason" with falsifying reality (TI III: 2, 5) (pp. 317–18). As Anderson acknowledges, Clark claims that by "reason" here Nietzsche means "pure reason," a

adjecto [a contradiction in terms]" and he exhorts us to "free ourselves from the seduction of words" (BGE: 16). But this merely states the conclusion of an argument that has yet to be made. What might that argument be? Poellner (1995: 79–111) offers a plausible reconstruction, drawing on both published and *Nachlass* writings. According to Poellner, the crux of Nietzsche's argument against the intelligibility of things-in-themselves comes to this:

> [W]hat an object is, its 'whatness' or essence, is something that can only be established, indeed only contentfully conceived, from

"nonnatural faculty . . . capable of knowledge of reality uncontaminated by connection to the senses" (1990: 106), which is why he puts "reason" in scare quotes throughout the section. Anderson retorts: "If 'reason' named a faculty that no one had, then this faculty could not have *succeeded* in falsifying the 'testimony of the senses,' as Nietzsche insists it has" (p. 318). But what Nietzsche means, of course, is that philosophers have taken categories that they *believed* to be deliverances of "pure reason" and applied them to reality, and in doing so *falsified* the real world. So Anderson's retort leaves Clark's interpretation of the text untouched.

A more serious challenge to Clark's reading appears to come from GS: 354 (Anderson 1996: 314 n. 21, 320–1), in which Nietzsche says in part, "This is the essence of phenomenalism and perspectivism as I understand them: Owing to the nature of *animal consciousness*, the world of which we can become conscious is only a surface-and-sign-world, a world that is made common and meaner. . . . [A]ll becoming conscious involves a great and thorough corruption, falsification, reduction to superficialities, and generalization."

Yet it would be surprising if even this passage reflected Nietzsche's belief in the falsification thesis (as Anderson claims), since, on its face, it also presupposes the truth of "physiology and the history of animals," the sciences which ground the passage's (purportedly true) claims about the origin of consciousness and language. The clue to what he is getting at comes from the fact that he equates "phenomenalism" and "perspectivism" in this passage (something he does not do in GM III: 12): he is presumably talking about "consciousness" in the sense of immediate sensory (phenomenal) experience, as distinct from that *theoretical* understanding of the world (for example, via sciences like physiology) we might arrive at through experiment and systematic inquiry; only the former, not the latter, "falsifies" reality.

Finally, in the last paragraph of GS: 354, when Nietzsche denies that we have any "organ for knowledge, for 'truth,'" he is quite clearly denying only that we have any knowledge of Kant's phenomenal/noumenal distinction ("the opposition of 'thing-in-itself' and appearance") – precisely the point central to Clark's developmental hypothesis about Nietzsche!

some determinate perspective or point of view (or sets of perspectives or points of view). ... What is designated by [the] term ["perspective"] in this context is simply the determinate manner in which the object appears in perception or conception. For example, if I visually imagine a building, I imagine it from some point of view (or successively, from several). ... [U]nlike certain other characteristics of the mental representation of some object, we cannot "discount" the perspectival, and thus subject-implying, character of it without the representation ceasing to represent anything in a contentful manner. It is because we cannot do this that every contentful conception of an object involves subject-implying (perspectival) characteristics. ... Nietzsche includes in the perspectival, subject-implying character of an object the aspect of it under which it always (necessarily) is of some degree of "concern" [or "interest"] to a subject, so that, for him, it is meaningless to speak of a really existing object that is of no concern to *any* subject.

(1995: 83–5)[19]

A *noumenal* world, however, would be a world of objects seen from *no perspective at all*, a world characterized without any reference to human concerns. Therefore, granting Nietzsche's argument (as reconstructed by Poellner) about the necessary conditions for conceiving of objects, it follows that there can be no *noumenal* objects, i.e., no things-in-themselves.

Arguments of this form may seem, at first glance, to conflate *inconceivability* with *impossibility*: could not something exist even though we cannot intelligibly conceive of it? Poellner's response is to observe that "inconceivability ... is ... the only criterion we have for considering some ostensible state of affairs to be impossible" (1995: 85). This, of course, overstates the point in one respect. For example, if we say it is impossible for there to be life after death, we do not say it because we cannot *conceive* of such a possibility (surely we can), but rather because such a possibility cannot be reconciled with a scientific understanding of the human mind and body (it is *nomically* impossible, but conceptually possible). But the point has more

[19] Cf. Poellner (2001) on "essential representation-dependence."

19

force when directed against a claim of conceptual possibility, like the claim that there exists a noumenal world, a world-in-itself. For the possibility of such a world is manifestly *not* established through empirical evidence (how could it be, since we know nothing about the noumenal world, other than that it (allegedly) exists); rather, such a world is a conceptual posit, a necessary logical link in the Kantian idealist system. But if a conceptual posit is, in fact, inconceivable – as Nietzsche (via Poellner) argues – then we have good reason for thinking it an impossibility. If that is correct, then the *only* world about which we can intelligibly speak is the world as it appears to human beings.

Nietzsche's view, as the preceding discussion already suggests, is extremely difficult to state in a way that is satisfyingly clear.[20] But if perspectivism does *not* entail the Skeptical Reading, what is the significance of the doctrine? It is perhaps easiest to see what the doctrine does mean if we take seriously the optical analogue that Nietzsche explicitly employs in GM III: 12 (Leiter 1994: 344 ff.). For seeing is clearly perspectival: for example, we *necessarily* see an objective from a particular perspective; the idea of seeing something from no perspective at all is a nonsensical one. Similarly, it seems we can adopt a plurality of visual perspectives on an object, each of which will illuminate different features of the object. But none of these features of visual perspectivism require us to deny that some perspectives will *distort* the true nature of a viewed object, or that the viewed object has a determinate character that transcends any particular perspective we adopt upon it.

In the case of knowledge, Nietzsche's point seems to be similar with the important difference that epistemic perspectives are not constituted spatially but in terms of our "affects" or "interests": we *necessarily* know an object from the standpoint of certain interests that direct our attention to only certain aspects of the object of knowledge. For example, if we want to create a map to give us knowledge of a particular region, what our map represents will vary with our interests, i.e., whether we are interested in the topography of the region, or the major arteries, or the tourist attractions. Similarly, as we multiply

[20] See Chapter 8 for further development of the points that follow.

interests we can expect to know more about the object of knowledge. But this perspectivism still allows for the possibility that certain perspectives can be simply *wrong* about the object, that they can "distort" its true nature. (Some maps do not portray the region accurately in any respect.) Perspectivism, construed thus, emphasizes that knowledge is always interested (and thus partial) and that differing interests will increase the breadth of knowledge, but it does not imply that knowledge lacks objectivity or that there is no truth about the matters known.

Skepticism about science

No philosopher can be a naturalist who thinks that the claim of science to a special epistemic status is bunk, yet this is precisely the view often attributed to Nietzsche. Nietzsche's position is often thought to be basically Rortyan (cf. Rorty 1989): science is just one "perspective" on the world, no more justified or true than any other perspective one might adopt (however useful it may be). For Nietzsche, then, to want to make philosophy continuous with science in the manner of M-Naturalism would seem utterly arbitrary and bizarre.

In the mid-1870s, Nietzsche did, in fact, go through a phase of "science worship" and hardcore "positivism," viewing natural science as the paradigm of all genuine knowledge, the culmination of which was *Human, All-too-Human*. This gave way, however, in the early 1880s to a quasi-Schopenhauerian, quasi-Langian skepticism about whether science could plumb the depths of reality, of the world-as-it-is-in-itself. Yet we have just seen that Nietzsche eventually repudiated the metaphysical distinction between a noumenal and phenomenal world on which this skepticism rests. Thus, unsurprisingly, in his later works, Nietzsche's skepticism vanishes and he repeatedly endorses a *scientific* perspective as the correct or true one. Even in the often misunderstood Third Essay of the *Genealogy* – in which Nietzsche attacks only the *value* of truth, not its objectivity or our ability to know it (see Chapter 8)[21] – Nietzsche refers to "there being so much useful

[21]   There is a related theme about the *value* of science that permeates Nietzsche's works, early and late. It is best expressed in the 1886 preface to *The Gay*

work to be done" in science and adds, regarding the "honest workers" in science, that, "I delight in their work" (GM III: 23). In works from earlier in the 1880s, he still lauds science for "the severity of its service, its inexorability in small as in great matters . . . the most difficult is demanded and the best is done without praise and decorations" (GS: 293) and says that "the *ideal* scholar in whom the scientific instinct, after thousands of total semi-failures, for once blossoms and blooms to the end, is certainly one of the most precious instruments there are" (BGE: 207). His complaint about science here, and elsewhere, isn't that it fails to provide objective knowledge of the truth, but rather that it cannot entirely preempt "philosophy," in Nietzsche's special sense of that term, since "genuine" philosophy is concerned with the creation of values. In short, contrary to the Rortyean image, all of Nietzsche's final, major works – the *Genealogy*, *Twilight of the Idols*, *The Antichrist*, *Ecce Homo* – "exhibit a uniform and unambiguous respect for facts, the senses, and science" (Clark 1990: 105).

Skepticism about causation

Nietzsche's alleged skepticism about causation falls prey to similar considerations. Recall that the naturalistic Nietzsche is purportedly looking for causal explanations of people's beliefs and actions. Yet this seems an odd undertaking for the Nietzsche who says that "one should use 'cause' and 'effect' only as pure concepts [*reiner Begriffe*], that is to say, as conventional fictions for the purpose of designation and communication – *not* for explanation" (BGE: 21). Yet the oddity disappears if we situate the quoted remark in context, for the passage continues, importantly, as follows:

> In the "in-itself" [*An-sich*] there is nothing of "causal connections," of "necessity," or of cause. . . . It is *we* alone who have

Science when he praises the Greeks for being "superficial – *out of profundity*" (GS Pref: 4). In other words, the Greeks recognized that *truth* and *knowledge* were not always conducive to life; that a certain amount of ignorance and superficiality might, indeed, be a precondition of life. Thus, the scientific pursuit of truth at any cost is a *normative* ideal that Nietzsche rejects. We shall revisit this issue in detail in Chapter 8.

devised cause, sequence, for-each-other, relativity, constraint, number, law, freedom, motive, and purpose; and when we project and mix this symbol world into things as if it existed "in itself," we act once more as we have always acted – *mythologically*.

The criticism here is familiar from Nietzsche's contemporary, the NeoKantian Lange (see Chapter 2), who had criticized scientists precisely for their false belief that science gives us knowledge of the noumenal world, when in fact science only concerns the phenomenal world. "Cause" and "effect" are "pure concepts" (obviously Kantian language), imposed by the human mind upon a world that, in-itself, contains "nothing of 'causal connections'" and the like. Notice, of course, that even in the Kantian perspective, this point does *not* undermine the objectivity of claims about causes; it simply confines their objective truth to the world as it appears to us. But since Nietzsche comes to repudiate the intelligibility of the noumenal/phenomenal distinction, it is unsurprising that his mature works should show none of the NeoKantian skepticism about causation (see Clark 1990: 103–5).

Hostility towards materialism

Given Nietzsche's oft-expressed hostility to materialism, including in the *Genealogy*, how can we construe him as a philosophical naturalist? He identifies himself, for example, as being one of "the ferocious opponents of all materialism" (GM III: 16) and he complains that the scientistic view that "the only justifiable interpretation" of the world would be one in which one does "research scientifically in *your* sense (you really mean, mechanistically?) – an interpretation that permits counting, calculating, weighing, seeing, and touching, and nothing more . . . is a crudity and naivete, assuming that it is not a mental illness or idiocy" (GS: 373). He adds, rhetorically, "Do we really want to permit existence to be degraded for us like this – reduced to a mere exercise for a calculator and an indoor diversion for mathematicians? Above all, one should not wish to divest existence of its *rich ambiguity*" (GS: 373).

But what *exactly* is Nietzsche's complaint in passages like these? Here again, their context proves decisive: for Nietzsche's critique is plainly directed against one type of S-Naturalism, i.e., the attempt to "reduce" everything that exists to material or physical facts that stand in mechanical relations with each other. But Nietzsche's naturalism, as we have seen it so far, is not substantive in this contemporary way; what Nietzsche signals in passages like those just quoted is precisely that he does *not* want his naturalism to be construed as involving materialism or physicalism as well – a position that was, indeed, popular in Nietzsche's own time (see Chapter 2).

This is clearest in the passage from the *Genealogy*. For the passage reads (in relevant part) as follows:

> [E]ven "psychic suffering" does not seem to be a fact to me at all, but simply an interpretation (causal interpretation) of facts which could not up to now be formulated exactly: thus, as something which is still completely in the air and has no scientific standing – actually just a fat word in place of a spindly question mark. If someone cannot cope with his "psychic suffering," this does *not* stem from his psyche, to speak crudely; more probably from his stomach (I did say I would speak crudely: which does not in any way signify a desire for it to be heard crudely, understood crudely ...). ... If [one] "cannot cope" with an experience, this sort of indigestion is as much physiological as any other – and often in fact just one of the consequences of that other – with such a point of view we can, between ourselves, still be the ferocious opponents of all materialism.
>
> (GM III: 16)

The concluding disclaimer about materialism here is clearly motivated by the fact that *in every other respect* the view endorsed in this passage is naturalistic: psychological claims are, says Nietzsche, *explicable* in terms of physiological facts. But Nietzsche does not, it appears, want to be understood as making the *metaphysical* claim that psychological facts are *nothing other than* physiological facts – the type of contemporary S-Naturalistic view associated with materialism.

It is a similar sentiment that underlies the passages from *The*

Gay Science. For in the section at issue (GS: 373), Nietzsche also writes as follows:

> Assuming that one estimated the *value* of a piece of music according to how much of it could be counted, calculated, and expressed in formulas: how absurd would such a "scientific" estimation of music be! What would one have comprehended, understood, grasped of it? Nothing, really nothing of what is "music" in it!

This criticism, again, is aimed only at the hardcore S-Naturalist who thinks that all facts – psychological, aesthetic, ethical, etc. – must be reducible to physical facts, to the sort of facts that can be "counted, calculated, and expressed in formulas." Many philosophers, including Nietzsche, reject this kind of S-Naturalism, but doing so does not require them to abandon the idea that many features of human beliefs and actions admit of naturalistic explanation. Indeed, Nietzsche's argument against reductive materialism here is evocative of one that has been current in our own time. According to this argument, it is a fatal problem for materialistic accounts that they omit the *qualitative* or *phenomenological* aspect of experience, e.g., what it is like to *experience* a piece of music as *beautiful*. It hardly seems plausible, though, that the beauty of a late Beethoven quartet is expressible in purely physical or mechanical terms – and yet it is beautiful nonetheless.

So Nietzsche is, indeed, hostile to "materialism"; the mistake is to equate "materialism" with naturalism *simpliciter*. Rather, the type of reductive materialism about which Nietzsche is skeptical is only one type of *naturalistic* position, one whose rejection is compatible with a thorough-going M-Naturalism, as well as opposition to supernaturalism.

Skepticism about human nature and essence

Nietzsche is widely thought to be a great opponent of *metaphysics*, and thus it might seem that he must also be an opponent of the idea that there is something called "human nature" which has certain *essential* properties. Such an inference seems plausible as long as the notion of "metaphysics" (in the pejorative sense) is kept suitably vague. For while it is clear that Nietzsche is opposed to certain classic metaphysical doctrines – like the doctrine of metaphysical realism, according to which there exists "a true world" (as discussed above) – it is far from clear that he rejects all claims about the *essence* or *nature* of various kinds of things. Thus, he calls on us "to complete our de-deification of nature . . . [and] to 'naturalize' humanity in terms of a pure, newly discovered, newly redeemed nature" (GS: 256). But more strikingly he makes claims about *essences* with some frequency – for example, concerning "the *essence* [*Wesen*] of what lives" (BGE: 259), "the essence [*Wesen*] of life" (GM II: 12), or "the weakness of the weak . . . – I mean [their] *essence* [*Wesen*]" (GM I: 13). The mistake of most of the anti-metaphysical readings of Nietzsche is to conflate Nietzsche's opposition to non-empirical or non-naturalistic claims (which he does, indeed, repudiate) with an opposition to any and all claims about a thing's essence or nature. But the latter claims are quite colorable within a naturalistic framework (for example, Quine's), as long as we understand them as *empirical* or *naturalistic* claims made from within our best-going theory of the world. As Quine puts it: "relative to a particular inquiry, some predicates may play a more basic role than others, or may apply more fixedly; and these may be treated as essential" (Quine 1981: 120–1; cf. Quine 1969: 114 ff.). Nietzsche needs neither more nor less than this view of essences in order to be the type of philosophical naturalist described here.

Nietzsche's project: the revaluation of values

Nietzsche's naturalism is enlisted on behalf of a "revaluation of all values," and before proceeding further, it will help the reader to have a brief sketch of this central philosophical project.

Throughout his mature work (from the 1881 *Daybreak* through his last productive year of 1888), Nietzsche's overriding concern is what he comes to call the revaluation of values or the critique of morality. Nietzsche attacks morality, most simply, because he believes its unchallenged cultural dominance is a threat to human excellence and human greatness. As he puts it in a crucial passage from the Preface to the *Genealogy* (6):

What if a regressive trait lurked in "the [morally] good man," likewise a danger, an enticement, a poison, a narcotic, so that the present *lived at the expense of the future?* Perhaps in more comfort and less danger, but also in a smaller-minded, meaner manner? . . . So that morality itself were to blame if man never attained the *highest power and splendor* [*Mächtigkeit und Pracht*] possible for the type man? So that morality itself was the danger of dangers?

This basic worry – about the possibilities for human greatness – animates all his writings, even some of the earliest. In the 1870s, he was already speaking of "the goal of culture" as "the production of genius" (U III: 6), though at this time he worried less about the effect of morality on genius than about "the crudest and most evil forces, the egoism of the money-makers and the military despots" (U III: 4). The major work of the early 1880s, *Thus Spoke Zarathustra*, begins with Zarathustra's image of a world in which all human excellence and creativity is gone, in which all that will remain is the "last man":

Alas, the time of the most despicable man is coming, he that is no longer able to despise himself. Behold, I show you the *last man*.

"What is love? What is creation? What is longing? What is a star?" thus asks the last man, and he blinks.

The earth has become small, and on it hops the last man, who makes everything small. . . .

"We have invented happiness," say the last men, and they blink. They have left the regions where it was hard to live, for one needs warmth. One still loves one's neighbor and rubs against him, for one needs warmth.

No shepherd and one herd! Everybody wants the same, everybody is the same: whoever feels different goes voluntarily into a madhouse.

"Formerly, all the world was mad," say the most refined, and they blink.

One is clever and knows everything that has ever happened: so there is no end to derision. One still quarrels, but one is soon reconciled – else it might spoil the digestion.

"We have invented happiness," say the last men, and they blink.
(Z Pref: 5)

In the last man, we encounter precisely the *moral* norms that Nietzsche attacks: the last man embraces happiness, comfort, peacefulness, neighbor love, equality (see Chapter 4). As a result, the last man can only ask, "What is creation?" thus signaling the distance between himself and any type of human greatness – for, as Zarathustra says later "the great – that is, the creating" (Z I: 12). Finally, in his last productive year, Nietzsche speaks of Christian morality as having "waged war unto death . . . against the *presupposition* of every eleva-tion, of every growth of culture" (A: 43), and he claims that acting in accord with what "has been called morality" "would deprive existence of its *great* character" (EH IV: 4).

Not all values are *moral* values for Nietzsche, however, and a crucial issue (to which we return in Chapter 3) is how to demarcate those values he attacks under the heading of "morality." Like Marx, Nietzsche conceives of particular systems of value as in the "inter-ests" of particular classes or *types* of people. (Unlike Marx, he believes this because he thinks it is fundamentally natural, not socio-economic facts, that determine one's interests.) So although "morality" is, in Nietzsche's view, well-suited to the great "herd" of mankind, it is, in fact, a danger to those potentially higher human beings, who mark any great historical or cultural epoch. Nietzsche's real aim, then, is to free these nascent higher types from their "false consciousness," i.e., their false belief that the dominant morality is, in fact, *good for them*. It is precisely this polemical project that the *Genealogy* carries out: by investigating the *origin* of morality Nietzsche hopes to *undermine* morality or, more precisely, to loosen the attachment of potentially great human beings to this morality. How exactly an inquiry into the *origin* of morality can facilitate a *critique* of morality is a matter to which we will return at length in Chapter 5.

We have now set out the basic contours of Nietzsche's project and philosophical views, and cleared aside some of the common misunderstandings that present obstacles to appreciating Nietzsche's naturalistic ambitions and commitments. We will find further support for the general interpretation outlined in this chapter, as well as set the stage for the discussion of the *Genealogy*, by considering with some care the intellectual milieu in which Nietzsche's philosophical sensibilities were nurtured.

Chapter 2

Intellectual history and background

Nietzsche was born in Röcken, Germany, a small village in the Prussian province of Saxony on October 15, 1844, the son and grandson of Lutheran ministers. His father died in 1849, a younger infant brother early the next year. In 1850, the family moved to Naumberg, to live with the father's mother and her sisters. Nietzsche entered Pforta, Germany's preeminent school for classical studies, in 1858. Upon graduation in 1864, he enrolled first at the University of Bonn (as a theology student, ironically enough), and then transferred a year later to Leipzig, to follow the eminent classical philologist Friedrich Ritschl. A brilliant student, he was appointed professor of classical philology at the University of Basel (Switzerland) in 1869 without a doctorate, on the strength of Ritschl's recommendation alone (the doctorate was subsequently awarded, without a dissertation).[1] He served briefly in

---

[1] The recommendation is stunning. Ritschl wrote: "However many young talents I have seen develop under my eyes for

1870 as a medical orderly in the Franco-Prussian war of 1870–1, but illness forced him out of service after only two months. A lifelong battle with ill health was now beginning in earnest.

In 1872, Nietzsche published his first book, *The Birth of Tragedy*, which effectively ruined his professional reputation in classical philology. Not content simply to solve academic puzzles, Nietzsche looked at the role of tragedy in Greek culture with an eye to the condition of German culture at the present. Dedicated to his friend, the German composer Richard Wagner, the book clearly implies that if "it is only as an *aesthetic phenomenon* that existence and the world are eternally *justified*" (BT: 5), then it is only Wagner's music that might justify the world of the present, a world too suffused with the Socratic rationalism against which the book's argument is mainly directed. Such polemical aims, in a work of scholarship, did not please his academic peers. Fourteen years later, he himself called the book "badly written, ponderous, embarrassing, image-mad and image-confused, sentimental, in places saccharine to the point of effeminacy, uneven in tempo, without the will to logical cleanliness, very convinced and therefore disdainful of proof. . . ." (BT Attempt: 3). The reviews at the time were not much more favorable,[2] though subsequent scholarship has actually vindicated Nietzsche on both certain broad themes,

> thirty-nine years now, *never yet* have I known a young man, or tried to help one along in my field as best as I could, who was so mature as early and as young as this Nietzsche. . . . He is the first from whom I have accepted any contribution [for publication] at all while he was still a student. If – God grant – he lives long enough, I prophesy that he will one day stand in the front rank of German philology. He is now twenty-four years old: strong, vigorous, healthy, courageous physically and morally, so constituted as to impress those of a similar nature. On top of that, he possesses the enviable gift of presenting ideas, talking freely, as calmly as he speaks skillfully and clearly. He is the idol and, without wishing it, the leader of the whole younger generation of philologists here in Leipzig who – and they are rather numerous – cannot wait to hear him as a lecturer. You will say, I describe a phenomenon. Well, that is just what he is – and at the same time pleasant and modest." Even though Nietzsche had yet to finish the Ph.D., Ritschl wrote, "I should stake my whole philological and academic reputation that the matter would work out happily" (quoted in PN: 7–8).

2   Though as Whitman (1986: 454) points out, the main "professional response to Nietzsche's book was in fact silence."

as well as certain technical issues of classical scholarship (for a balanced assessment, see Silk and Stern 1981: 132–224). All of Nietzsche's subsequent work abandoned even the pretense of aiming for an academic audience of classicists, and turned to the central cultural and philosophical issues about which he cared most deeply.

By 1878, with the first volume of *Human, All-too-Human*, Nietzsche signaled his philosophical break with Wagner (whom he had stopped seeing two years earlier). In this new book, he now privileged not art, but science, as the mark of high culture. A year later, his recurring health problems – bouts of "uninterrupted three-day migraine[s], accompanied by laborious vomiting of phlegm" (EH I: 1), not to mention insomnia and eye problems – forced him in to retirement, with a small pension. The serious health problems plagued him for the remainder of his life.

During most of 1880 and early 1881, he wrote his first *mature* work, *Daybreak: Thoughts on the Prejudices of Morality*, sounding most of the themes which would receive their final expression in the *Genealogy* (see Clark and Leiter 1997). Through the 1880s, he lived an itinerant existence in various inns in Italy, Switzerland, Germany, and France, as he composed his most famous works, including *Thus Spoke Zarathustra* (1882–5), *Beyond Good and Evil* (1885–6), the *Genealogy* (1886–7), *Twilight of the Idols* (1888), *The Antichrist* (1888) and *Ecce Homo* (1888). His books sold poorly, were rarely reviewed, and, in some cases, Nietzsche had to pay for their printing himself.[3] In early 1888, the influential Danish critic Georg Brandes began lecturing on Nietzsche's ideas, as well as corresponding with Nietzsche himself. Just as he began to enjoy his first real recognition, however, Nietzsche suffered a nervous and physical collapse in the city of Turin (Italy) in early January 1889. He spent the next eleven years a mental and physical invalid, under the care, variously, of professional institutions, his mother and then his proto-nationalist and anti-semitic sister, Elizabeth, who also assumed control of his literary estate. He died on August 25, 1900, his long illness likely the product of an undiagnosed and untreated syphilitic infection acquired in his youth. In the years before his death, he was quickly becoming

---

[3] On the publication history, see Schaberg (1995).

an intellectual celebrity, with admirers paying reverent visits to the invalid. Within a decade of his death, he was probably the most famous and influential intellectual figure in all of Europe, a position he continues to hold to the present day (see Chapter 9).

Nietzsche's productive life coincided with a transformative period in German history. The industrialization of Germany began in earnest after 1850 which brought about the first real working class movement in Germany from 1873 onwards. By the 1880s "industry for the first time began to employ more workers than agriculture" (Williamson 1986: 48, 46). The pivotal political figure, Otto von Bismarck, became Prime Minister of Prussia in 1861. By early 1871 "Bismarck's diplomacy and Prussian military power" had unified Germany under "an authoritarian State that recognized neither the theory nor the practice of popular sovereignty and self-government" (Craig 1991: 33; cf. Williamson 1986: 57). The ultra-nationalism and anti-semitism that culminated more than sixty years later with Nazism, first began to flower during this time – which may account for Nietzsche's tireless polemics against nationalism, militarism, statism, and anti-semitism (as well, perhaps, as his complete contempt for Germany and Germans[4]). Indeed, Nietzsche viewed both the rise of industrial capitalism – which Bismarck also championed (Williamson 1986: 12) – and proto-nationalism as adding simply another layer of obstacles to the development of culture in Germany. The following passage from a work of the early 1870s is typical of his attitude towards the country and people whom he loathed above all others:

> Certainly, he who has to live among Germans suffers greatly from the notorious greyness of their life and thought, from their formlessness, their stupidity and dull-mindedness, their coarseness in more delicate affairs, even more from their envy and a certain secretiveness and uncleanliness in their character; he is pained and offended by their rooted joy in what is false and ungenuine, in bad imitations, in the translation of good foreign things into bad native ones: now, however, that one has in addition, and as the most painful experience of all, their feverish

---

[4]   Cf. EH III: CW-4: "It is part of my ambition to be considered a despiser of the Germans *par excellence*."

restlessness, their search for success and profit, their overestimation of the moment, one is limitlessly indignant to think that all these maladies and weaknesses are on principle never to be cured but only painted over.

(U III: 6)

In the same essay, he attributes the sorry state of German culture in this period to the "crudest and most evil forces, the egoism of the money-makers and the military despots" (U III: 4). Notice, of course, that his objection to capitalism and militaristic nationalism is not *moral* in any conventional sense of that term,[5] but almost *esthetic*: they pose obstacles to the flourishing of cultural greatness.

These are the bare facts of Nietzsche's life and times; the details have been told well and at length by others.[6] What concerns us especially here are the profound intellectual influences on the young Nietzsche, influences that shaped his naturalism and which remain visible even in a mature work like the *Genealogy*. These may, for our purposes, be confined to essentially four: Nietzsche's training in the discipline of classical philology; his exposure to the early Greek philosophers, especially the Presocratics and Sophists; his encounter with the philosophy of Schopenhauer; and the influence of the German Materialism of the 1850s and after.

Classical philology

The modern research university was a German creation reflecting an ideal developed by Wilhelm von Humboldt in the early nineteenth century. It was only after 1850, though, that Humboldt's vision of universities as "the homes of scholars dedicated to *Wissenschaft* (pure learning as opposed to utilitarian skills) and *Bildung* (the cultivation of the whole person)" (Craig 1991: 173) really came to fruition in Germany, eventually becoming the paradigm for higher education everywhere. It was also during this century that Germany became the

---

5 For example, it reflects no concern for the effect of capitalism and nationalism on the well-being of the majority of human beings.

6 See, e.g., Kaufmann (1974: 23–71); Janz (1978); Hayman (1980); Craig (1991); and for another brief overview, see Clark (1998a).

world's leading center for classical philology – what we now call simply "classics" – that is, the careful study of the literary and philosophical texts of the ancient Greek and Roman worlds.

Classical philology, importantly, understood itself to be a *Wissenschaft*, that is, a "science" (though the English-language connotation of *natural* science, like physics, is misleading). This meant, in particular, that, "The ancient world, its texts and its history, were submitted to critical analysis with an unprecedented thoroughness, sense of system and concern for evidence that was, in intention at least, dispassionate and . . . disinterested" (Silk and Stern 1981: 11). Nietzsche's philological work while still a student "exhibit[ed] all the familiar features of nineteenth-century 'scientific' scholarship," i.e., "collating manuscripts, emending texts or . . . investigating date, authorship, provenance or genesis of ancient writings" (Silk and Stern 1981: 16).[7] His youthful studies, for example, of Diogenes Laertius (the third-century commentator on early Greek philosophy) are in the opinion of one modern scholar,

> brilliant. Nietzsche's subject is esoteric, he is obliged to argue in complex and tortuous turns, he carries a heavy burden of erudition. Yet the studies proceed with astonishing clarity and penetration. Their style is plain – sometimes pugnacious, sometimes witty, but never bombastic and never obscure. The argument is elegantly articulated, and its flow is sustained with unusual skill and sinew.
>
> . . . the Laertian studies were written by an industrious, erudite, disciplined and brilliant young mind.
>
> (Barnes 1986: 39–40)

This retrospective assessment may help us appreciate why Nietzsche's mentor Ritschl recommended him so highly that Basel would appoint

---

7   His teacher Ritschl could still write in 1873 about Nietzsche's "most rigorous methodology of schooled, scientific research," even as he lamented the metaphysical excesses of *The Birth of Tragedy*. For the most subtle treatment of the state of classical philology at the time, see Whitman (1986). As Whitman argues, part of what made *The Birth of Tragedy* an "embarrassment to classicists" was that it represented a return to "the magisterial tradition" of philology, then in disrepute due to the influence of the newer "scientific" model for the discipline. Ibid. at 466.

the twenty-four-year-old Nietzsche to its faculty without a dissertation in hand. Nietzsche was simply a first-rate classical scholar in the nineteenth-century German mold.

Of course, the adoption of a "scientific" paradigm of research in classical philology brought with it increasingly narrow specialization, so that by the 1860s there was a "fragmentation of classical studies from 'life outside'" as "[y]oung scholars gravitated towards ... the problems ... of single texts" (Silk and Stern 1981: 13). Nietzsche reacted against this narrow "professionalization" of classical philology throughout his productive life, especially in his many piercing observations regarding professional scholars (e.g., GS: 366; BGE: 45; EH II:8). But his antipathy to "professionalized" classical scholarship was surely most inflamed by the poor reception the profession accorded his *The Birth of Tragedy*, which observed none of the canons of the *Wissenschaft* as then constituted (Silk and Stern 1981: 132; Whitman 1986: 465–8). Indeed, Nietzsche is obviously speaking autobiographically when just a couple of years later he remarks on the "distress" one must feel when the work of genius is treated "with indifference" by "the arid self-satisfaction of the scholars" (U III: 6).

Yet his hostility to the "aridity," complacency and insularity of academic classicists should not obscure what Nietzsche clearly retained from his early training at their hands – for example, their characteristic "reverence for every kind of mastery and competence, and ... [their] uncompromising opposition to everything that is semblance, half-genuine, dressed up, virtuosolike, demagogical, or histrionic in *litteris et artibus* – to everything that cannot prove ... its unconditional *probity* in discipline and prior training" (GS: 366). Even in one of his very last works he still speaks, with admiration, of "scholarly culture," one characterized by "scientific *methods*" including "the great, the incomparable art of reading well" (A: 59). And lest his meaning be missed, he explicitly defends "philology" as "the art of reading well – of reading facts [*Thatsachen*] without falsifying them by interpretation [*Interpretation*], without losing caution, patience, delicacy, in the desire to understand" (A: 52).

Nietzsche's continuing loyalty to many of the canons of the philological *Wissenschaft* is typically ignored by those anachronistic commentators (e.g., DeMan 1979, Nehamas 1985) who take Nietzsche's recurring talk about "interpretation" and "texts" to anticipate deconstructionist orthodoxies of the present, like the idea "that literary texts can be interpreted *equally well* in vastly different and *deeply incompatible* ways" (Nehamas 1985: 3, emphases added). But such an approach forgets that Nietzsche learned how to read texts from Ritschl, not Derrida. And for a Ritschl, or any other nineteenth-century practitioner of "the art of reading well – of reading facts without falsifying them by interpretation," the existence of "deeply incompatible" ways of reading a single text is merely evidence of mediocre philology (Leiter 1992).[8] With respect to this attitude, at least, Nietzsche remained his master's loyal pupil.[9]

We should note, in particular, that Nietzsche freely characterizes his naturalism in the literary language that writers like DeMan and Nehamas misunderstand in the anachronistic way just noted. For example, his famous naturalistic proclamation in BGE 230 (discussed in Chapter 1) speaks in terms of the "eternal basic text [*ewigen Grundtext*] of *homo natura*." But in calling this text of man (understood as a natural organism) "eternal" and "basic," Nietzsche plainly does not mean to suggest that it is like a literary text that "can be interpreted equally well in vastly different and deeply incompatible ways" (Nehamas 1985: 3). To the contrary, the point is precisely that non-naturalistic readings "falsify" the "facts" about this "text." It is the aim of Nietzsche – ever the "good philologist" – to correct these *mis*readings (Westphal 1984b; Leiter 1992).

---

[8]   Postmodernist readers frequently lift from context Nietzsche's quip that "facts is precisely what there is not, only interpretations" (WP: 481). In context, however, two things are clear about this remark: it is an attack on the positivist idea of a "naked" or "brute" fact; and it presupposes the distinction between the noumenal and phenomenal world that, as we saw in Chapter 1, Nietzsche ultimately rejects. This should be clear enough from the line that immediately follows the famous remark: "We cannot establish any fact 'in itself.'" That we can not have epistemic access to "any fact 'in itself'" is, however, compatible with the mature Nietzsche thinking there *are* facts in the only real world, i.e., the so-called "phenomenal" world.

[9]   Because Ritschl also embodied aspects of "the magisterial tradition," Nietzsche was his master's pupil in other ways as well. See Whitman (1986: 461 ff.).

The Presocratics and the Sophists

An even more important legacy of Nietzsche's training in classical philology is the sympathetic (indeed, highly partisan) interest he acquired in many of the Greek thinkers known as the "Presocratics" and "Sophists," who were active in the sixth and fifth centuries BC.[10] He expresses his attitude most simply in a note of 1888: "The real philosophers of Greece are those before Socrates" (WP: 437) (cf. EH III: BT-3: "the *great* Greeks in philosophy" are "those of the two centuries *before* Socrates"). By contrast, he views "the Greek philosophers from Socrates onward" as "a symptom of decadence; the anti-Hellenic instincts come to the top" (WP: 427). "For the whole phenomenon Plato I would sooner use the phrase 'higher swindle'" (TI X: 2), he says. Writing a decade earlier, he puts the point as follows:

> With the Greeks, things go forward swiftly, but also as swiftly downward; the movement of the whole mechanism is so intensified that a single stone, thrown into its wheels, makes it burst. Such a stone was Socrates, for example; in one night, the development of philosophical science [*philosophische Wissenschaft*], until then so wonderfully regular but, of course, all too swift, was destroyed.

(HAH: 261)

What is it that the Presocratic philosophers stand for that Nietzsche finds so attractive – so much so that he views them as "the real philosophers of Greece" in contrast to Socrates and Plato? Four themes in the early Greek philosophers are of particular importance for Nietzsche: their *methodological naturalism* (M-Naturalism); their appreciation of the *limitations of knowledge;* their *empiricism*; and their *realism*.[11]

---

[10]   These thinkers do not speak univocally, and Nietzsche's interest is somewhat selective. He is, for example, most taken with Thales, Heraclitus, Thucydides, and aspects of Democritus, while he is more critical of Parmenides and the Eleatic school. I shall speak loosely in the text of "Presocratics" and "Sophists" without noting all the divergences, and the respects in which Nietzsche is unsympathetic to certain doctrines associated especially with certain Presocratic figures.

[11]   Nietzsche's understanding of the Greeks is also almost certainly influenced by the teachings of his Basel contemporary, the great historian Jacob Burckhardt. On Burckhardt's influence, see especially Gossman (2000).

Methodological naturalism

For many of the Presocratics (as well as later Greek thinkers), philosophy is not distinct from disciplines like biology or the natural sciences more generally: philosophy aims for a general explanatory account of the world and its elements (Guthrie 1962: x). In this approach to theorizing, the Presocratics give us (according to Nietzsche) "*the archetypes of philosophic thought*," so much so that "[a]ll posterity has not made an essential contribution to them since" (PTAG: 1). The basic archetype is to be found in the first Greek philosopher, Thales. Nietzsche analyzes his contribution this way:

> Greek philosophy seems to begin with an absurd notion, with the proposition that *water* is the primal origin and the womb of all things. Is it really necessary for us to take serious notice of this proposition? It is, and for three reasons. First, because it tells us something about the primal origin of all things; second, because it does so in language devoid of image or fable; and finally, because contained in it, if only embryonically, is the thought, "all things are one."

> (PTAG: 3)

Two things distinguish Thales on this account: first, his attempt to give a *naturalistic* account of the origin (by discarding image and fable, he "shows him[self] as a natural scientist" (PTAG: 3)); and second, his commitment to the idea that there is a certain (perhaps explanatory) unity to the diverse surface of things as we experience them.[12] While Thales thought water could do the required naturalistic unifying work, other Presocratics posited air (Anaximenes, Diogenes), fire (Heraclitus),[13] and water, fire, air and earth (Empedocles)[14] as the

---

[12] Although in this early essay, Nietzsche characterizes this latter commitment as a "metaphysical conviction" akin to a "mystic intuition," it is in fact quite clear that such explanatory unification of seemingly disparate phenomena is a characteristic aim of empirical science. Of course, at the time Nietzsche wrote this essay, he was still in the thrall of Schopenhaurian monism – the doctrine that all is "will" – which may also explain his attraction to Thales at this stage.

[13] "Fire," though, functions more metaphorically and heuristically for Heraclitus, making him less like the other figures noted.

[See facing page for n. 14.]

basic constituent elements of everything else. Like later philosophical naturalists such as Spinoza, the early Greek philosophers viewed nature as continuous throughout, so that even the understanding of human beings must proceed apace with the understanding of the rest of nature. For Heraclitus, for example, the study of "men – their soul, institutions and ideas . . . was in no way separate from the study of the outside world; the same materials and the same laws are found in each sphere" (Kirk *et al.* 1983: 203). In short, "Human behavior, as much as changes in the external world, is governed by the same *Logos* [i.e., roughly, the same explanatory principles or forces]" (Kirk *et al.* 1983: 212).[15] Similar naturalistic themes are found in the Sophists, who shared a "common interest in anthropology . . . [i.e.,] the evolution of man as a product of nature" (Guthrie 1971: 46).

Limitations of knowledge

While in "Thales for the first time the man of science triumphs over the man of myth," there is more to his significance according to Nietzsche: for in Thales "the man of wisdom [*Weisheit*] triumphs in turn over the man of science [*Wissenschaft*]" (PT: 145). What distinguishes, then, Thales from the mere man of science? According to Nietzsche:

> Science rushes headlong, without selectivity, without "taste," at whatever is knowable, in the blind desire to know all at any cost. Philosophical thinking, on the other hand, is ever on the scent of those things which are most worth knowing, the great and the important insights. Now the concept of greatness is changeable in the realm of morality as well as in that of aesthetics. And so philosophy starts by legislating greatness.
>
> (PTAG: 3)

What distinguishes, in other words, the philosopher from the scientist, is that the latter is committed to knowledge *for the sake of knowledge itself*, and thus pursues knowledge "at any cost." The philosopher –

---

[14] Empedocles also adds "Love" and "Strife" as the *motivating* forces that operate upon the four basic elements.

[15] On the meaning of *Logos*, see Guthrie (1962: 38).

the "man of wisdom" – by contrast is interested in knowledge for the sake of some particular value (Nietzsche's example, above, is "greatness"), other than the presumed absolute value of truth which the scientist takes for granted (cf. GS: 344). This is why, for Nietzsche, "*Genuine philosophers . . . are commanders and legislators*: they say, '*thus* it *shall* be!'" (BGE: 211). The philosopher explicitly legislates those values in whose service knowledge is then enlisted.

What is quite remarkable about this passage from the early 1870s is that it expresses a view that Nietzsche held *throughout his productive life*: the same points are made, again and again, in *The Birth of Tragedy* (e.g., 17–18), in the *Untimely Meditations* (III: 6), in *Beyond Good and Evil* (e.g., 204–13) in the new additions (of 1885–6) to *The Gay Science* (e.g., Pref: 4; GS: 344), and in the *Genealogy* (III: 23–5). Notice, in particular, that raising a question about the *value* of knowledge or truth is manifestly *not* an attack on the existence or possibility of knowledge or truth; rather, it is an expression of the lesson Nietzsche had learned from the early Greeks:

> No, this bad taste, this will to truth, to "truth at any price," this youthful madness in the love of truth, have lost their charm for us: for that we are too experienced, too serious, too merry, too burned, too *profound*. . . . Today we consider it a matter of decency not to wish to see everything naked, or to be present at everything, or to understand and "know" everything. . . .
>
> Oh, those Greeks! They knew how to live. What is required for that is to stop courageously at the surface, the fold, the skin, to adore appearance, to believe in forms, tones, words, in the whole Olympus of appearance. Those Greeks were superficial – *out of profundity [Tiefe]*.
>
> (GS Pref: 4)

It is not, then, that the Greeks lacked knowledge; rather they *chose* to remain superficial because they knew all too well the *deep* truths – for example, about "the irrationality and suffering of human existence" (PT: 136). They understand – as Socrates and his heirs do not – that knowledge can be dangerous and terrible, that we may want to put limits on knowledge for the sake of other values: e.g., preserving the will to live in the face of a terrible and irrational world.

What is objectionable for Nietzsche about Socrates and the arrival of Socratic rationalism is precisely that it marks a "new and unprecedented value set on knowledge" (BT: 13). Socrates, as "the prototype of the theoretical optimist . . . ascribes to knowledge and insight the power of a panacea" (BT: 15). Socrates, in short, fails to realize what the Presocratic writers understood all too well: that knowledge need not be a panacea, that the pursuit of truth is simply one *value*, a value whose realization may be incompatible with others.

It is important to notice that Nietzsche's M-Naturalism is quite compatible with rejecting Socratic optimism, i.e., the view that truth is the highest value and knowledge the highest pursuit. In fact, as we shall see, Nietzsche pursues his naturalistic inquiries only so far as is necessary to achieve his overriding *normative* goal: what he calls the revaluation of all values. This is particularly important to keep in mind in reading the *Genealogy*. For while the *Genealogy* purports to make *true* or *factual* claims about the origins of morality, it is manifestly not a conventional *scholarly* or *scientific* treatise, reflecting a "desire . . . for cold, pure, inconsequential knowledge" (U III: 6). Its aim is *not* to know the truth about morality's origins for the sake of knowing that truth; rather, it is animated by the same profound normative commitment as all Nietzsche's mature work: to *revalue* existing morality. Nietzsche wants to explore the origins of morality in order to force a reassessment of the *value* of our morality as we now find it. The pursuit of knowledge in the *Genealogy* – just as his general pursuit of a naturalistic understanding of human beings – is an instrument in the service of this overriding aim of formulating a critique of morality. In this regard, Nietzsche exhibits the "wisdom" of the Presocratics: he seeks a naturalistic understanding of the world, but he does not seek such an understanding as a mere end-in-itself, to be pursued at any cost; rather, his M-Naturalism is an instrument in the service of the revaluation of values.

Empiricism

Nietzsche's empiricism – his view that genuine knowledge comes from the senses – has always proved an embarrassment for Nietzsche's postmodernist and deconstructionist interpreters. Yet we repeatedly find

Nietzsche saying things like, "All credibility, all good conscience, all evidence of truth come only from the senses" (BGE: 134) or, more elaborately:

> Today we possess science precisely to the extent to which we have decided to *accept* the testimony of the senses – to the extent to which we sharpen them further, arm them, and have learned to think them through. The rest is miscarriage and not-yet-science . . . [in which] reality is not encountered at all.
>
> (TI III: 3)

Yet it is precisely many of the Presocratics and Sophists who provide a model of uncompromising empiricism.[16] For the great dispute of antiquity, initiated by the Eleatics, is precisely between those philosophers who accept the testimony of the senses – which shows us a world of constant change and passing away (a world of "becoming") – and those who reject this testimony, and posit an ideal world of "being" which is timeless and unchanging. Nietzsche clearly sides with the empiricist-minded Presocratics against their "idealist" brethren. Thus, in the same chapter of *Twilight of the Idols* just quoted, Nietzsche singles out Heraclitus for parting company with "the rest of the philosophic folk" who "rejected the testimony of the senses" (TI III: 2). He continues: "Insofar as the senses show becoming, passing away, and change, they do not lie." This empiricism of the Presocratics stands in marked contrast to the "Platonic slander of the senses" (WP: 427); Plato, according to Nietzsche, "flee[s] from reality and . . . see[s] things only in pallid mental picture" (D: 448).

In the case of the Sophists, however, empiricism is often associated with *relativism* – roughly, the view that judgments are only "valid" relative to a "framework" or "perspective," so that conflicting judgments can, in principle, both be true. Since knowledge comes from

---

16 During the nineteenth-century, "empiricism [also] came to be the defining characteristic of real science" (Schnädelbach 1983: 82). Hermann von Helmholtz (1821–94) "whose numerous addresses were widely read" and who enjoyed "almost unassailable authority as a famous natural scientist" claimed that "'true science is . . . nothing but a methodically and deliberately completed and purified experience'" (quoted in Schnädelbach 1983: 85). As we will see shortly, Nietzsche was likely influenced by these sources as well.

the senses, but each person's sensory experience may be different, it follows that there may be no objective knowledge. As Guthrie explains:

> [T]he Sophists could not, any more than other pretenders to serious thought, brush aside the Eleatic dilemma, which forced a choice between being and becoming, stability and flux, reality and appearance. Since it was no longer possible to have both, the Sophists abandoned the idea of a permanent reality behind appearances, in favour of an extreme phenomenalism, relativism and subjectivism.

> (1971: 47; cf. p. 50)

But if empiricism entails a *relativism* to the effect that the truth or falsity of judgments is always relative (e.g., to the perceiver, as in the infamous Protagorean doctrine that "man is the measure of all things"), then it is hard to see how it can be squared with naturalism. For naturalism presupposes that the naturalistic claims provide *epistemically superior* explanations of phenomena. We seem ensnared in a dilemma similar to that originally posed by the Skeptical Reading (Chapter 1).

Recent scholarship, however, rejects Guthrie's view that the Sophists were, in fact, relativists in any pernicious sense, i.e., in a sense incompatible with *objectivity* (e.g., Bett 1989; Woodruff 1999). The Sophists did, of course, embrace a trivially relativistic doctrine that we now call "relationalism" (Railton 1986a: 10–11), according to which certain predicates apply *objectively*, but *not absolutely*: their applicability is relative to certain *types* of situations or circumstances.[17] So, for example, the notion of something being "good for" or "bad for" a person – in the sense of contributing to or harming the person's well-being – is a relational notion: philosophy may be *good for* me, but bad for someone else; cow's milk may be good for calves, but bad

---

[17] Both Bett (1989: 145) and Guthrie (1971: 166, 187–8) note this point, though without using the label "relationalism." Hunt (1991: 132) makes much out of Nietzsche's alleged "relativism," but all he in fact has in mind is the trivial doctrine of relationalism. Of course, relationalism about the predicate "true" itself would give us relativism in the pernicious sense, i.e., a relativism incompatible with objectivity.

for human babies. Although such judgments are relational, they are also objectively true or false, i.e., given certain natural facts about the digestive system of human babies, it is objectively (but relationally) true that cow's milk upsets that system. Even Protagoras – who *may* be the only genuine relativist among the Sophists (cf. Bett 1989) – is said to acknowledge relationalism in Plato's dialogue bearing his name:

> I know plenty of things – foods, drinks, drugs, and many others – which are harmful to men, and others which are beneficial, and others again which, so far as men are concerned, are neither, but are harmful or beneficial to horses, and others only to cattle or dogs. Some have no effect on animals, but only on trees, and some again are good for the roots of trees but injurious to the young growths. Manure, for instance, is good for all plants when applied to their roots, but utterly destructive if put on the shoots or young branches. Or take olive oil. It is very bad for plants, and most inimical to the hair of all animals except man, whereas men find it of service both to the hair and to the rest of the body. So diverse and multiform [i.e., relational] is goodness that even with us the same thing is good when applied externally but deadly when taken internally.

> (334a–c)

The view expressed here is clearly related to Protagoras's crucial concession in Plato's *Theaetetus* (178b–179b) that judgments about what is advantageous or beneficial *are* objective. In our terminology, even Protagoras concedes that it is an objective relational fact that, e.g., olive oil is *bad* for the skin of animals, but *good* for the skin of humans. We shall see, in fact, that such a view of objective relational goodness is crucial for Nietzsche as well: for Nietzsche holds that particular *moralities* can be good for certain types of people, but bad for others (see Chapter 3).

Since *relationalism* is not a relativist doctrine that undermines objectivity, the fact that the Sophists were relationalists does not show them to be relativists in a sense incompatible with naturalism (cf. Bett 1989: 145–50). In fact, the critiques mounted by the Sophists and their allies in the so-called "new learning" of the fifth century BC were "founded not on relativism but on views about the fixed natures of things. The traditional view that sophists are relativists must give way to the recognition that what most characterizes the Sophists as a group is their commitment to human nature as a subject of study" (Woodruff 1999: 305). The Sophists (and their contemporaries) were, in fact, quite interested in the distinction between *physis* (roughly, "nature") and *nomos* (roughly, "norm" or "convention"). Some (like Antiphon and Callicles) clearly defended the propriety of what is *natural* (e.g., selfishness) *against* prevailing conventions that would restrain this nature (Guthrie 1971: 101–13; Bett 1989: 162–3), while others (like Protagoras) defended moral and political conventions as crucial to human well-being (Bett 1989: 163–4; cf. Guthrie 1971: 60–79). In neither approach is there evidence of relativism.

In fact, it is only the Sophist Protagoras, with his doctrine that "man is the measure of all things," who seems to embrace relativism; but what is missing is any indication that other Sophists followed Protagoras on this score. While the Sophists as a group may have been unified by their empiricism, their skepticism, and their interest in rhetoric (Bett 1989: 153, 167–8), there is no evidence that they conceived of empiricism as entailing relativism, in the manner Guthrie suggests and which Protagoras perhaps embodies.

Realism

That Nietzsche's attraction to the Sophists was not motivated by his perception of them as relativists should be apparent from the striking fact that he most often holds up as the embodiment of Sophistic culture not Protagoras or Gorgias or Thrasymachus, but rather the great Greek historian Thucydides, author of *History of the Peloponnesian War*.[18] In Thucydides, Nietzsche says,

---

[18] Cf. Guthrie (1971: 84): "To understand the temper of the age in which the Sophists lived, one cannot do better than start with the philosophic historian Thucydides." Brobjer (2001), in arguing that Nietzsche was "disinterested" in and "ambivalent" about the Sophists, only manages to sustain his argument by discounting Nietzsche's identification of Thucydides as the embodiment of Sophistic culture. But once we grant Nietzsche his own understanding of the Sophistic movement, Brobjer's argument that there are few references

that *culture of the most impartial knowledge of the world* [*unbefangenste Weltkenntnis*] finds its last glorious flower: that culture which had in Sophocles its poet, in Pericles its statesman, in Hippocrates its physician, in Democritus its natural philosopher; which deserves to be baptized with the name of its teachers, the Sophists.

(D: 168, cf. WP: 428).

Similarly, in one of his last works, he remarks that in Thucydides, "the culture of the Sophists, by which I mean the culture of the realists [*die Realisten-Cultur*], reaches its perfect expression" (TI X: 2). What distinguishes Thucydides and the Sophists for Nietzsche – what makes them most attractive to his way of thinking – is their *realism*. This is *not* "realism" in the contemporary sense of a metaphysical doctrine about the mind-independence of the world, but rather in an older sense, still familiar from popular parlance in phrases like "Realpolitik." Realism in this sense refers to a certain hard-headed, unromantic, uncompromising attitude, which manifests itself in a brutal honesty and candor in the assessment of human motives and the portrayal of human affairs – what we might call "Classical Realism" (Leiter 2001b), to distinguish it from contemporary metaphysical realism. "The Sophists are no more than realists," says Nietzsche; "they possess the courage of all strong spirits to *know* their own immorality" (WP: 429). Thucydides is

the great sum, the last revelation of that strong, severe, hard factuality [*starke, strenge, harte Thatsächlichkeit*] which was instinctive with the older Hellenes. In the end, it is *courage* in the face of reality that distinguishes a man like Thucydides from Plato: Plato is a coward before reality, consequently he flees into the ideal; Thucydides has control of *himself*, consequently he also maintains control of things.

(TI X: 2)

to the "Sophists" is vitiated; indeed, Brobjer's own research elsewhere has shown that Thucydides is one of the ancient authors Nietzsche refers to most often *and* most positively (Brobjer 1995, Appendix 3). For a thorough critique of Brobjer's position, see Mann (2000).

"Thucydides and, perhaps Machiavelli's *Principe* [*The Prince*]," Nietzsche adds, "are most closely related to myself by the unconditional will not to gull oneself and to see reason in *reality* – not in 'reason,' still less in 'morality'" (TI X: 2).

Nietzsche's view of Thucydides as the quintessential Classical Realist is not novel: throughout the *History*, Thucydides portrays with unflinching candor a world in which actors are driven by lust for power and glory, and in which talk about morality and justice is largely claptrap and window-dressing. Perhaps the most famous example of this in the *History* is the dialogue between the Athenians and the vanquished Melians – a dialogue that Guthrie calls "the most famous example of amoral realism" (Guthrie 1971: 85). Negotiating over the terms of surrender, the Athenians address the Melians, in relevant part, as follows:

> For our part, we will not make a long speech no one would believe, full of fine moral arguments – that our empire is justified because we defeated the Persians, or that we are coming against you for an injustice you have done to us. . . . Instead, let's work out what we can do on the basis of what both sides truly accept: we both know that decisions about justice are made in human discussions only when both sides are under equal compulsion [i.e., only among equals does right prevail over might]; but when one side is stronger, it gets as much as it can, and the weak must accept that. . . .
>
> Nature always compels gods (we believe) and men (we are certain) to rule over anyone they can control. We did not make this law, and we were not the first to follow it; but we will take it as we found it and leave it to posterity forever, because we know that you would do the same if you had our power, and so would anyone else.
>
> (Woodruff 1993: 89, 105)

Nietzsche's own commentary on this particular dialogue highlights what he regards as "realistic" about Thucydides' rendering of the event:

> Do you suppose perchance that these little Greek free cities, which from rage and envy would have liked to devour each other, were guided by philanthropic and righteous principles?

49

Does one reproach Thucydides for the words he puts into the mouths of the Athenian ambassadors when they negotiated with the Melians on the question of destruction or submission?

Only complete Tartuffes [i.e., Socrates and Plato] could possibly have talked of virtue in the midst of this terrible tension – or men living apart, hermits, refugees, and emigrants from reality – people who negated in order to be able to live themselves –

The Sophists were Greeks: when Socrates and Plato took up the cause of virtue and justice, they were *Jews* [i.e., promulgators of Judeo-Christian, or slave, morality[19]] or I know not what – Grote's[20] tactics in defense of the Sophists are false: he wants to raise them to the rank of men of honor and ensigns of morality – but it was precisely their honor not to indulge in any swindle with big words and virtues.

(WP: 429)[21]

Thucydides, in short, dispenses with the fiction that would deny that *strength*, *power*, and *selfishness* are the driving forces in human affairs; in its place, he offers a picture in which the *true* amoral motives now appear in the mouths of the actors themselves. As one commentator remarks:

[A] frequent purpose of the speeches [in Thucydides's *History*] is to reveal the [true] motives of the speakers. The speeches are part of Thucydides' larger project of bringing submerged realities to the surface. . . . Thucydides wants to bring the darker side of human nature to light by revealing motives . . . that speakers would want to conceal in real life. . . . Thucydides' speakers are made to say what Thucydides thinks they actually believe, whether they would have said those things in public or not. . . . He shows us their speeches refracted through a lens of honesty.

(Woodruff 1993: xxiii)

[19] On Nietzsche's use of "Jew" and "Christian" interchangeably to mean essentially adherents of a particular morality, see Chapter 6.

[20] The reference is to George Grote, the famous nineteenth-century English classicist.

[21] This is in part a quotation from Victor Brochard, *Les sceptiques grecs* (1887). For discussion, see Brobjer (forthcoming).

Thucydides, of course, is not alone among the Sophists in evincing this realistic view of the amoral motives operative in human affairs. The Sophist Gorgias, as well as Glaucon and Thrasymachus in Plato's *Republic*, are also Classical Realists, in the sense of sharing the same "attitude of hard-headed realism or fact-facing which without passing judgment declares that the more powerful will always take advantage of the weaker, and will give the name of law and justice to whatever they lay down in their own interests" (Guthrie 1971: 60). These Classical Realists, according to Guthrie, all agree with Glaucon in the *Republic* that "[s]elf-interest . . . is what every nature (*physis*) naturally pursues as good" (1971: 99).

Although Classical Realism is the hallmark of Sophistic culture for Nietzsche, realistic themes are in evidence in some of the Presocratics as well. Among the Presocratics, for example, Nietzsche says he finds "no fanatics looking at the world through rose-colored glasses" (PT: 200). "With Empedocles and Democritus," for example, "the Greeks were well on the way toward *assessing correctly* the irrationality and suffering of human existence; but thanks to Socrates, *they never reached the goal*. An unbiased view of man is something which eludes all Socratics, who have those horrible abstractions, 'the good' and 'the just' on their minds" (PT: 136). Indeed, Nietzsche thinks the admirably "scientific" mindset cultivated by the Presocratics is anathema to Socrates:

> [S]cience takes things seriously that have nothing to do with "good" and "evil," consequently [it] makes the feeling for "good" and "evil" seem less important. For morality demands that the whole man and all his forces should stand in its service. . . . This is why scientific procedures rapidly declined in Greece once Socrates had introduced into science the disease of moralizing; the height attained in the disposition of Democritus, Hippocrates, and Thucydides was not attained a second time.
>
> (WP: 443)

Heraclitus, too, represents the realistic repudiation of "moralizing," though for somewhat different reasons as Nietzsche explains:

> Who could possibly demand from such a philosophy [as Heraclitus'] an ethic with its necessary imperatives "thou shalt," or

worse yet, accuse Heraclitus of lacking such! Man is necessity down to his last fibre, and totally "unfree," that is if one means by freedom the foolish demand to be able to change one's *essentia* arbitrarily, like a garment – a demand which every serious philosophy has rejected with the proper scorn.

(PTAG: 7)

This crucial point of realistic (and fatalistic) insight – that man "is necessity down to his last fibre," that one cannot "change one's *essentia* arbitrarily" – is one Nietzsche finds not only in Heraclitus, but in Spinoza, Schopenhauer, and his German Materialist contemporaries. We shall have occasion to consider Nietzsche's *fatalism*, as it was influenced by Schopenhauer, shortly.

There is one final aspect of Sophistic Classical Realism on which we have not yet touched, for the Sophists, and their contemporaries like Callicles, often advanced accounts of the *origin* of morality that resonate strikingly with views Nietzsche expresses.[22] Consider, for example, the Calliclean view that the inferior employ morality to make "slaves of those who are naturally better" (*Gorgias*, 491e–492a), that "the weaker folk, the majority . . . frame the laws [and, we might add, the moral norms] for their own advantage" in order to "frighten [the strong] by saying that to overreach others is shameful and evil" (*Gorgias*, 483b–d). We surely hear echoes of Callicles in the *Genealogy* when Nietzsche writes:

When the oppressed, downtrodden, violated say to each other with the vindictive cunning of powerlessness: "Let us be different from evil people, let us be good! And a good person is anyone who does not rape, does not harm anyone, who does not attack, does not retaliate . . ." – this means, if heard coolly and impartially, nothing more than "We weak people are just weak: it is good to do nothing *for which we are not strong enough*."

(GM I: 13)

22 I should note that it has been well established that Nietzsche did *not* embrace (as, e.g., Guthrie thinks) Calliclean hedonism, i.e., the view that "anyone who is to live aright should suffer his appetites to grow to the greatest extent and not check them" (*Gorgias*, 491e) (contrast, Guthrie 1971: 106–7). But Nietzsche clearly appreciated the value of checking desire and accepting limitations (e.g., BGE: 188). On this whole issue, see the useful discussion in Nehamas (1985: 202–3); cf. Leiter (2000: 295, n. 42).

So too is Callicleanism in evidence when Nietzsche observes that "everything that elevates an individual above the herd and intimidates the neighbor is . . . called *evil*" (BGE: 201); when he suggests that "[m]oral judgments and condemnations constitute the favorite revenge of the spiritually limited against those less limited" (BGE: 219); finally, too, when he claims that the "chief means" by which the "weak and mediocre . . . weaken and pull down the stronger" is "the moral judgment" (WP: 345).[23] We shall see these Calliclean themes regarding the origin of morality repeatedly in evidence in the *Genealogy* and Nietzsche's critique of morality more generally (see Chapters 4 and 6).

Schopenhauer

Commentators have written more about the influence of the philosophy of Arthur Schopenhauer (1788–1860) on Nietzsche than any of the other thinkers discussed in this chapter. And while Nietzsche's encounter with Schopenhauer is undeniably important, it is hardly more important than the other figures and movements discussed here. For these others, as much as Schopenhauer, shaped Nietzsche's sensibility and demarcated the range of problems which concerned him. Indeed, in many respects, Schopenhauer simply *reinforces* ideas and sentiments that Nietzsche would have found in the other intellectual sources discussed in this chapter.

Although Schopenhauer published his major work – Volume I of *The World as Will and Representation* – in 1818 (the second volume appeared in 1844), it was not until the middle of the nineteenth century that he became a prominent and influential intellectual figure. In 1818, Hegel's "absolute" idealism still dominated the philosophical scene in

---

23 Compare also Glaucon in Plato's *Republic* (esp. *circa* 360c, discussing the ring of Gyges), who maintains that the putatively just would prefer to be unjust if they could get away with it; under such circumstances, "We should then watch the just man in the very act of resorting to the same conduct as the unjust man because of the self-advantage which every creature by its nature pursues as a good." The resonance here is striking with Zarathustra's warning about those "who talk much of their justice" that "when they call themselves good and the just, do not forget that they would be pharisees, if only they had – power" (Z II: "On the Tarantulas").

Germany, whereas Schopenhauer wanted to revive aspects of the Kantian distinction between the world as it really is in-itself (the world as "will" for Schopenhauer) and the world as it *appears* to us (i.e., the world as "representation"). Yet an historically sensitive reading of Nietzsche must recognize that by the time of Hegel's death in 1831, the Hegelian system was falling into disrepute. Hegel's death, in effect, marks the death of Idealism for the next century in Germany (cf. Lange 1865: 245; Schnädelbach 1983: 3). "Materialists" (see below) and NeoKantians were the dominant philosophical figures by the time Nietzsche was being educated. While there is inconclusive evidence that Nietzsche had some modest first-hand familiarity with Hegel's texts,[24] his remarks about Hegel suggest that he absorbed a caricature of Hegelian philosophy from Schopenhauer's often hilarious and always wicked anti-Hegelian polemics.[25] The now widespread pedagogical practice of teaching Hegel and Nietzsche together as major figures of "Nineteenth-Century Philosophy" actually does considerable violence to the real intellectual history of that period.

Nietzsche discovered Schopenhauer by accident in October 1865, when he happened to pick up a copy of *The World as Will and Representation* in a bookstore in Leipzig. The work made an enormous impression on the 21-year-old Nietzsche. As he wrote at the time:

> I do not know which demon whispered to me: "Take this book home with you." In any case, it went against my usual custom of avoiding over-hasty book purchases. At home I threw myself into the corner of the sofa with the treasure I had acquired, and started to allow that energetic, sombre genius to work upon me. Here every line screamed renunciation, denial, resignation, here I saw a mirror which caught sight of world, of life, and of my own mind in terrifying grandeur. Here the full, disinterested,

[24] The issues are discussed in Brobjer (forthcoming), though even he notes that when Nietzsche applied for the philosophy chair at Basel in 1871, he emphasized his knowledge *only* of ancient philosophy, Kant, and Schopenhauer.

[25] This fact makes the construal of Nietzsche as a critic of Hegel in Deleuze (1962) particularly odd; Hegel was simply a dead issue in academic German philosophy at the time Nietzsche was writing.

sun-like eye of art looked upon me, here I saw sickness and
healing, exile and sanctuary, hell and heaven.

(Quoted in Janaway 1998b: 16)

The composer Richard Wagner, whom Nietzsche met three years later,
shared this enthusiasm for Schopenhauer, thus only amplifying the
philosopher's importance for the young Nietzsche (who remained for
several years in Wagner's thrall as well). This thinker whom he called
the "greatest philosophical demi-god in the whole of the last thousand
years" (Janaway 1998a: 1) is omnipresent in early works like *The
Birth of Tragedy*, though he becomes increasingly an object of critique
in the mature works. We have already seen in Chapter 1 how Schopenhauer's quasi-Kantian skepticism about our ability to know the *noumenal* world affected Nietzsche's early epistemological views, and
how he eventually moved beyond Schopenhauer on this issue. Here,
we may concentrate on three additional aspects of Schopenhauer's
thought that prove especially important for a reading of the *Genealogy*:[26] his pessimism or nihilism; his ethics of compassion; and his
theory of agency and character.

Pessimism/nihilism

The world as it really is in-itself, according to Schopenhauer, is essentially "will," a famously obscure concept in the Schopenhauerian
system. Roughly, we may think of it as some sort of formless, undif-
ferentiated blind striving force that underlies everything (cf. Janaway
1994: 28–34). As individual human beings, in the phenomenal world,
each of us is essentially will as well, although here Schopenhauer's
notion is less opaque. As one commentator writes:

The will has no overall purpose, aims at no highest good, and
can never be satisfied. Although it is our essence, it strikes us
as an alien agency within, striving for life and procreation
blindly, mediated only secondarily by consciousness. Instinctive
sexuality is at our core, interfering constantly with the life of

[26] For an excellent overview of Schopenhauer's philosophy, see Janaway
(1994), which also contains a useful bibliography.

the intellect. To be an individual expression of this will is to lead a life of continual desire, deficiency, and suffering. Pleasure or satisfaction exists only relative to a felt lack; it is negative, merely the cessation of an episode of striving or suffering, and has no value of itself. Nothing we can achieve by conscious act of will alters the will to life within us. There is no free will. Human actions, as part of the natural order, are determined. . . . As individual parts of the empirical world we are ineluctably pushed through life by a force inside us which is not of our choosing, which gives rise to needs and desires we can never fully satisfy, and is without ultimate purpose. Schopenhauer concludes that it would have been better not to exist – and that the world itself is something whose existence we should deplore rather than celebrate.

(Janaway 1998a: 2–3)

Hence Schopenhauer's pessimistic verdict: in a world of continual, senseless suffering – in which we endlessly strive and desire, with only temporary satisfactions, and all to no end, except to restart the painful cycle anew – how can life itself be justified? Would we not, in fact, be better off dead? Nietzsche accepted Schopenhauer's pessimistic challenge and "[m]uch of his own thought may be regarded as an attempt to meet this challenge, and to establish a viable alternative verdict" (Schacht 1983: 478).[27] For the young Nietzsche, it is art, especially music, that holds the key to justifying existence (cf. Schacht 1983, Chapter VIII), but in his mature work a more important role is played by the *revaluation of values*. The question becomes, in other words: what is the *value* of those values that underwrite the pessimistic verdict? The *Genealogy* is part of Nietzsche's mature project of attacking those moral values in the perspective of which life itself seems to lack all value.

Ethics of compassion

As the foregoing remarks suggest, it is ultimately Schopenhauer's moral perspective with which Nietzsche must take issue. Central to

[27] We shall return to this point, significantly, in Chapter 8.

Schopenhauer's ethical view is the idea that pity or compassion (*Mitleid*) is the only morally valuable motive, while egoism or self-ishness lacks moral value; indeed, for Schopenhauer, compassion is the true *basis* of morality (Schopenhauer 1841). Schopenhauer's moral views were not, however, unconnected to his general Kantianism. For Schopenhauer

> believed that Kant had already shown that time and space do not belong to the thing-in-itself, and therefore that individuality and plurality are foreign to the "true essence of the world" [Schopenhauer 1841a: 207]. ... To the extent that we fail to recognize our individuality as mere appearance, we are moved to action only by egoistic concerns. ... If we care about the welfare of others, this is due not to our natural inclinations, but only to the recognition in others of something that lies beyond nature, of our "own self," our "own true inner nature" [1841a: 209]. ... [C]ompassion [*Mitleid*], immediate concern for the welfare of another, possesses a higher worth than egoistic incli-nation because, rather than being part of our natural equipment, it is a sign of our connection to a reality that goes beyond the phenomenal or natural world.
>
> (Clark and Leiter 1997: xix–xx)

Mitleid has higher moral value than egoism, in short, because in *Mitleid* we transcend the illusion of our individuality, which is a mere artifact of our existence in the phenomenal world, the world of "mere" appearance.

Nietzsche's well-known polemics against *Mitleid* as a moral ideal (e.g., HAH: 50, 103; D: 134; GS: 99; BGE: 201, 225) are clearly directed at Schopenhauer's ethics. (This point is obscured in English by the fact that most translators of Schopenhauer render *Mitleid* as "compassion," while most translators of Nietzsche render the same German word as "pity.") Indeed, he announces in the preface to the *Genealogy* that in addressing "the question of the *value* of morality,"

> I had to confront my great teacher Schopenhauer. ... [and deal] with the value of the "unegoistic," the instincts of compassion [*Mitleid*], self-denial, self-sacrifice which Schopenhauer had for

so long gilded, deified and transcendentalized until he was finally left with them as those "values as such" on the basis of which he *said* "*no*" to life and to himself as well.

(GM Pref: 5)

The *Genealogy* then sets out to ask about "the *value* of compassion and of the morality of compassion" and to explore the possibility that such a morality might turn out to be "the danger of dangers" (GM Pref: 6). In so doing, Nietzsche is setting himself in opposition to Schopenhauer in order to resist Schopenhauer's pessimistic verdict: for, as we have just seen him say, it is "on the basis" of this morality of compassion that Schopenhauer is led to say "'no' to life" (GM Pref: 5). To critique this morality is, then, to critique the evaluative perspective on the basis of which life appears to lack value. As he puts it in *Daybreak*: by challenging the "higher value" assigned to the unegoistic over the egoistic,

we shall restore to men their goodwill towards the actions decried as egoistic and restore to these actions their *value – we shall deprive them of their bad conscience*! And since they have hitherto been by far the most frequent actions, and will continue to be so for all future time, we thus remove from the entire aspect of action and life its *evil appearance*! This is a very significant result!

(D: 148)

The *Genealogy*, as we shall see, aims for the same "significant result" (see especially Chapter 4).

Theory of agency and character

If Nietzsche resists Schopenhauer's pessimism and his moral philosophy, Nietzsche follows him much more closely in his theory of agency and character. For Schopenhauer, of course, the "self" as manifest in the merely phenomenal world is an illusion: in the noumenal world – i.e., the world as it *really* is – there are no individual selves; all is "will." Since Nietzsche rejects this aspect of Schopenhauer's view, what matters is what Schopenhauer taught him about the self as it is found in the "phenomenal" world – the only world, for Nietzsche, that there is.

Certain aspects of Schopenhauer's view are familiar. Schopenhauer denied the freedom of the will in the empirical realm,[28] in virtue of the truth of determinism, which follows from "the principle of sufficient reason," which holds that "all necessity is the relation of consequent to ground" (1818: 113). Since "the principle of sufficient reason is the universal form of every phenomenon, and man in his action, like every other phenomenon, must be subordinated to it" (1818: 113), it follows that all human actions are *necessary*, i.e., causally determined. As conscious intellects, we are like "spectators" upon our actions; while they may appear "undetermined" to us, in reality, they are completely determined, though the causes are opaque to the intellect (1818: 291).

Schopenhauer's picture is, in fact, richer than this, and important for understanding Nietzsche. For Schopenhauer also held that each person has an "unalterable . . . empirical character" (1818: 301). "[T]he tendency of his innermost nature and the goal he pursues in accordance therewith," says Schopenhauer, "these we can never change by influencing him from without, by instructing him" (1818: 294). The necessity of one's actions, then, actually follows from the causal interaction of one's unalterable character with "motives," that is, conscious representations that, for example, portray the world as being in such-and-such a way: e.g., "There is a glass of water on that table" or "This job will pay well." "Just as everything in nature has its forces and qualities that definitely react to a definite impression, and constitute its character," observes Schopenhauer, "so man also has his *character*, from which the motives call forth his actions with necessity" (1818: 287; cf. 1818: 290, 292, 301). Since "every individual action follows with strict necessity from the effect of the motive on the character" (1818: 113), and since the character is constant, it follows that every

[28] The exception to this generalization occurs when the merely phenomenal self "abandons all knowledge of individual things as such, "and makes contact, as it were, with the thing-in-itself, i.e., the will (1818: 301; cf. 1818: 404). There is, again, no reason to think that Nietzsche accepted this part of Schopenhauer's view, depending as it does on the very distinction Nietzsche repudiates.

action we perform *had to be performed*, as though fated. Indeed, the principle of sufficient reason – which rules in the phenomenal world for Schopenhauer – entails that "everything can be regarded as irrevocably predetermined by fate . . . by means of the chain of causes" (1818: 302). Fatalism about human action is just a particular instance of this broader thesis, as Schopenhauer makes plain: "Just as events always come about in accordance with fate, in other words, according to the endless concatenation of causes, so do our deeds always come about according to our intelligible character" (1818: 302). This leads Schopenhauer to the following remarkable comment on the Christian doctrine of "predestination" according to which a man's

> life and conduct, in other words his empirical character, are only the unfolding of the intelligible character, the development of decided and unalterable tendencies already recognized in the child. Therefore his conduct is, so to speak, fixed and settled even at his birth, and remains essentially the same to the very end. We too agree with this [doctrine].
>
> (1818: 293)

Schopenhauer goes on to dissociate himself from some of the theological baggage associated with the Christian doctrine of predestination, but the point to note is that he endorses the key elements of its fatalistic conception of human life: it is just not God that does the determining for Schopenhauer, but rather the interaction of motive and unalterable character operating under the principle of sufficient reason (i.e., the law of cause-and-effect).

The many resonances in Nietzsche of this Schopenhauerian view are striking. In an early work, for example, he explicitly praises Schopenhauer for his "insight into the strict necessity of human actions" adding that we confront "a brazen wall of fate [*des Fatums*]: we *are* in prison, we can only *dream* ourselves free, not make ourselves free" (HAH II: 33). In his next (and first mature) work, *Daybreak*, he suggests that what looks like purposive and intentional action is nothing more than the *necessary* course of events playing itself out:

> [P]erhaps there exists neither will nor purposes, and we have only imagined them. Those iron hands of necessity which shake the

dice-box of chance play their game for an infinite length of time; so that there *have* to be throws which exactly resemble purposiveness and rationality of every degree. *Perhaps* our acts of will and our purposes are nothing but just such throws – and we are only too limited and too vain to comprehend our extreme limitedness: which consists in the fact that we ourselves shake the dice-box with iron hands, that we ourselves in our most intentional actions do no more than play the game of necessity.

(D: 130)

Anticipating the later themes of *Ecce Homo* (see Chapter 3), Nietzsche writes in *The Gay Science*: "*What does your conscience say*? – 'You shall become the person you are'" (GS: 270). A few years later, in *Beyond Good and Evil*, Nietzsche observes that:

[A]t the bottom of us, really "deep down," there is, of course, something unteachable, some granite of spiritual *fatum* [personl fate or destiny], of predetermined [*vorherbestimmer*] decision and answer to predetermined selected questions. Whenever a cardinal problem is at stake, there speaks an unchangeable [*unwandelbares*] "this is I."

(BGE: 231)

In his last productive year, Nietzsche writes that, "The single human being is a piece of *fatum* from the front and from the rear, one law more, one necessity more for all that is yet to come and to be" (TI V: 6). In *Nachlass* notes from the same year, he claims that "the voluntary is absolutely lacking ... everything has been directed along certain lines from the beginning" (WP: 458) and that, not surprisingly, "one will become only that which one is (in spite of all: that means education, instruction, milieu, chance, and accident)" (WP: 334).

If all the foregoing sounds a lot like Schopenhauer, it should give one pause that Nietzsche also strikes some discordant notes. In several places in *Daybreak*, for example, he appears to repudiate Schopenhauer's view of character. For example, he writes:

One can dispose of one's drives like a gardener and, though few know it, cultivate the shoots of anger, pity, curiosity, vanity as productively and profitably as a beautiful fruit tree on a trellis.

> ... All this we are at liberty to do: but how many know we are at liberty to do it? Do the majority not *believe* in *themselves* as in completely *fully-developed facts*? Have the great philosophers [i.e., Schopenhauer] not put their seal on the prejudice with the doctrine of the unchangeability of character?
>
> (D: 560)

Nietzsche voices this same theme more than once (e.g., D: 364, 382), suggesting that he did not simply take over Schopenhauerian fatalism wholesale.

In fact, Schopenhauer's own view in this regard is a bit more complex. For Schopenhauer also argues that there is something called "acquired character" which consists, essentially, in learning what one's unalterable character is really like (1818: 304–5). Once we have "acquired character," says Schopenhauer,

> we shall no longer be novices, wait, attempt, and grope about, in order to see what we really desire and are able to do; we know this once for all, and with every choice we have only to apply general principles to particular cases, and at once reach a decision.
>
> (1818: 305)

Schopenhauer's idea, here, seems to be this: once we know the facts about our character, we can (via intellect presumably) proceed in realizing our character more efficiently and effectively. To "acquire character," in other words, is to know our "limits," and thus to be spared the experience of being "often ... driven back on to our own path by hard blows from outside" (1818: 304) when we exceed those "limits."

But if this is Schopenhauer's view, then it is not clear that it is really very different from Nietzsche's. For Nietzsche asks us – repeatedly in *Daybreak* – to think of ourselves as analogous to plants; and the view he opposes is simply the view that there is no work for a "gardener" to do, whether on the roots (as in a plant) or on the drives (as in a person). Yet it appears that this is precisely Schopenhauer's view as well (though Nietzsche seems not to have recognized it): the "unalterability" of character for Schopenhauer does not, it seems, entail that there is no "gardening" work to be done on the basic ingredients (e.g., the drives) which constitute the "character." As Schopenhauer writes later on, the "will" is like "the strong blind man carrying the sighted lame man [i.e., the intellect] on his back" (1844: 209). This suggests, though, that there is work for the intellect to do in guiding the character – precisely what we can do when we "acquire" character in Schopenhauer's sense. So the passages in *Daybreak* are not a repudiation of Schopenhauer's view, but a reiteration of it.

But does this modification of the view refute the fatalism? In fact, it does not (though Schopenhauer, at least, is unclear on this issue). We shall have to wait, however, for the discussion of Nietzsche's theory of agency in Chapter 3 before setting out the detailed answer to this question.

German Materialism

"Materialism" is a venerable philosophical position from Leucippus, Democritus, Epicurus, and Lucretius in antiquity, to La Mettrie and d'Holbach in the eighteenth century, to the German Materialists of the mid-nineteenth century, to Smart, Quine, and the Churchlands in the twentieth century.[29] Many materialists are Substantive Naturalists (in the terminology of Chapter 1), i.e., they believe, more or less strictly, that everything that exists is physical. *Reductive* materialists think that seemingly non-physical phenomena (like mental experiences) are *reducible* to physical phenomena; *eliminative* materialists think that some non-physical stuff cannot be reduced and so must be "eliminated" from our best picture of the world, much as we have eliminated witches and the ether. Some who have claimed the "materialist" label were less committed to Substantive Naturalism than to the Methodologically Naturalistic idea we have seen in Spinoza, Heraclitus, and Nietzsche that everything that exists is naturalistically explicable. Thus, the eighteenth-century "materialist" Baron d'Holbach (best known for his 1770 book *The System of Nature; or the Laws of the Moral and Physical World*) held that "human consciousness, value-making, and morality are ... mechanically predetermined by

[29] See generally, Lange (1865) and Vitzthum (1995).

natural forces" (Vitzthum 1995: 70) so that a human being is "nothing more than a passive instrument in the hands of necessity" (quoting d'Holbach, Vitzthum 1995: 71).

German Materialism of the 1850s (influenced, in part, by d'Holbach) embodied a similarly naturalistic world-view, well captured by one of its leading proponents, the medical doctor Ludwig Büchner (older brother of the proto-existentialist playwright Georg), in his 1855 best-seller *Force and Matter*: "the researches and discoveries of modern times can no longer allow us to doubt that man, with all he has and possesses, be it mental or corporeal, is a *natural product* like all other organic beings" (p. lxxviii). "Man is a product of nature," declared Büchner, "in body and mind. Hence not merely what he is, but also what he does, wills, feels, and thinks, depends upon the same natural necessity as the whole structure of the world" (p. 239). So spoke the "German Materialists" of the 1850s and after.

German Materialism had its origins in Ludwig Feuerbach's works of the late 1830s and early 1840s, but it really exploded onto the cultural scene in the 1850s, under the impetus of the startling new discoveries about human beings made by the burgeoning science of physiology.[30] After 1830 in Germany, "Physiology ... became the basis for modern scientific medicine, and this confirmed the tendency, identifiable throughout the whole of the nineteenth century, towards integration of human and natural sciences" (Schnädelbach 1983: 76). In his 1843 *Philosophy of the Future*, Feuerbach could write that, "The new philosophy makes man, along with nature as the basis of man, into the one and only universal and highest object of philosophy: anthropology, including physiology, becomes the universal science" (Sec. 54). In 1850, the physiologist Jacob Moleschott published two books in this Materialistic spirit: the scholarly *The Physiology of Food* and a popular companion volume, *The Theory of Food: For the People*. These were followed in 1852 by the work that made Moleschott famous, *The Cyclical Course of Life*. The year 1855 also

---

[30] Schnädelbach distinguishes the "vulgar materialism" of the German Materialists proper – Büchner, Vogt and Moleschott – from the "anthropological materialism" of Feuerbach and the "historical materialism" of Marx. The German Materialists accepted scientism: "science itself satisfies all philosophical requirements" (1983: 96).

saw the publication of two influential and polemical treatises: the physiologist Karl Vogt's *Blind Faith and Science* and Büchner's *Force and Matter*, the latter of which "soon earned the reputation as the Bible of materialism," going through 12 editions in 17 years, and being translated into 17 foreign languages (Gregory 1977: 105).

Given their tremendous impact, it would have been impossible for the young Nietzsche to have been unfamiliar with the Materialists. "[T]he German materialists . . . took the German intellectual world by storm during the 1850s" (Vitzthum 1995: 98). A critic of materialism writing in 1856 complained that, "A new world view is settling into the minds of men. It goes about like a virus. Every young mind of the generation now living is affected by it" (quoted in Gregory: 10).[31] Yet the crucial event for Nietzsche was his discovery in 1866 of Friedrich Lange's recently published *History of Materialism*, a book which opened up for him the whole history of philosophical materialism up to and including German Materialism, as well as introducing him to the profound developments in modern natural science, especially chemistry and physiology.[32] As with Schopenhauer, the impact on the young Nietzsche was dramatic. "Kant, Schopenhauer, this book by Lange – I don't need anything else," he wrote in 1866 (quoted in Janz 1978 I: 198). He viewed the work as "undoubtedly the most significant philosophical work to have appeared in recent decades" (ibid.), and called it in a letter of 1868 "a real treasure-house," mentioning,

---

[31] Brobjer (forthcoming) reports that Nietzsche had read Feuerbach as a young man, as well as the journal *Anregungen für Kunst, Leben und Wissenschaft* which, in the early 1860s, published many articles about materialism, including by Büchner.

[32] See generally, Salaquarda (1978) and Stack (1983). Stack, in my view, overstates Nietzsche's debt to Lange, and fails to note their many differences, e.g., Nietzsche was less critical of materialism than Lange, and Nietzsche plainly repudiated Lange's Kantianism (e.g., Lange's view that "[w]e must therefore recognize the existence of a transcendent order of things . . ." (1865: 230)). Stack's book does usefully demonstrate that an influence on Nietzsche can be profound (as evidenced by the views he would later express) without Nietzsche acknowledging that fact. Thus, for example, his *Nachlass* references to Büchner tend to be rather dismissive and rude. Cf. KSA 7: 596, 740. The similarities, however, between Materialist thought and Nietzsche's own turn out to be striking.

among other things, Lange's discussion of the "materialist movement of our times" (quoted in Stack 1983: 13) – including such figures as Feuerbach, Büchner, Moleschott, Heinrich Czolbe, and the pioneering physiologist Hermann von Helmholtz. From Lange, Nietzsche would have acquired a clear picture of contemporary German Materialism, of its "mechanical understanding of man as a mere natural creature" (Lange 1865: 213), of its view that, "The nature of man is . . . only a special case of universal physiology, as thought is only a special case in the chain of physical processes of life" (Lange 1865: 248).

Lange, himself, was one of a number of "neo-Kantian" critics of Materialism who held, first, that modern physiology vindicated Kantianism by demonstrating the dependence of knowledge on the peculiarly human sensory apparatus (Lange 1865: 322 [discussing the "confirmation from the scientific side of the critical standpoint in the theory of knowledge"] and 3rd Sec., Ch. IV ["The Physiology of the Sense-Organs and the World as Representation"]); and, second, that the Materialists were naive in believing science gives us knowledge of the thing-in-itself rather than the merely phenomenal world (cf. p. 84 ["the physiology of the sense-organs has . . . produced decisive grounds for the [epistemological] refutation of Materialism"]; pp. 277 ff.; p. 329).[33] At the same time, Lange's general intellectual sympathies were clearly with the Materialists as against the idealists, theologians, and others who resisted the blossoming scientific picture of the world and of human beings. Thus, for example, he remarks: "if Materialism can be set aside only by criticism based upon the [Kantian] theory of knowledge . . . in the sphere of positive questions it is everywhere in the right . . ." (1865: 332). Since Nietzsche, as we have seen, eventually abandoned the residual Kantianism he inherited from both Schopenhauer and Lange, what matters most for understanding Nietzsche is Lange's basically favorable attitude toward Materialism.

While a reaction to German Materialism did set in by the 1870s and 1880s, Nietzsche's youthful engagement with the Materialists made a profound and lasting impression on him. In early 1868, he briefly contemplated switching from the study of philology to chem-

[33] Another such NeoKantian critic, interestingly, was Helmholtz; see Schnädelbach (1983: 104–5).

istry, and starting in the late 1860s, he began an intensive reading of books on natural science (Brobjer forthcoming), readings which continued into the 1880s (Janz 1978 II: 73–4; Hayman 1980: 234). He admits that in the late 1870s, "A truly burning thirst took hold of me: henceforth I really pursued nothing *more* than physiology, medicine and natural sciences" (EH III: HAH-3). This impression is evident even in his mature work of the 1880s. In *Ecce Homo*, he complains of the "blunder" that he "became a philologist – why not at least a physician or something else that opens one's eyes?" (EH II: 2). The same year, he comments (in a passage evocative of La Mettrie's 1748 *Man a Machine*) that, "Descartes was the first to have dared, with admirable boldness, to understand the animal as *machina*: the whole of our physiology endeavors to prove this claim. And we are consistent enough not to except man, as Descartes still did" (A: 14).

Indeed, the importance of German Materialism to the intellectual climate of the period is evidenced by Nietzsche's repeatedly felt need to distance himself from certain Materialist doctrines that he found unpalatable. For example, the whole of Chapter Six of *Beyond Good and Evil* – "We Scholars" (BGE: 204–13) – is plainly a polemic against the Materialist view that "official philosophy could be replaced with natural science," as the historian Frederick Gregory puts it (1977: 146). The Materialists felt "that their system was merely a systematization of the knowledge gained in the natural sciences and thus had finally put an end to the need for philosophy" (Schnädelbach 1983: 103). Thus, an "increasing contempt for philosophy" became common (ibid., p. 92). So when Nietzsche complains of the "arrogant contempt for philosophy" coming from "the lips of young natural scientists and old physicians" (BGE: 204), he is not only talking about the Materialists in general, but also about the physician Büchner in particular, who by the mid-1880s was an old man, yet still enjoying the fame sustained by the repeated printings of his *Force and Matter*, which expressed precisely this "arrogant contempt."[34] Recall, however, our discussion from Chapter 1: Nietzsche's objection in passages like

---

[34] Nietzsche does concede that given the "wretchedness of most recent philosophy" – he cites Dühring as one example – "a solid man of science *may* feel that he is of a better type and descent" (BGE: 204).

these are not to science, *per se*, or to the relevance of science and scientific methods to philosophy, but rather to the idea that science could dispense with the role of "genuine philosophers" as creators of values (cf. BGE: 211; Chapter 1). As he says elsewhere, it is, "Around the inventors of new values [that] the world revolves," albeit "invisibly" and "inaudibly" (Z I: 12; Z II: 18). Of course, Nietzsche is eager to utilize the information provided by "physiologists and doctors" as to which values might contribute to "the preservation of the greatest number" or to "producing a stronger type" (GM I: Note), but he is equally keen to resist the Materialist conceit that the creative role of philosophy might be dispensed with altogether.

Nietzsche is similarly hostile to the tendency toward *reductive* materialism evinced by many of the German Materialists, who often appeared to embrace a mind-brain identity theory, i.e., the view that all mental states are simply identical with physical states in the brain.[35] As we saw in Chapter 1, Nietzsche argued against this view in now familiar *phenomenological* terms (associated, for example, with Thomas Nagel and Charles Taylor), attacking the ability of reductive materialism to capture the distinctive qualitative character of experience (cf. GS: 373). Indeed, when he describes himself as "the sternest opponent of all materialism" (GM III: 16), he must plainly mean *reductive* materialism, since this remark comes immediately on the heels of his claim that, "When someone cannot get over a 'psychological pain,' that is *not* the fault of his 'psyche' but, to speak crudely, more probably even that of his belly" (GM III: 16). (Natural facts may be explanatorily primary for Nietzsche – part of Nietzsche's Methodological Naturalism – but that does not entail that he embraces the substantive naturalism favored by many of the Materialists.)

In fact, this latter passage is just one example of Nietzsche's unabashed appropriation of ideas of clear Materialist pedigree. We saw in discussing Nietzsche's Doctrine of Types in Chapter 1[36] evidence of his view that persons are best understood physiologically, a view clearly supported by the whole Materialist movement. He also shares

35 See, e.g., Lange (1865: 155–7); Büchner (1870), Chapter XII ["Brain and Soul"]; note Schopenhauer's own flirtation with the same view [1844: 272 ff.]).
36 See pp. 8–10.

with the Materialists a blanket repudiation of the idea of free will (Büchner 1870: 239–40; Gregory 1977: 34),[37] and, in fact, must be taking for granted the intellectual ascendancy of the Materialists when he quips that the "will was firmly accepted as given" but "[t]oday we no longer believe a word of all this" (TI VI: 3). One can surely recognize, too, the (anachronistically) Nietzschean flavor of Büchner's claim that,

> Man is subject to the same laws as plants and animals. . . . [M]an [is] physically and mentally the product of such external influences [as "congenital physical and mental dispositions," as well as "sex, nationality, climate, soil"], and develops accordingly – certainly not that morally independent, free-willing creature as he is represented by moralists.

> (1870: 243)

Nietzsche plainly echoes Feuerbach's famous dictum that, "The body in its totality is my ego [*Ich*], my very essence" (Gregory 1977: 30) when Zarathustra says "body am I entirely, and nothing else; and soul is only a word for something about the body" (Z I: 4). (Echoes of Schopenhauer are apparent here too; cf. 1818: 100).

Perhaps most strikingly, Nietzsche's notorious speculations about the role of nutrition, climate, and bodily fluids like bile on the thoughts and character of persons were clearly inspired by the Materialists. Moleschott's influential *Physiology of Food* (Moleschott 1859), for example, consisted of more than 500 pages of detailed information about the physiological and chemical aspects of food and human digestion, while the popular companion volume recommended different diets for "artisans" than for "thinkers and scholars," in view of the differing intellectual demands made upon each (1853, Third Book, Chs. VI and VII). In reviewing Moleschott's book, Feuerbach

---

37 The Materialists seem to have been drawn to this conclusion, however, primarily by their reductive theory of mind, which led them to the view that there is (as Thomas Nagel describes it) "no room for agency in a world of neural impulses, chemical reactions, and bone and muscle movements" (1986: 111). Nietzsche, in fact, sometimes flirted with a similar view (as did Schopenhauer): e.g., "one has a nervous system (– but no 'soul' –)" (WP: 229).

expressed the core idea as follows: "If you want to improve the people then give them better food instead of declamations against sin. Man is what he eats" (quoted in Gregory 1977: 92). According to Lange, Moleschott taught that "man is the sum of parents and nurse, of place and time, of air and weather, of sound and light, of food and dress" (1865: 241). Büchner's work is full of remarks like, "A copious secretion of bile has, as is well-known, a powerful influence on the mental disposition" (1870: 119), as well as discussions of the effects of climate on national character-types (1870: 241–2). The whole intellectual *Zeitgeist* of the period encouraged pursuit of *physiological* explanations of intellectual traits or dispositions, as reflected in Büchner's claim that, "Newton's atrophied brain caused him in old age to become interested in studying the books of Daniel and Revelation in the Bible" (1870: 111).

With figures like Moleschott and Büchner ascendant on the intellectual scene, it is not surprising, then, that we should find Nietzsche meditating on "the moral effects of different foods" and calling for a "philosophy of nutrition" (GS: 7); or speculating that, "Wherever a deep discontent with existence becomes prevalent, it is the aftereffects of some great dietary mistake made by a whole people over a long period of time that are coming to light" (GS: 134); or arguing that:

> Whatever proceeds from the stomach, the intestines, the beating of the heart, the nerves, the bile, the semen – all those distempers, debilitations, excitations, the whole chance operation of the machine of which we still know so little! – had to be seen by a Christian such as Pascal as a moral and religious phenomenon, and he had to ask whether God or Devil, good or evil, salvation or damnation was to be discovered in them! Oh what an unhappy interpreter.
>
> (D: 86)

He reiterates the point several years later in the *Genealogy*: "'sinfulness' in man is not a fact, but rather the interpretation of a fact, namely a physiological upset, – the latter seen from a perspective of morals and religion which is no longer binding on us" (GM III: 16). From the Materialist Movement of Nietzsche's Germany, in short, Nietzsche would have learned to think of persons as essentially natural, bodily organisms, organisms for whom free will was an illusion, and for whom questions of physiological traits, nutrition and climate were decisive in determining their ideas, their values, and their development. Ahistorical commentators who too readily dismiss Nietzsche's interest in physiological questions (e.g., DeMan 1979: 119; Nehamas 1985: 120) miss the centrality of such ways of thinking to Nietzsche's naturalism and to the whole intellectual climate of the period. "The naturalization of the image of man under the influence of natural science was the work of the materialist movement of the middle of the century" (Schnädelbach 1983: 229). In this regard, Nietzsche was very much a thinker of his times.

Summary

It may help to conclude this chapter by recapping briefly the main intellectual influences on Nietzsche, as set out above. These influences fall into essentially six categories.

First, an appreciation for "*good philology*," for the art of reading well, of getting things "right" in interpretive matters, which Nietzsche learned from his training in classical philology.

Second, a commitment to *methodological naturalism* – to the idea that the world, and in particular human beings, can be explained in essentially *scientific* terms – which Nietzsche found in both the Presocratics and the German Materialists.

Third, a commitment (not always strict) to *empiricism*, to the idea that genuine knowledge must have some basis in sense experience, an epistemological posture he admired in many of the Presocratics and Sophists, and which was also present in the Materialists.

Fourth, a tendency to look at matters *realistically*, in the manner of the Classical Realism of the Sophists and Presocratics, thinkers who candidly and unflinchingly assessed human motives and actions, and who appreciated the extent to which self-interest figured in human affairs, even (importantly) in the types of *moralities* people preached and adopted.

Fifth, an acceptance of an essentially *fatalistic* conception of human agency, according to which human beings lack free will, and are determined to do what they do, and believe what they believe, by largely *natural* facts about their physiology and their psychological drives – a view Nietzsche found, in related forms, in both Schopenhauer and the Materialists.

Sixth, an acceptance of the *problem of suffering* as a central challenge, one that raised fundamental questions about the justification of life itself – a challenge posed most powerfully by Schopenhauer, but which resonates with concerns Nietzsche finds in the Presocratics as well.

Good Philology, M-Naturalism, Empiricism, Classical Realism, Fatalism, and the Problem of Suffering are recurring themes in Nietzsche's work, including the *Genealogy*. Recent anachronistic readings (like Danto 1965, Foucault 1971, DeMan 1979, Nehamas 1985) have largely obscured the importance of many of these to Nietzsche by ignoring the actual influences on his thought and the historical context in which he was writing. But once we locate Nietzsche in his intellectual world, as opposed to ours, these themes leap to the fore. It remains to be seen, now, how these themes figure in Nietzsche's moral philosophy and in the *Genealogy* itself.

Chapter 3

Nietzsche's critique of morality I

The scope of the critique and the critique of moral agency

Unlike many of the great philosophers of the past, Nietzsche did not set out his ideas systematically in one or two central works. There is no analogue to Kant's *Critique of Pure Reason* or Hume's *Treatise of Human Nature* in the Nietzschean corpus. The *Genealogy* perhaps comes closest, which is why it is the ultimate subject of this volume and the most widely assigned Nietzschean text. But the subject of Nietzsche's *Genealogy* – the critique of morality – is hardly unique to that work, and it has both a conceptual prehistory in earlier works and receives further important development in contemporaneous and later works. We can only read the *Genealogy* effectively against the backdrop of a more systematic picture of Nietzsche's mature critique of morality. This chapter and the next endeavor to put such a picture in place.

The scope problem

One of the standing problems in the interpretation of Nietzsche is how to define the precise *scope* of his critique of morality. This problem remains because of perplexing features of Nietzsche's discussion which rule out two initially attractive accounts: on the one hand, that Nietzsche is simply a critic of *all* morality; on the other, that he is only a critic of some particular kind of morality – for example, "Christian" morality or "European" morality. Neither account, however, proves adequate.

Nietzsche could not be a critic of *all* "morality" for two reasons. First, he explicitly embraces the idea of a "higher morality" which would inform the lives of "higher men" (Schacht 1983: 466–9). Moreover, in so doing, he employs the same German word – typically, *Moral*, sometimes *Moralität* – for both what he attacks and what he praises. Labels alone will thus not permit us to sort out the values he attacks from those he affirms. Second, Nietzsche aims to offer a revaluation of existing values in a manner that appears, itself, to involve appeal to broadly "moral" standards of some sort. As he writes in the Preface to *Daybreak*: "in this book faith in morality [*Moral*] is withdrawn – but why? *Out of morality [Moralität]*! Or what else should we call that which informs it – and *us*? . . . [T]here is no doubt that a 'thou shalt' [*du sollst*] speaks to us too" (4). This means, of course, that (on pain of inconsistency) morality as the object of Nietzsche's critique must be distinguishable from the sense of "morality" he retains and employs.

At the same time, Nietzsche does not confine his criticisms of morality to some single religiously, philosophically, socially or historically circumscribed example. Thus, it will not do to say that he simply attacks Christian or Kantian or European or utilitarian morality – though he certainly at times attacks all of these. The question then is what Nietzsche takes to be characteristic generally of "morality" in his pejorative sense – hereafter, "MPS" – that is, morality as the object of his critique.

To date, four approaches have dominated treatments of this question in the secondary literature. Defenders of what we may call the "Catalogue Approach" characterize MPS in terms of its distinctive normative content, i.e., a catalogue of its characteristic normative demands. Defenders of the "Origins Approach" characterize MPS in terms of the motives which explain its genesis. Defenders of the "Universality Approach" characterize MPS in terms of its view that one moral code ought to apply to all. Finally, defenders of the "Presuppositions Approach" characterize MPS in terms of its distinctive empirical and metaphysical presuppositions. Let us begin by briefly reviewing each of these interpretive approaches in turn.

According to the Catalogue Approach, Nietzsche characterizes morality by – and criticizes it for – its specific content. Walter Kaufmann's gloss is typical in this respect:

> What Nietzsche opposed in Christian morality . . . were such features as these: . . . an antagonism against excellence, a predisposition in favor of mediocrity or even downright baseness, a leveling tendency, the conviction that sex is sinful, [and] a devaluation of both body and intellect in favor of the soul.

> (1959: 213–14)

Other common candidates for the catalogue of distinguishing objectionable features of MPS include its endorsement of pity (Foot 1973: 156–7; Schacht 1983: 359 ff.), selflessness (Schacht 1983: 360), equality (Schutte 1984: 169), and the extirpation of the instincts (Danto 1965: 148; Kaufmann 1974, Chapter 7).

According to the Origins Approach, MPS is characterized by its distinctive genesis: namely, its development out of *ressentiment*.[1] That is, MPS is distinguished by the fact that its particular normative demands issue from the resentment and hatred felt by certain types of people ("slaves," the "weak," the mediocre) toward those better off. (For more on *ressentiment*, see Chapter 6.) This picture of MPS typically is supplemented with the Catalogue Approach, that is with an enumeration of what specific normative demands are in fact produced by *ressentiment* (e.g., Kaufmann 1959: 213–14). The Origins Approach is also distinguished by the account it then gives of Nietzsche's critique of MPS: on this picture, Nietzsche's critique is an

---

[1]   Kaufmann 1959: 213–14; Kaufmann 1974: 374; Foot 1973: 157–9; Magnus 1978: 13–16.

"internal" critique, that is a critique of MPS on the grounds that its own proclaimed standards (e.g., "love one another") require a condemnation of MPS itself given its typical motives (e.g., hatred) on Nietzsche's account. Here, again, Kaufmann's summary is representative: "The revaluation [of values] is thus the alleged discovery that our morality is, *by its own standards*, poisonously immoral" (1974: 113).[2]

According to the Universality Approach, MPS is marked by its view that one moral code of conduct is appropriate for all, without exception. One commentator has even gone so far as to claim that Nietzsche's "main objection to morality is its absolutism" in precisely this sense (Nehamas 1985: 223).[3]

Finally, the Presuppositions Approach holds that MPS is marked not by its distinctive content, its origins or its universality but rather by its special empirical and metaphysical presuppositions – presuppositions that Nietzsche challenges. One commentator has characterized this as Nietzsche's rejection of "the apparatus of agency, selfhood, freedom, responsibility, blame, and guilt [which] furnished the accoutrements for the modality [of the morality] to which we are accustomed" (Bergmann 1988: 34). Thus, on this account, MPS has "one quite particular modality," that is, it presupposes a particular descriptive account of agency, including "the substantivized and reified 'ego' which undergirds all of this" (Bergmann 1988: 35, 45).[4]

We may summarize, then, the standard accounts of Nietzsche's conception of MPS as follows: the Catalogue Approach characterizes MPS in terms of a catalogue of its distinctive normative contents; the

[2] Cf. Foot 1973: 114; Geuss 1981: 44.
[3] Cf. Nehamas 1985: 209, 214; see also Foot 1973: 165; Solomon 1973b: 216; Schutte 1984: 169; Geuss 1997: 7.
[4] Cf. Deleuze 1962: 21; Danto 1965: 105–6; Schacht 1983: 441 ff.; Williams 1993a; Geuss 1997: 7. Notice, too, that we are focusing here only on the *logical* presuppositions of morality, i.e., those claims that must be true for the practice of moral judgment to be intelligible. But morality may also have *causal* presuppositions, i.e., claims which, as an historical matter, stand in some *causal* connection to our present moral beliefs. Examples of these kinds of presuppositions would include the belief in God (Schacht 1983: 443) or certain feelings of "reverence" towards supposed authorities that are leftovers of more superstitious times (Clark and Leiter 1997: xxxi–xxxiv).

Origins Approach, in terms of its genesis out of *ressentiment*; the Universality Approach in terms of its commitment to the universal applicability of one moral code; and the Presuppositions Approach in terms of its (untenable) empirical and metaphysical presuppositions.

Does Nietzsche, then, have a unified target in attacking MPS? It is important *not* to confuse this exegetical question with the question of whether Nietzsche thinks the concept of morality is itself "unified," i.e., whether morality has some *essential* character.[5] We can agree with Nietzsche that "only something which has no history can be defined" (GM II: 13), that what we call "morality" has a history, and that, consequently, morality cannot be "defined" (see Chapter 5). But neither the *definition* of "morality," nor the *essential meaning* of morality qua real historical phenomenon, is what is called for here. The exegetical question is simply whether that particular construct Nietzsche attacks under the label "morality" can be coherently characterized. Some commentators are skeptical of finding an answer to this latter, more modest question. Philippa Foot, for example, declares that, "there is no single answer to the question as to what he was attacking or as to what the basis might be for the attack" (1973: 167).

In fact, this skepticism is unwarranted, for there exists a plausible account of Nietzsche's target and of his grounds for attacking it, one that explains the coherence of his critical project and its compatibility with his commitment to "moral" beliefs of his own. MPS, here, is an heuristic, not an historical, category. Such an account combines the insights of the Catalogue and Presuppositions Approaches, and subsumes the pertinent parts of the Universality and Origins Approaches under these first two. Importantly, however, we should reject the idea associated with the Origins Approach that Nietzsche offers an *internal* critique of MPS. We will return to this latter topic, however, in Chapter 5.

---

5   Cf. Clark 1994: 21–3; Geuss 1997: 1–2. As we will see in Chapter 5, Nietzsche's view is that while "morality" has meant different things at different times, that is also compatible with there being stable characteristics of anything that counts as a morality.

"Morality" as the object of Nietzsche's critique: a formal account

Nietzsche believes that all normative systems which perform some-thing like the role we associate with "morality" share certain structural characteristics.[6] In particular, all normative systems have both *descriptive* and *normative* components, in the sense that: (a) they presuppose a particular descriptive account of human agency – in the sense that for the normative claims comprising the system to have intelligible application to human agents, particular metaphysical and empirical claims about agency must be true; and (b) they embrace norms which favor the interests of some people, perhaps at the expense of others. Any particular morality will, in turn, be the object of Nietzsche's critique (i.e., an MPS) only if it:

1   presupposes three *particular* descriptive claims about the nature of human agents pertaining to free will, the transparency of the self, and the essential similarity of all people ("the Descriptive Component"); and/or

2   embraces norms that harm the "highest men" while benefiting the "lowest" ("the Normative Component").

It may be useful to begin by asking two questions. First, what is the connection between the two general components of morality, the descriptive and the normative? And second, how essential are these two components in fact?

On Nietzsche's view, the conjunction of the descriptive and normative components of morality is not simply an accident. As we learned from the discussion of naturalism and type-facts in Chapter 1, Nietzsche believes a person's views are explicable by natural facts about that person. More precisely, on Nietzsche's account, agents typi-cally hold *any* belief – e.g., any philosophical or metaphysical view – because it favors or supports the type of life those agents are capable of living. Thus, Nietzsche claims that:

1   agents (generally) hold particular philosophical and metaphys-ical views because they support their moral beliefs; and

6   The meaning or value of these normative systems, however, may vary con-siderably.

2   agents (generally) hold particular moral beliefs because they favor the interests of those agents (i.e., favor the conditions under which those agents enjoy their maximum feeling of power, given what they are like).[7]

Thus, Nietzsche thinks that agents will typically believe in the metaphysical and empirical claims presupposed by morality only when the normative agenda of morality serves the interests of those agents – and this is because the intelligibility of the normative demands of morality depends (generally) on agents holding the right descriptive views.

It is also clear, however, that for Nietzsche what ultimately defines MPS as against unobjectionable normative systems is the distinctive normative agenda. Thus, while he criticizes at length the description of agency that is typically part and parcel of MPS (for the reasons just discussed), he also holds that "[i]t is *not* error as error that" he objects to fundamentally in MPS (EH IV: 7): that is, it is *not* the falsity of the descriptive account of agency presupposed by MPS, per se, that is the heart of the problem, but rather its distinctive normative commitments.[8] Thus, strictly speaking, it is true that an MPS would be objectionable even if it did not involve a commitment to an untenable descriptive account of agency.[9] Because Nietzsche's two most common – and closely related – specific targets are, however, Christian and Kantian morality, the critique of the descriptive component of MPS figures prominently in Nietzsche's writing, and any account of the logic of his critique that omitted it would not do justice to his concerns.

---

[7]   Note the parenthetical "generally": for Nietzsche draws attention to important exceptions to each of these claims. Thus, with respect to our philosophical and metaphysical beliefs, he sometimes suggests that these are also due to certain assumptions built into the grammar of our language (BGE: 20; TI III: 5). With respect to our moral beliefs, it is central to his whole critical project that there are at least some people – "higher men" – for whom such beliefs are distinctly disadvantageous: and it is them that Nietzsche hopes to reach with his critique.

[8]   A point missed in Geuss (1997: 7 ff.).

[9]   Certain forms of utilitarianism fit this description. See, e.g., Smart (1984) and Williams (1985: 178).

The Descriptive Component of MPS

MPS for Nietzsche depends for its intelligibility on three descriptive theses about human agency:

1   Human agents possess a will capable of free and autonomous choice.
2   The self is sufficiently transparent that agents' actions can be distinguished on the basis of their respective motives.
3   Human agents are sufficiently similar that one moral code is appropriate for all.[10]

We may call these, respectively, the theses of "Free Will," "Transparency of the Self," and "Similarity." These three theses must be true in order for the normative judgments of MPS to be intelligible because the normative judgments of MPS are marked for Nietzsche by three corresponding traits; namely, that they:

1'   hold agents responsible for their actions;
2'   evaluate and "rank" the motives for which agents act;[11]
3'   presuppose that "morality" has universal applicability.

Thus, the falsity of the picture of agency would affect the intelligibility of moral judgments in the following three ways:

1"   If agents lacked "free will" they could not be held responsible for their actions.
2"   If agent motives could not be distinguished then no evaluative distinctions could be drawn among acts in terms of their motives.

---

10   See, e.g., BGE: 32; GM I: 13; TI VI; EH III: 5; EH IV: 8; and also Leiter (1995) for a detailed defense of this reading. Geuss (1997: 3–4) offers a related account, though he complicates things unnecessarily. Geuss speaks of Nietzsche's target as "the traditional European morality derived from Christianity" and describes it as committed to six characteristic theses. But these six are naturally reduced to the three theses I treat as characteristic of the Descriptive Component of morality: Geuss's theses 1 and 2 reduce to what I call the Similarity Thesis; Geuss's theses (3)–(6) reduce to the Free Will and Transparency Theses.

11   This is not a commitment *necessarily* shared, of course, by consequentialist moral theories, though most of these will endorse (1') and (3'). Nietzsche, though, appears to concur with Kant in viewing "ordinary" morality as fundamentally concerned with motives.

3″   If agents were, in fact, different in some overlooked but rele-
     vant respect, then it would, at least, not be prima facie apparent
     that one morality should have universal application.

It is the burden, then, of Nietzsche's critique of the Descriptive
Component of MPS to show that, in fact, none of these latter theses
about the nature of agency hold. To understand this critique we must
first revisit the topic of Nietzsche's fatalism which we first encountered in Chapter 2.

The critique of the Descriptive Component: fatalism and agency

Following (though modifying) Schopenhauer, Nietzsche holds that a
person's life proceeds along a fixed trajectory, fixed by "natural" facts
about that person.[12] Nietzsche, the fatalist, views a person like a plant:
just as, say, the essential natural facts about a tomato plant determine
its development (e.g., that it will grow tomatoes and not, say, corn),
so, too, the essential natural facts about a person determine its development as well. Of course, the precise development of a tomato plant
– whether it "flourishes" or wilts – is affected (causally) by a host
of other factors that don't constitute the "essence" of the plant: for
example, the soil in which it is planted, the amount of water it receives,
and the like. So the natural facts about the tomato plant *circumscribe*,
as it were, the possible trajectories, though they themselves do not
uniquely determine which of these is realized. Nietzsche seems to hold
the same view about persons: natural facts about a person circumscribe
what that person becomes, though within the limits set by the natural
facts, the precise details of what a person becomes depend (causally)
upon other factors. More formally, then, we can say that according to
Nietzschean Fatalism:

> Natural facts about a person are *causally primary* in fixing the
> trajectory of that person's life.

Natural facts, in turn, are "causally primary" with respect to some
effect (i.e., some life trajectory) insofar as:

[12]   See pp. 58–63, Chapter 2.

1   they are always *necessary* for that effect; although

2   they may not be *sufficient* for it.

So, for example, natural facts (e.g., about metabolism, bone structure, body and muscle type, propensity to disease or illness) may be causally primary with respect to being a professional basketball player, in the sense that; (i) to become a professional basketball player it is always *necessary* to have the right natural characteristics (height being only the most common); though (ii) these natural characteristics are typically not *sufficient* to guarantee that one becomes a professional basketball player (e.g., not all tall, physically-fit people become professional basketball players). Nietzschean Fatalism is compatible, then, with the idea that factors other than natural facts about the person may still play a causal role in the trajectory of a person's life – within the limits circumscribed, of course, by the natural facts. For Nietzsche's fatalism to have any bite, of course, it must turn out that the natural facts significantly circumscribe the possible trajectories. We may assume, with Nietzsche, that they do so, in this sense: the fundamental facts about one's *character and personality* are fixed by natural facts, and thus how one responds to differing circumstances and environments is also causally determined by natural facts. But the actual circumstances in which a person finds himself are plainly not fixed in advance by the natural facts about a person.

Indeed, we should be careful at this point to distinguish several related doctrines that might seem to be in play: let us call them Classical Determinism, Classical Fatalism, and Causal Essentialism.[13] Classical Determinism is the view that for any event p at a time t, p is necessary given the totality of facts prior to t, together with the actual laws of nature. Classical Fatalism, by contrast, is the view that whatever happens had to happen, but not in virtue of the truth of Classical Determinism. (Strictly speaking, Classical Determinism would not entail Classical Fatalism, since the outcomes necessitated under Classical Determinism are *contingent* on the past and on the laws of nature.) Classical Fatalism involves the notion of some sort of non-deterministic, perhaps even non-causal *necessity*, and in that sense is a rather cryptic view. Finally, Causal Essentialism is the doctrine

[13]   I am grateful to R. C. Koons for guidance on this issue.

that for any individual substance (e.g., a person or some other living organism) that substance has "essential" properties that are causally primary with respect to the future history of that substance, i.e., they non-trivially determine the space of possible trajectories for that substance. Notice that Causal Essentialism entails neither Classical Determinism nor Fatalism. Unlike Determinism, Causal Essentialism is compatible with there being no laws of nature. Unlike Fatalism, Essentialism does not entail that any particular outcome to a person's life is *necessary* (since Causal Essentialism only *circumscribes* trajectories, but does not necessitate any particular one).

Nietzsche's fatalism involves *only* Causal Essentialism; Nietzsche is neither a Classical Determinist nor a Classical Fatalist. That is, he holds only that there are essential natural facts about persons that significantly circumscribe the range of life trajectories that persons can realize and that, as a result, make each individual's life "fated," not in the classical sense, but in the sense that what an individual can become is severely constrained from the start.

We saw substantial evidence of Nietzsche's fatalism in Chapter 2, in our discussion of Schopenhauer.[14] Yet we only mentioned in passing there the most striking evidence of how deep Nietzsche's own fatalism runs: namely, that he tells the story *of his own life* in fatalistic terms in *Ecce Homo*. This should be plain enough from the subtitle of the work: "How One Becomes What One Is" (*Wie man wird, was man ist*).[15] Indeed, Nietzsche's highly stylized "autobiography" is

[14] See pp. 60–2 in Chapter 2.

[15] Surprisingly, interpreters like Nehamas and Rorty resist the fatalistic implications. Thus, Rorty, commenting on the subtitle, writes as follows:

> In the sense Nietzsche gave to the phrase, "who one actually is" does not mean "who one actually was all the time" but "whom one turned oneself into in the course of creating the taste by which one ended up judging oneself." The term "ended up" is, however, misleading. It suggests a predestined resting place.

(1989: 99)

Rorty does not, in fact, try to ground this interpretive claim in a reading of *Ecce Homo* (he cites only Nehamas as authority!). Yet the misunderstanding of Nietzsche's point is suggested immediately by the mistranslation: one becomes "what" [*was*] one is, according to Nietzsche, not "who" [*wer*] one

organized around a double irony. The first concerns the real purpose of the autobiographical undertaking itself: namely, as an extended exercise in self-congratulation. But whereas the typical autobiography pursues this end while trying not to be obvious about it, Nietzsche simply declares plainly the point of the project with his chapter titles: that is, to show "Why I Am So Wise" (EH I), "Why I Am So Clever" (EH II), and the like. This is autobiography as *unabashed* self-congratulation.

Or so it first appears until the second irony of *Ecce Homo* becomes visible. For though Nietzsche, indeed, thinks himself wise, clever, and the author of good books, there is nothing, in fact, self-congratulatory about his answer to the questions *why* he is so wise,

is. But to speak of "what" rather than "who" suggests precisely the objectification of the person that one would expect from a philosopher who views persons as having immutable, determining characteristics, such that one may ask of a human being, as one may ask of a tree, "*What* is it made of essentially?".

Nehamas' own misreading of the EH subtitle is defended on different, but equally problematic, grounds. For example, commenting on the famous section "On the Despisers of the Body" (Z I: 4), Nehamas claims that those who despise the body do so because of "the belief that they have a stable self" (1985: 251 n. 6). But Zarathustra nowhere in the passage disputes the existence of a stable self; to the contrary, he equates the real self with the body, and describes how this body determines what we do even as we imagine otherwise. "Your self [the body]," says Zarathustra, "laughs at your ego and at its bold leaps. 'What are these great leaps and flights of thought to me' it says to itself. 'A detour to my end. I am the leading strings of the ego and the prompter of its concepts.'"

Elsewhere, Nehamas argues that the idea of an underlying, essential self is incompatible with Nietzsche's "general denial of the idea of a reality that underlies appearance" (1985: 173). Yet *this* denial is for Nietzsche a denial of the *metaphysical* distinction between the "merely" apparent, sensible realm and a supra-sensible, unknowable reality (as drawn, e.g., by Kant; cf. TI IV); it could hardly involve a denial of the difference between superficial states (like consciousness) and the underlying, causally efficacious states (which are, in principle, knowable), like the unconscious drives or the body. For this latter distinction is plainly central to Nietzsche: for example, when he calls consciousness "surface and skin – which, like every skin, betrays something but *conceals* even more" (BGE: 33) (cf. EH II: 9: "consciousness *is* a surface").

so clever, and the rest. This is because the argument of *Ecce Homo* is imbued with fatalism. Indeed, the book begins on precisely that note: "The good fortune of my existence," says Nietzsche in the first line, "lies in its fatality [*Verhängnis*]" (EH I: 1). As a result, the answer to the apparently self-congratulatory "why" questions is roughly this: "It was a lucky fact of nature that I, Nietzsche, was a healthy organism, that is, the type of creature that instinctively does the right things to facilitate its flourishing."[16] "I have always *instinctively* chosen the *right* means against wretched states" (EH I: 2; first emphasis added), declares Nietzsche. As the argument of *Ecce Homo* makes explicit, this means choosing (instinctively or necessarily) the right nutrition, the right climate, the right forms of recreation, "everything that deserves to be taken seriously in life" (EH IV: 8).[17] Nietzsche wrote such wise and clever books for the same reason the tomato plant grows tomatoes: *because it must*, because it could not have done otherwise. But there is no self-congratulation involved in simply reporting what had to be, and Nietzsche displays none. To the contrary, as he remarks in the quotation with which the book opens: "How could I fail to be grateful [*dankbar*] to my whole life?" This very way of putting the question, however, suggests a sharp divide between the "life" – which runs its necessary course – and the conscious "self" which views the life as though a (grateful) spectator upon it.

Fatalistic themes recur throughout *Ecce Homo*.[18] Explaining why he returned to Rome while writing *Zarathustra*, Nietzsche comments that "some fatality was at work" (EH III: Z-4). He declares that "*amor*

16 Cf. EH I: 2: "I took myself in hand, I made myself healthy again: the condition for this – every physiologist would admit that – is *that one be healthy at bottom*."

17 Cf. EH II: 10: "these small things – nutrition, place, climate, recreation, the whole casuistry of selfishness – are inconceivably more important than everything one has taken to be important so far."

18 One might worry that Nietzsche's comment about "[a]ccepting oneself as if fated" (EH I: 6) suggests that he does not really believe in fatalism: hence the "as if." Here Kaufmann's rendering is problematic (and probably reflects his own discomfort with finding Nietzsche to be a fatalist), for Nietzsche says simply "*wie*," not "*als ob*." Thus, the phrase might have been rendered, more aptly, as "accepting oneself as fated" – which, on Nietzsche's view, one really is!

fati" is the mark of "greatness": that one does not merely "bear what is necessary . . . but *love*[s] it" (EH II: 10). Later he remarks (not surprisingly) that "*amor fati* is my inmost nature" (EH III: CW-4). The depth of Nietzsche's fatalism regarding his own life becomes most apparent in a long passage from the second chapter of *Ecce Homo*. Nietzsche is here discussing his development as a philosopher, after noting that, "To become what one is, one must not have the faintest notion *what* one is" (EH II: 9). He continues:

> Meanwhile the organizing "idea" that is destined to rule [*die zur Herrschaft berufne*] keeps growing deep down – it begins to command; slowly it leads us *back* from side roads and wrong roads; it prepares *single* qualities and fitnesses that will one day prove to be indispensable as means toward a whole – one by one, it trains all *subservient* capacities before giving any hint of the dominant task, "goal," "aim," or "meaning."
>
> Considered in this way, my life is simply wonderful. For the task of a *revaluation of all values* more capacities may have been needed than have ever dwelt together in a single individual – above all, even contrary capacities that had to be kept from disturbing, destroying one another. . . . [Their] *higher protection* manifested itself to such a high degree that I never even suspected what was growing in me [*was in mir wächst*] – and one day all my capacities, suddenly ripe [*reif*], *leaped forth* [*hervorsprangen*] in their ultimate perfection.
>
> (EH II: 9)

Nietzsche here views his own life as, say, an apple tree – unaware of its true nature – might view itself: although not "suspect[ing] what was growing" in it, the tree one day finds its fruit "suddenly ripe" and "leap[ing] forth."[19] We now have the answer to the book's subtitle: how one becomes what one is. The answer: by making no special effort *directed toward that end*, because one becomes what one is *necessarily*.

19 Cf. Schopenhauer's observation in *On the Freedom of the Will* that trying to use "talk and moralizing" to "reform" a man's "character . . . is exactly like the attempt . . . by means of careful cultivation to make an oak produce apricots" (1841b: 45).

Against the background of Nietzsche's fatalism, we may now consider the three aspects of his critique of the Descriptive Component of MPS.

The critique of free will

Ordinary moral thought supposes that agents are morally responsible for their actions, except under special circumstances (e.g., when they are asleep, insane, drugged, and the like). To be responsible for what one does, agents must act freely or autonomously. Let us call "the Autonomy Condition" the condition that must be satisfied for ascriptions of moral responsibility to be justified. Nietzsche's theory of agency involves a sustained attack on the Autonomy Condition, hence on the idea that agents are morally responsible for what they do.

Now if Nietzsche were a systematic philosopher, we could expect to find a fully developed theory of mind *and* action in his work. For an account of free action – one that explains how action can meet the Autonomy Condition – can easily flounder at the level of the mind–body problem. If, for example, the most plausible metaphysics of mind eliminates mentality, or renders mentality epiphenomenal, or reduces mentality to the physical (thus rendering it subject, perhaps, to deterministic natural laws), then it may be hard to see how we could locate an agent that satisfies the Autonomy Condition within a mind so conceived. Nietzsche, however, has no worked-out theory of mind; his arguments against the Autonomy Condition all arise from his theory of action. We may identify two distinct arguments against the Autonomy Condition in Nietzsche's writings. First, Nietzsche argues that an autonomous agent would have to be *causa sui* (i.e., self-caused, or the cause of itself); but since nothing can be *causa sui*, no one could be an autonomous agent. The second argument grows out of Nietzsche's claim that our conscious life is essentially epiphenomenal, that what rises to the level of consciousness is simply an effect of something unconscious, or perhaps even something physical. Assuming that conscious states would have to figure in the causation of *autonomous* actions, it follows that there are no such actions, since actions are simply determined by the natural facts that determine consciousness. Let us call this the "Naturalistic Argument."

If Nietzsche is correct in his Naturalistic Argument, this will prove fatal even to those popular attempts to reconcile free agency with deterministic processes. Moreover, as a picture of action, it will underwrite the fatalism we have seen Nietzsche give expression to in the many passages noted above and in Chapter 2.

Before turning to an explication of these two arguments, two initial points warrant comment. Philosophers usually distinguish the problem of whether the *will* is free from the problem of whether *action* or *agency* is free (e.g., Watson 1987). In fact, of course, the problems are deeply related: a free action, for example, is often thought to be one that is caused (or "determined") by a free will. For purposes of this discussion, in any event, this is how we shall think of the issue, even if this does not do justice to the full range of possible philosophical complications.

Although Nietzsche's repudiation of free will – the "error of free will" as he calls it (TI VI: 7) – is well known, his reasons for rejecting it do not depend on the truth of Classical Determinism. From the standpoint of contemporary philosophical interests, this is a considerable virtue of Nietzsche's approach for two reasons. First, many, perhaps most, philosophers since Hume have thought free will compatible with determinism. Second, determinism may, in fact, be false: the universe of quantum physics is often thought to be indeterministic.[20] Happily, we find in Nietzsche arguments against the Autonomy Condition that still have force against compatibilists in a quantum world.

The Causa Sui *Argument*

According to Nietzsche, "the concept of a *causa sui* is something fundamentally absurd" (BGE: 15). If this is correct, many philosophers take it to pose a fundamental challenge to the possibility of free will. As Gary Watson explains the intuitive point: "If the will is the product of culture and physiology, then there is no room for the idea that the agent is the author of his or her will" (Watson 1987: 164).

---

[20] This fact (if it is a fact!) still leaves us very far from having shown that the will or action is free. For an attempt to exploit quantum indeterminacy in defense of free will, see Kane (1996).

If all your actions arise from "choices" (that arise from the will), but all your choices are determined by facts about your nature (say, your unconscious psyche and your physiology), then your actions appear determined not *by you*, but by facts about you. This, so the argument goes, is not sufficient for autonomous action or a free will, since what you do is determined, as it were, by what you already are.

Nietzsche seems to have drawn precisely the same conclusion:

> The *causa sui* is the best self-contradiction that has been conceived so far, it is a sort of rape and perversion of logic; but the extravagant pride of man has managed to entangle itself profoundly and frightfully with just this nonsense. The desire for "freedom of the will" in the superlative metaphysical sense ... the desire to bear the entire and ultimate responsibility for one's actions oneself, and to absolve God, the world, ancestors, chance, and society involves nothing less than to be precisely this *causa sui* and ... to pull oneself up into existence by the hair, out of the swamps of nothingness.

> (BGE: 21)

But we cannot, needless to say, pull ourselves up "out of the swamps of nothingness," and so we cannot have ultimate responsibility for our actions. Our "will" is an artifact of the facts about us, and thus cannot be the source of genuinely autonomous action (the sort that would ground responsibility).

Notice that the problem is not resolved by suggesting that, even if our initial "character" is fixed by natural facts about us, we may, later on, strive to alter this basic character through the choices we make – for example, by choosing to undergo psychoanalysis, or to "turn over a new leaf." For this move simply pushes the requirement of a *causa sui* back one more level, yielding an infinite regress. As Galen Strawson has helpfully put the point:

> We may later engage in conscious and intentional shaping procedures – call them S-procedures – designed to affect and change our characters, motivational structure, and wills. ... The question is then why we engage in the particular S-procedures that we do engage in, and why we engage in them in the particular

way we do. The general answer is that we engage in the particular S-procedures that we do engage in, given the circumstances
in which we find ourselves, because of certain features of the
way we already are.

(1994: 18)

If, in other words, we are not *causa sui*, then everything about our
will (and, consequently, about our actions) is causally determined by
something about the "way we already are" – including those opera-
tions of will in which we attempt to alter the "way we already are."
The result appears to be a picture of agency in which "the person
serves merely as the arena for these events: he takes no active part"
(Velleman 1992: 461). Indeed, as we shall see shortly, this is a view
Nietzsche (unlike Schopenhauer) explicitly ends up embracing.

Many philosophers[21] have thought that the *causa sui* argument
disproves something no one need believe – namely, that the will be
uncaused. Free will and moral responsibility, these philosophers hold,
are not only compatible with, but may require that, the will be causally
determined. As a result, these philosophers adopt a fairly cavalier
posture towards the *Causa Sui* Argument. As Galen Strawson has
correctly observed, however, "Belief in the kind of absolute moral
responsibility [and autonomy] that [the argument] shows to be impossible has for a long time been central to the Western religious, moral
and cultural tradition" (1994: 8).[22] Arguably, it is only certain academic philosophers who think the need to be a self-caused agent is
superfluous, something that can be finessed via some adroit dialectical
moves. Yet as Strawson's comment nicely brings out, the concept of
"free will" in play in the culture at large may be far more wedded

---

[21] Not, however, those who embrace various libertarian theories of free will –
those who think freedom of the will depends on its being outside the causal
order altogether – or those (notably Roderick Chisholm) who think free will
requires putting the agent, as an irreducible primitive, into the causal order. I
sympathize with the dominant sentiment that libertarian, and agent-causation,
theories make no sense. For representative critiques, see Strawson (1994:
18–20); Velleman (1992: 468–9); and Watson (1987: 161–9).

[22] In unpublished work, Peter Poellner has argued that this is not correct. The
historical issues are complex, and dealing with them adequately would take
us too far afield.

to the notion of autonomous action which is rendered impossible by the argument under consideration here than the concept of "free will" favored by compatibilists. As we shall see later, this focus is consistent with Nietzsche's critical occupation with *actual* cultural practices, rather than the theories of philosophers.

The Naturalistic Argument

The *Causa Sui* Argument just considered already presupposes a certain view of persons: namely, that each person has certain characteristics that causally determine that person's "will." Nietzsche's full-blown theory of action builds upon this idea. We may state Nietzsche's view, in bold outline, as follows.

Recall Nietzsche's "Doctrine of Types" from Chapter 1: each person has a fixed psycho-physical constitution, which defines him as a particular *type* of person. Call the relevant psycho-physical facts here "type-facts." Type-facts, for Nietzsche, are either *physiological* facts about the person, or facts about the person's unconscious drives or affects. The claim, then, is that each person has certain largely immutable physiological and psychic traits, that constitute the "type" of person he or she is.

Type-facts, for Nietzsche, are *causally primary* with respect to the course of a person's life – in the sense of "causally primary" noted already. Type-facts are also *explanatorily primary*, in the sense that all other facts about a person (e.g., his beliefs, his actions, his life trajectory) are explicable by type-facts about the person (perhaps in conjunction with other natural facts about the circumstances or environment). This means, among other things, that a person's conscious mental states are "Kind-Epiphenomenal."[23] Consciousness is Kind-Epiphenomenal in the sense that conscious states are only causally effective in virtue of type-facts about the person (that is, not simply in virtue of their being conscious states). Put more simply:

[23] A property is "Kind-Epiphenomenal" when it has no causal powers in virtue of being the kind of property it is, but only in virtue of its relation to some other set of properties. In the literature, this is standardly called "type epiphenomenalism," but since "type" has a term-of-art usage in the discussion of Nietzsche, I've used "kind" instead.

consciousness is not causally efficacious in its own right. While a person's conscious states may be part of the causal chain leading up to action, they play that role only in virtue of type-facts about the person. (At times, however, Nietzsche seems to embrace the more radical (and less plausible) view, that consciousness is Token-Epiphenomenal: i.e., that conscious states are simply *effects* of under-lying type-facts about the person, and play no causal role whatsoever.)

This basic theory generates the following picture of action. We typically locate the "will," as the seat of action, in various conscious states: for example, our beliefs and desires (cf. Velleman 1992). According to Nietzsche, however, the "will" so conceived is nothing but the effect of type-facts about the person. This means that the real story of the genesis of an action begins with the type-facts, which explain both consciousness *and* a person's actions. Here is how Nietzsche puts it, after suggesting that the "will" is related to, but conceptually prior to, the concepts of "consciousness" and "ego":

> The "inner world" is full of phantoms . . .: the will is one of them. The will no longer moves anything, hence does not explain anything either – it merely accompanies events; it can also be absent. The so-called *motive*: another error. Merely a surface phenomenon of consciousness – something alongside the deed that is more likely to cover up the antecedents of the deeds than to represent them. . . .
>
> What follows from this? There are no mental [*geistigen*] causes at all.
>
> (TI VI: 3)[24]

In the last line, Nietzsche must mean only that there are no *conscious* mental causes. Indeed, in other passages, he is explicit that the target of this critique is the picture of conscious motives as adequate to account for action. As he writes in *Daybreak*, "we are accustomed to exclude all [the] unconscious processes from the accounting and to reflect on the preparation for an act only to the extent that it is

[24] Cf. WP: 666: "why could a 'purpose' not be an epiphenomenon in the series of changes in the activating forces that bring about purposive action – a pale image sketched in consciousness beforehand that serve to orient us concerning events, even as a symptom of events, *not* as their cause."

conscious" (D: 129), a view which Nietzsche plainly regards as mistaken, both here and in the passage quoted above. Indeed, the theme of the "ridiculous overestimation and misunderstanding of consciousness" (GS: 11) is a recurring one in Nietzsche. "[B]y far the greatest part of our spirit's activity," says Nietzsche, "remains unconscious and unfelt" (GS: 333; cf. GS: 354). And in a *Nachlass* note of 1888, he writes (perhaps a bit hyperbolically): "everything of which we become conscious is a terminal phenomenon, an end – and causes nothing" (WP: 478). His strongest argument for the epiphenomenality of the mental is the following phenomenological argument against the *causal autonomy* of consciousness: namely, "that a thought comes when 'it' wishes, and not when 'I' wish" (BGE: 17). But if that is right – as it surely is – and if actions are apparently "caused" by thoughts (by particular beliefs and desires), then it follows that actions are not caused solely by our conscious mental states, but rather by whatever it is (i.e., type-facts) that determines the "thoughts" that enter consciousness. Thus, it is the (autonomous) causal power of our conscious mental life that Nietzsche must be attacking. Given, then, that Nietzsche claims consciousness is epiphenomenal,[25] and given our identification of the "will" with our conscious life, Nietzsche would have us dispense with the idea of the will as causal altogether.[26]

This latter point is significant in understanding the depth of Nietzsche's repudiation of the doctrine of free will. Compatibilists since Hume have argued that free action is compatible with the will being causally determined; all that is required for free action (and, accordingly, for moral responsibility), compatibilists maintain, is that the will be causally determined *in the right sort of way*. According to the influential "hierarchical" or "identification" accounts – associated, most prominently, with Harry Frankfurt (1988) – what is required for

---

[25] Some of the passages just quoted are, admittedly, ambiguous as between Kind-Epiphenomenalism and Token-Epiphenomenalism (the latter doctrine holding that conscious states are simply not causally effective at all, not even in virtue of underlying type-facts).

[26] This gives us the real import of Nietzsche's demand that we should dispense with both the idea of "free will" *and* of "unfree will" (BGE: 21): the point is that we should dispense with the idea that there is such a thing as the *will*, some internal locus of agency that is *either* determined or free.

free action is that we *identify* with those desires that causally determine the will, that we regard these effective desires "as our own" (in some precise sense over which philosophers differ, though the details do not matter here). Frankfurt puts the point by describing a hierarchy of desires, in which we have second-order desires that only certain of our first-order desires should actually be effective (in generating action); our action is "free" when these second-order desires are realized – even though, of course, the ensuing action is causally determined by a first-order desire.

After a quarter of a century of philosophical debate, it should be plain that hierarchical accounts of free will have failed.[27] They all stumble over two obstacles (Watson 1987: 148–50; Velleman 1992: 470–3). First, these theories have no account of the *source* of our second-order desires or volitions, the ones that account for which first-order desires we "identify" with in action. For all the hierarchical accounts tell us, our second-order desires could be causally determined in a way that is not *compatible* with freedom and responsibility. To put this in Nietzschean terms: since second-order desires are not, themselves, *causa sui*, they could not possibly underwrite autonomy; what second-order desires we happen to have is just a consequence of the way we already are (an effect of the type-facts). Second, hierarchical accounts present the specter of an infinite regress: for even if our effective first-order desires are those picked out by certain second-order desires, the question still remains why it is one identifies with *these particular* second-order desires. What is it about these second-order desires that make them one's own? For obvious reasons, it had better not be a third-order desire that a particular second-order desire be effective *vis-à-vis* one's first-order desires! But in that case, it remains unclear how the "identification" process even gets off the ground.

---

[27] One should not think that this feature is peculiar to hierarchical accounts. Indeed, it is striking that all philosophical defenses of free will (at least the ones designed to underwrite moral responsibility) are dismal failures; the peculiarity, of course, is that the bulk of philosophical energy continues to be expended upon defending free will, rather than upon exploring the philosophical consequences of abandoning free will. For a refreshingly different suggestion along these lines, see Strawson (1994): 22.

What bears noting now is that Nietzsche presents yet a *third* objection to the compatibilist account. For on Nietzsche's picture of action, the sorts of desires that hierarchical accounts point to are mere epiphenomena in consciousness; the genuine causal determinants of action both lie below the surface of consciousness (in type-facts about the person) *and* are generally unknown to us. But as long as they remain unknown, then we could not possibly "identify" with them (assuming a satisfactory account of identification were even forthcoming), and thus could not, as the hierarchical accounts would have us do, "identify" with the *real* determinants of our action. The latter point is one Nietzsche repeatedly emphasizes. He says that "all actions are essentially unknown" (D: 116) and that "nothing . . . can be more incomplete than" a person's "image of the totality of *drives* that constitute his being" (D: 119). Later, he writes that our actions "remain impenetrable," for "every action is unknowable" (GS: 335) – not in principle, of course, but in fact. If each action is caused by type-facts about the person – facts about that person's physiology and unconscious make-up – then it is easy to understand why our actions, for Nietzsche, would be unknowable (or certainly very hard to know). The picture that emerges is, of course, similar to Freud's (later) psychic determinism, and like Freud's it entails that the real cause of our actions may be opaque.

So, for Nietzsche, each of us has an essential psycho-physical constitution – a set of type-facts that make us what we are – and our actions, and even our conscious life, are all causally determined by these natural facts about us. Although the language of "type-facts" is not Nietzsche's, this concept does figure centrally in his mature writings as discussed in Chapter 1. As he puts it in a famous passage from the *Genealogy* itself:

> [O]ur thoughts, values, every "yes," "no," "if" and "but" grow from us with the same inevitability as fruits borne on the tree – related and each with an affinity to each, and evidence of one will, one health, one soil, one sun.

> (GM Pref: 2)

Thus, just as natural facts – type-facts – about a tree determine the fruit that tree necessarily bears, so too natural type-facts about a person determine the "fruit" that person necessarily bears – that is, the ideas and values he comes to embrace. Although ahistorical interpreters like Nehamas (1985: 120) and Paul DeMan (1977: 119) simply dismiss all this physiological and naturalistic talk as tangential to Nietzsche's "real" concerns, it should now be plain how much violence such a move does to the integrity of the texts. The foregoing remarks express a view that is not marginal, but absolutely central, to any serious understanding of persons for Nietzsche.

But is there not yet a final way to save a role for the "autonomous" agent? Nehamas (1985), for example, suggests that Nietzsche believes people "create" themselves, where such creation presumably involves satisfaction of something like the Autonomy Condition. Nehamas observes that for Nietzsche, "The people who 'want to become those they are' are precisely 'human beings who are new, unique, incomparable, who give themselves laws, who create themselves' (GS: 335)" (1985: 174). Unfortunately, Nehamas truncates the quote from *The Gay Science* precisely at the point at which it becomes troubling for his thesis that Nietzsche believes the self can be autonomously created. For Nietzsche, in the full passage, continues as follows:

> To that end [of creating ourselves] we must become the best learners and discoverers of everything that is lawful and necessary in the world: we must become *physicists* in order to be *creators* in this sense [*wir müssen Physiker sein, um, in jenem Sinne, Schöpfer sein zu können*] – while hitherto all valuations and ideals have been based on *ignorance* of physics. . . . Therefore: long live physics!
>
> (GS: 335)

Creation "in this sense" is, then, a very special sense indeed: for it presupposes the discovery of what is "lawful and necessary" as revealed by physical science. The passage begins to make more sense when we recall its context: this is the section in which Nietzsche claims that "every action is unknowable," though he adds:

> our opinions, valuations, and tables of what is good certainly belong among the most powerful levers in the involved

> mechanism of our actions, but . . . in any particular case the law
> of their mechanism is indemonstrable [*unnachweisbar*].

This observation leads Nietzsche immediately to the suggestion that we should create "our own new tables of what is good," presumably with an eye to effecting the causal determination of our actions in new ways. However, we need help from science to identify the lawful patterns into which values and actions fall; even if the mechanisms are undemonstrable, science may at least reveal the patterns of value-inputs and action-outputs. So to create one's self, "in this sense," is to accept Nietzsche's basically deterministic picture of action – as determined by sub-conscious causes that are hard to identify – but to use science to help identify those "values" which figure in the causal determination of action in new, but predictable, ways.[28] If this is the right way of understanding this passage, then Nietzsche's frequent remarks elsewhere about "creating" values would also be evidence (as Nehamas suggests [1985: 174]) for the claim that we may create ourselves: for values figure, causally, in our actions (hence, in who we become); hence the creation of values is causally connected to the creation of ourselves.

But now recall our earlier concession that Nietzsche cannot sensibly hold the view that type-facts determine all aspects of a person's life, for some of what happens to a person depends on circumstances and environment, which themselves are not causally determined by type-facts. Quite importantly, as we've just seen, among the factors that constitute the "circumstances" and "environment" – and which, in turn, exert a causal influence on a person's life trajectory – are values. (This, of course, is why Nietzsche considers it important to undertake a revaluation of values: values *do* make a causal difference.) Insofar, then, as a person creates these values, he participates in the creation of the environment which, in turn, can change the course

---

[28] GS: 290 (another passage on which Nehamas relies) is problematic for a somewhat different reason. Strictly, all it does is *describe* the type of person who gives style to his character; it does not suggest, or presuppose, that simply anyone *can* give such style. But a person constituted by the right type-facts could, of course, be enabled to "give style" in the sense Nietzsche describes here.

of a person's life trajectory. So while type-facts may circumscribe the range of possible trajectories, it now seems that a person can "create" his life – and thus be morally responsible for it – insofar as he can create those values that (causally) determine which of the possible trajectories is in fact realized.

As we saw in Chapter 2, this view appears to be precisely the view that both Nietzsche and Schopenhauer embrace. We can speak, for example, of the nurturing of a tomato plant as a "creative" act, even though, of course, no amount of creative input into the process will yield an apple tree. But what we can contribute, qua gardeners, is to shape the environment in ways that will affect which of the possible trajectories – wilting, flourishing, or any of the possible stages in between – the plant will realize. So, responsibility is saved, it seems, by simply recognizing the limited domain for autonomous, creative work, while allowing for the underlying fatalism which entails only that one's possibilities are circumscribed. A place for autonomy and responsibility is found precisely in the conceptual space between Causal Essentialism (the heart of Nietzsche's fatalism) and Classical Determinism.

Unfortunately, this seemingly attractive defense of autonomy simply does not square with the theory of action that underlies the basic fatalistic doctrine. Recall Galen Strawson's observation that insofar as one is not a *causa sui*, then "the particular way in which one is moved to try to change oneself . . . will be determined by how one already is" (1994: 7). In other words, even the choice to "create" particular values does not, in fact, satisfy the Autonomy Condition: for what values the person "chooses" to "create" is simply determined by the type-facts about that person – by "how [*he*] already is." So the fact that values play a causal role in a person's life trajectory only means a person can create his life *if* we can rightly speak of his having "created" these values. But the arguments against the Autonomy Condition considered above speak against this possibility, as much as they do against the idea of creating one's life directly (without the mediation of values).

Could this really be Nietzsche's view? Could it be the case that by "creation," Nietzsche means something radically different from its ordinary sense? In general, such a conclusion ought not to be surprising: Nietzsche retains lots of concepts – "free will" for example (e.g., BGE: 19; GM II: 2; TI IX: 8) – in senses that are foreign to their conventional meanings.[29] But there is an even clearer precedent for thinking that this is what happens to the concept of "creation" in Nietzsche's work. It is to be found in a fascinating, but little-noted passage, in *Daybreak* on "self-mastery" (*Selbst-Beherrschung*) (D: 109).[30] We should first grant, plausibly enough, that to speak of *mastering* oneself, just as to speak of *creating* oneself, presupposes – conventionally – that the Autonomy Condition is satisfied: there must be, in ordinary parlance, an autonomous self that *does the mastering* and *does the creating*. Someone who, for example, masters his burning desire for alcohol through a medication that moderates his desire for alcohol has not, it seems, engaged in "self-mastery": the drive has been mastered, to be sure, but it is not an autonomous *self* that did the mastering, but rather the drug.

Section 109 of *Daybreak* begins by canvassing six different ways of "combating the vehemence of a drive [or urge] [*eines Triebes*]." What follows is Nietzsche at his most psychologically astute, as he documents six different ways of mastering a powerful urge: for example, by avoiding opportunities for gratification of the drive, thus weakening it over time; or by learning to associate painful thoughts with the drive, so that its satisfaction no longer has a positive valence.

Interesting as these observations are, the real significance of this

---

[29] A particularly confusing case of this flaunting of conventional meanings concerns the discussion in GM II: 2 of "responsibility" – an "extraordinary privilege" of which only the "sovereign" individual is capable. In the latter case, Nietzsche is concerned with the difficulty of *breeding* a type of person (whom he calls "responsible") who will act in calculable and predictable ways – e.g., keeping his promises. He is *not* arguing, however, that people deserve *praise* and *blame* for their acts because they are responsible for them, in the sense of having freely chosen to perform them. It is this latter notion that is under attack throughout Nietzsche's works.

[30] This passage, I hasten to add, is not atypical. For one thing, it squares with the theory of action already defended and documented above. But similar claims also appear in BGE: 117 ("The will to overcome an affect is ultimately only the will of another, or of several, other affects") and underlie the extended discussion in GM III: 17.

passage lies elsewhere. For Nietzsche is also concerned here to answer the question as to the "ultimate motive" for "self-mastery." He explains it as follows:

> [*T*]*hat* one *wants* to combat the vehemence of a drive at all, however, does not stand within our own power; nor does the choice of any particular method; nor does the success or failure of this method. What is clearly the case is that in this entire procedure our intellect is only the blind instrument of *another drive*, which is a *rival* of the drive whose vehemence is tormenting us. . . . While "we" believe we are complaining about the vehemence of a drive, at bottom it is one drive *which is complaining about the other*; that is to say: for us to become aware that we are suffering from the *vehemence* of a drive presupposes the existence of another equally vehement or even more vehement drive, and that a *struggle* is in prospect in which our intellect is going to have to take sides.
>
> (D: 109)

Even if the intellect must "take sides" (*Partei nehmen*) this plainly does not mean that the intellect determines which side prevails: to the contrary, the intellect is a mere spectator upon the struggle. Thus, the fact that one masters oneself is *not* a product of autonomous choice by the person, but rather an effect of the underlying type-facts characteristic of that person (i.e., the physical arena in which these drives struggle): namely, which of his various drives happens to be strongest. There is, as it were, no "self" in "self-mastery": that is, no conscious "self" who contributes anything to the process. "Self-mastery" is merely an effect of the interplay of certain drives, drives over which the conscious self exercises no control (though it may, as it were, "take sides"). David Velleman describes an account of agency in which there is, in fact, no autonomous agent as one in which "the person merely serves as the arena for [certain] events: he takes no active part" (1992: 461). But we have now seen clearly that this is precisely Nietzsche's view. A "person" is an arena in which the struggle of drives (type-facts) is played out; how they play out determines what he believes, what he values, what he becomes. But, qua conscious self or "agent", the person takes no active part in the process.

Nietzsche, unlike his "great teacher" Schopenhauer, draws the correct conclusion from the initial fatalistic premises about agency.[31]

Transparency of the self

Nietzsche agrees with Kant (and also Schopenhauer) in viewing ordinary morality as concerned with the *motives* for which agents act (BGE: 32). Given that assumption, the intelligibility of the practice of moral judgment requires that we be able to know *which* motives

---

[31] Commentators, even those sensitive to naturalistic and quasi-fatalistic themes in Nietzsche's work, have often resisted this conclusion about the depth of Nietzsche's fatalism (e.g., May (1999) pp. 19 ff.; Schacht (1983)). Schacht, for example, tries to show that Nietzsche reserves "the possibility of a genuine and significant role for intentions in the genesis of action" (1983: 303). In support, Schacht quotes (ibid.) the following passage: "People are accustomed to consider the goal (purposes, volitions, etc.) as the *driving force* [behind actions], in keeping with a very ancient error; but it is merely the *directing* force – one has mistaken the helmsman for the steam" (GS: 360). From this, Schacht concludes that, "it is at least possible for intention to perform a significant 'directing' function where human action is concerned. And if this is so, it follows that [Nietzsche] would not have all human action thought of as determined invariably and exclusively by non-conscious forces and environmental factors" (1983: 303–4).

Yet Schacht, uncharacteristically, chops the quotation from *The Gay Science* at a misleading point. For the full passage continues as follows: "Is the 'goal,' the 'purpose' not often enough a beautifying pretext, a self-deception of vanity after the event that does not want to acknowledge that the ship is *following* the current into which it has entered accidentally? that it "wills" to go that way *because – it must*? that it has a direction, to be sure, but no helmsman at all?" In fact, then, Nietzsche is rejecting the suggestion that intentions (goals, purposes) function like helmsmen on ships, determining the direction of the ship, although the "steam" (the "drives" perhaps) provide the energy. The helmsman may, out of vanity, think of himself as "choosing" a direction, but he is simply doing what he "must": indeed, he is altogether expendable (there may be "no helmsman at all"). So, too, we may interpret ourselves as intentionally willing certain things, when really that "willing" itself, like the direction we fancy ourselves to be choosing, is simply what we "must" do, the mere necessary effect of something else. Nietzsche, then, repudiates the very possibility that Schacht embraces; that he should do so, however, is precisely what one should expect given the fatalism we have seen he embraced throughout his career.

are the cause of *which* actions. It is this descriptive premise that Nietzsche challenges.[32]

His primary ground for skepticism grows out of the theory of action described above: Nietzsche thinks, as we have seen, that "every action is unknowable" (GS: 335; cf. WP: 291, 294), for it is determined by non-conscious type-facts about the agent. As he writes in *Daybreak*:

> The primeval delusion still lives on that one knows, and knows quite precisely in every case, *how human action is brought about*. . . . 'I know what I want, what I have done, I am free and responsible for it, I hold others responsible, I can call by its name every moral possibility and every inner motion which precedes action; you may act as you will – in this matter I understand myself and understand you all!' – that is how . . . almost everyone still thinks. . . . [But] [a]ctions are *never* what they appear to us to be! We have expended so much labor on learning that external things are not as they appear to us to be – very well! the case is the same with the inner world! Moral actions are in reality "something other than that" – more we cannot say: and all actions are essentially unknown.
>
> (D: 116)

Actions are unknown because "nothing . . . can be more incomplete than [one's] image of the totality of *drives* which constitute [a man's]

---

[32] Curiously, Kant *also* concedes that the actual motives may, in fact, be unknowable. So, for example, at the beginning of Chapter II of the *Groundwork of the Metaphysics of Morals*, Kant admits that "it is absolutely impossible for experience to establish with complete certainty a single case in which the maxim of an action in other respects right has rested solely on moral grounds and on the thought of one's duty" (407). And in *The Metaphysics of Morals*, he notes that, "A man cannot see into the depths of his own heart so as to be quite certain, in even a *single* action, of the purity of his moral intention and the sincerity of his disposition." (392). Kant, of course, here lays great emphasis on *certainty*, whereas Nietzsche's skepticism holds even when the epistemic demand is less stringent than certainty. But more generally, it is one of many peculiarities of Kantian ethics that Kant does not take these admissions to be more damning for his moral philosophy than he does.

being" (D: 119). One "can scarcely name even the cruder ones: their number and strength, their ebb and flow, their play and counterplay among one another, and above all the laws of their *nutriment* remain wholly unknown" (D: 119). But as Nietzsche has already told us (e.g., D: 109, discussed above), the self is merely the arena in which the struggle of drives plays itself out, and one's actions are the outcomes of the struggle. As he puts the point somewhat later in the same work:

> [B]efore an act there step into our reflective consciousness one after another the *consequences* of various acts all of which we believe we can perform. . . . We believe we have resolved upon an act when we have decided that its consequences will be more favorable than those of any other. . . . [W]e would then . . . possess in our *picture of the consequences* of a certain action a *motive* for performing this action. . . . But at the moment when we finally do act, our action is often enough determined by a different species of motives than the species here under discussion. . . . What . . . comes into play [rather] is the way we habitually expend our energy; or some slight instigation from a person whom we fear or honor or love; or our indolence, which prefers to do what lies closest at hand; or an excitation of our imagination brought about at the decisive moment by some immediate, very trivial event; quite incalculable physical influences come into play; caprice and waywardness come into play; some emotion or other happens quite by chance to leap forth: in short, there come into play motives in part unknown to us, in part known very ill. . . . *Probably* a struggle takes place between these as well, battling to and fro, a rising and falling of the scales . . .: something quite invisible to us of which we would be quite unconscious. . . . [T]he struggle itself is hidden from me, and likewise the victory as victory; for, though I certainly learn what I finally *do*, I do not learn which motive has therewith actually proved victorious. *But we are accustomed to exclude* all these unconscious processes from the accounting and to reflect on the preparation for an act only to the extent that it is conscious.
>
> (D: 129)

So the motives for actions may, indeed, be different: the difficulty is that we do not have epistemic access to what the causally effective motives really are. Consequently, we cannot assess actions in terms of their motives, since we lack knowledge of the relevant differentiating features.[33] Thus, Nietzsche's critique of the descriptive presuppositions of MPS is simply that if motives are to be the basis for the moral evaluation of actions, then such evaluation is impossible, since the motives for action are largely unknown.

Universality and similarity

MPS always claims universal applicability, "it says stubbornly and inexorably, 'I am morality itself, and nothing besides is morality'" (BGE: 202). Nietzsche wants to resist this move. All moralities, he says, are "baroque and unreasonable . . . because they address themselves to 'all,' because they generalize where one must not generalize" (BGE: 198). But why must one *not* generalize this way? What kind of mistake is involved in MPS claiming universal applicability?

Nietzsche thinks that MPS can only get away with claiming universal applicability because it is perceived to be "in the general interest," as it were. Thus, the general applicability of MPS is predicated on an assumption about *similarity* among persons and their interests: people are essentially *similar*, and so the MPS that is good for one will be good for all. It is this assumption that Nietzsche denies.

Recall Nietzsche's central explanatory principle, introduced in Chapter 1: "Every animal . . . instinctively strives for an optimum of

---

33 Curiously, in the *Nachlass*, Nietzsche toys with a somewhat different critique of this descriptive presupposition of MPS. Actions can not be morally evaluated on the basis of motives not because the motives are unknown, but because they are all the same! So, for example, in a *Nachlass* note of 1887, he writes, "My purpose: to demonstrate the absolute homogeneity of all events . . .; to demonstrate how everything praised as moral is identical in essence with everything immoral" (WP: 272; cf. WP: 375). This thesis is in obvious tension with the thesis in the published works that motives are unknown, which may explain why Nietzsche never published this idea of the "homogeneity of all events." The thesis also depends, of course, on a very strong form of the doctrine of the will to power, a doctrine, as we shall see later, that Nietzsche did not ultimately accept.

favorable conditions in which fully to release his power and achieve his maximum feeling of power" (GM III: 7). Applied to morality, it yields the *Classically Realist* conclusion à la Sophists) that even particular moralities are adopted because they contribute to the power of certain animals. Morality, says Nietzsche, is "prudence, prudence, prudence [*Klugheit*], mixed with stupidity, stupidity, stupidity" (BGE: 198). The "prudence" (or "cleverness") consists in getting others to adhere to a morality that is advantageous to oneself, while the "stupidity" Nietzsche refers to is that involved when others, for whom such a morality is disadvantageous, adhere to it nonetheless. "*Morality in Europe today is herd animal morality*," says Nietzsche, "in other words . . . merely *one* type of human morality beside which, before which, and after which many other types, above all *higher* moralities, are, or ought to be, possible" (BGE: 202). Nietzsche's central worry, as we shall see below, is that MPS, which may be good for the herd, is *harmful* for higher types of human beings. As he writes later in *Beyond Good and Evil*:

> [T]he question is always who *he* is, and who the *other* person is. In a person, for example, who is called and made to command, self-denial and modest self-effacement would not be a virtue but the waste of a virtue: thus it seems to me. Every unegoistic morality that takes itself for unconditional and addresses itself to all does not only sin against taste: it is a provocation to sins of omission, one *more* seduction under the mask of philanthropy – and precisely a seduction and injury for the higher, rarer, privileged.
>
> (221)

As we have already seen, Nietzsche views persons as constituted by type-facts, i.e., the psycho-physical facts that make each person who he or she is. Insofar as people possess differing type-facts, they are dissimilar. But is this dissimilarity *relevant*? Nietzsche thinks it is, because he (tacitly) holds the crucial premise that type-facts determine what is in one's interests: what is *good* for a person (hereafter "prudential goodness") depends on the type-facts about that person. Since this idea is crucial to Nietzsche's whole critique of MPS, it warrants considering this idea in some detail.

Start with the intuitive notion that what is prudentially good for a person is whatever facilitates that person's *flourishing* – where what counts as flourishing is *relative* to type-facts about that person. Let us, following Railton (1986a), call the doctrine that goodness is relative to type-facts "relationalism." Peter Railton offers the following apt analogy to illustrate the sense in which prudential or non-moral goodness is a "relational" (or trivially relative) property:

> In a naturalistic spirit, we might think of goodness as akin to nutritiveness. All organisms require nutrition, but not the same nutrients. Which nutrients a given organism or type of organism requires will depend upon its nature. Cow's milk nourishes calves and many humans, but it won't nourish those organisms, including some humans, who cannot produce the enzymes needed to digest it; and some elements essential to human nutrition are toxic to other organisms. There is, then, no such thing as an *absolute* nutrient, that is, something that would be nutritious for all possible organisms. There is only *relational* nutritiveness: substance *S* is a nutrient for organisms of type *T*.
>
> (1986a: 10)

This kind of claim will prove crucial for Nietzsche's critique of morality: it is precisely Nietzsche's claim that, like nutrients, *values* can also be good or bad (nutritional or non-nutritional, even harmful) for different types of persons, depending on their nature. Moral values are harmful, claims Nietzsche, to potentially great human beings; while moral values are well suited to ("nutritious for") the herd animal and the slave. In this sense, what is non-morally good is relative or relational.

This idea of relational goodness, as we saw in Chapter 2, was familiar in antiquity. Early expression to it is given, for example, in Heraclitus: "Sea is the most pure and the most polluted water; for fishes it is drinkable and salutary, but for men it is undrinkable and deleterious" (Fr. 61 in Kirk *et al.* 1983: 188). And it is elaborated upon in a famous speech by Protagoras in Plato's dialogue of the same name:

> I know plenty of things – foods, drinks, drugs, and many others – which are harmful to men, and others which are beneficial,

and others again which, so far as men are concerned, are neither, but are harmful or beneficial to horse, and others only to cattle or dogs. Some have no effct on animals, but only on trees, and some again are good for the roots of trees but injurious to the young growths. Manure, for instance, is good for all plants when applied to their roots, but utterly destructive if put on the shoots or young branches. Or take olive oil. It is very bad for plants, and most inimical to the hair of all animals except man, whereas men find it of service both to the hair and to the rest of the body. So diverse and multiform is goodness that even with us the same thing is good when applied externally but deadly when taken internally.

(334a–c)

In both Heraclitus and Protagoras, we see the notion of relational goodness at work: what is good for fish, may be bad for men; and what is good for men, may be bad for all other animals. This amounts precisely to a denial of what Railton also denies: *absolute* goodness. As W. K. C. Guthrie explains, one sense of the "relativity" of value found in the Sophists is the view that:

There is nothing to which the epithets good, bad or the like can be applied absolutely and without qualification, because the effect of everything is different according to the object on which it is exercised, the circumstances of its application and so on. What is good for A may be bad for B, what is good for A in certain circumstances may be bad for him in others, and so on.
(1971: 166)

It is precisely because the Sophists were primarily concerned with relational prudential goodness that they liked to compare their task with a doctor's, for "it was the medical writers above all who insisted (as success in their craft demanded) on the relativity of 'good' and 'bad' to the individual" (Guthrie 1971: 169) (cf. Plato's *Theaetetus*, 167b–c). The Sophist, unlike the physician, was concerned with the social and practical well-being of the individual, not his physical well-being; but the same notion of relational goodness was at work. As Guthrie again aptly summarizes the view:

> [M]en and societies differ widely, and so therefore do their needs.
> There is no all-embracing "good for man." To diagnose the par-
> ticular situation and prescribe the best course of action for a man
> or a state under given conditions, as a doctor does for his patient
> is, as Protagoras saw it, the task of the Sophist.
>
> (1971: 187)

Thus, we find in some of the Sophists – and in earlier Greek thinkers
who influenced them, like Heraclitus – the notion of relative or relational goods, things that are good for some particular *type* of creature,
but not for all creatures.[34]

But what accounts for the *objectivity* of relational goodness?[35]
Here consideration of Railton's view will prove particularly useful.

[34] The Sophists often expressed the same idea about relational goodness through
analogies to husbandry and the care of plants, a comparison also made in the
Hippocratic *Law* (see Guthrie (1971), 168–9): what is good for the flourishing of a plant, the health of an individual, and the general well-being of the
individual is, in each case, relational, and thus the attention of the husband-
man, the doctor, and the Sophist must be directed to the facts peculiar to each.
The plant analogy is clearly the one that made the most profound impression
on Nietzsche. Indeed, it is striking how often the rhetoric of breeding, growth,
and other plant-related concepts appears in Nietzsche's work. In an early
work of 1880, he suggests that we should think of ourselves as gardens that
require special gardening to "cultivate [*ziehen*] the shoots of anger, pity,
curiosity, vanity as productively and profitably as a beautiful fruit tree on a
trellis . . ." (D: 560; cf. D: 532). And in his last work, *Ecce Homo*, he speaks
of his own flourishing in terms of, e.g., the climate and nutrition that made it
possible; and he remarks that, "I never even suspected what was growing in
me [*was in mir wächst*] – and one day all my capacities, suddenly ripe [*reif*],
leaped forth in their ultimate perfection" (EH II: 9).

[35] Note that even the Sophists thought such judgments were objective. For example, in the passage from Guthrie quoted above in the text concerning one sense
of "relativity" in Sophistic thought, Guthrie concludes by observing that, for
some of the Sophists, "The objectivity of the good effect is not denied, but it
varies in individual cases" (1971: 166) – i.e., it is an objective *relational*
good. Guthrie explicitly contrasts this sense of relativity with another,
more skeptical sense (expressed in the Protagorean "man is the measure"
doctrine), according to which "'there is nothing either good or bad, but
thinking makes it so'" (1971: 166). As Myles Burnyeat has also observed,
the so-called "new formulation" of the Protagorean position later on in
the *Theaetetus* (178b–179b) allows "one element of objectivity . . . [namely]

If there is a real, objective fact about what is non-morally or prudentially good for a person, then it must, according to Railton, have two
features:

> (1) *independence*: it exists and has certain determinate features
> independent of whether we think it exists or has those features,
> independent, even, of whether we have good reason to think this;
> (2) *feedback*: it is such – and we are such – that we are able to
> interact with it, and this interaction exerts the relevant sort of
> shaping influence or control upon our perceptions, thought, and
> action.

(1986b: 172)

Railton argues for the intuitively plausible idea that what is non-
morally good for a person consists in "what he would want himself
to seek if he knew what he were doing" (1986b: 177). More precisely,
Railton holds that what is non-morally good for a person is what would
satisfy an *objective interest* of that person (1986b: 176). Something is
in the objective interest of a person when his "ideal" self would want
his non-ideal self to want or seek it.[36] A person's ideal self is just a
self with "unqualified cognitive and imaginative powers, and full
factual and nomological information about his physical and psychological constitution, capacities, circumstances, history, and so on"

the objectivity of judgments about what is advantageous or beneficial"
(1990: 39).

In the *Theaetetus*, however, the modified Protagorean view is admitted
because of the difficulties and paradoxes generated both by giving a relativistic account of expertise and by applying the subjectivist "man is the
measure" doctrine to prospective judgments about what is prudentially good
or advantageous. (The latter is well-discussed in Burnyeat (1990: 39–42).)
These arguments do not seem to figure in Nietzsche's thinking on this issue.

36 This way of putting it is not quite faithful to Railton's usage, as will become
clear shortly. According to Railton, it is the existence of what he calls "the
reduction basis" that makes something an objective interest of a person, and
not the fact that his ideal self would want his non-ideal self to want it (1986b:
175). The reduction basis, in turn, is just the set of facts which the ideal
self takes into account in formulating what he would want his non-ideal self
to want.

(1986b: 174–5). Railton offers the homely example of Lonnie, the foreign traveler, suffering from an upset stomach and desirous of a glass of milk. In fact, however, "hard-to-digest" milk would "further unsettle Lonnie's stomach and worsen his dehydration" (1986b: 174–5). Drinking milk would not be prudentially good for Lonnie; which is to say it is not in his objective interest; which is to say Lonnie's ideal self would not want Lonnie to want a glass of milk. Why not? Because (among other reasons) Lonnie's ideal self knows the effects of milk on the human digestive system and thus knows that milk will aggravate rather than ameliorate the symptoms. It is these "natural" facts – about Lonnie's physical condition, the nature of milk, and milk's effect on the human system – that make it the case that drinking the milk is *not* in Lonnie's objective interest, i.e., is not prudentially good for him. Hence, too, the *independence* of prudential goodness: these natural facts about Lonnie, about human biology, and about milk are what they are whatever we may think.

What about feedback, then? Here the story of Lonnie continues. Without any ideal self to direct his wants, Lonnie still has a way of interacting with and finding out about what is in his objective interest. Should he drink the milk, his condition will only worsen. Should he, however, on a subsequent occasion drink a clear, carbonated liquid, he may notice that his condition improves markedly. Thus, Lonnie may develop "some conscious or unconscious, reasoned or super-stitious, tendency to seek out" this kind of drink when feeling ill (1986b: 180). Railton describes this type of feedback from what is non-morally good for a person as operating via "the *wants/interests mechanism*,"

> which permits individuals to achieve selfconscious and unself-conscious learning about their interests through experience. In the simplest sorts of cases, trial and error leads to the selective retention of wants that are satisfiable and leads to satisfactory [i.e., prudentially good] results for the agent.
>
> (1986b: 179)

And thus we have a contemporary moral philosopher's account of non-moral goodness as consisting in "what [a person] would want himself to seek if he knew what he were doing" (1986b: 177).

To be sure, the details of this account are not to be found in Nietzsche, but it still resonates remarkably well with what Nietzsche does say. For Nietzsche, much like Railton, conceives of persons as *natural* creatures whose psychological and physiological characteristics importantly determine what they are capable of, hence also what would be good for them. Consider, for example, Nietzsche's discussion of the case of the Italian writer Cornaro in *Twilight of the Idols* (VI: 1). Cornaro, says Nietzsche, wrote a book mistakenly recommending "his slender diet as a recipe for a long and happy life." But why was this a mistake? Nietzsche explains:

> The worthy Italian thought his diet was the *cause* of his long life, whereas the precondition for a long life, the extraordinary slowness of his metabolism, the consumption of so little, was the cause of his slender diet. He was not free to eat little *or* much; his frugality was not a matter of "free will": he became sick when he ate more. But whoever is not a carp not only does well to eat properly, but needs to.

This little account echoes Railton's theory of objective but relational goodness at several points. There is an independent natural fact about Cornaro that explains why a slender diet is good for him: namely, "the extraordinary slowness of his metabolism." There is feedback, via the wants/interests mechanism: given his slow metabolism, if Cornaro ate more "he became sick"; conversely, when he stuck to his slender diet, he did well. The natural facts also constrained him: "[h]e was not free to eat little *or* much." Cornaro's mistake consists, in effect, in his belief in *absolute* – rather than relational – prudential goodness: he thought the "good" diet was good for everyone, when in fact it was only good for certain types of bodies (namely, those with slow metabolisms). Like Railton, the contemporary naturalist, Nietzsche, the nineteenth-century naturalist, holds the view that what is non-morally good for a person is importantly constrained and determined by natural facts about him.

Let us be clear, however, about what is at stake here. The claim is *not* that Nietzsche clearly articulates something like the view Railton describes. Rather, the claim is that Nietzsche holds the view that facts about prudential goodness are both relational and objective, and

Railton's view explains how this could be so, providing the philosophical underpinnings and detail that are missing in Nietzsche's own account.

To return, then, to our main theme, Nietzsche's critique of the Similarity Thesis: Nietzsche holds that agents are essentially *dissimilar*, insofar as they are constituted by different type-facts. Since type-facts determine what is good and bad for an agent, it follows that one morality cannot be good for all, since people differ in a respect relevant to their interests. Thus, the Similarity Thesis, like the Transparency of the Self and Free Will Theses, turns out to be false, given Nietzsche's conception of persons and agency.

Chapter 4

Nietzsche's critique of morality II

The critique of moral norms

The core of Nietzsche's critique of morality is his attack on the normative component of MPS: even a morality which presupposed no false descriptive theses would still be the object of Nietzsche's attack if it contained norms that benefited the "lowest" men while harming the "highest." To begin, we must demonstrate that this claim is central to Nietzsche's critique and ask what Nietzsche means by "higher" and "lower" men.

As we saw in Chapter 3, Nietzsche has been saddled with a variety of different accounts and critiques of MPS. But in fact, all his criticisms turn out to be parasitic upon one basic complaint. For example, contrary to Nehamas (1985) and Geuss (1997), Nietzsche never objects to the universality of moral demands, per se, as an *intrinsically* bad feature of MPS. Rather, he finds universality objectionable because he holds that "the demand of one morality for all is detrimental to the higher men" (BGE: 228). Universality would be unobjectionable if agents were relevantly similar, as we saw at the end of the previous

chapter. But because agents are relevantly different, a universal morality must necessarily be harmful to some. As Nietzsche writes elsewhere: "When a decadent type of man ascended to the rank of the highest type [via MPS], this could only happen at *the expense of its countertype* [emphasis added], the type of man that is strong and sure of life" (EH III: 5). Finally, consider the illuminating preface to the *Genealogy*, in which Nietzsche sums up his basic concern particularly well:

> What if a symptom of regression lurked in the "good," likewise a danger, a seduction, a poison, a narcotic, through which the present lived *at the expense of the future*? Perhaps more comfortably, less dangerously, but at the same time in a meaner style, more basely? – So that morality itself were to blame if the *highest power and splendor* [*Mächtigkeit und Pracht*] possible to the type man was never in fact attained? So that morality itself was the danger of dangers?
>
> (GM Pref: 6; cf. BT Attempt: 5)

This theme is sounded throughout Nietzsche's work. In a book of 1880, for example, he writes that, "Our weak, unmanly social concepts of good and evil and their tremendous ascendancy over body and soul have finally weakened all bodies and souls and snapped the self-reliant, independent, unprejudiced men, the pillars of a *strong* civilization" (D: 163). Similarly, in a posthumously published note of 1885, he remarks that "men of great creativity, the really great men according to my understanding, will be sought in vain today" because "nothing stands more malignantly in the way of their rise and evolution . . . than what in Europe today is called simply 'morality'" (WP: 957). In these and many other passages,[1] Nietzsche makes plain his fundamental objection to MPS: simply put, that MPS thwarts the development of human excellence, i.e., "the highest power and splendor possible to the type man." This is the very heart of Nietzsche's challenge to MPS.

More precisely, then, Nietzsche's view poses the following interpretive questions:

---

[1]   See, e.g., BGE: 62, 21; GM III: 14; A: 5, 24; EH IV: 4; WP: 274, 345, 400, 870, 879.

1   *What is characteristic of the "highest power and splendor actu-
     ally possible to the type man"?* What, in other words, marks the
     higher men that Nietzsche sees as threatened by MPS?

2   *In what respects does MPS prevent the development or flour-
     ishing of higher men?* What is it, in other words, about the norms
     of MPS that harms higher men while favoring lower men?
     Through what causal mechanism exactly does MPS work its
     pernicious effects? If there is to be any issue for Nietzsche, then
     it must be the case that MPS *really does have harmful effects*
     on higher men. If MPS did not harm higher men – whoever,
     precisely, they are – then Nietzsche's central complaint about
     MPS fails.

3   *What value is to be assigned to the flourishing of higher men
     such that it counts against MPS that it prevents their flourishing?*
     If MPS is objectionable because it thwarts the "highest power
     and splendor" possible for man, that must be because a very
     high value is to be assigned to the flourishing of these higher
     men. This presents several questions: value for whom? and why?
     and what is supposed to be the upshot for MPS?

     The rest of this chapter will attempt to answer these questions,
with the most attention accorded the first two.

"Higher men"

Who, then, are Nietzsche's "higher men"?[2] Notice that Nietzsche
provides several examples in his writings of those he regards un-
equivocally as "higher men": Goethe, Beethoven, and (perhaps most
importantly) Nietzsche himself.[3] Nietzsche, of course, often expresses

---

[2]   In *Thus Spoke Zarathustra*, Nietzsche spoke of the "superman" as a kind
      of ideal higher type. This particular concept, however, simply drops out of his
      mature work (except for a brief mention in EH in the context of discuss-
      ing *Zarathustra*). Unfortunately, it has received far more attention from com-
      mentators than it warrants: the higher type of human being (a Goethe or a
      Nietzsche) is more important for understanding Nietzsche than the hyperbolic,
      and often obscure, Zarathustrian rhetoric about the *Über-mensch*.

[3]   The point in the text should be distinguished from the idiosyncratic view
      defended in the final chapter of Nehamas (1985). According to Nehamas,

admiration for other people – Napoleon, sometimes Caesar, the "free spirits" discussed throughout *The Gay Science* – but creative geniuses like Goethe and Nietzsche, himself, stand out for the esteem they enjoy in Nietzsche's work.[4] What makes these figures paradigms of the "higher" type for Nietzsche, beyond their great creativity (since, as he says, "the men of great creativity" are "the really great men according to my understanding" (WP: 957))?[5] Nietzsche's writings, in fact, depict five distinctive, and closely related, characteristics of the higher type of human being. Taken together, they are plainly sufficient to make someone a higher type in Nietzsche's view, though it is not obvious that any one of these is necessary, and various combinations often seem sufficient for explaining how Nietzsche speaks of higher human beings.

1   *The higher type is solitary and deals with others only instrumentally.* "Every choice human being," says Nietzsche, "strives instinctively for a citadel and a secrecy where he is saved from the crowd, the many, the great majority . . ." (BGE: 26). Such solitude, though, is "not . . . chosen, but . . . given" (WP: 943): a "well-turned-

---

Nietzsche does not *describe* his ideal person – his "higher man" – but rather "exemplifies" such a person in the form of the "character" that is constituted by and exemplified in his corpus. Nietzsche, however, *describes* at great length and in many places (e.g., D: 201; GS: 55; BGE: 287; NCW Epilogue: 2; WP: 943) the types of persons he admires; and he also *describes* himself as such a person – see, for example, EH I: 2. For further criticism of Nehamas on this and other points, see Leiter (1992).

4   Brobjer (1995, Appendix 2) has shown that no one is referred to more in the Nietzschean corpus than Goethe (135 references), and the references are uniformly very positive. (Schopenhauer is a close second with 122 references, but their content is far more mixed.) Beethoven is referenced 27 times by Nietzsche – still making him one of the people Nietzsche discusses most often (Napoleon, for example, is mentioned 26 times, and Spinoza and Voltaire 25 times each) – and, more significantly, the references to Beethoven are, as with Goethe, uniformly positive.

5   A capacity for "self-overcoming" is often mentioned in this connection as well, but this notion is so vague, that it is hard to know what it amounts to without specification in terms of characteristics like those discussed in the text that follows.

out person" "is always in his own company, whether he associates with books, human beings, or landscapes" (EH II: 2). The higher type is thus solitary by necessity: "There is a solitude within him that is inaccessible to praise or blame, his own justice that is beyond appeal" (WP: 962). "[T]he concept of greatness entails being noble, wanting to be by oneself, being able to be different, standing alone and having to live independently [*auf-eigne-Faust-leben-müssen*]" (BGE: 212). Indeed, the higher type pursues solitude with something of a vengeance, for he "knows how to make enemies everywhere, . . . [He] constantly contradicts the great majority not through words but through deeds" (WP: 944).

Unsurprisingly, then, the great or higher man lacks the "congeniality" and "good-naturedness" so often celebrated in contemporary popular culture. "A great man . . . is incommunicable: he finds it tasteless to be familiar" (WP: 962). More than that, though, the higher type deals with others, when he has to, in a rather distinctive way: "A human being who strives for something great considers everyone he meets on his way either as a means or as a delay and obstacle – or as a temporary resting place" (BGE: 273). Thus, "a great man . . . wants no 'sympathetic' heart, but servants, tools; in his intercourse with men, he is always intent on *making* something out of them" (WP: 962). The great man approaches others instrumentally not only because of his fundamental proclivity for solitude, but because of another distinguishing characteristic: he is consumed by his work, his responsibilities, his projects.

2 *The higher type seeks burdens and responsibilities, as he is driven towards the completion of a unifying project.* "What is noble?" Nietzsche again asks in a *Nachlass* note of 1888. His answer: "That one instinctively seeks heavy responsibilities" (WP: 944). So it was with Goethe: "he was not fainthearted but took as much as possible upon himself, over himself, into himself" (TI IX: 49). But the higher type does not seek out responsibilities and tasks arbitrarily. "A great man," says Nietzsche displays "a long logic in all of his activity . . . he has the ability to extend his will across great stretches of his life and to despise, and reject everything petty about him" (WP: 962). This is the trait Nietzsche sometimes refers to as having "style" in

"character" (GS: 290).[6] Indeed, we have seen already how Nietzsche saw his own life as manifesting precisely this trait:

> [T]he organizing "idea" that is destined to rule [in one's life and work] keeps growing deep down – it begins to command; slowly it leads us *back* from side roads and wrong roads; it prepares *single* qualities and fitnesses that will one day prove to be indispensable as means toward a whole – one by one, it trains all *subservient* capacities before giving any hint of the dominant task, "goal,' "aim," or "meaning."
>
> Considered in this way, my life is simply wonderful. For the task of a *revaluation of all values* more capacities may have been needed than have ever dwelt together in a single individual. ... I never even suspected what was growing in me – and one day all my capacities, suddenly ripe, *leaped forth* in their ultimate perfection.

(EH II: 9)

We know from earlier in *Ecce Homo* that Nietzsche views himself as a higher type, "a well-turned-out-person" (EH I: 2), and thus we may conclude that it is a characteristic *only* of the higher type that he is driven in pursuit of a project in the way described here. Indeed, it turns out to be precisely this kind of instinctive drivenness that Nietzsche has partly in mind when he praises "health."

3 *The higher type is essentially healthy and resilient.* One essential attribute of the "well-turned-out-person" is that he "has a taste only for what is good for him; his pleasure, his delight cease where the measure of what is good for him is transgressed. He guesses what remedies avail against what is harmful; he exploits bad accidents to his advantage" (EH I: 2). But this is just to say that a higher type is *healthy*, for health, Nietzsche tells us, means simply "instinctively cho[osing] the *right* means against wretched states" (EH I: 2). This permits us to understand Nietzsche's own declaration in *Ecce Homo*

---

6   It is important to note that this famous passage (GS: 290) merely *describes* those – "the strong and domineering natures" – who are *able* "'to give' style" to their character; it does not presuppose that just anyone can do so and it is not a recommendation that everyone try to do so.

that he was "*healthy at bottom*" (EH I: 2), a seemingly paradoxical claim for a philosopher whose physical ailments were legion. Yet "health," for Nietzsche, is a term of art, meaning not the absence of sickness, but something closer to *resilience*, to how one deals with ordinary (physical) sickness and setbacks.[7] "For a typical healthy person," Nietzsche says, "being sick can even become an energetic *stimulus* for life, for living more. This, in fact, is how [my own] long period of sickness appears to me *now* ... it was during the years of my lowest vitality that I *ceased* to be a pessimist; the instinct of self-restoration *forbade* me a philosophy of poverty and discouragement" (EH I: 2). To cease to be a pessimist is to reject MPS, for only under the color of MPS does life appear to lack value. Thus, being healthy, in turn, entails a distinctive non-pessimistic attitude towards life – which is yet a fourth mark of the higher type.

4   *The higher type affirms life, meaning that he is prepared to will the eternal return of his life.* In *Beyond Good and Evil*, Nietzsche describes "the opposite ideal" to that of moralists and pessimists like Schopenhauer as "the ideal of the most high-spirited, alive, and world-affirming human being who has not only come to terms and learned to get along with whatever was and is, but who wants to have *what was and is* repeated into all eternity" (BGE: 56). Put more simply: the higher type embraces the doctrine of the eternal recurrence and thus evinces what Nietzsche often calls a "Dionysian" or "life-affirming" attitude.

Talk about "affirming" life is, however, rather vague; happily, we can say something more precise about what Nietzsche means. A person, for Nietzsche, has a *Dionysian attitude* toward life insofar as he affirms his life unconditionally; in particular, insofar as he affirms it *including* the "suffering" or other hardships it has involved. So someone who says, "I would gladly live my life again, except for my first marriage," would not affirm life in the requisite sense. Thus, we may say that a person *affirms* his life in Nietzsche's sense only insofar

---

7   There is also, to be sure, a kind of psychological sickness characteristic of the "priest" and the man of *ressentiment*, which is also incompatible with "health." We will return to these topics in Chapters 6 and 8.

as he would gladly will its eternal return: i.e., will the repetition of his entire life through eternity. In fact, Nietzsche calls "the idea of the eternal recurrence" the "highest formulation of affirmation that is at all attainable" (EH III: Z-1; cf. BGE: 56). Higher men, then, are marked by a distinctive Dionysian attitude toward their life: they would gladly will the repetition of their life eternally.

Notice that Nietzsche claims precisely this attitude characterized both himself and Goethe. Speaking, for example, of the neglect by his contemporaries of his work, Nietzsche writes: "I myself have never suffered from all this; what is *necessary* does not hurt me; *amor fati* [love of fate] is my inmost nature" (EH III: CW-4). Regarding Goethe, Nietzsche says that, "Such a spirit . . . stands amid the cosmos with a joyous and trusting fatalism, in the *faith* . . . that all is redeemed and affirmed in the whole. . . . Such a faith, however, is the highest of all possible faiths: I have baptized it with the name of *Dionysus*" (TI IX: 49). We shall shortly see how this distinctive attitude of higher men – their Dionysian attitude toward life – figures in Nietzsche's critique of the normative agenda of MPS.

5 *The higher man has a distinctive bearing towards others and especially towards himself: he has self-reverence.* "The 'higher nature' of the great man," says Nietzsche in a striking *Nachlass* note of 1888 "lies in being different, in incommunicability, in distance of rank, not in an effect of any kind – even if he made the whole globe tremble" (WP: 876; cf. GS: 55). This is perhaps the most unusual feature of Nietzsche's discussion of the higher type, for it suggests that, at bottom, being a higher type is a matter of "attitude" or "bearing." In a section of *Beyond Good and Evil*, Nietzsche once again answers the question, "What is noble?," this time as follows: "It is not the works, it is the *faith* that is decisive here, that determines the order of rank . . .: some fundamental certainty that a noble soul has about itself, something that cannot be sought, nor found, nor perhaps lost. *The noble soul has reverence [Ehrfurcht] for itself*" (BGE: 287). Self-reverence – to revere and respect oneself as one might a god – is no small achievement, as the proliferation of "self-help" programs and pop psychology slogans like "I'm OK, you're OK" would suggest. Self-loathing, self-doubt, and self-laceration are the norm among

human beings; to possess a "fundamental certainty" about oneself is, Nietzsche thinks quite plausibly, a unique state of affairs.[8]

Allied with this posture of self-reverence are other distinctive attitudes that distinguish the bearing of the higher man. "The noble human being," says Nietzsche, "honors himself as one who is powerful, also as one who has power over himself, who knows how to speak and be silent, who delights in being severe and hard with himself and respects all severity and hardness" (BGE: 260).[9] (The higher man, unsurprisingly, is no hedonist: "What is noble?" asks Nietzsche: "That one leaves happiness to the great majority: happiness as peace of soul, virtue, comfort, Anglo-angelic shopkeeperdom à la Spencer" (WP: 944).) In an earlier work, Nietzsche explains that:

[8] I return to this topic in Chapter 6. Note, too, that there are echoes in Nietzsche's discussion of the higher man of Aristotle's famous discussion of *megalopsychia* in the *Nicomachean Ethics* (1123b–1125a16). *Megalopsychia* has been variously translated, but for our purposes, "greatness of soul" is the most illuminating English equivalent. Kaufmann (1974: 382–3) notices the similarity between Nietzsche's "higher" man and Aristotle's "great-souled" man, but never explains or examines it in any detail. This is a serious omission, since there are as many differences as similarities. But among the interesting similarities are the following Aristotelian comments about the "great-souled" man: "the man is thought to be great-souled who thinks himself worthy of great things, being worthy of them" (1123b); "honor from casual people and on trifling grounds he will utterly despise" (1124a10); "he is the sort of man to confer benefits, but he is ashamed of receiving them; for the one is the mark of a superior, the other of an inferior" (1124b10); "it is characteristic of the great-souled man not to aim at the things commonly held in honor" (1124b20); "He must be unable to make his life revolve around another, unless it be a friend; for this is slavish" (1125a); "Nor is he mindful of wrongs; for it is not the part of a great-souled man to have a long memory, especially for wrongs, but rather to overlook them" (1125a); "a slow step is thought proper to the great-souled man, a deep voice, and a level utterance; for the man who takes few things seriously is not likely to be hurried" (1125a10).

[9] That Nietzsche does not think there is any contradiction between revering oneself and also being "severe and hard" with oneself helps illuminate his understanding of self-reverence. Self-reverence is not, as it were, a matter of putting oneself on a pedestal; it means being "severe and hard" with oneself *not* out of doubt and self-loathing, but as a result of "fundamental certainty" about one's own worth and mettle, as someone who is capable of severity and hardness as needed.

> [T]he passion that attacks those who are noble is peculiar. . . .
> It involves the use of a rare and singular standard cold to every-
> body else; the discovery of values for which no scales have been
> invented yet; offering sacrifices on altars that are dedicated to
> an unknown god; a courage without any desire for honors; self-
> sufficiency that overflows and gives to men and things.
>
> (GS: 55)

Indeed, the ability to set his own standard of valuation is one of the
most distinctive achievements of the higher type, as we saw already
in the discussion of solitude. And "the *highest* man," says Nietzsche,
is "he who *determines* values and directs the will of millennia by
giving direction to the highest natures" (WP: 999).

Considered all together, it becomes clear why creative geniuses
like Goethe, Beethoven, and Nietzsche himself should be the preferred
examples of the higher human being: for the characteristics of the
higher type are precisely those that lend themselves to *artistic* and
creative work. A penchant for solitude, an absolute devotion to one's
tasks, an indifference to external opinion, a fundamental certainty
about oneself and one's values (that often strikes others as hubris) –
all these are the traits we find, again and again, in artistic geniuses.

Take the case of Beethoven. The leading modern biographical
study (Solomon 1977), for example, tells us that,

> Beethoven was possessed of an unswerving sense of "mission,"
> of "vocation," and filled with a deep conviction as to the signifi-
> cance of his work and his art. All else was subordinated to the
> fulfillment of this mission . . . by 1798 [when Beethoven was
> 28] an elitist, almost Caesarist element has entered his thought;
> in that year, he wrote to Zmeskall: "The devil take you. I refuse
> to hear anything about your whole moral outlook. *Power* is the
> moral principle of those who excel others, and it is also mine."
> And in 1801, he referred to two of his friends as "merely . . .
> instruments on which to play when I feel inclined. . . . I value
> them merely for what they do for me."
>
> (p. 86)

This remarkable passage reveals several of the traits Nietzsche associates with the higher human being: tremendous self-assurance, drivenness and devotion to one's creative task, an instrumental attitude towards others. Beethoven displayed a resilience to match these other traits; the "several years of considerable anguish" (when, among other things, he began to lose his hearing) were also "years of extremely high productivity and creative accomplishment" (p. 114); indeed, Beethoven's biographer suspects that "the former may have been a necessary precondition of the latter" (p. 115) and finally concludes that, "All of Beethoven's defeats were, ultimately, turned into victories" (p. 124). This is, in a nutshell, Nietzsche's very notion of the "health" that is so distinctive of the higher human being.

That Nietzsche's paradigmatic higher type is the artistic genius is worth emphasizing, given Nietzsche's many infamous illiberal sentiments.[10] For, ultimately, Nietzsche admired creative individuals the most: in art, literature, music, and philosophy – "the men of great creativity, the really great men according to my understanding" (WP: 957). His critique of MPS is, in an important sense, driven by the realization that the *moral* life is essentially inhospitable to the truly creative life – a point to which we shall return below.

This use of examples, however, only indirectly illuminates what Nietzsche means by "lower men." Beyond observing, however, that Nietzsche thought the "lower" types were the vast majority, it is not clear we need to say more to understand Nietzsche's critique. As Nietzsche says in the *Genealogy*, the "physiological casualties and the disgruntled" are "the *majority* of mortals" (III: 1). Or similarly in *Beyond Good and Evil*: "There is among men as in every other animal species an excess of failures, of the sick, degenerating, infirm, who suffer necessarily; the successful cases are, among men, too, always the exception" (p. 62). We do not need more than this recognition of Nietzsche's rather dim view of the vast bulk of humanity, since the *core* of Nietzsche's critique is simply that MPS has a *deleterious effect on higher men* (i.e., men who manifest human excellence). While Nietzsche also seems to think that MPS is in the interests of other persons – "lower men" – this by itself is *not* objectionable; recall that Nietzsche says that "The ideas of the herd should rule in the herd –

10   On the latter, see Chapter 9.

but not reach out beyond it" (WP: 287). It is this "reaching out beyond" then that is at issue because it is this that *harms* "higher men." If there were a social order in which morality existed – and in which it served the interests of "lower" types – without having any effects on potentially "higher men" then one would imagine that Nietzsche should have no objections. In that case, one could leave the issue of who "lower men" are pleasantly vague without any cost to the analytical task of getting clear about Nietzsche's critique of morality.

At the same time, Nietzsche does hold the basically Calliclean view (see Chapter 2) that moral values are, in fact, *in the interest* of certain types of people, namely "lower men" – and to understand and assess this claim we would need to know who precisely he means in speaking of "lower men." Ordinarily, of course, we think that the hallmark of "moral" views is precisely that they are not self-interested. But on Nietzsche's account, this is an illusion: the general *prevalence* of moral values is in fact in the interests of certain *types* of people (in Nietzsche's typical terminology: they serve the will to power of these people). After all, it is a basic explanatory principle of Nietzsche's (as first noted in Chapter 1) that, "Every animal . . . instinctively strives for an optimum of favorable conditions in which fully to release his power and achieve his maximum feeling of power" (GM III: 7). As applied to morality, it leads naturally to claims like the following:

> [I]n the history of morality a will to power finds expression, through which now the slaves and oppressed, now the ill-constituted and those who suffer from themselves, now the mediocre attempt to make those value judgments prevail that are favorable to *them*.

> (WP: 400)

In a similar vein, Nietzsche claims elsewhere that only certain types of people "praise selflessness *because it brings* [*them*] *advantages*" (GS: 21; cf. WP: 246). And so too, he holds that slave morality simply reflects "the prudence of the lowest order" (GM I: 13) because it legitimizes the characteristics and desires of the "lowest order" by casting them in a morally praiseworthy light. Thus, Nietzsche suggests (in GM I: 14) that the "lowest order" or "the slaves" effect (through MPS) the following prudential moral translations:

1   their impotence becomes "goodness of heart";
2   their anxious lowliness becomes "humility";
3   their "inoffensiveness" and their "lingering at the door" becomes "patience";
4   their inability to achieve revenge becomes their *unwillingness* to seek revenge;
5   their desire for retaliation becomes a desire for justice;
6   their hatred of the enemy becomes a hatred of injustice.

In each case, then, MPS assigns moral value to the attitude or desire on the right-hand side of the translation, thereby legitimizing the *real* attitudes and desires (on the left-hand side) of the "lowest order." In *legitimizing* these attitudes and desires, MPS, prima facie, serves the interests of those who hold them.

Higher men and the critique of MPS: objections

MPS, then, is marked by a distinctive normative agenda that is harmful to higher men; and it is because it harms higher men that Nietzsche centrally objects to MPS. One final challenge to this interpretation merits consideration. According to this objection, Nietzsche attacks MPS not because it is harmful to higher men but because MPS is: (i) harmful to "life"; or (ii) "anti-nature." Both of these interpretations of Nietzsche's complaint find ample textual support in Nietzsche, but in each case, as we shall see, "life" and "anti-nature" must be construed as reflecting his concern for the preservation and cultivation of "higher men."

Consider first the charge that Nietzsche sees MPS as a threat to "life" itself. Geuss, for example, says that, "There is little doubt that 'Life' . . . in Nietzsche does seem to function as a criterion for evaluating moralities" (1997: 10). So, too, Schacht claims that Nietzsche "takes 'life' in this world to be the sole locus of value, and its preservation, flourishing, and above all its enhancement to be ultimately decisive for determinations of value" (1983: 359). Thus, the question of the value of MPS is really the question of its "value for life" (p. 354).[11]

As it stands, such an account is too vague: what exactly does "life" refer to here? Schacht, following a suggestion of Nietzsche's

---

[11]   See also May (1999): 25 ff.

from the *Nachlass* (WP: 254), suggests that life is will to power, and thus degree of power constitutes the standard of value. But this involves no gain in precision. Nietzsche may, indeed, have thought that more "power" – in his sense – was more valuable than less, but that still leaves us with the question: power of *what* or of *whom*? The only plausible candidate – given especially his other remarks discussed above – is power *of people*; just as the only plausible candidate for the "life" that Nietzsche considers it valuable to preserve and enhance must be the *lives of people*.

From this it does not follow, however, that only the "highest men" are the locus of value; one could imagine a philosopher who used "life" to gloss the lives of *all* people (so that the maximum power of *all* people was what was valuable); or even an environmentally-minded philosopher who used "life" to gloss all forms of life, human and non-human. But here the more explicit remarks about higher men quoted in the prior section suggest that in Nietzsche's case when he speaks of the value for "life" he means simply the value for the preservation and enhancement of the highest men.

That this is what Nietzsche in fact has in mind is revealed by the context of his actual remarks about the "value for life." For example, he comments that "a higher and more fundamental *value for life* might have to be ascribed to deception, selfishness, and lust" (BGE: 2, emphasis added). But what sort of "life" is, e.g., "selfishness" valuable for? As Nietzsche writes elsewhere (e.g., GM Pref: 5–6), it is simply that life which manifests "the highest power and splendor actually possible to the type man." And similarly, when Nietzsche says that a "tendency hostile to life is therefore characteristic of morality," it is clear in context that what "life" refers to is "the type man" who might be "raised to his greatest splendor and power" (that is, but for the interference of MPS) (WP: 897). In short, then, the things Nietzsche identifies as "valuable" for life are those he takes to be necessary for the flourishing of the highest types of life (or human excellence), while those that he identifies as harmful to it are those that he takes to be things that constitute obstacles to such flourishing. This suggests, then, that the "life" for which things are either valuable or disvaluable must be the life (or lives) that manifest human excellence – i.e., the lives of "higher men."

Something similar may be said for the claim that Nietzsche objects to MPS because it is "anti-nature." For example, when Nietzsche says in *Ecce Homo* (IV: 7) that "it is the lack of nature, it is the utterly gruesome fact that *antinature* itself received the highest honors as morality" that he centrally objects to in a morality, his claim will remain obscure unless we can say precisely what about MPS makes it "anti-natural." Nietzsche, himself, offers guidance on this in the same section when he explains that an MPS is anti-natural insofar as it has the following sorts of characteristics: it teaches men "to despise the very first instincts of life" and "to experience the presupposition of life, sexuality, as something unclean"; and it "looks for the evil principle in what is most profoundly necessary for growth, in *severe* self-love" (EH IV: 7).

But from this it should be apparent, then, that it is not anti-naturalness itself that is objectionable, but the consequences of an anti-natural MPS that are at issue: for example, its opposition to the instincts that are "profoundly necessary for growth." This point is even more explicit in *The Antichrist*, where Nietzsche notes that Christian morality "has waged deadly war against this higher type of man; *it has placed all the basic instincts of his type under ban*" (5, emphasis added). In other words, the anti-naturalness of MPS is objectionable because the "natural" instincts MPS opposes are precisely those necessary for the growth of the "higher type of man." Thus, underlying Nietzsche's worries about the anti-naturalness of MPS – just as underlying his worries about the threat MPS poses to life – is a concern for the effect of MPS on "higher men."

The normative content of MPS and the causal mechanism of harm

Nietzsche objects to the normative agenda of MPS because it is harmful to the highest men. In Nietzsche's various accounts of what the objectionable agenda of MPS consists, he identifies a variety of normative positions, of which the following is a representative list.[12] We may

12 See D: 108, 132, 174; GS: 116, 294, 328, 338, 345, 352, 377; Z I: 4, II: 8, III: 1, 9, IV: 13, 10; BGE: 197, 198, 201–2, 225, 257; GM Pref: 5, III: 11 ff.; TI II, V, IX: 35, 37–8, 48; A: 7, 43; EH III: D-2, IV: 4, 7–8; WP: 752.

characterize these simply as "pro" and "con" attitudes, and we may say that a morality is the object of Nietzsche's critique (i.e., it is an MPS) if it contains one or more of the following normative views:

Pro	Con
Happiness	Suffering
Altruism/selflessness	Self-love or self-interest
Equality	Inequality
Peacefulness, tranquillity	Danger
Social/communal utility	That which endangers such utility
Pity/compassion	Indifference to the suffering
Extirpation of the instincts	Enjoyment or satisfaction of the instincts
Well-being of the "soul"	Well-being of the body

Three preliminary observations about this picture of Nietzsche's critique are in order:

First: the various possible normative components of MPS should be construed as *ideal-typical*: they single out for emphasis and criticism certain important features of larger and more complex normative views. Nietzsche himself remarks that while there is "a vast realm of subtle feelings of value and difference of value which are alive, grow, beget, and perish," we still need "attempts to present vividly some of the more frequent and recurring forms of such living crystallizations – all to prepare a *typology* of morals" (BGE: 186). In criticizing MPS, we should see Nietzsche as criticizing some of the "frequent and recurring forms" that mark various ideal types of MPS.

Second: morality does not, of course, consist only of pro and con "attitudes": to the contrary, associated with each of these attitudes could be various prescriptive and proscriptive commands, suitable to the plethora of particular circumstances to which such attitudes might be relevant. Yet Nietzsche is typically concerned with the underlying (ideal-typical) attitude – or "spirit" of MPS – rather than the particular rules of conduct.

Third: let us say that that which morality has a "pro" attitude towards is the "Pro-Object," while that which morality has a "con" attitude towards is the "Con-Object." Keeping in mind that what seems to have *intrinsic* value[13] for Nietzsche is human excellence or human greatness, we can say that Nietzsche's criticisms consist of two parts.

[See facing page for n. 13.]

a   With respect to the Pro-Object, Nietzsche argues either: (i) that the Pro-Object has no *intrinsic* value (in the cases where MPS claims it does); or (ii) that it does not have any or not nearly as much *extrinsic* value as MPS treats it as having; and

b   with respect to the Con-Object, Nietzsche argues *only* that the Con-Objects are *extrinsically* valuable for the cultivation of human excellence – and that this is obscured by the "con" attitude endorsed by MPS.

Here, then, we come to the core of the proposed interpretation of Nietzsche's critique of MPS. What unifies Nietzsche's seemingly disparate critical remarks – about altruism, happiness, pity, equality, Kantian respect for persons, utilitarianism, etc. – is that he thinks a culture in which such norms prevail as morality will be a culture which eliminates the conditions for the realization of human excellence – the latter requiring, on Nietzsche's view, concern with the self, suffering, a certain stoic indifference, a sense of hierarchy and difference, and the like. Indeed, when we turn to the *details* of Nietzsche's criticisms of these norms we find that, in fact, this is precisely what he argues. Let us now consider three examples.

1   According to Nietzsche, the "spirit" of MPS is that happiness is good, and suffering bad. What, one wonders, could be harmful about this sort of seemingly innocuous valuation? An early remark of Nietzsche's suggests an answer:

> Are we not, with this tremendous objective of obliterating all the sharp edges of life, well on the way to turning mankind into *sand*? Sand! Small, soft, round, unending sand! Is that your ideal, you heralds of the sympathetic affections?

(D: 174)

---

[13]   What has *intrinsic* value has value in-itself; what has *extrinsic* value has value only as a means to something else (e.g., something with intrinsic value). (Something can, of course, have *intrinsic* value without having unconditional value, i.e., value *no matter what*. Nietzsche is skeptical quite generally about claims of unconditional value. I am indebted to Aaron Ridley on this point.)

In a later work, Nietzsche says – referring to hedonists and utilitarians – that, "Well-being as you understand it – that is no goal, that seems to us an *end*, a state that soon makes man ridiculous and contemptible" (BGE: 225). By the hedonistic doctrine of well-being, Nietzsche takes the utilitarians to have in mind "*English* happiness," namely, "comfort and fashion" (BGE: 228) – a construal which, if unfair to *some* utilitarians (like Mill), may do justice to our ordinary aspirations to happiness.[14] In a similar vein, Nietzsche has Zarathustra dismiss "wretched contentment" as an ideal (Z Pref: 3), while also revealing that it was precisely "the last men" – the "most despicable men" – who "invented happiness [*Glück*]" in the first place (Pref: 5).

Thus, the first part of Nietzsche's objection is this: happiness is not an intrinsically valuable end; men who aim for it – directly or through cultivating the dispositions that lead to it – would be "ridiculous and contemptible." Note, of course, that Nietzsche allows that he himself and the "free spirits" will be "cheerful" or "gay" (*fröhlich*) – they are, after all, the proponents of the "gay science." But the point is that such "happiness" is not *criterial* of being a *higher* person, and thus it is not something that the higher person – in contrast to the adherent of MPS – aims for.

But why is it that aiming for happiness would make a person so unworthy of admiration? Nietzsche's answer appears to be this: because *suffering* is positively necessary for the cultivation of human excellence – which is the only thing, on Nietzsche's view, that warrants admiration. Nietzsche writes, for example, that:

> The discipline of suffering, of *great* suffering – do you not know that only *this* discipline has created all enhancements of man so far? That tension of the soul in unhappiness which cultivates its strength, its shudders face to face with great ruin, its inventiveness and courage in enduring, persevering, interpreting, and exploiting suffering, and whatever has been granted to it of

14   Nietzsche thought, wrongly, that the "British utilitarians . . . walk clumsily and honorably in Bentham's footsteps" and that they have "[n]ot a new idea, no trace of a subtler version or twist of an old idea" (BGE: 228). Mill, of course, wanted to reject Benthamite hedonism (a more apt target for Nietzsche) as the criterion of utility.

profundity, secret, mask, spirit, cunning, greatness – was it not granted to it through suffering, through the discipline of great suffering?

(BGE: 225; cf. BGE: 270)

Now Nietzsche, of course, is not arguing here that – in contrast to the view of MPS – suffering is really *intrinsically* valuable (not even MPS claims that). The value of suffering, according to Nietzsche, is only extrinsic: suffering – "great" suffering – is a prerequisite of any great human achievement. As Nietzsche puts the point elsewhere: "Only great pain is the ultimate liberator of the spirit. . . . I doubt that such pain makes us 'better'; but I know that it makes us more profound" (GS Pref: 3). Nietzsche's attack, then, conforms to the model sketched above: (i) he rejects the view that happiness is *intrinsically* valuable; and (ii) he thinks that the negative attitude of MPS toward suffering obscures its important extrinsic value.

In regard to (ii), it is worth recalling a biographical fact about Nietzsche: namely, that perhaps no philosopher in history knew suffering more intimately than he did (see Chapter 2). For many years, he endured excruciating headaches and nausea, lasting for days at a time, and during which he was bedridden and often alone. Yet notwithstanding his appallingly bad health throughout the 1880s, he produced in less than a decade the bulk of his remarkable philosophical corpus. In fact, he believed that his suffering contributed essentially to his work; here is a typical – admittedly hyperbolic – remark from *Ecce Homo*:

In the midst of the torments that go with an uninterrupted three-day migraine, accompanied by laborious vomiting of phlegm, I possessed a dialectician's clarity *par excellence* and thought through with very cold blood matters for which under healthier circumstances I am not mountain-climber, not subtle, not *cold* enough.

(EH I: 1)

Even as early as 1880, he writes in a letter that, "My existence is a fearful burden. I would have thrown it off long ago if I had not been making the most instructive tests and experiments on mental and moral questions in precisely this condition of suffering and almost complete renunciation" (quoted in Hayman 1980: 219). Thus, on Nietzsche's picture of his own life, it was absolutely essential and invaluable that he suffered as he did: hence his willingness to will his life's eternal return, *including all its suffering*. We might add, too, that if Nietzsche had taken seriously MPS's evaluation of happiness and suffering, then he should not have been able to maintain his Dionysian attitude toward life; to the contrary, rather than will its repetition, he should have judged his life a failure because it involved so much hardship. Indeed, he explicitly stands that moral valuation on its head. "Never have I felt happier with myself," he declares, "than in the sickest and most painful periods of my life" (EH III: HAH-4).

Now it may perhaps be quite true – even uncontroversial – that great achievements (certainly great artistic achievements) seem to grow out of intense suffering – there is no shortage in the history of art and literature of such cases. But granting that, we come up against a serious objection to Nietzsche's position: namely, why should anyone think MPS is an obstacle to this phenomenon? This is what we may call the "Harm Puzzle," and the puzzle is this: why should one think the general moral prescription to alleviate suffering must stop the suffering of great artists, hence stop them from producing great art? One might think, in fact, that MPS could perfectly well allow an exception for those individuals whose own suffering is essential to the realization of central life projects. After all, a prescription to alleviate suffering does not arise in a vacuum: presumably it reflects a concern with promoting well-being, under some construal. But if some individuals – nascent Goethes, Nietzsches, and other geniuses – would be *better off* with a good dose of suffering, then why would MPS recommend otherwise? Why, then, should it be the case that MPS "harms" potentially "higher men"?

This challenge involves a serious misunderstanding of Nietzsche's critique: for Nietzsche's point, we might say, is not about *theory* but about *culture*. (Indeed, Nietzsche claims that Christian morality has "waged war unto death . . . against the *presupposition* of every elevation, every growth of culture" (A: 43), and that what "has been called morality" threatens to "deprive existence [*Dasein*] of its *great* character" (EH IV: 4).) Nietzsche's point is that when moral values come to predominate in a culture, their valuations will subtly affect the attitudes of all members of that culture. If moral values emphasize the badness of suffering and the goodness of happiness, that will surely have an effect on how individuals with the potential for great achievements will understand, evaluate and conduct their own lives. If, in fact, suffering is a precondition for these individuals to do anything great, and if they have internalized the norm that suffering must be alleviated, and that happiness is the ultimate goal, then we run the risk that, rather than – to put it crudely – suffer and create, they will instead waste their energies pursuing pleasure, lamenting their suffering and seeking to alleviate it. Moral values may not explicitly prohibit artists or other potentially "excellent" persons from ever suffering; but the risk is that a culture – like ours – which has internalized the norms *against* suffering and *for* pleasure will be a culture in which potential artists – and other doers of great things – will, *in fact*, squander themselves in self-pity and the seeking of pleasure.

Nietzsche's response to the Harm Puzzle, then, essentially involves an empirical claim about what the *real effect* of MPS will be. That is, we can understand Nietzsche to argue as follows: the normative component of MPS is harmful not because its specific prescriptions and proscriptions explicitly require potentially excellent persons to forgo that which allows them to flourish; that is, the claim is *not* that a conscientious application of the "theory" of MPS is incompatible with the flourishing of higher men. Rather, Nietzsche's claim is that MPS *in practice* simply does not make such fine distinctions: under a regime of moral values – and importantly because of MPS's commitment to the idea that one morality is appropriate for all – potentially higher men will come to adopt such values as applicable to themselves as well. Thus, the normative component of MPS is harmful because, in reality, it will have the effect of leading potentially excellent persons to value what is in fact not conducive to their flourishing and devalue what is, in fact, essential to it.[15]

[15]   Note the contrast with the traditional Christian view of suffering. While the traditional Christian, like Nietzsche, is no hedonist or Benthamite utilitarian, his attitude towards suffering is still fundamentally different. The Christian views suffering as an *objection* to life, the recompense for which is to be found in another, after-life. The Nietzschean, by contrast, does not view

We have seen, then, a paradigmatic example of Nietzsche's critique of MPS. His central objection to MPS is that it thwarts the development of human excellence. And his argument for this, in each case, turns on identifying distinctive valuations of MPS, and showing how – as in the case of norms favoring happiness and devaluing suffering – they undermine the development of individuals who would manifest human excellence. Let us conclude this section by sketching some comparable arguments with respects to two other important aspects of the normative component of MPS.

2   That MPS takes a positive attitude toward altruism and the "unegoistic" generally is central in many places to Nietzsche's attack on MPS. In the *Genealogy*, Nietzsche suggests that the whole question of "the *value* of morality" is importantly a question about "the value of the 'unegoistic'" (Pref: 5). In a later work, he even goes so far as to claim that, "The loss of the center of gravity, resistance to the natural instincts – in one word, 'selflessness' – that is what was hitherto called 'morality'" (EH III: D-2). His view on the value of this particular Pro-Object of MPS was also unequivocal; as he puts it in an early work: "'Selflessness' has no value either in heaven or on earth. All great problems demand *great love*" (GS: 345). In a similar vein, he writes that, "An 'altruistic' morality – a morality in which self-interest wilts away – remains a bad sign under all circumstances. ... The best is lacking when self-interest begins to be lacking" (TI IX: 35). Thus, Nietzsche claims that altruism and selflessness are extrinsically *disvaluable* for the pursuit of "great problems" and for the "best" more generally. Moreover, Nietzsche claims that the Con-Object of MPS – self-love or self-interest – is extrinsically valuable for these same ends: as he puts it most simply in *Ecce Homo*, "*severe* self-love" is among the things "most profoundly necessary for growth" (IV: 7).

It should be emphasized that Nietzsche's defense of the value of self-love against altruism is *not* a defense of mere indulgence or greed: it is, after all, "severe" self-love that has extrinsic value; and elsewhere Nietzsche attacks "the selfishness of the sick" (Z I: 22;

suffering as an *objection* to life, and thus does not view it as requiring compensation in any form.

contrast Z III: 10) and derides the "self-interested çattle and mob" (WP: 752) – indicating that there are types of "self-interest" (e.g., "self-seeking") that must lack extrinsic value.[16] The distinction is, roughly, between self-interest which manifests itself in gratification of immediate desires and self-interest (or self-love) which has as its aim the cultivation or flourishing of the self, quite apart from desire-gratification. So, for example, Nietzsche praises the demanding, self-centered obsessiveness the artist requires to do his creative work; Nietzsche writes, for example, that:

> Every artist knows how far from any feeling of letting himself go his "most natural" state is – the free ordering, disposing, giving form in the moment of "inspiration" – and how strictly and subtly he obeys thousandfold laws precisely then.

> (BGE: 188)

Now insofar as "virtue, art, music, dance, reason, spirituality" – all things "for whose sake it is worthwhile to live on earth" (BGE: 188) – require that their creators concentrate on them to the exclusion of all other concerns and interests (including those of other persons), then it is easy to see why severe self-love – the sort of single-minded focus characteristic of the disciplined artist at work – may possess considerable extrinsic value in Nietzsche's view.

3 MPS endorses equality and condemns inequality: more exactly, it endorses equality of regard and treatment (if not equality of outcomes and conditions). Nietzsche attacks the modern doctrine of equality in many places (GS: 377; Z IV: 13; TI IX: 48; A: 43; WP: 752), but the clearest statement of his criticism comes in Section 257 of *Beyond Good and Evil*:

---

[16] Kaufmann's translation actually makes the distinctions much easier to draw; in the original, Nietzsche, in fact, uses the *same* word – *Selbstsucht* – in two of the passages (EH IV: 7; Z I: 22). Literally, Nietzsche recommends "severe selfishness" while also attacking the "selfishness of the sick." By contrast, the WP passage speaks of *eigennützig* cattle and mob – what Kaufmann renders as "self-seeking" (and I have translated as "self-interested"). Kaufmann's different renderings are, however, largely warranted by the context, and do serve to highlight the point made in the text.

> Every enhancement of the type "man" has so far been the work
> of an aristocratic society . . . that believes in the long ladder of
> an order of rank and differences in value between man and man.
> . . . Without that *pathos of distance* which grows out of the
> ingrained difference between strata – when the ruling caste con-
> stantly looks afar and looks down upon subjects and instruments
> . . . – that other, more mysterious pathos could not have grown
> up either – the craving for an ever new widening of distances
> within the soul itself, the development of ever higher, rarer . . .
> more comprehensive states – in brief, simply the enhancement of
> the type "man," the continual "self-overcoming of man."

Here, then, Nietzsche defends the extrinsic value of inequality (the
Con-Object for MPS) for the "enhancement of the type 'man'" by
arguing that there is some sense in which the social practice of unequal
regard – of looking down on those of lower social rank – conditions
people, similarly, to be able to look down upon themselves. Since,
however, when one looks down on oneself one is not looking down
on something *other*, Nietzsche's thought is that this practice of unequal
"self-regard" will drive the individual to "overcome" his contemptible
current condition, to make of himself something higher and better. The
alternative attitude – which Nietzsche regards as "democratic" and
which embraces "equal regard" – has the opposite result: as Nietzsche
says: "Democracy represents the disbelief in great human beings . . .:
'Everyone is equal to everyone else.' 'At bottom we are one and all
self-seeking cattle and mob'" (WP: 752).

Metaethics: realism about value?

Nietzsche wants to effect a revaluation of values, that is, a new assessment of the value of our "moral" values. He holds that MPS is not
conducive to the flourishing of human excellence, and it is by reference to *this* fact that he proposes to assess the value of MPS. This
kind of critical project naturally invites the question: what exactly is
the *value* of the flourishing of human excellence, and why does it
trump the values served by MPS (e.g., the preservation of the herd)?
These kinds of questions are, broadly speaking, metaethical in nature:

we are asking about the status – metaphysical, epistemological – of the values used to undertake the "revaluation" ("the assessing values"). Are the assessing valuations veridical, while those of MPS are not? Are the assessing valuations justified (in some sense to be specified) while MPS valuations are not?

What animates these kinds of questions is precisely a worry about Nietzsche's critical project that might be summed up simply as follows: in offering a revaluation of morality is Nietzsche doing anything more than giving his idiosyncratic opinion from his idiosyncratic evaluative perspective? Is there, in short, anything about Nietzsche's evaluation of morality that ought to command *our* attention and assent? While a foray into Nietzsche's metaethical views risks taking us far afield of the *Genealogy*, the metaethical questions must have already occurred to the reader, and so something must be said about them here.

Roughly speaking, Nietzsche must be either a *realist* or an *anti-realist* about value. Realists about value think there are *objective* facts about value: there is an "objective" fact about what is good and bad, valuable and disvaluable, and thus there is a fact of the matter about, e.g., whether MPS lacks value because it is harmful to higher men.[17] Anti-realists deny that there are such "objective" facts about value. *Objectivity* is a crucial variable in this debate. The intuitive idea behind it is simple enough: facts are objective just in case their character and

---

[17] Contemporary Anglo-American philosophy, especially as influenced by Michael Dummett, characterizes the realism/anti-realism debate in *semantic* terms, reflecting the "linguistic turn" of this century's philosophy, i.e., the tendency towards framing classic metaphysical or ontological questions in semantic terms. Thus, the realist about some class of entities holds not simply that these entities have some suitably objective existence in the real world, but that the discourse in which we talk about such entities is genuinely and successfully referential, and that the truth-conditions for this discourse are, in principle, evidence-transcendent.

Most philosophers prior to the twentieth century, of course, did not have elaborate views about semantics. This is hardly an inexcusable failing. For surely it is the metaphysical questions about value that have animated the debate about the objectivity of ethics from the Sophists to the present. Thus, the discussion of "realism" and "anti-realism" in the text will proceed in indifference to the *semantic* issues at stake. Nothing is lost, however, in such an approach given Nietzsche's silence on semantics.

existence is *independent* of the states of mind of persons in some appropriate sense. *Epistemic* independence is most often what is at issue: a fact is objective if its character and existence does not depend on what people believe or would have reason to believe about it.

Many commentators have thought Nietzsche was a realist about value. Some writers think that Nietzsche's doctrine of will to power provides some objective criterion of value.[18] Others (like Foot 1973) make a more modest claim: that Nietzsche's evaluative perspective resonates with concerns we all share, and thus enjoys a kind of inter-subjective appeal. There are reasons to be skeptical about both kinds of accounts. We may say why, briefly, here.[19]

1 *Value realism and will to power* Schacht (1983) is representative of those commentators who see Nietzsche as "grounding" his evaluative perspective in his doctrine of the will to power. According to Schacht, Nietzsche "is proposing to evaluate [moral values] by reference to a standard of valuation independent of them, from a perspective which transcends them. ... [T]his perspective is a privileged one, which an understanding of the fundamental character of life and the world [as will to power] serves to define and establish" (1983: 348–9). Schacht defends this reading by appeal to *Nachlass* passages like "assuming that life itself is the will to power" then "there is nothing to life that has value, except the degree of power" (WP: 55) (Schacht 1983: 349).

But what exactly is the *argument* here? When pressed, commentators are never able to say. Schacht, for example, writes:

> Human life, for Nietzsche, is ultimately a part of a kind of vast game ... [which] is, so to speak, the only game in town. ... The nature of the game, he holds, establishes a standard for the evaluation of everything falling within its compass. The availability of this standard places evaluation on footing that is as firm as that on which the comprehension of life and the world stands.
>
> (1983: 398)

[18] See, e.g., Morgan 1941: 118 ff.; Kaufmann 1974: 199–200; Wilcox 1974: 194–9; Schacht 1983: 348 ff.; Hunt 1991, Chapter 7.

[19] The interested reader should consult Leiter (2000) for a detailed critique.

Talk of "the only game in town" is far too metaphorical, however, to bear the philosophical weight demanded. From the fact that "life itself is the will to power," how does it follow that *power* is the only standard of value? From the fact, for example, that all life obeys the laws of fundamental physics, nothing follows about the appropriate standard of value. What Schacht and others seem to have in mind is something like John Stuart Mill's argument for utilitarianism, which proceeds from the premise that since happiness is the only thing people desire or aim for, it follows that happiness is the only thing that possesses intrinsic value. This argument, though, is famously unsuccessful: from the fact that only happiness *is* desired, nothing at all follows about what *ought* to be desired. Attempts to construe Nietzsche's argument in an analogous way encounter similar problems (cf. Leiter 2000).

There is a further problem. The view at issue presupposes an unusually strong doctrine of the will to power: a doctrine, to the effect, that *all* life (actions, events) reflects the will to power. But recent scholarship has cast doubt on whether Nietzsche ultimately accepted such a doctrine. The single most famous passage on will to power in the Nietzschean corpus, for example, is the concluding section (1067) of *The Will to Power*, where he affirms that, "*This world is the will to power – and nothing besides*! And you yourselves are also this will to power – and nothing besides!" Although a favorite of commentators for many years, the passage has now been conclusively discredited by the leading scholar of the *Nachlass*, the late Mazzino Montinari. Montinari has shown that Nietzsche had, in fact, discarded the passage by the spring of 1887 (1982: 103–4)! It was, as Montinari notes, made part of the Köselitz-Forster compilation of *The Will to Power* (the basis for the English-language edition by Kaufmann and Hollingdale) notwithstanding "Nietzsche's literary intentions" (1982: 104).

More recently, Maudemarie Clark has argued that Nietzsche could not have accepted the very strongest form of the doctrine of the will to power – namely, that all *force*, animate and inanimate, is will to power – given the putative argument he gives for it. Clark points out that the *only argument* for this doctrine of the will to power in Nietzsche's published works – in Section 36 of *Beyond Good and Evil* – is cast in the conditional form: if we accept certain initial hypotheses, then, Nietzsche thinks, the strong doctrine of the will to power follows. But one of the antecedents of this conditional is the "causality of the will," and Clark argues that Nietzsche clearly *rejects* such causality elsewhere in his work (e.g., GS: 127; TI II: 5; TI VI: 3). Therefore, this section cannot constitute an argument for the strongest doctrine of the will to power that Nietzsche, himself, would actually accept! Rather than embracing the strongest form of the doctrine, Clark argues that Nietzsche is, somewhat ironically, illustrating the very flaw of philosophers he warns against in the surrounding passages: namely, their tendency to propound theories of the essence of reality that are just projections of their own evaluative commitments (Clark 1990: 212–27). Thus, Nietzsche says of the Stoic talk of living "according to nature" that "while you pretend rapturously to read the canon of your law in nature, you want something opposite. . . . Your pride wants to impose your morality, your ideal, on nature" (BGE: 9). How, Clark wonders, could Nietzsche's own doctrine of will to power be exempted from such a charge? (Note, too, that Montinari claims that the one surviving relic of 1067 of *The Will to Power* in the published works is precisely the ironic Section 36 of *Beyond Good and Evil* (1982: 104).)

Of course, Clark could be right about the strongest form of the doctrine (encompassing animate *and* inanimate nature), but wrong about the only form at issue here: namely, that all *organic* phenomena are will to power. Indeed, one might think it is precisely this latter view that Nietzsche endorses in the Second Essay of the *Genealogy* when he lambasts the

> prevailing instinct and fashion which would much rather come to terms with absolute randomness, and even the mechanistic senselessness of all events, than the theory that a *power-will* is acted out in all that happens. The democratic idiosyncrasy of being against everything that dominates and wants to dominate . . . has already become master of the whole of physiology and biology. . . . But this is to misunderstand the essence of life, its *will to power*.

(GM II: 12)

Of course, this passage seems equally open to the charge Nietzsche levelled against the Stoics: namely, of wanting to "impose your morality, your ideal, on nature" (BGE: 9). After all, even Nietzsche admits that "what formerly happened with the Stoics still happens today, too, as soon as any philosophy begins to believe in itself. It always creates the world in its own image" (BGE: 9). The passage at issue (GM II: 12) seems especially vulnerable to these charges, for the affirmation about "the essence of life" being will to power follows upon an *evaluative* proposition Nietzsche clearly sympathizes with: "man's sacrifice *en bloc* to the prosperity of one single *stronger* species of man – that *would* be progress" (GM II: 12). As a rhetorical matter, however, it is far easier to win support for that proposition by casting it as following from a general "truth" *about nature*, namely that all of nature involves precisely such sacrifices and overcomings of others for the sake of something more powerful (GM II: 12). But that the real concern is evaluative, and not with theories of nature, should be obvious from the evaluative proposition he wants to establish and from his description of the opposition: the proponents of mechanism, a "democratic idiosyncrasy."

Those less inclined to give weight to these kinds of rhetorical subtleties in Nietzsche's style will, of course, insist on taking the strong claims about will to power at face value. Yet such a reading confronts the difficulty that Nietzsche *repeatedly* makes claims inconsistent with the thesis that "the essence of life" is will to power. So, for example, he writes:

> Life itself is to my mind the instinct for growth, for durability, for an accumulation of forces, for *power*: where the will to power is lacking there is decline. It is my contention that all the supreme values of mankind *lack* this will.

> (A: 6)

But if all actions manifested this *will*, then this *will* could never be found lacking. Yet Nietzsche thinks it can be lacking, which means he must countenance the possibility that not all organic phenomena are will to power. This passage is not atypical. Later in the same work, he returns to the same theme concerning "[w]herever the will to power declines in any form" (A: 17). In the immediately preceding work he claims that the "effects" of liberal institutions are "known well enough: they undermine the will to power" (TI IX: 38). And in the immediately subsequent work (his last), Nietzsche refers to "the terrible *aspects* of reality (in affects, in desires, in the will to power)" (EH IV: 4),[20] which certainly sounds as if will to power is simply one among various characteristics of life – *alongside* affects and desires, rather than the essential core of them all.

Indeed, if, as the defenders of the strong doctrine of will to power believe, "his fundamental principle is the '*will to power*'" (Jaspers 1965: 287), then it is hard to understand why he says almost nothing about will to power – and nothing at all to suggest it is his "fundamental principle" – in the two major self-reflective moments in the Nietzschean corpus: his last major work, *Ecce Homo*, where he reviews and assesses his life and writings, including specifically all his prior books (EH III); and the series of new prefaces he wrote for *The Birth of Tragedy*, *Human, All-too-Human*, *Daybreak*, and *The Gay Science* in 1886, in which he revisits his major themes. That this putative "fundamental principle" merits no mention on either occasion strongly suggests that its role in Nietzsche's thought has been greatly overstated.

But what, then, does Nietzsche believe about will to power? As Kaufmann and Clark, among others, have noted, Nietzsche's doctrine of will to power in its origin and most of its later development is *psychological* in character: the will to power is posited as the best psychological explanation for a wide variety of human behaviors (Kaufmann 1974, Ch. 6; Clark 1990: 209–12). But as the preceding considerations make clear, Nietzsche could not have believed that will to power was the fundamental explanation for *all* human behavior. To the extent he sometimes seems to embrace this stronger claim,[21] we must simply take Nietzsche to have overstated his case for the reasons already given (something his penchant for hyperbolic rhetoric and polemics often leads him to do).

There is a larger worry for the argument that will to power provides an objective criterion of value lurking here as well. Nietzsche only makes the remarks that seem to suggest that power is an objective

[20] Nietzsche speaks here of the *Furchtbarkeiten* of reality, for which there is no ordinary English equivalent (literally, it would be "terriblenesses"); Kaufmann's rendering – "terrible aspects" – seems fair.

[21] See, e.g., Z II: 12; GS: 349; BGE: 259; GM II: 12.

criterion in passages from the *Nachlass*, work that Nietzsche never published during his lifetime.[22] Thus, even if one thought that Nietzsche really held the strong descriptive doctrine of the will to power – the doctrine that all animate force (perhaps *all* force) is will to power – in his published works, it is still the case that he only uses this doctrine to argue for the normative conclusion in *Nachlass* material.

In recent years, important doubts have been raised about the canonical status of this *Nachlass* material.[23] It appears that Nietzsche wanted this material destroyed, and it was only the intervention of others, independent of Nietzsche, that resulted in the material being saved for posterity. These sorts of considerations suggest that a view ought not to be attributed to Nietzsche *solely* on the basis of its articulation in these notebooks. But this is precisely what the defender of

---

[22] There are also some remarks in books he published (or intended to publish) that might be misconstrued as realism about value based on the doctrine of will to power. For example, Nietzsche writes: "What is good? Everything that heightens the feeling of power in man, the will to power, power itself" (A: 2). But in the context, it is clear that this is not a proposal for a definition (reforming or otherwise) of "good" but rather simply an endorsement: power is what is good, while, as he says in the next sentence, "[e]verything that is born of weakness" is "bad" (A: 2).

Similarly, John Wilcox points to the "Note" at the end of GM I – where Nietzsche calls for "physiologists and doctors" to get involved in the study "of the *value* of existing valuations" – as evidence that Nietzsche recognized the need for scientific help in his realist construal of value as power (1974: 200–1). Yet this passage concludes, "*All* sciences must, from now on, prepare the way for the future work of the philosopher: this work being understood to mean that the philosopher has to solve the *problem of values* and that he has to decide on the *hierarchy of values.* Now as Wilcox himself earlier notes (1974: 41), the *philosophers* are precisely the ones who "*create values,*" who "*are commanders and legislators*" (BGE: 211). Thus, what Nietzsche must be calling for is for scientific illumination of the effect of particular values on different types of persons (do they contribute, as Nietzsche puts it in the Note, to "the preservation of the greatest number" or to "producing a stronger type"), as an aid to the philosopher's creative work. But the values themselves are creations; the "physiologists and doctors" simply help the philosopher understand the effects of different sorts of values.

[23] See Montinari 1982: 92–104; Hollingdale 1985: 166–72, 182–6; Magnus 1988: 222–32, 234 n. 18.

the realist reading of Nietzsche under consideration here must do. Instead of pursuing this textually suspect course, we might, in the spirit of interpretive charity, simply surmise that Nietzsche recognized the untenability of the kind of argument Schacht finds in Nietzsche and that this is why the explicit textual support for this realist view of Nietzsche is found only in material Nietzsche never published.

2 *Value realism and intersubjectivity*   Perhaps value is objective in the more modest sense of *not* being merely subjective, i.e., not varying with each individual or each community. Foot (1973) appears to endorse such a reading of Nietzsche's metaethics. According to Foot, in the revaluation of values, Nietzsche is doing something more than simply expressing his idiosyncratic view, a view that admits of no interpersonal justification. While agreeing that Nietzsche's intention is, in part, "to present us with a clash of interests – the good of the strong against that of the weak," Foot adds that "this is not all he wants to suggest" (1973: 162). Noting that Nietzsche "seems to want to say that anyone who is strong, independent, and so on – anyone who fits his description of the higher type of man – is one who *has value* in himself" (1973: 163), Foot goes on to explicate this notion of "value" as follows:

> [I]t does make sense to say that *we value* strong and exceptional individuals. . . . We do find patterns of reaction to exceptional men that would allow us to see here a valuing rather similar to valuing on aesthetic grounds. . . . I am thinking of the interest and admiration which is the common attitude to remarkable men of exceptional independence of mind and strength of will. . . . [Nietzsche] is appealing to our tendency to *admire* certain individuals whom we see as powerful and splendid. . . . [There is] a similarity between the way we attribute *value* (aesthetic value) to art objects and the *value* that Nietzsche attributes to a certain kind of man, both resting on a set of common reactions.
>
> (1973: 163)

Nietzsche, on this picture, does not claim that his evaluative perspective is true; he simply claims that it enjoys a certain sort of interpersonal appeal, owing to our "common attitude to remarkable men,"

"our tendency to *admire* certain individuals," to find them aestheti-
cally appealing. There may be no fact-of-the-matter as to whether
higher men are or are not *really* valuable, but Nietzsche's evaluative
standpoint is privileged by virtue of its appeal to all of us. We're all
interested, it seems, in the flourishing of higher men.

What is right about this picture is that Nietzsche sometimes
(at least in the *Nachlass*) *seems* to conceive of the appeal of higher
men in "aesthetic" terms. For example, Nietzsche says that whether to
prefer the cultivation of higher or lower men is "at bottom a question
of taste and aesthetics" (WP: 353), and he suggests that evaluating
a man in terms of "how much he costs, or what harm he does" is as
inappropriate as "apprais[ing] a work of art according to the effects it
produces" (WP: 878). Yet, as an interpretive claim about Nietzsche,
Foot's account is ultimately untenable. For Nietzsche could not hold
that the flourishing of "higher men" will appeal to "*our* tendency" to
admire such men or to any sort of "common" attitude: the aesthetic
appeal of flourishing higher men, in short, is not for all.

This point follows from Nietzsche's Callicleanism, which we
first introduced in Chapter 2. Recall that Nietzsche embraces the
Calliclean doctrine that the inferior employ MPS to make "slaves of
those who are naturally better" (*Gorgias*, 491e–492a), that "the weaker
folk, the majority ... frame the laws [and, we might add, the morals]
for their own advantage" in order to "frighten [the strong] by saying
that to overreach others is shameful and evil" (*Gorgias*, 483b–d). In
short, the Calliclean view is that morality is simply the prudence of
the weak who, unable to do what the strong can do, opt instead to put
the actions of the strong under the ban of morality.

What obstacle, then, does Nietzsche's Callicleanism present for
Foot's reading? Recall that Foot wanted to resist the view that in his
revaluation Nietzsche simply "present[s] us with a clash of interests
– the good of the strong against that of the weak" (1973: 162); instead,
Foot suggests that Nietzsche is appealing to a "common" tendency to
admire higher men, men who would otherwise be thwarted by the
reign of moral values.

But Nietzsche's Callicleanism suggests something quite different: namely, that it is part of the very appeal of MPS that it *does* thwart
the flourishing of higher men. If that is right, then it would simply be

145

bizarre for Nietzsche to think that the *flourishing* of "higher men" would appeal to everyone. It is precisely because it doesn't that MPS arises in the first place, as a means for the low and base to thwart the flourishing of the high. This is not to deny that higher men may still be admirable in the eyes of the base and low (hence their envy); it *is* to deny, however, that Nietzsche's evaluative perspective – that it is an *objection* to MPS that it thwarts the high – could enjoy a privilege in virtue of this shared admiration. On the Calliclean picture, there is a fundamental hostility between the high and low, the strong and the weak, one which will not be bridged by inviting the low to admire the high, or the weak, the strong. "The well-being of the majority and the well-being of the few are opposite viewpoints of value," Nietzsche says in the "Note" at the end of the first essay of the *Genealogy*. And in Nietzsche's revaluation, we might add, "never the twain shall meet."[24]

Metaethics: anti-realism about value

If Nietzsche is not a *realist* about value – in either Foot's or Schacht's sense – then he must be an anti-realist: he must ultimately deny that there is any objective vindication for his evaluative position. (This, in fact, is the most familiar reading *outside* the secondary literature on Nietzsche; one finds this view of Nietzsche's metaethics, for example, in the sociologist Max Weber and the moral philosopher Alasdair MacIntyre, among many others.) We must be clear, however, about the kinds of judgments to which this metaethical position applies. For recall that Nietzsche appears to hold that, e.g., "herd" morality is *good for* the herd, but that it is *bad for* higher men. He says, for example,

---

[24] This is not to deny, however, that, as Nietzsche puts it, "in all the higher and more mixed cultures there also appear attempts at mediation between these two moralities [master and slave moralities], and yet more often the inter-penetration and mutual misunderstanding of both, and at times they occur directly alongside each other – even in the same human being, within a *single* soul" (BGE: 260). That there are (clearly failed) *attempts* [*Versuche*] at mediation or that both viewpoints can exist in one soul does not, of course, show that there is an evaluative standpoint from which one could successfully mediate and reconcile the normative claims of the opposing moralities.

that, "The ideas of the herd *should* rule in the herd – but not reach out beyond it" (WP: 287; emphasis added); and elsewhere he describes slave morality as simply "the prudence of the lowest order" (GM I: 13). When it comes to value judgments pertaining to welfare or prudential goodness – what is good or bad for particular sorts of persons – Nietzsche seems to believe there is an objective fact of the matter (that's his "relationalism," discussed earlier).[25] Nietzsche cannot be an anti-realist about *these* judgments of value. Rather, his anti-realism applies to the "revaluative" judgment that *follows upon* these judgments of welfare: that is, the judgment that *because* herd morality is *good for* the herd but *bad for* higher men, herd morality (or the universal reign of herd morality) is bad or disvaluable.

Nietzsche certainly says much that sounds like he is denying the objectivity of moral value.[26] Zarathustra tells us that, "Verily, men gave themselves all their good and evil [*Gutes und Böses*]" (Z I: 15) and that "good and evil that are not transitory do not exist" (Z II: 12). In *The Gay Science*, Nietzsche explains that, "Whatever has *value* in our world now does not have value in itself, according to its nature – nature is always value-less, but has been *given* value at some time" (301; cf. D: 3). Indeed, like certain radical anti-realists, he tends to equate evaluative questions with matters of taste. "What is now decisive against Christianity is our taste [*Geschmack*], no longer our reasons" (GS: 132), he writes, noting later in the same work that what counts as "justice . . . is by all means a matter of taste, nothing more" (GS: 184).[27]

---

[25] See pp. 106–8.
[26] One frequently cited, but actually inapposite passage, is TI VII: 1: "*there are altogether no moral facts*" (e.g., Danto 1965: 133; Hunt 1991: 108). If not taken out of context, however, it is clear that Nietzsche is not denying the objectivity of value in this passage. Rather, he is denying the descriptive presuppositions about agency that are necessary for moral judgment to be intelligible.
[27] Zarathustra also remarks that "all of life is a dispute [*Streit*] over taste and tasting. Taste – that is at the same time weight and scales and weigher; and woe unto all the living that would live without disputes over weight and scales and weighing!" (Z II: 13). This does not amount to a concession that one can "dispute" taste on the basis of objective reasons. Here the German is more revealing; the authoritative *dtv – Wortebuch der deutschen Sprache* defines

Nietzsche's central argument for anti-realism about value is *explanatory*: moral facts don't figure in the "best explanation" of experience, and so are not real constituents of the objective world. Moral values, in short, can be "explained away." Such a conclusion follows from Nietzsche's naturalism.[28] As we have seen, Nietzsche thinks a person's moral beliefs can be explained in naturalistic terms, i.e., in terms of type-facts about that person. Thus, to explain a person's moral judgments, one needn't appeal to the existence of objective moral facts: psycho-physical facts about the person suffice. Thus, since non-evaluative type-facts are the primary explanatory facts, and since explanatory power is the mark of objective facts, it appears that there cannot be any value facts.

Now Nietzsche never says outright, "Since we can explain why agents make the value judgments they do in terms of type-facts about agents – i.e., since we can explain values away – we shouldn't be realists about value," but how else are we to construe his relentless pursuit of the psycho-physiological roots of our value judgments? Given that Nietzsche makes claims that sound like anti-realism about value, it is natural to read Nietzsche's naturalistic explanations of value judgments as buttressing the core anti-realist thought, which Nietzsche accepts, namely that there are no objective facts about value.

Nietzsche even makes some more explicit remarks that do invite precisely this reading. For example, in his first mature work, *Daybreak*, of 1880, Nietzsche repeatedly attacks the moral – in contrast to the

---

Streit as follows: "*Zustand der Uneinigkeit, bei dem jeder Beteiligte versucht, seinen Willen durchzusetzen*" (a state of disagreement, in which each party tries to enforce his will). It is this idea of trying to "enforce" one's will that is closer to the sort of "dispute" in which Nietzsche thinks competing tastes – e.g., his versus the Christian's – might really engage. Indeed, the startling "Decree Against Christianity" at the end of *The Antichrist* gives a clear indication of the kind of means for enforcing one's will that Nietzsche has in mind. (The "Decree" was, in fact, excised by Nietzsche's early editors: see KSG, vol. 6: 254.) Thus, for example, he declares that "Against the priest one doesn't use reasons, but prison" and that all churches "should be flattened to the ground and be regarded as *the most wicked* places of the earth, to the terror of all posterity. Poisonous snakes should be bred there."

28   For a detailed account of the explanatory argument for moral anti-realism, see Leiter (2001a).

naturalistic – interpretation of phenomena as an error. This theme is voiced near the very beginning of the work:

> When man gave all things a sex he thought, not that he was playing, but that he had gained a profound insight: – it was only very late that he confessed to himself what an enormous error this was, and perhaps even now he has not confessed it completely. – In the same way man has ascribed to all that exists a connection with morality and laid an *ethical significance* on the world's back. One day this will have as much value, and no more, as the belief in the masculinity or femininity of the sun has today.
>
> (D: 3; cf. p. 100)

The suggestion here is that we are guilty of a projective error: just as, previously, we projected gender onto the sun, we now project "ethical significance" onto the natural world. But these natural things – the sun, the world – are not themselves gendered or ethically significant (cf. HAH: 4). As Nietzsche puts it in a later work: "There are no moral phenomena at all, but only a moral interpretation of phenomena" (BGE: 108). Nietzsche's naturalism raises a question precisely about the adequacy of this moral interpretation: he shows it to be a *mis*-interpretation. The proper, naturalistic interpretation, by contrast, is one in which the moral categories figure only as an explanandum. As Nietzsche puts it, moral judgments and evaluations are "images" and "fantasies," the mere effects of type-facts about agents (D: 119).

If we assume that Nietzsche is an anti-realist about non-prudential value, then another feature of his writing – one typically ignored by commentators – also makes considerably more sense: namely, that he is quite concerned to circumscribe his audience. As he puts it most simply at the beginning of *The Antichrist*: "This book belongs to the very few"; in particular Nietzsche's ideal reader is marked by "Reverence for oneself" (A Pref) – one of the defining traits, he tells us elsewhere, of the "noble" person (BGE: 287). Similarly, in his autobiography Nietzsche says regarding "the air of my writings" that "[o]ne must be made for it" (EH Pref: 3). He claims, too, that, "Ultimately, nobody can get more out of things, including books, than he already knows" (EH III: 1; cf. BGE: 87). And in a related vein, he says that, "Nobody is free to have ears for Zarathustra" (EH Pref: 4), presumably because "Zarathustra experiences himself as the *supreme type of all beings*" (EH III: Z-6). Elsewhere he remarks that, "Today's ears resist . . . our truths" (BGE: 202). And he recognizes that, "Our highest insights must – and should – sound like follies and sometimes like crimes when they are heard without permission by those who are not predisposed and predestined for them" (BGE: 30). In another work, finally, he gives perhaps his fullest exposition of this theme:

> It is not by any means necessarily an objection to a book when anyone finds it impossible to understand: perhaps that was part of the author's intention – he did not want to be understood by just "anybody." All the nobler spirits and tastes select their audience when they wish to communicate; and choosing that, one at the same time erects barriers against "the others." All the more subtle laws of any style have their origin at this point: they at the same time keep away, create a distance, forbid "entrance," understanding, as said above – while they open the ears of those whose ears are related to ours.

> (GS: 381)

Now if we assume that Nietzsche, in the revaluation, is simply giving expression to the evaluative taste of a certain type of person – a "higher" or "noble" person; and if we assume further, consistent with the anti-realism, that there are no objective facts about non-prudential value; then it would, indeed, make sense for Nietzsche to want to circumscribe his audience to those who share Nietzsche's evaluative taste, those for whom no justification would be required: those who are simply "made for it," "whose ears are related to ours," who are "predisposed and predestined" for Nietzsche's insights.

Two aspects of Nietzsche's work may, however, seem to be in tension with value anti-realism: first, his reliance on the distinction between "higher" and "lower" types of human beings; and second, the force and seriousness with which he presents his evaluative judgments.

As we have seen, Nietzsche speaks constantly of higher and lower types of people; indeed, such a distinction is central in his critique of MPS. But doesn't Nietzsche seem to think there are objective facts about who is "high" and who is "low"? And if he does, is such a view compatible with anti-realism?

One possible response might run as follows. Yes, one might concede, there are objective facts about "high" and "low": Goethe *really* is a higher type, and the herd animal *really* is a lower type. But there is still no objective fact about whether MPS is non-prudentially *disvaluable* just because it has the effect of thwarting the flourishing of objectively higher types. Realism about "high" and "low" does not entail realism about non-prudential value.

Such a response confronts at least two difficulties. First, it seems that the judgment that "X is a higher person" includes a significant evaluative component: "Goethe is a *higher* type" is not evaluatively neutral in the manner of "Goethe is a *taller* than average type." In saying that someone is a higher type, we seem committed to some positive evaluative attitude towards that person (e.g., that it is good to have persons like that around). If there is an objective fact that "X is a higher type," and it is a fact that MPS thwarts the flourishing of higher types, then it would seem that at least some objective weight must accrue to the Nietzschean position that MPS is disvaluable because of this effect it has.

Here is a second difficulty. If it is an objective fact that Goethe is a higher type and, say, Hitler is a herd animal, then the following counterfactual would seem to be true:

(C) If Hitler had been like Goethe, he would have been better off.

He would have been better off because he would have been a higher type, instead of a lower type – and it is an objective fact that the high are *really* high, and the low are *really* low. But this seemingly objective judgment – that Hitler would have been *better off* had he been more like Goethe – is a non-prudential value judgment; it is not a judgment about what is good for Hitler under the circumstances, but rather a judgment about what would make Hitler better off, but for his circumstances. In general, it seems that conceding the objectivity of "high" and "low" permits one to make objective non-prudential value judgments like: the good of the higher type is superior to the good of the lower type.

For these reasons, it seems important that Nietzsche's judgments of "high" and "low" do not turn out to be objective. It may be an objective fact that MPS thwarts the flourishing of those Nietzsche views as higher types; but it is not an objective fact that they are *really* higher. The suggestion, then, is that Nietzsche be construed as an anti-realist about "high" and "low," just as he is about all non-prudential value concepts.

In fact, there are good grounds for thinking this is Nietzsche's view. For example, in *Thus Spoke Zarathustra*, Nietzsche writes that, "Good and evil, and rich and poor, and high and low [*Hoch und Gering*], and all the names of values – arms shall they be and clattering signs that life must overcome itself again and again" (Z II: 7). Here Nietzsche is explicit that "high and low" are simply "names of values," just like "good and evil." But since, as we have just seen, Nietzsche is an anti-realist about these latter evaluative concepts, it seems he should be an anti-realist about the former.

Further support for this reading comes from consideration of the actual contexts in which he marks traits as "high" and "low." Consider, for example, the exposition in the *Genealogy* (I: 14) of the sense in which slave morality is the "prudence of the lowest order" (GM I: 13). According to Nietzsche, slave morality takes certain typical characteristics of the "lowest order" and redescribes them in morally praiseworthy lights. So, for example, their impotence becomes "goodness of heart," their anxious lowliness becomes "humility," their "inoffensiveness" and "lingering at the door" becomes "patience," and their desire for retaliation becomes a desire for justice.

Now if Nietzsche were really a realist about the concept of "lowness," then we ought to be able to identify the objective facts in virtue of which something is really low. Yet surely, as this example suggests, there is good reason for skepticism about what they would be: for when Nietzsche tries to describe *all* patience as nothing more than a "lingering at the door" and *all* humility as simply "anxious lowliness," it is natural to think that there is no "objective" fact about "lowness" here but simply a polemical and evaluatively loaded characterization. To think that all humility is really "anxious lowliness" is just to identify oneself as one who shares Nietzsche's evaluative sensibility, one "whose ears are related to ours" (GS: 381), one "predisposed and predestined" for Nietzsche's insights (BGE: 30). In short, given the way in which Nietzsche actually speaks of the "high" and "low," we should understand Nietzsche's metaethical position as also characterizing these terms: to say that "X is low" is not to describe an objective fact, but rather to identify oneself as sharing in a certain evaluative sensibility or taste.

We come, then, to a more compelling concern: namely, that Nietzsche simply does not write like someone who thinks his evaluative judgments are merely his idiosyncratic preferences. As John Wilcox put it many years ago: Nietzsche's "works are full of valuations; he took sides" (1974: 2). But the problem is not only that: rather it is that he takes sides with such force, such polemical ferocity, that it seems hard to think of Nietzsche as really believing, as the preceding account of his metaethics would have it, that the evaluative judgments he thrusts upon his readers reflect no objective fact of the matter, that they admit of no objective grounding for those who do not share what simply happens to be Nietzsche's idiosyncratic evaluative tastes. On the metaethical position elaborated here, it seems Nietzsche must believe that if, in response to his point that "morality were to blame if the *highest power and splendor* actually possible to the type man was never in fact attained" (GM Pref: 6), someone were to say, "So much the better for morality!," there would be nothing further to say to that person: at the best, Nietzsche might turn his back and say, "Oh well – doesn't share my evaluative tastes."

The difficulty is that there seems to be a substantial amount of Nietzschean rhetoric that cannot be reconciled with this metaethical view, and that cries out instead for some sort of realist construal. It is worth recalling some examples of this rhetoric. Nietzsche calls "morality" "an *idiosyncrasy of degenerates* which has caused immeasurable harm" (TI V: 6). He says, "Christian morality" is that "which *corrupted* humanity" (EH IV: 7). He says that the moral principle requiring, "Refraining mutually from injury, violence, and exploitation and placing one's will on a par with that of someone else," once it becomes "the *fundamental principle of society* ... immediately proves to be what it is – a will to the *denial* of life, a principle of disintegration and decay" (BGE: 259). The dominance of MPS "would deprive existence of its *great* character and would castrate men and reduce them to the level of desiccated Chinese stagnation" (EH IV: 4). "An 'altruistic' morality," says Nietzsche, "a morality in which self-interest wilts away . . . remains a bad sign under all circumstances. . . . The best is lacking when self-interest begins to be lacking" (TI IX: 35). And near the end of *Ecce Homo* – a singularly strident work – he writes:

> [T]his is what is most terrible of all – the concept of the *good* man signifies that one sides with all that is weak, sick, failure, suffering of itself . . . – an ideal is fabricated from the contradiction against the proud and well-turned out human being who says Yes, who is sure of the future, who guarantees the future – and he is now called *evil* – And all this was believed, *as morality*! – *Ecrasez l'infame*!
>
> (EH IV: 8)

But if Nietzsche is really an anti-realist about non-prudential value – including his own revaluative judgment – then it would have to be the case that in response to the question, "Is it a fact that one ought to crush this infamy [is it a fact that it is *infamy*?]?" Nietzsche's "official" answer would be: "No; only crush it – and only view it as infamy – if you share my evaluative taste for the flourishing of higher men." The challenge now is to understand how such an answer could possibly be compatible with the volume of Nietzsche's rhetoric.

In fact, the style in which Nietzsche writes about value is *only* rhetoric, and from his rhetorical style we are entitled to no inference regarding his real metaphysics of value. Three sorts of considerations should block this inference:

First, *the rhetoric is forceful, but the language of truth and falsity is conspicuously absent*. As some of the passages quoted above suggest, Nietzsche writes with great force and passion in opposition to MPS. But it is striking that he does not use the epistemic value terms – the language of truth and falsity, real and unreal – in this context. This, of course, might not be notable, except for the fact that in his equally forceful attacks on, e.g., Christian cosmology, or religious interpretations of natural events, he invokes the conceptual apparatus of truth and falsity, truth and lie, reality and appearance, all the time (cf. Leiter 1994: 336–8). Thus, for example, Nietzsche lampoons Christian cosmology as lacking "even a single point of contact with reality" and as "pure fiction" which "falsifies . . . reality" ("*die Wirklichkeit fälscht*") (A: 15). Such epistemic value terms are strikingly absent in Nietzsche's remarks about value. One natural explanation for this difference in rhetoric – natural especially in light of the substantial evidence for his anti-realism – is precisely that in the moral case he does not think there is any fact of the matter.

Second, recall what Nietzsche's goal is in undertaking a "revaluation of all values": he wants to alert "higher" types to the fact that MPS is not, in fact, conducive to their flourishing. Thus, he needs to "wake up" his appropriate readers – those whose "ears are related" to his – to the dangers of MPS, a task made all the more difficult by MPS's pretension to be "morality itself." Given, then, that Nietzsche's target is a certain sort of misunderstanding on the part of higher men, and given the difficulty of supplanting the norms that figure in this misunderstanding (the norms of MPS), it should be unsurprising that Nietzsche writes with passion and force: he must shake higher types out of their intuitive commitment to the moral traditions of two millennia! Moreover, Nietzsche's naturalism, and the prominent role it assigns to non-conscious drives and type-facts, leads him to be skeptical about the efficacy of reasons and arguments. But a skeptic about the efficacy of rational persuasion might very well opt for persuasion through other rhetorical devices.

Third, and perhaps most importantly, a rhetorical tone like Nietzsche's – looked at in the context of his life – does not really suggest realism about the content, but rather desperation on the part of the author to reach an increasingly distant and uninterested audience. The Nietzsche who was almost completely ignored during the years before illness erased his intellect and deprived him of his sanity might have resorted to more and more strident and violent rhetoric in frustration over not being heard – and not because he was a realist. Indeed, in the absence of explicit evidence of value realism, this seems the most plausible explanation for the vast majority of the passages with which we have been concerned in this section.

For these various reasons, then, the character of Nietzsche's rhetoric can be understood as compatible with his anti-realism about moral value.

Two final puzzles

Nietzsche's basic philosophical and explanatory stance – what we have been calling "naturalism" – is perhaps best captured in his discussion of the strange case of Cornaro (TI VI: 1, 2). Nietzsche, recall, explains the case as follows:

> Everybody knows the book of the famous Cornaro in which he recommends his slender diet as a recipe for a long and happy life. . . . I do not doubt that scarcely any book (except the Bible, as is meet) has done as much harm. . . . The reason: the mistaking of the effect for the cause. The worthy Italian thought his diet was the *cause* of his long life, whereas the precondition for a long life, the extraordinary slowness of his metabolism, the consumption of so little, was the cause of his slender diet. He was not free to eat little *or* much; his frugality was not a matter of "free will": he became sick when he ate more.
>
> (TI VI: 1; cf. WP: 229)

Nietzsche takes "Cornarism" to involve a widespread kind of mistake, which we might characterize as follows: given effects E1 and E2 and their mutual "deep cause" DC, Cornarism involves construing E1 as the cause of E2, while ignoring the existence of DC altogether.

Now as Nietzsche makes clear in the section following the above (TI VI: 2), the major culprits of Cornarism are morality and religion: that is, while the basic "formula on which every religion and morality is founded is: 'Do this and that, refrain from that and that – then you will be happy! Otherwise . . . ,'" Nietzsche holds – *contra* Cornarism – that,

> a well-turned out human being . . . *must* perform certain actions and shrinks instinctively from other actions; he carries the order, which he represents physiologically, into his relations with other human beings and things.
>
> (TI VI: 2)

Thus, both the moralist and Cornaro prescribe conduct in order to effect certain other ends, when, in fact, the prescribed conduct (E1) and the desired end (E2) are only possible for an agent of the appropriate type; for such an agent, the conduct occurs necessarily (he "*must* perform certain actions"). The real error of Cornarism, in short, consists in its failure to understand that type-facts about an agent (psycho-physiological facts) are the *primary* causal/explanatory facts; everything else – including the various normative codes (moral, dietary) that agents embrace – are themselves either *secondary* causes – i.e., causally effective in virtue of the presence of the requisite type-facts – or, alternately, *effects* of the underlying type-facts. That is why Nietzsche declares that, "A man as he *ought* to be: that sounds to us as insipid as 'a tree as it ought to be'" (WP: 332). Moral (or dietary) prescriptions are not primary causes but effects in a double sense: (a) they lack primary causal efficacy because only type-facts about agents have primary causal efficacy; and (b) they are themselves effects, that is, they are only embraced because of one's *type*. What moralists fail to understand is that, "Reality shows us an enchanting wealth of types" (TI V: 6) – each with values and behaviors appropriate to that type – and that, as a result, "the demand of one morality for all is detrimental to the higher men" (BGE: 228), because higher types require different values than other types of persons.

Nietzsche's view that the prevalence of MPS is harmful to higher types of men – the claim central, as we have seen, to Nietzsche's critique of MPS – seems to pose a puzzle when juxtaposed with Nietzsche's naturalistic critique of Cornarism. That is, the critique of MPS as described earlier in this chapter seems to suppose precisely that moralities can be causally effective: they can cause higher types of men not to flourish, precisely because higher types will accept moral values as applicable to themselves, even though such values do not contribute to their flourishing. That suggests both that some values are causally effective, and that some values are embraced *not* because they are effects of type-facts about the agent. How can these claims be reconciled with Nietzsche's naturalistic critique of Cornarism as described above?

Our earlier discussion (Chapter 3) of Nietzsche's fatalism and theory of agency suggests an answer. Recall that when Nietzsche affirms the explanatory *primacy* of type-facts about agents, he is only ruling out causal efficacy that is not ultimately traceable to causal efficacy in virtue of type-facts. Thus, Nietzsche can, as we saw, admit the plausible view that the values an agent is exposed to can affect the agent – but only in virtue of type-facts about that agent. Thus, if

MPS hinders the flourishing of higher types, it is only because there are type-facts about higher types that make them susceptible to the influence of these values. So, too, agents can come to accept values that are, overall, harmful to that type of agent only in virtue of type-facts about agents that would lead them to do so – this, in fact, is the very essence of "decadence" for Nietzsche. Noting that he equates "corruption" and "decadence," Nietzsche explains that: "I call an animal, a species, or an individual corrupt when it loses its instincts, when it chooses, when it prefers, what is disadvantageous for it" (A: 6). Thus, when higher men come to believe in MPS this is simply a case of decadent type-facts about agents doing the work of belief-fixation: an agent with corrupt instincts – a type-fact about that agent – will embrace "disadvantageous" values *because of this type-fact*.

Now this proposed solution to the puzzle may seem to suggest an equally paradoxical possibility: namely, that Nietzsche's higher men are *decadent* insofar as they embrace MPS values, values that are not conducive to their flourishing. But there is nothing paradoxical about this – surely one can be both excellent and self-destructive – and it is a possibility Nietzsche frankly acknowledges. For example, Nietzsche wastes no time at the beginning of his autobiography in announcing: "I have a subtler sense of smell for the signs of ascent and decline than any other human being before me . . . – I know both, I am both" (EH I: 1); adding, "Need I say after all this that in questions of decadence I am *experienced*?" (EH I: 1). Yet Nietzsche, as we have seen, takes himself ultimately to be an example of a higher type of person. Not surprisingly, then, Nietzsche continues in *Ecce Homo* by saying:

> Apart from the fact that I am a decadent, I am also the opposite. My proof for this is, among other things, that I have always instinctively chosen the *right* means against wretched states; while the decadent typically chooses means that are disadvantageous for him. As *summa summarum* [over-all], I was healthy; as an angle, as a specialty, I was a decadent.
>
> (EH I: 2)

Thus, insofar as the higher type has, like Nietzsche, a decadent streak (a type-fact about the higher type), he may succumb to MPS; insofar as he is fundamentally "healthy," he will, like Nietzsche, overcome his attachment to MPS. Higher types post-Nietzsche have the advantage of having Nietzsche help them recognize the competing natural tendencies within themselves (towards health or decadence). As one commentator puts it, "Nietzsche's writings themselves are another part of the earthly causal order, and as such, may well influence many of his readers" (Gemes 1992: 51). We might only qualify this by saying that Nietzsche only expects that his writings will influence *certain* readers, those who are "predisposed and predestined" for his insights (BGE: 30) – in virtue of their type.

There remains one final puzzle about Nietzsche's critique of MPS and his metaethics as presented above. For if Nietzsche is right that MPS presupposes descriptive claims about agency that are not true (the arguments discussed in Chapter 3), then hasn't Nietzsche given the adherents of MPS *reasons* to stop embracing MPS?

Recall why this creates a problem for the interpretation of Nietzsche as an anti-realist. If value is not objective, then there can be no mistakes of cognitive judgment; there can be no *theoretical* reasons – as opposed, e.g., to prudential or practical ones – for believing one way rather than the other. But surely *false premises or presuppositions* constitute theoretical reasons for not believing in values that involve them. In that case, it starts to look like MPS judgments and Nietzsche's own evaluative perspective are not, as the anti-realism would imply, on the same epistemological plain: MPS judgments have objective problems that Nietzschean values don't.

Two observations are in order at this point. First, recall Nietzsche's goal: to free nascent higher types from the "grip" of MPS. That being his ultimate aim, there seems no reason why he should not want to employ all the rhetorical resources available – including resources that depend on the fact that most readers *will* find falsity to be an objection to a view. Insofar as most readers still think truth has "absolute value" (the view that Nietzsche attacks in GM III), then Nietzsche can take advantage of that fact in trying to dissuade them from accepting MPS.[29]

[29] To be sure, Nietzsche can reject the *absolute* value of truth and still think truth has *some* value (as he plainly does) and that *falsity* can *sometimes* constitute an objection to a belief. For further discussion, see Chapter 8.

But as a matter of Nietzsche's own theoretical posture, notice that Nietzsche has only given reasons for rejecting MPS values if we grant a particular epistemic norm: one should not believe X if X is unsupported by theoretical reasons. A view that presupposes false-hoods is, a fortiori, unsupported by theoretical reasons. Once we embrace this as a norm for belief, then it seems to follow that, granted the soundness of Nietzsche's criticisms, we are *not* equally justified in believing MPS values as opposed to values which do not presuppose falsehoods.

Ordinarily, of course, this norm for belief would not warrant much attention. But in the context of Nietzsche's view, it becomes significant, for Nietzsche does not accept it without qualification. Here we come upon a theme in Nietzsche's thought that has often received *too much* attention: his emphasis on the necessity of error. Nietzsche, following some of the Presocratics, thinks that to live and flourish we must believe a multitude of things that are not true. He gives expression to this theme in the early sections of *Beyond Good and Evil*:

> The falseness of a judgment is for us not necessarily an objection to a judgment. ... The question is to what extent it is life-promoting, life-preserving, species-preserving, perhaps even species-cultivating. And we are fundamentally inclined to claim that the falsest judgments ... are the most indispensable for us. ... [R]enouncing false judgments would mean renouncing life and a denial of life. To recognize untruth as a condition of life.
> (BGE: 4; cf. BT Attempt: 5)

If untruth can be a condition of life – if, in other words, we ought to believe errors and falsehoods when they are necessary for our flour-ishing – then the fact that moral judgments presuppose falsehoods does not necessarily constitute a reason – at least for the suitably Nietzschean reader – for rejecting such norms. As Nietzsche puts it elsewhere: "Even if a morality has grown out of an error, the realiza-tion of this fact would not so much as touch the problem of its value" (GS: 345). That is, such a morality might still be valuable, i.e., worth accepting, notwithstanding its dependence on errors.

Nietzsche's emphasis on the necessity of error entails a very different norm for belief than the mundane one described above.

Nietzsche's view seems to be that we ought to believe X if it is a condition of our life to believe X and *even if* X is unsupported by theoretical reasons (e.g., because it involves contradictions or presupposes falsehoods). Granted this norm for belief, then, Nietzsche can still hold that, notwithstanding his criticisms of the false presuppositions of MPS, belief in moral values and non-moral values both lack objective justification. This does not preclude him from taking rhetorical advantage of the conventional norm for belief acceptance, but it does permit him to maintain the coherence of his own meta-ethical stance.

This approach, moreover, is wholly consistent with Nietzsche's actual critical strategy against MPS: namely, that he criticizes MPS centrally for its harmful effects on the flourishing of higher men who would manifest various forms of human excellence. While Nietzsche disputes the conception of agency presupposed by MPS, he does not argue that MPS should be rejected *because* of its false presuppositions. As Ken Gemes has again nicely put it: "Nietzsche's attack on Christianity [and Christian morality] is based on the fact that it enfeebles strong wills, not that it is false" (1992: 58). Thus, even in criticizing MPS, Nietzsche respects the new epistemic norm that grows out of his recognition of the necessity of error.

Conclusion

We began in Chapter 3 with three interpretive puzzles: (i) what the scope of Nietzsche's attack on morality might be; (ii) how to circumscribe this critique without recourse to known types of morality (historical, philosophical, religious); and, at the same time, (iii) how to distinguish it from the "moral" beliefs Nietzsche himself seems to continue to hold. We may now summarize the answers defended in Chapters 3 and 4 as follows.

Nietzsche is a critic of morality (MPS) in the sense of values that: (a) presuppose for the intelligibility of their application specific empirical and metaphysical claims about human agency; and centrally (b) harm the highest men. Values, then, that do *not* presuppose an untenable account of agency and that *are* conducive to the flourishing of higher men are not the object of Nietzsche's critique.

To make his full case against MPS, Nietzsche must show: (i) that moral values do depend on a picture of agency, which is (ii) untenable; (iii) that moral demands do in fact harm higher men; and (iv) that the value of higher men is such that it ought to count against moral demands that they have this effect.

Philosophers who would defend MPS against Nietzsche's attack must show: either (i') that moral values do not depend on an untenable picture of agency (either (a) because they don't depend on it or (b) because it is not untenable); or (ii') that even if they do depend on such a picture, this does not undermine the appropriateness of their application to human affairs; *and* either (iii') that MPS is not a threat to human excellence; or (iv') that even if it is a threat, this does not count significantly against the value of moral demands. We will return in Chapter 9 to the question of whether or not Nietzsche's critique is successful.

A final challenge to the account of Nietzsche's critique of morality developed in Chapters 3 and 4 now merits consideration. One might object that the conception of MPS described above is simply an arbitrary mish-mash of views that does not deserve a unitary label. Surely, one might say, the descriptive component of MPS has a distinctively Kantian flavor to it, from which all manner of consequentialists will dissent; and similarly, one might worry that no known moral system – philosophical or historical – embraces the full normative agenda of MPS described above. In what sense, then, is this a critique of "morality," rather than simply a shot-gun approach to a vast array of normative views?

There is, in fact, a simple two-part answer to this worry. First, Nietzsche does indeed take a critical stand against a wide array of normative views – that is precisely part of the point of the preceding characterization of MPS. But second, Nietzsche perceives these views to have something important in common – admittedly something that most of their philosophical and non-philosophical proponents do not typically acknowledge: namely, that they favor the lowest men at the expense of the highest. If it is this latter feature that Nietzsche centrally objects to, then surely it is fair to consider together the whole range of normative views that are marked by this characteristic. It is true, of course, that the descriptive component of MPS may not characterize all otherwise objectionable normative systems; but even here one finds that the Similarity Thesis is extremely common and, at least within the Kantian tradition, so too are the Free Will and Transparency Theses. But if what unites all Nietzsche's targets is their endorsement of a normative agenda that, in some way, is incompatible with the realization of human excellence, then that is "unity" enough to justify reading Nietzsche as a critic of "morality" in this broad sense captured by the account of his critique presented here.

We turn now to an examination of how Nietzsche's critique of morality – of MPS – is developed in the *Genealogy* itself.

Chapter 5

What is "genealogy" and what is the *Genealogy*?

Much of the *Genealogy*'s fame rests on its perceived introduction of a new method to philosophy – namely, "genealogy" – which is importantly different from ordinary historical inquiry (Foucault 1971; MacIntyre 1990; Geuss 1994). Nietzsche, of course, brings this new method to bear on morality, but the method itself is supposed to be of general applicability, as Foucault's genealogies of the hospital, the prison, and the insane aslyum are often taken to illustrate.

Now Nietzsche himself explicitly enlists genealogy in the service of a *critique* of morality (more precisely, MPS) (GM Pref: 5). But how could a quasi-historical method have any bearing on an essentially evaluative project? If that is not puzzling enough, the reader soon discovers a further complication: for the *Genealogy* consists of three essays, each telling three rather different kinds of stories (so it appears) about the "origins" of MPS. So is this, one wonders, a genealogy, or *genealogies*, and is this a genealogy of morality, or of *moralities*? Is this book merely united

in virtue of its putatively new method – whatever exactly that turns out to be – or does it have a thematic or dialectic unity as well? In this chapter, we set out answers to these questions.

The principles and method of "genealogy"

Foucault (1971) popularized the idea that "genealogy" represents a new historico-philosophical method. Foucault claims that genealogy is different from traditional history in that genealogy "opposes itself to the search for 'origins'" (1971: 77), where this means a search for "the exact essence of things . . . the existence of immobile forms that precede the external world of accident and succession" (1971: 78). The genealogist, says Foucault, "refuses to extend his faith in metaphysics" and instead,

> finds that there is "something altogether different" behind things: not a timeless and essential secret, but the secret that they have no essence or that their essence was fabricated in a piecemeal fashion from alien forms. . . . A genealogy of values, morality, asceticism, knowledge will never confuse itself with a quest for their "origins," will never neglect as inaccessible the vicissitudes of history. On the contrary, it will cultivate the details and accidents that accompany every beginning; it will be scrupulously attentive to their petty malice; it will await their emergence, once unmasked, as the face of the other.
>
> (1971: 78, 80)

There is a kernel of truth in this account, as we shall see, but also much that is misleading. To start, Foucault's "traditional" historian sounds too much like a clumsy Platonist to be a plausible opponent: what practicing historian believes that the "origin" is to be sought in "immobile forms that precede the external world"? (Indeed, Foucault draws a false distinction between *Historie* and *Genealogie*, when, in fact, Nietzsche uses the terms interchangeably.)[1] So, too, Foucault's

---

[1] Cf. Nehamas (1985: 246 n. 1): "Nietzsche does not, as Foucault does, contrast genealogy with history but insists that genealogy simply *is* history correctly practiced." See generally Pizer (1990).

claim that the genealogical object has no "essence" suggests an anachronistic affinity with postmodern skepticism about facts and objectivity. Whether Foucault intended this latter affinity or not, he has certainly been read that way. Thus, two influential commentators have explained Foucault's theory of genealogy as follows:

> For the genealogist . . . [t]he more one interprets the more one finds not the fixed meaning of a text, or of the world, but only other interpretations. These interpretations have been created and imposed by other people, not by the nature of things. In this discovery of groundlessness the inherent *arbitrariness* of interpretation is revealed.
>
> (Dreyfus and Rabinow 1983: 106–7, emphasis added)

But this cannot be what Nietzsche means by "genealogy," for Nietzsche says that the *Genealogy* is concerned with "a real *history of morality*" [*wirklichen Historie der Moral*],[2] in contrast to mere "hypothesis-mongering" (GM Pref: 7). And a genealogist is only interested in "that which can be documented, which can actually be confirmed, and has actually existed" (GM Pref: 7). Nietzsche's genealogist appears to be very much interested in "the nature of things" as they *really* are, not simply as some arbitrary interpretation would have them be.

In the standard dictionary definition, "genealogy" is the study of family pedigree. In particular, it is often the study of pedigree with an eye to producing a "positive valorization" of some object by showing it to have a distinguished origin: the value of the distinguished ancestor is, as it were, transmitted to the present-day descendants (Geuss 1994: 275). (Those with disreputable forebears are typically less interested in advertising their own genealogy precisely because they share the assumption that the value at the point of the origin is transmitted to those later on in the genealogical tree.)

Nietzsche's genealogical practice is different. In the genealogy of morality, his aim is critical not positive, and he is concerned *precisely* to break the chain of value transmission by showing that the

---

2   Foucault (1971) renders *wirkliche Historie* as "effective history" ("*l'histoire effective*"), no doubt because "real" history sounds like it is claiming an epistemic privilege for its claims – much like traditional history!

value or meaning of the genealogical object is discontinuous over time for two reasons: first, because there is no unitary value or meaning transferred from point of origin to contemporary object; and, second, because there is more than one point of origin. Thus, while the traditional study of pedigree presupposes something like the following picture:

Present object (possessing value X)

↑ (value X)

↑ (value X)

Point of Origin (value X)

Nietzschean genealogy replaces it with a very different picture, in which the present object of study is shown to have multiple points of origin, with multiple valuations:

Present object (possessing value X)

↗ (value C)	↑ (value T)	↑ (value O)
↗ (value B)	↑ (value S)	↑ (value N)
Point of Origin 1	Point of Origin 2	Point of Origin 3
(value A)	(value R)	(value M), etc.

Notice, however, that genealogy does require that there be some *stable* object throughout the genealogical tree, for only if there is such a stable object does it make sense to speak of a genealogy of *morality* or of any *particular* object. The crucial contention, then, is that the *stable* or individuating feature of the genealogical object – say, morality – is *not* its value or meaning or purpose. It is this connection in particular that Nietzsche wants to sever: from the present value/meaning/purpose of an object, we are entitled to no inference about its origin. (Indeed, the failure to sever the two is precisely the mistake attributed to prior historians of morality (GM I: 1–3).) On this point, Nietzsche follows Darwin, who cautioned against "the mistake of inferring current function or meaning from ancestral function or meaning" (Dennett 1995: 465; cf. Clark 1998a: xxiv).

Nietzsche himself makes these points explicitly in the one methodological discussion of genealogical practice in the *Genealogy*, which appears in the exact middle of the book: GM II: 12 (cf. Clark

1994). Nietzsche has here embarked upon a seemingly tangential discussion about the genealogy of punishment. But, in fact, he uses the opportunity to articulate (and illustrate via a case study) what is distinctive of genealogy. He writes as follows:

> Now another word on the origin and purpose of punishment – two problems which are separate, or ought to be: unfortunately people usually throw them together. How have [prior, non-Nietzschean] moral genealogists reacted so far in this matter? Naively, as is their wont – : they highlight some "purpose" in punishment, for example, revenge or deterrence, then innocently place the purpose at the start ... and have finished. ... [But] the origin of the emergence of a thing and its ultimate useful-ness ... are *toto coelo* separate; that anything in existence, having somehow come about, is continually interpreted anew, ... transformed and redirected to a new purpose by a power superior to it. ... [E]very purpose and use is just a *sign* that the will to power has achieved mastery over something less powerful, and has stamped upon it its own functional meaning [*und ihm von sich aus den Sinn einer Funktion aufgeprägt hat*]. ... The "development" of a thing, a tradition, an organ is there-fore certainly not its *progressus* towards a goal, still less is it a logical *progressus*.

So the genealogist of punishment does not view the *present* purpose of punishment as having evidential value regarding the origin of punishment: at the point of origin, punishment may have had a wholly other purpose. Indeed, throughout its history, punishment may have had multiple purposes (meanings), as appropriated by different peoples and historical epochs, so that its present purpose is but *the latest* "func-tional meaning" imposed upon the practice.

But what then makes this a genealogy of *punishment*: how do we know it is *punishment* whose history we are tracing throughout, and not simply different practices? Nietzsche explains: "we have to distinguish between two of its aspects: one is its relative *permanence*, a traditional practice [*Brauch*], a fixed form of action, a 'drama,' a certain strict sequence of procedures, the other is its *fluidity*, its meaning [*Sinn*], purpose and expectation, which is linked to the carrying out of such procedures" (GM II: 13). Genealogy, then, presupposes that its object has a stable or essential character – its *Brauch* – that permits us to individuate it intelligibly over time. What the genealogist denies is that this stable element is to be located in the object's purpose or value or meaning (its *Sinn*): it is precisely *that feature* which is discontinuous from point of origin to present-day embodiment.

In the case of punishment, for example, the "stable" element might simply be "the act of inflicting a harm or loss on a person based on a judgment that the person deserves this loss owing to something he or she has done" (Clark 1994: 21). What changes is the *purpose* of inflicting such a harm or loss: sometimes it is done as "a means of rendering harmless," sometimes it is "payment of a debt," sometimes "a means of inspiring fear of those who determine and execute punishment," sometimes "an *aide memoire*," etc. (GM II: 13). As Nietzsche writes:

> With regard to the other element in punishment, the fluid one, its "meaning," the concept "punishment" presents, at a very late stage of culture (for example, in Europe today), not just one meaning but a whole synthesis of "meanings": the history of punishment up to now in general, the history of its use for a variety of purposes, finally crystallizes in a kind of unity which is difficult to dissolve back into its elements, difficult to analyse and, this has to be stressed, is absolutely *undefinable*. (Today it is impossible to say precisely *why* people are actually punished: all concepts in which an entire process is semiotically concentrated defy definition; only something which has no history can be defined.)
>
> (GM II: 13)

"Concepts influenced by history," as Clark notes (borrowing the Wittgensteinian image), "are like ropes held together by the intertwining of strands, rather than by a single strand running through the whole thing" (1994: 22; cf. Geuss 1997: 1; HA: 33). Genealogy, then, would be a matter of separating "the various strands that may have become so tightly woven together by the process of historical development that they seem inseparable" (Clark 1994: 22). We will ask shortly *why* one would want to untangle the strands, as Nietzsche wants to do in the *Genealogy*.

Remember, however, that Nietzsche's mini-genealogy of punishment is significant primarily for what it tells us about the practice of genealogy *generally*, hence about the genealogy of morality. This means, in particular, that there must be a *stable* or *essential* element in morality, even as the genealogy of morality reveals its multifarious meanings and purposes. Paradoxically, of course, the genealogist cannot appeal to the *values* of morality to individuate it as an object of genealogy: a genealogy of an evaluative or purposive concept cannot appeal to the value or purpose to identify its object! (Recall that the genealogical hypothesis is precisely that value and purpose are fluid.) But how then do we *fix* the object? Why is it, for example, that the transformation from "master morality" to "slave morality" recounted in the first essay of the *Genealogy* is part of a genealogy *of morality*: why not just say that slave morality "changed the topic," as it were, given its radically different normative and metaphysical apparatus (see Chapter 6)? The question, in short, is what in morality is "relatively *permanent*" (GM II: 13)?

Nietzsche is not ideally clear on this point, but we may make a proposal on his behalf.[3] Let us say that the "permanent" element in morality is *the practice of evaluating oneself and others* – call it the Anthropocentric Evaluative Practice (hereafter AEP).[4] The claim, then, is that a "morality" qua object of genealogy is necessarily an AEP.

---

[3]   Although there is no reason to think Nietzsche picked up on this point, it is worth noting that the "relatively permanent" element need not be present in *all* instances of morality for the analogy to genealogy to work. Even a family genealogy does not presuppose that there is one element shared in common by a living member of the family and his ancestor twenty generations ago. It suffices that between each generation there is an appropriate, shared element (e.g., a blood tie). So, too, with a genealogy of morality it suffices if at each *transformative* stage in the genealogy there is a shared element that allows us to individuate the transformation as one *involving morality*. Even if our present-day morality shares nothing in common with its various ancestors that the *Genealogy* exposes, it suffices to establish the overall story as a genealogy of *morality* if at each transformative stage in the genealogy there are shared elements. (Here I have benefited from comments by Ken Gemes and Itai Sher.)

[4]   Note that this characterization is compatible with the currently fashionable idea that morality places restrictions on how we treat non-human animals. For

(The claim is *not* that every AEP is a morality, however.) In this sense, both slave and master moralities are examples of *morality*: they are both evaluative practices, concerned not with things or texts or foods, but with *human beings*, both the actor himself and his fellow humans. This allows conceptual space in which "moralities" can still differ dramatically as to their value or purpose.

So a genealogy of morality shows "morality" (qua AEP) to have several different origins and multiple meanings. In particular, the genealogist resists the mistaken inference from the present purpose of morality to any conclusions about its history or origin. But this, so far, is only part of what is distinctive of genealogy qua method. For equally central to genealogical practice, in Nietzsche's view, is a commitment to *naturalism*.[5] The genealogy is not only a *history* of morality that rejects the evidential value of morality's present meaning for discovering its origin, but it is also a distinctively *naturalistic* history, an account of the origins of morality without appeal to supernatural causes. Nietzsche reiterates this methodological point in both the Preface of the *Genealogy*, and his summary of the *Genealogy*'s argument two years later in *Ecce Homo*.

In the Preface, he contrasts his own adolescent approach to the question of the origin of good and evil – "I quite properly gave God credit for it" (GM Pref: 3) – with the mature approach in the *Genealogy*: "I learnt, in time, to separate theological from moral prejudice and I no longer searched for the origin of evil *beyond* the world," an approach for which his "innate fastidiousness with regard to all psychological questions" naturally suited him (GM Pref: 3). In *Ecce Homo*, he repeatedly emphasizes his naturalistic posture. He describes the "truth" of the first essay as "the birth of Christianity out of the spirit of *ressentiment*, not, as people, may believe out of the 'spirit'" (EH III: GM). That is, the origin of Christianity (more precisely, the morality associated with Christianity (see Chapter 6))

even proponents of this idea do not claim that we should morally evaluate the character or conduct of non-human animals; all they claim is that the conduct of humans towards such animals has *moral* significance.

5   This point is missed in both Foucault (1971) and Geuss (1994), but correctly emphasized by Clark (1998a).

is explicable in terms of a certain kind of psychological mechanism found in creatures like us – namely, *ressentiment* – not in terms of some supernatural spiritual inspiration or source. So, too, the "psychology of the *conscience*" proferred in the second essay locates the origin of conscience *not* as " 'the voice of God in man' " but rather as the result of the conflict between man's animal nature and the constraints imposed by civilized intercourse with other human beings (see Chapter 7) (EH III: GM). Indeed, Nietzsche characterizes the whole volume as "three decisive preliminary studies by a psychologist" (EH III: GM). It is, in short, naturally occurring psychological mechanisms – *ressentiment* (GM I), internalized cruelty (GM II), the will to power (GM III) – that suffice to explain morality's origin in Nietzsche's view; we need no recourse to non-natural or supernatural forces and entities.

"Genealogy" and critique

Nietzsche employs his genealogical method in order to *critique* morality (more precisely, MPS). As he notes in the Preface:

> I was preoccupied with something much more important than the nature of hypotheses, mine or anybody else's, on the origin of morality (or, to be more exact: the latter concerned me only for one purpose, to which it is one means among many). For me it was a question of the *value* of morality.
>
> (GM Pref: 5)

But how does an investigation of the origins of MPS shed light on the *value* of MPS? The question is particularly pressing, since, as we have seen, Nietzsche denies the conventional idea that value is transmitted from point of origin to contemporary object. So why think a genealogy should even be "one means among many" towards a critique of MPS?

One problem that seems to haunt the *Genealogy* is the genetic fallacy, the fallacy of thinking the origin of X demonstrates something about the value of X. But Nietzsche is aware of the genetic fallacy, remarking, for example, that "Even if a morality has grown out of an error, the realization of this fact would not so much as touch the problem of its value" (GS: 345). Yet it is precisely the question of the value of MPS that Nietzsche's critique means to raise. Thus, if Nietzsche is not committing the genetic fallacy, why, then, does he think the origin of MPS has *any* bearing on a critique of MPS? As we saw in Chapter 3, a number of commentators have thought Nietzsche mounts an *internal* critique of MPS, that is, a critique of MPS on the grounds that its own proclaimed standards (e.g., "love one another") require a condemnation of MPS itself given its typical motives (e.g., hatred) on Nietzsche's account.[6] An internal critique suggests, then, one way in which genealogy could be relevant to the revaluation of values without committing the genetic fallacy: for insofar as the genealogy identifies the motives in which MPS has its origin, and insofar as these motives stand condemned by MPS itself, then the genealogy contributes to a critique of MPS by the latter's own ("internal") standards.

Notice, of course, that the genealogy has to identify *not simply* the motives that explain the origin of MPS, but the motives which are still operative in MPS today, for only if MPS is *still* motivated by hatred would it seem that a "morality of love" would have any reason to condemn itself. That "once upon a time" MPS arose because of hatred might be somewhat embarrassing for the morality of love, but it is hardly a refutation: to think otherwise would, once again, involve the genetic fallacy. A first reason for being skeptical, then, about the "internal critique" interpretation of Nietzsche is that it is not at all clear from the text of the *Genealogy* that he is claiming that present-day morality is motivated by hatred or *ressentiment*. Indeed, were he to be claiming that, he would run afoul of one of the central tenets of genealogy discussed above: namely, that there can be radical discontinuities of purpose or meaning from an object's point of origin to its contemporary form. So even if, at its origin, MPS served the "purpose" of expressing the hatred of "slaves" towards those better off, genealogical method is predicated precisely on the assumption that the purpose of MPS might have changed dramatically over time.

There is a further, related, textual consideration counting against the internal critique reading: for while Nietzsche clearly wants his readers to appreciate the irony that a morality of "love" should have

---

[6] See, e.g., Foot (1973): 114; Kaufmann (1974): 113; Geuss (1981): 44.

its origins in hatred, careful examination of Nietzsche's texts reveals that he does *not* seize upon this contradiction (even in the *Genealogy*) in mounting his criticism of MPS.[7] This, in fact, is fortunate, since as we have just seen, for him to seize upon this contradiction would involve him in the genetic fallacy that he disowns.[8]

[7] This claim requires at least two qualifications. First, in at least one place, Nietzsche does remark upon "the fundamental contradiction in the morality that is very prestigious nowadays: the *motives* of this morality stand opposed to its principle" (GS: 21). But his point in this context concerns the putatively selfish motives people have for assigning moral value to selflessness: as Nietzsche puts it, "The 'neighbor' praises selflessness *because it brings him advantages*" (GS: 21). Nietzsche does not, however, make this contradiction central to his *criticism* of the moral ideal of selflessness (as I discuss below); nor is it this "contradiction" commentators have in mind when they attribute an internal critique to Nietzsche (e.g., Geuss 1981: 44).

Second, it is also true that Nietzsche holds that there is an important sense in which Christian morality (in particular) self-destructs: namely, the value assigned to truthfulness in the Christian tradition becomes, over time, "translated and sublimated into a scientific conscience, into intellectual cleanliness at any price"; and it is under the demand of this new conscience that morality – and particularly its metaphysical suppositions – collapses (GS: 357; also, EH IV: 3). But this, again, does not amount to an internal critique of morality: rather, morality is criticized from a broadly "scientific" and "truth-seeking" standpoint, a standpoint which is *not* internal to Christian morality, but which Christian morality helped produce.

[8] There is one other reason for rejecting the suggestion that genealogy lays the foundation for an internal critique of MPS, for one typical interest of an internal criticism of any view is that it should force those who hold the view to reconsider their commitment. If this were not the critical motivation, then criticism of a view might proceed more directly to the merits of the view itself (as measured by some other standard), independent of any consideration of the standards that commend it to those who hold it. Thus, one reason for offering an internal critique of MPS would be to challenge the commitment of the adherents of MPS to these values by showing that the reasons for their commitment are unacceptable by the standards of MPS itself. Yet Nietzsche is explicit that this is *not* his aim: he does not want to force the *majority* of people (the "herd" as he often calls them) to abandon MPS; to the contrary, he claims that MPS is, indeed, appropriate for certain types of people. Thus, he proclaims, "The ideas of the herd should rule in the herd – but not reach out beyond it." (WP: 287), noting elsewhere that "we demand that herd morality should be held sacred unconditionally" (WP: 132) and that "being an immoralist, one has to take steps against corrupting innocents" (GS: 381).

But we should be careful, at this point, not to overstate Nietzsche's aversion to the genetic fallacy. For the ultimate goal of the *Genealogy*, remember, is to free nascent higher human beings from their false consciousness about MPS, i.e., their false belief that MPS is *good for them*. From the standpoint of that normative end, Nietzsche has no reason to disown fallacious forms of reasoning as long as they are rhetorically effective. From the Sophists, as we saw in Chapter 2, Nietzsche learned the importance of good rhetoric, whose aim is "to influence action, nothing more" (Woodruff 1999: 308; cf. Mourelatos 1987). Or as Guthrie puts it, citing *Phaedrus* 267a, "Rhetoric teaches from the first that what matters is not what is the case, but what appears, what men can be persuaded of" (Guthrie 1971: 179). Thus, even if it is *not* the case that MPS's origin makes it vulnerable to internal critique, Nietzsche would hardly be sorry if his readers drew that (fallacious) inference.

The foregoing considerations, however, simply return us to the original puzzle of how, except at the level of rhetoric, genealogy contributes to critique. Nietzsche writes, for example, that, "[W]e need a *critique* of moral values, *the value of these values should itself, for once, be examined* – and so we need to know about the conditions and circumstances under which the values grew up, developed and changed" (GM Pref: 6; cf. GM I: Note).[9] Here Nietzsche makes the link explicit: we need genealogical knowledge – "about the conditions and circumstances under which the values grew up, developed and changed" – in order to "critique . . . moral values." But why? Why do the conditions and circumstances surrounding MPS's origin matter to the critical project?

We must, at this point, heed Nietzsche's parenthetical qualification in section 5 of the Preface, namely that the genealogy "(concerned me only for one purpose [i.e., to critique morality], to which it is one

Nietzsche's real aim, as we have seen, is simply to put an "end to [the] tyranny" of MPS (WP: 361), that is, to the tendency of MPS to say "stubbornly and inexorably, 'I am morality itself, and nothing besides is morality'" (BGE: 202). Given his aims, then, Nietzsche has no particular reason to prefer "internal critique" as his critical *modus operandi*.

9 In fact, as we shall see, "need" is too strong: a genealogy is one way of getting at the critique, but it is not, strictly speaking, necessary for it.

means [*Mittel*] among many)" (GM Pref: 5). The genealogy of morality, then, is but *one* instrument for arriving at a particular end, namely a critique of morality. This should alert us to the possibility that the critique of morality does not *depend* on the genealogy of morality, though the genealogy may help us arrive at it.

As we saw at length in Chapter 4, the centerpiece of Nietzsche's critique of MPS is the claim that MPS thwarts the flourishing of human excellence. The real question, then, is how genealogy is a means towards this kind of critique. Consider, again, the Preface, where Nietzsche writes as follows:

> [U]nder what conditions did man invent the value judgments good and evil? *and what value do they themselves have?* Have they up to now obstructed or promoted human flourishing? Are they a sign of distress, poverty and the degeneration of life? Or, on the contrary, do they reveal the fullness, vitality and will of life, its courage, its confidence, its future?
>
> (GM Pref: 3)

This passage suggests the following connection between genealogy and critique. The point of origin of a morality has a special *evidential* status as to the *effects* (or causal powers) of that morality, for example, as to whether morality obstructs or promotes human flourishing. This point follows from Nietzsche's Classically Realist view (see Chapter 2) that all moralities (except in cases of false consciousness) are adopted for prudential reasons, i.e., because they are in the interests of *certain types of people*. Recall that on this Calliclean picture, persons adopt moralities for self-interested reasons, because each "instinctively strives for an optimum of favourable conditions in which fully to release his power" (GM III: 7). Thus, people wouldn't have adopted morality in the first place if its *effect* wasn't to produce "favorable conditions in which" they can "release [their] power." That is, morality must have the creation of those conditions in which certain types of people flourish as one of its effects. As Nietzsche puts it in the *Nachlass*:

> Thus in the history of morality a will to power finds expression, through which now the slaves and oppressed, now the

> ill-constituted and those who suffer from themselves, now the
> mediocre attempt to make those value judgments prevail that are
> favorable to *them*.
>
> (WP: 400; cf. BGE: 187; Z I: 15;
> WP: 134, 254, 258, 675)

If this is right, then it follows that insight into the origin of MPS gives us insight into the *causal powers* of MPS: by understanding the origin, we understand the effects of adopting a particular morality. But as we saw in Chapter 4, the core of Nietzsche's critique of MPS is precisely that it has pernicious causal powers: it thwarts the flourishing of great human beings. The genealogy of morality is but one way of discovering this fact: for we discover, in the *Genealogy*, that, at its origin, MPS (because of its distinctive effects) was in the interests of the weak, base, and wretched. Notice that, in the passage from the Preface quoted above (GM Pref: 3), Nietzsche translates the question "what value do [moral values] themselves have?" into the question, "Have [these values] up to now obstructed or promoted human flourishing?" The question about the value of MPS is a question about the causal powers of MPS – its effect upon flourishing. By discovering the conditions under which these values were invented, we shed light on this question – *given* the assumption that people typically create values that are in their self-interest in virtue of those values having certain kinds of effects on the "conditions" under which they can succeed (GM III: 7).

This idea – that the origin of MPS sheds evidential light on the causal powers of MPS – is still compatible with the genealogical hypothesis that the meaning or purpose of morality is fluid over time. The causal powers belong, as it were, to the "permanent" element of MPS,[10] but it is perfectly intelligible that some object might have stable causal powers, but very different meaning or value for different peoples at different times. Thus, for example, the causal powers of the sun have been stable over time, yet its "meaning" or "purpose" as understood by human beings has been remarkably various.

---

[10] More precisely, we should say that all AEPs have causal powers – indeed, that follows from the Classically Realist view of value that Nietzsche accepts (see Chapter 2). What distinguishes MPS is that it has pernicious causal powers.

An additional virtue of this reading of the connection between genealogy and critique is that it explains why Nietzsche describes the genealogy as "one means among many" towards a critique of morality (GM Pref: 5), for we can criticize MPS on the grounds that it thwarts the flourishing of human excellence simply by showing that it *does in fact* have this effect. No recourse to the genealogy of MPS is required to establish this causal claim. (Notice, in particular, that most of Nietzsche's attacks on MPS elsewhere in his corpus proceed without any recourse to genealogical claims.) Indeed, it bears emphasizing that only the genealogy in conjunction with the thesis that the causal powers of the object are stable over time, supports the claim that MPS in fact has the pernicious effects Nietzsche attributes to it. This latter thesis would, of course, require independent defense, a defense absent in the *Genealogy*. In this respect, it really may be more accurate to say that by revealing the "shameful origin" of MPS, the *Genealogy* simply brings "a *feeling* of diminution in value of the thing that originated thus and *prepares the way* to a critical mood and attitude toward it" (WP: 254; cf. GS: 345; second emphasis added). It prepares this way by giving evidence of the pernicious causal powers of MPS, without establishing that MPS still possesses them.

Even to produce a "feeling of diminution" and to "prepare the way" for a critique is already to accomplish a project of some importance. Indeed, the style of argument involved here is familiar from many contexts. Suppose an acquaintance recommends a restaurant in glowing terms, making it sound almost too good to believe. You then learn that the origin of the acquaintance's enthusiasm for this restaurant is that he is a part-owner of the establishment! The origin does not, to be sure, refute the acquaintance's reasons to patronize the restaurant, but the discovery of this "shameful origin" surely "prepares the way to a critical mood and attitude toward[s]" these reasons. One will revisit the reasons with a skeptical eye, knowing what one now knows about the origin. So, too, Nietzsche clearly hopes that the readers of the *Genealogy* will stand ready to revisit (indeed, revalue) MPS given what he shows them about its origin and its effects.

What is the *Genealogy*?

The *Genealogy*, as we have just seen, employs the genealogical method – history rightly practiced – in order to criticize MPS. This observation constitutes only a partial answer, however, to the question of what Nietzsche's book – *On the Genealogy of Morality* – is supposed to be. Are the genealogies it recounts, for example, mere suggestive fictions, or do they claim some special epistemic standing? Does the book tell one story about the origin of MPS, or three different stories? Do the three essays that comprise the *Genealogy* bear any relation to each other, or do they stand or fall independently of each other?

Some commentators have described the "stories" in the *Genealogy* as having a "mythic quality,"[11] but we do well to remember that Nietzsche claims much more on their behalf. He professes to be offering a "real *history of morality*," one that focuses only on "that which can be documented, which can actually be confirmed and has actually existed" (GM Pref: 7). Even when describing the *Genealogy* in *Ecce Homo* two years later, he speaks of the "truth" that each essay reveals, noting that in each essay "a *new* truth [*Wahrheit*] becomes visible every time" (EH III: GM). Nietzsche clearly means the *Genealogy* to present the facts about MPS's multiple and complex origins.

A skeptical reader, however, might call attention to the complete absence of the scholarly apparatus one would associate with an inquiry into the *real* origins of MPS. In fact, almost *nothing* is documented and almost no confirming evidence (other than some etymological evidence) is cited in the text of the *Genealogy*. This decidedly unscholarly-looking book simply does not live up to the exacting standards set down in the Preface. Should we, then, discount the rhetoric of the Preface and *Ecce Homo* as mere posturing and bravado, and treat the *Genealogy* as a (perhaps) "useful fiction" about the origin of MPS?

Drawing such an inference from the absence of scholarly apparatus would, however, be too hasty. For one thing, the reader must remember that Nietzsche subtitles the book "A Polemic," and his goal,

[11] Bergmann (1988): 29; see also, May (1999), p. 52: "Nietzsche's genealogical accounts, of which that of the masters and slaves is a paradigm, are best taken as fictional."

as we have seen above and in Chapters 3 and 4, is to critique MPS, in particular, in order to free nascent higher human beings from their false consciousness about MPS. To that end, the tone and trappings of a scholarly treatise would simply be an impediment. The burden of the *Genealogy* is to force people to think the unthinkable, to question the value of MPS, a task made all the more difficult by the fact that "*the slave revolt in morality* . . . has a two thousand-year history behind it and which has only moved out of our sight today because it – has been victorious" (GM I: 7). Thus, while the *Genealogy* purports to make *true* or *factual* claims about the origins of MPS, it is manifestly not a conventional *scholarly* or *scientific* treatise, reflecting a "desire . . . for cold, pure, inconsequential knowledge" (U III: 6). Its aim is *not* to know the truth about MPS's origins for the sake of knowing that truth; rather, it is animated by the same profound normative commitment as all Nietzsche's mature work: to *revalue* existing morality.

So the normative and rhetorical ends of the *Genealogy* explain why it does not have a conventional scholarly form. Yet it certainly bears remarking that modern scholars have now largely supplied the scholarly annotations that are missing, demonstrating that in writing the *Genealogy*, Nietzsche did rely extensively on contemporary scholarly literature.[12] While not all his claims admit of simple "confirmation" in this way, many of them do. What this suggests is precisely that Nietzsche eschewed the conventional scholarly format precisely because his normative and rhetorical goals were far more important and demanded a "polemic," not a dry academic treatise.

The unity of the *Genealogy*

A more difficult interpretive question concerns the unity of the three essays that comprise the *Genealogy*. The question has often been prejudged by the practice of many English translators (most famously Kaufmann) of rendering the title as "On the Genealogy of Morals"

---

[12] See the Endnotes in Clark and Swensen (1998); see also Thatcher (1989); KSA 14: 377–82. Unpublished work by Thomas Brobjer on the sources for the *Genealogy* complements the cited sources. For additional, sympathetic confirmation of Nietzsche's etymological evidence, see Migotti (1998): 767–70.

(*Zur Genealogie der Moral*), thus implying (in principle) that the book is a genealogy not of one thing (namely, morality) but of something with a possibly plural nature (namely, morals). As Clark observes: "Kaufmann's translation of the singular '*Moral*' as 'morals,' while not wrong, has tended to encourage those who deny that the book offers any kind of unified theory" (1994: 22; cf. Clark and Swensen 1998: 119). But a translation should not prejudice the issue in this way; rather, it should reflect the conclusions of an interpretive argument about the unity of the book. Since the book, as we shall see shortly, is best construed as a unified account, not just methodologically but thematically, translating the title as "Morality" makes more sense.[13]

We have already alluded, of course, to the *methodological* unity of the *Genealogy*, namely, to its attempt to explain the origin of morality in naturalistic terms, in particular by appeal to naturally occurring psychological mechanisms found in creatures like us: *ressentiment* (GM I), internalized cruelty (GM II), will to power (GM III). The general project, however, is not entirely new with the *Genealogy*. Nietzsche first broaches the question of the origin of morality in *Human, All-too-Human*, and revisits the theme in *Daybreak* and *Beyond Good and Evil*.[14] It is worth pausing for a moment to look at how the critique of morality, and its naturalistic explanation, evolved through these earlier works.

As its very title suggests, *Human, All-too-Human* seeks to "explain the so-called 'higher' activities – art, religion, and morality

13 Some commentators have also contested the translation of "Zur" as "on," instead of "towards." Once again, the German commands neither translation; a sensible decision must be predicated on a plausible interpretive hypothesis about the book and how the title would bear on that hypothesis. Those who favor "towards" generally do so because they are under the influence of "postmodernist" readings of Nietzsche, and thus think it more appropriately "modest" as a title, implying as it does that Nietzsche does not think he has offered the final word on the subject. It seems odd, though, to think of the *Genealogy* – a long, systematic polemic, distinguished by its often contemptuous dismissal of other historians of morality, as well as its immodest aim of overturning MPS – as reflecting any modesty of method or ambition.

14 A particularly useful feature of the Cambridge edition of the *Genealogy* is that it contains translations of all the earlier texts by Nietzsche to which he alludes in the *Genealogy*, and thus is an excellent place to begin for an overview of Nietzsche's earlier attempts at genealogy.

– which are often taken as signs of human participation in a higher or metaphysical realm (HA: 10) ... in terms of the 'lower,' the merely human" (Clark and Leiter 1997: xx). This naturalistic ambition, as we have seen, remains intact in the *Genealogy*. But in *Human, All-too-Human*, the primary explanatory device involves exposing the egoistic roots of what *appear*, initially, to be non-egoistic phenomena. Thus, in this early work, Nietzsche attacks morality very much in the spirit of the French aphorist LaRochefoucauld, revealing apparently "moral" actions as concealing selfish motives.

Maudemarie Clark, who has done the most to illuminate the evolution of Nietzsche's philosophical views, has argued that Nietzsche's critique of morality progresses beyond the early strategy evinced in *Human, All-too-Human*. In Nietzsche's next major work, *Daybreak*, Clark argues that Nietzsche no longer assumes that morality is merely a veneer, behind which selfish motives lurk; rather he assumes that morality is a *real* phenomenon, in the sense that moral reasons *really* motivate people. Thus, in *Daybreak*, he attacks the reasons morality offers as *bad* reasons (Clark 1998a: 17–18; cf. Clark and Leiter 1997: xx–xxvi). By contrast, "By the time he wrote *Genealogy*, Nietzsche's position has changed [from that in *Daybreak*]. ... His ultimate problem with morality is no longer that it does not give us good reasons but, as he suggests in ... [the] preface, that it stands in the way of a kind of human perfection" (Clark 1998a: 18, 19).[15] Thus, Clark concludes:

> The project of a genealogy of morality is thus to explain in purely naturalistic terms, without appeal to the voice of God or an immortal soul in touch with eternal values, the origins of morality: how it came about that human beings are guided by

[15] Cf. Clark and Leiter (1997): xxxiv: "Nietzsche reached the perspective of his *Genealogy* only by overcoming the accounts of the origins of morality offered [in *Daybreak*, i.e., in terms of a "naturalized Kantian interpretation of the morality of custom". *Daybreak*'s] importance to us may lie primarily in its ability to show that his later genealogy of morality did not emerge from thin air nor spring full-blown from Nietzsche's head, but was the product of a serious and sustained effort to understand what morality is and how it could have arisen on the assumption that it is a purely natural phenomenon." On the "morality of custom," see Clark and Leiter (1997): xxviii–xxxiv.

morality. The question is not why we are morally good, but why it is that human animals accept (hence act on the basis of) specifically *moral* reasons or values.

(1998a: 26–7)

We may agree with this account in two respects: first, of course, in its contention that Nietzsche seeks a *naturalistic* explanation for morality; and second, in the suggestion that the question is "not why we are morally good, but why it is that human animals accept" morality. Where we must be cautious is – perhaps surprisingly – with respect to Clark's parenthetical: it is not at all clear that Nietzsche thinks most people "act on the basis of morality" or that they "are guided by morality."

The distinction we must attend to here is between (a) what people *actually* do as well as their *real* reasons for doing it, and (b) how they publicly *evaluate* actions (theirs and others), that is, the standards of value they profess allegiance to in their judgments. As we saw in Chapter 2, the Classical Realism of Thucydides is manifest, in part, in his intentional collapse of this distinction: that is, Thucydides' actors say openly what they are *really* doing and *why* they are doing it. In portraying them this way, Thucydides is exposing the farcical hypocrisy of ordinary life, in which the distinction is honored, in which all actors profess allegiance to altruism and justice, while in reality they pursue their selfish interests and regard "justice" as a requirement only among those with equal power. Contrary to Clark, it is not clear that Nietzsche ever abandons this view. Thus, even in *Daybreak*, he still speaks of egoistic actions as having "hitherto been by far the most frequent actions," and notes that they "will continue to be [the most frequent] for all future time" (D: 148). (Nietzsche proposes only that we deprive such actions "*of their bad conscience*" (D: 148).) And in a work of his last productive year, he describes politicians as "anti-Christians through and through in their deeds," and remarks on the irony that they, nonetheless, "still call themselves Christians": "what a *miscarriage of falseness* [*eine Missgeburt von Falschheit*] must modern man be," he concludes (A: 38). But "modern man" is only a "miscarriage of falseness" because he professes "Christian" (i.e., moral) values, while acting in an unChristian (i.e., immoral) fashion.

This Realistic picture is not fundamentally different from the one that informs *Human, All-too-Human*.

If Nietzsche does not, in fact, think most people act in accordance with morality, but simply profess allegiance to it, then why does he think MPS is so harmful? Recall the core of Nietzsche's critical worry about MPS as outlined in Chapter 4: namely, that a nascent creative genius should come to take MPS so seriously that he fails to realize his genius. Rather than tolerate (even welcome) suffering, he will seek relief from hardship and devote himself to the pursuit of pleasure; rather than practice what Nietzsche calls "severe self-love," and attend to himself in the ways requisite for productive creative work, he will embrace the ideology of altruism, and reject "self-love" as improper; rather than learn how to look down on himself, to desire to overcome his present self and become something better, he will embrace the prevailing rhetoric of equality – captured nicely in the pop-psychology slogan "I'm OK, you're OK" – and thus never learn to feel the contempt for self that might lead one to strive for something more. It is not, then, that Nietzsche thinks people *practice* too much altruism – after all it is Nietzsche, as we have just seen, who notes that egoistic actions "have hitherto been by far the most frequent actions" (D: 148) – but rather that they *believe* too much in the value of altruism, equality, happiness, and the other characteristic norms of MPS. It is the prevalence of moral *ideology* that worries Nietzsche: for even if there is neither much altruism nor equality in the world, there is almost universal endorsement of the *value* of altruism and equality – even, notoriously (and as Nietzsche seemed well aware: e.g., A: 38), by those who are its worst enemies in practice. Nietzsche's claim is that a culture which embraces the ideology of MPS – even if it does not act in accordance with this ideology – presents the real threat to the realization of human excellence, because it teaches potential higher types to disvalue what would be most conducive to their creativity and value what is irrelevant or perhaps even hostile to it.

Now surely Nietzsche is right that individuals of great creativity and sensitivity are far more likely to take MPS seriously than the politicians whose hypocrisy he derides in the remark quoted earlier. As Nietzsche observes at one point: "What distinguishes the higher human beings from the lower is that the former see and hear immeasurably more, and see and hear more thoughtfully" (GS: 301). But it is precisely this trait of the "higher human beings" that makes them all the more susceptible to the deleterious effects of MPS: a thoughtless brute is hardly likely to worry about the morality of his acts – nor is he likely to become a creative genius. But the higher types that Nietzsche worries about are both likely candidates for critical self-reflection in light of moral norms and, at the same time, those for whom such norms are most harmful. Indeed, as we have argued, it is precisely Nietzsche's aim to help these higher human beings "see and hear" something more: namely, that moral values are really disadvantageous for them.

That Nietzsche's concern is with the prevalence of MPS as an ideology – not the prevalence of actions in accord with MPS – and, in particular, with the effect of this ideology on the *self-conception* of potentially higher types, is suggested in many places. In *Daybreak*, he speaks of wanting to deprive egoistic actions of "their bad conscience" (148). In *Beyond Good and Evil*, Nietzsche observes that in order to "[s]tand all valuations *on their head*," Christianity had to

> cast suspicion on the joy in beauty, bend everything haughty . . . conquering, domineering, all the instincts characteristic of the highest and best-turned-out type of "man," into unsureness, dilemma of conscience [*Gewissens-Noth*], self-destruction.
>
> (BGE: 62)

In *Twilight of the Idols*, he describes the "man" "improved" by MPS as

> a caricature of man, like a miscarriage: he had become a "sinner," he was stuck in a cage, *imprisoned among all sorts of terrible concepts* [*schreckliche Begriffe*]. And there he lay, sick, miserable, malevolent against himself: full of hatred against the springs of life, full of suspicion against all that was still strong and happy.
>
> (TI VII: 2, emphasis added)

In each case, we see that the thrust of the worry is that higher types will come to evaluate and think of themselves in terms of the *concepts* peculiar to MPS (and Christianity) – that they will become "imprisoned among all sorts of terrible concepts" – with the result that they will be cast into self-doubt and a destructive self-loathing, and thus never realize the excellences of which they are capable.

His general point is perhaps most strikingly put in a very Calliclean passage from *Beyond Good and Evil*:

> The highest and strongest drives, when they break out passionately and drive the individual far above the average and the flats of the herd conscience, wreck the self-confidence of the community. ... Hence just these drives are branded and slandered most. High and independent spirituality, the will to stand alone, even a powerful reason are experienced as dangers; everything that elevates an individual above the herd and intimidates the neighbor is henceforth called *evil*; and the fair, modest, conforming mentality, the *mediocrity* of desires attains moral designations and honors.

(BGE: 201)

"High and independent spirituality", "the will to stand alone": these traits clearly resonate with those we saw (in Chapter 4) that Nietzsche attributes to the higher human being. Yet it is these traits that MPS "brands" and "slanders" – and who would be surprised if someone should abandon their independent ways with the force of morality against them? It is not, then, that there is too much pity and altruism in the world, but rather that there is too much *belief in the value* of pity, altruism and the other distinctive norms of MPS.

Thus, we need to sever Clark's equation between "taking morality seriously" and "acting on the basis of moral reasons." Nietzsche does, indeed, conceive the puzzle as one of explaining why human beings would come to profess this kind of morality as the dominant standard of evaluation; but he does not, it appears, depart from the Classical Realist view that, whatever people say, most of them act on the basis of non-moral reasons. Frithjof Bergmann puts Nietzsche's question well and suitably dramatically:

> Nietzsche raises a question, not mildly, or in quietly bemused philosophical wonder, but in outrage, and consternation, in an

effort to ring a storm-bell and to wake us up. He asks: how was it ever possible for meekness, humility and self-denial, modesty, pity and compassion to become *values*? What happened? For it is weird and monstrous and dumbfounding, and precisely the kind of unnatural untowardness that cries out for explanation.

The question is not: why do so many feign modesty to hide their arrogance, or make a show of pity while they gloat with malice? Pretense and hypocrisy are not the issue. That query would be mild and common and would still reconfirm and bow before these values. And exactly that is what Nietzsche wants to undercut and to deny. The question, rather, is: how can one fathom or imagine the process through which these qualities were elevated into values? How were they placed upon this pedestal – since on the face of it they so clearly have no claim to this status?

(Bergmann 1988: 29)

Bergmann's framing of the question does bring out one respect in which Clark has correctly identified a change from the period of *Human, All-too-Human*: there, Nietzsche's goal was largely to expose the hypocrisy of people's moral posturing. But such a critique, as both Bergmann and Clark observe, continues to accept the view that pity or altruism *has* value. Beginning with *Daybreak*, Nietzsche's posture shifts, and he is now ready to ask about the value of these values themselves. (In that sense, *Daybreak* marks the beginning of the revaluation of all values, as Nietzsche himself remarks [EH III: D-1].) What we must reject is Clark's further suggestion that Nietzsche thinks people actually act *on the basis* of MPS. It suffices for setting Nietzsche's problem if people take MPS seriously, even if they continue to act amorally in reality. The question then is: why? Why do people take such a morality seriously at all?

We have now seen a unity of both *method* and *problematic* in the *Genealogy*. Each essay employs the method of genealogy, i.e., a naturalistic history which identifies the naturally occurring psychological mechanisms that figure in the origin of MPS; and each essay contributes to a solution of the problem of how human beings came to take MPS seriously. In a passage that justifies Bergmann's vivid rendering of the problem, Nietzsche himself writes in the third essay of the *Genealogy* regarding our "ascetic" (or life-denying) morality as follows:

> Such a monstrous method of valuation is not inscribed in the records of human history as an exception and curiosity: it is one of the most wide-spread and long-lived facts there are. Read from a distant planet, the majuscule script of our earthly existence would perhaps seduce the reader to the conclusion that the earth was the ascetic planet *par excellence*, an outpost of discontented, arrogant and nasty creatures who harboured a deep disgust for themselves, for the world, for all life and hurt themselves as much as possible out of pleasure in hurting: – probably their only pleasure.

(GM III: 11)

It is the central puzzle of the *Genealogy* to explain how such a state of affairs came to pass, how it is that Christianity, Judaism, Buddhism, Islam, Hinduism and, most importantly, their distinctively ascetic moralities came to have such a profound hold upon the human mind.

How it came to pass is precisely what the three essays of the *Genealogy* tell us. The origin of the now predominant "ascetic" morality is, of course, not unitary: three different kinds of phenomena – and three different kinds of naturally occurring psychological mechanisms – went into producing this morality in its present form. The first, textually but not chronologically (the subject of GM I), concerns an actual historical event: the triumph of Christianity and Christian morality in the late Roman Empire. Nietzsche does not purport to set out all the causes of this dramatic historical transformation, only to focus on the one central to the moral psychology of the event: the role of the psychological state Nietzsche calls *ressentiment* in the creation of the distinctive structure of evaluation characteristic of what Nietzsche calls "slave morality." But how is it that such a morality triumphed? Why would the "masters" of the ancient world adopt a morality that was, at bottom, a piece of prudence on the part of slaves? The answer is never explicitly set out in the First Essay.

The second major event (the subject of GM II) is actually the first chronologically:[16] it calls our attention to an event from pre-history, as it were, a psychological precondition of any type of human society at all, namely, that creatures like us give up the outward expression of our natural aggressive and cruel instincts. Civilized intercourse would, of course, be impossible if we gave such instincts free rein. But abandoning the external expression of such instincts is not without costs; these cruel instincts do not disappear, but turn inward, finding expression in *bad conscience*, a form of internalized cruelty to oneself. Most importantly, though, Nietzsche wants to examine how this capacity for bad conscience became transformed into a *moralized* form of internal regulation, one in which self-regulation is deeply inter-twined with self-flagellation, self-loathing and concepts like "guilt" and "sin." The difficulty is precisely that the Greeks and Romans, as members of civilized societies, *must*, given the argument of the Second Essay of the *Genealogy*, have had a bad conscience: what they did not have was a fully *moralized* bad conscience (i.e., they did not experience *guilt*). A puzzling feature of the Second Essay, as we shall see, is that it does not fully answer the question of how bad conscience became *moralized* – and yet it is this moralized bad conscience that is essential to the moral psychology of morality as we now find it.

The Third Essay answers the questions left open by the earlier essays – why did slave morality triumph? why did bad conscience turn into guilt? – and thus brings the book to a satisfying close.[17] What slave morality and the moralized bad conscience have in common is that they give expression to what Nietzsche calls "the ascetic ideal." Masters accept slave morality because, at bottom, they fall prey to the attractions of the ascetic ideal. Bad conscience becomes moralized because it serves the ascetic ideal. The crucial question then becomes: *why* would creatures like us have become so taken with the ascetic

---

[16] See Dennett (1995: 462).

[17] As Risse (2001: 55) points out, Nietzsche, in an 1888 postcard to Overbeck, suggested that more essays could have been added to the *Genealogy* and that, as a result, the book does not offer "a final account of morality." That point – penned two years, of course, after writing the *Genealogy* – is still compat-ible, however, with the three essays Nietzsche did write having more unity than Nietzsche himself calls attention to in the text.

ideal? At bottom, this is the critical explanatory question of the whole book. And its answer must meet the demands of Nietzsche's central naturalistic hypothesis: namely, that "every animal ... instinctively strives for an optimum of favourable conditions in which fully to release his power and achieve his maximum feeling of power" (GM III: 7). The surprise, as it were, of the Third Essay is that even the ascetic ideal – a seemingly life-denying ideal – fulfills such an instinctive striving. For the vast majority of creatures like us, Nietzsche claims, the ascetic ideal renders life bearable – hence its remarkable success, hence its global dominion.

This brief account of the dialectic unity of the *Genealogy*'s argument still omits mention of one variable: the role of those Nietzsche calls "the priests." For the priests are assigned a central role in bringing about the triumph of slave morality and the ascetic ideal in the First and Third Essays. Indeed, Nietzsche's own summary of the *Genealogy* two years later in *Ecce Homo* concludes with the claim that the former "contains the first psychology of the priest" (III: GM). Later, in the same book, he notes that the dominion of Christian or ascetic morality

> still leave[s] open the possibility that not humanity is degenerating but only that parasitical type of man – that of the *priest* – which has used morality to raise itself mendaciously to the position of determining human values – finding in Christian morality the means to come to *power*. – Indeed, this is *my* insight: the teachers, the leaders of humanity, theologians all of them, were also, all of them decadents: *hence* the revaluation of all values into hostility to life, *hence* morality –
>
> *Definition of morality*: Morality – the idiosyncrasy of decadents, with the ulterior motive of revenging oneself against life.
>
> (EH IV: 7)

In fact, as we shall see in Chapter 8, Nietzsche's claim here is not consistent with the argument of the Third Essay. While it is true that the priest plays an important instrumental role in bringing about the dominion of the ascetic ideal, the argument of the Third Essay depends on the assumption that there is a naturalistic explanation for why the vast majority of human beings would find such an ideal attractive once presented with it. The argument of the *Genealogy*, in short, seems to be precisely that "humanity" – or at least the vast bulk of humanity – "is degenerating."

Chapter 6

A commentary on the First Essay

The truth of the *first* inquiry is the birth of Christianity: the birth of Christianity out of the spirit of *ressentiment*, not, as people may believe, out of the "spirit" – a countermovement by its very nature, the great rebellion against the dominion of *noble* values.

(EH III: GM).

Nietzsche suggests the essential argument of the most famous of the three essays of the *Genealogy* in its title – "'Good and Evil', 'Good and Bad'" ["*Gut und Böse*", "*Gut und Schlecht*"] – and develops it in the summary he penned two years later in *Ecce Homo* (see above).[1] According to the First Essay, the morality associated with Christianity is not some timeless bequest from God, a case of divine inspiration implanted in the soul of man, but rather the prudent creation of *particular*

---

[1]   Actually, the best short guide to the core argument of the First Essay is BGE: 260, from which I will quote liberally in this chapter.

kinds of people (slaves or the oppressed) at a particular historical moment (roughly, the Roman Empire *circa* the 1st through 3rd centuries AD) and for reasons that are explicable in naturalistic (more precisely, psychological) terms. That this morality is the product of a particular historical event "has only been lost sight of because [this morality] was victorious" (GM I: 7). What we have lost sight of is that a morality which attaches a positive valence to a cluster of related practices and attitudes (like altruism, pity, and egalitarianism), and whose central evaluative axes revolve around the distinction between "good" and "evil" (*böse*) actions, is, in fact, a radically new and different mode of evaluation compared to the "noble" mode of evaluation that preceded it. Such a morality is the *self-interested* creation of a *class* of people who are reacting against their social and economic circumstances in the only way they can: unable to overthrow their oppressors by physical force, they *create* values that *devalue* the oppressors, which ultimately leads to their abnegation. In doing this, the oppressed must offer a new assessment of the radically different normative universe of their oppressors, one which revolves around the axes of evaluating "good" and "bad" (*schlecht*) persons. Driving this creation forward is a distinctive psychological state found in creatures like us: what Nietzsche calls *ressentiment*. The morality of Christianity is in fact the product of the *ressentiment* felt by the oppressed against their oppressors, which resulted in the *first* revaluation of values, the replacement of the "good/bad" evaluative scheme of the oppressors (roughly, the nobility of the late Roman Empire) with the "good/evil" evaluative scheme of the oppressed (the slaves and oppressed of the empire).

If the basic outline of the story of the First Essay is simple, the questions it raises are many and complex. Why exactly have we lost sight of this momentous historical event? In what sense is a psychological mechanism adequate to explain an historic transformation in values of the scope Nietzsche describes? How does such a mechanism operate? What precisely distinguishes a morality of "good and evil" from a morality of "good and bad"? And, most perplexing of all, why should this revaluation have been successful, given the advantage in resources and arms of the oppressors? We shall take up these questions in turn and, in the course of exploring the answers, examine the arguments of the First Essay.

Explaining historical blindness

If "noble" modes of evaluation were usurped roughly two millennia ago, why would this be unknown to Nietzsche's readers? Of course, in one sense it is not news that Christianity supplanted paganism, that Christians were, as legend has it, thrown to the lions by the Romans, and that the gradual spread of Christianity throughout the empire, initially among the oppressed classes but culminating with the conversion of the Emperor Constantine, marked a major historical transformation in values and attitudes (for example, towards sex).

What is supposed to constitute surprising information for Nietzsche's readers are not these textbook historical facts – which make little or no appearance in the First Essay – but something rather different: the claim that the *morality* associated with Christianity was a *creation* of certain kinds of people who were moved by prudential or self-interested considerations which led them to *revalue* or *invert* other moral values. The morality of altruism was, in fact, a piece of self-interested (albeit half-conscious) "calculation" by the oppressed.[2] That, a bit too crudely expressed, is what history has missed.

In this regard, it bears emphasizing that, despite the fact that Nietzsche speaks in *Ecce Homo* of "the birth of Christianity," he is not really interested at all in the origin of the religious cosmology, institutions, and rituals distinctive of Christianity; indeed, he is not even interested in *Christianity*, per se, as should be apparent from the way he uses Judaism and Christianity interchangeably in describing his target (e.g., GM I: 9 where he writes "everything is being made appreciably Jewish, Christian or plebeian (never mind the words!)"). What he is interested in is the *morality* distinctive of Judaism and Christianity. That is why he distinguishes himself from the so-called "free thinkers," whose slogan is: "We loathe the Church, *not* its poison. . . . Apart from the Church, we too love the poison" (GM I: 9). The poison – the fruit of the "slave revolt" in morals, the distinctive evaluative axes of the morality of "good and evil" – is what Nietzsche opposes.

Nietzsche, of course, tells us that "*the slaves' revolt in morality* begins with the Jews" (GM I: 7), but is equally clear that, "We know

---

2   Vengeance, to be sure, was another important motive for the "slave revolt," as will become clear in the discussion of *ressentiment*, below.

who became heir to this Jewish revaluation" (GM I: 7), namely, Christianity. And should anyone really miss his meaning – and his rhetoric about the Jews is, to be sure, inflammatory in the early sections of the Essay – the culminating section of the First Essay makes it clear. He writes:

> The two *opposing* values "good and bad," "good and evil" have fought a terrible battle for thousands of years on earth. . . . The symbol of this fight . . . is "Rome against Judea, Judea against Rome."
>
> Which of them has *prevailed* for the time being, Rome or Judea? But there is no trace of doubt: just consider whom you bow down to in Rome itself, today, as though to the embodiment of the highest values – and not just in Rome, but over nearly half the earth?

(GM I: 16)

In other words, the proof of the triumph of "Judea" is that the *Catholic Pope* now rules in Rome! Nietzsche even goes so far in this concluding section to identify how "the Jews feel about [classical] Rome" with the *New* (i.e., Christian) Testament's "Apocalypse of John, the wildest of all outbursts ever written which revenge has on its conscience," adding, parenthetically, a comment about "the profound consistency of *Christian* instinct in inscribing this book of hate to the disciple of love" (emphasis added). And although the Renaissance represented "a brilliant, uncanny reawakening of the classical ideal, of the noble method of valuing everything" it too was defeated by "Judea . . . thanks to that basically proletarian (German and English) *ressentiment*-movement which people called the Reformation" (GM I: 16).

"Judea" then, and even "Jew" are interchangeable for Nietzsche with Catholic, Protestant, and Christianity: and it is not the rituals, the institutions, the cosmology associated with these religions that he opposes (though he plainly rejects all that too), but the *morality* they promulgate, the mode of evaluation for which they stand.

Our failure to recognize the peculiar facts about the origin of Judeo-Christian morality is attributable by Nietzsche to three causes: (1) the triumph of this morality, (2) the misleading histories produced by "these English psychologists" (GM I: 1), and (3) lack of the relevant philological expertise and sensitivity (until Nietzsche). Let us consider these causes in turn.

"[T]he slaves' revolt in morality," says Nietzsche, "has two thousand years of history behind it and ... has only been lost sight of because – it was victorious." (GM I: 7). This, in a nutshell, is the primary obstacle to the story Nietzsche wants to tell: we simply no longer even realize that our morality is itself the outgrowth of an earlier *revaluation* of values, precisely because that earlier revaluation has been so successful. This morality now "says stubbornly and inexorably, 'I am morality itself, and nothing besides is morality'" (BGE: 202), so that the question never arises, "How did this morality come about?" or "What are alternatives to this morality?" The success of the slave revolt makes such questions seem idle or nonsensical: idle, because they seek an answer to a question no one feels the need to ask; nonsensical, because any "alternative" would not even be a "morality."

Of course, the success of the slave revolt in morals has not been total, since Nietzsche allows that remnants of the opposed "master morality" remain with us (BGE: 260). But the point is that what remains are evaluative concepts whose heritage can be traced to "master morality," not any self-conscious awareness of this heritage and how it differs from the dominant evaluative concepts which derive from the slave revolt.

Yet success alone is not enough to explain our historical blindness, since, after all, that blindness is not, as noted earlier, complete: we are dimly aware, for example, that pagan morality differs from Christian. What has compounded the problem, according to Nietzsche, is *bad* existing "histories" of morality and a general lack of appropriate intellectual tools, notably philological ones.

The existing histories are those he attributes to "[t]hese English psychologists" (GM I: 1), a term he is using extremely loosely, since the primary example he discusses is actually one by a *German*, his friend Paul Rée (1849–1901), author of *The Origin of Moral Feelings* (1877).[3] It is true that, in the early 1880s, Nietzsche had been reading

---

[3] Nietzsche met Rée in 1873, and the 1877 book "owed a great deal to discussions with Nietzsche," as Rée's own letters acknowledge. See Kaufmann (1974): 48. Brobjer (forthcoming) reports that Nietzsche's personal copy of

W. E. H. Lecky's *History of European Morals* (1869), a work which discusses authors such as the Scotsman Hume and the English philosophers Hutcheson, Bentham, and Mill, among others, all of whom were concerned in various ways with the nature and origin of moral sentiments. Yet the precise hypothesis about origins that Nietzsche actually criticizes is this one: "'Originally ... unegoistic acts were praised and called good by their recipients, in other words, by the people to whom they were *useful*; later, everyone *forgot* the origin of the praise and because such acts had always been *routinely* praised as good, people began to experience them as good'" (GM I: 2).[4] This argument, however, comes from Rée, not these other thinkers.[5]

Now these "English" histories (and their authors) are not without merit, as GM: 1 emphasizes, for, like Nietzsche, they are willing to entertain the possibility of "a plain, bitter, ugly, foul, unchristian, immoral truth" (GM I: 1). The difficulty is that they make the historical mistake we discussed in Chapter 5: from the *current* meaning or value of some practice they draw a (fallacious) inference about its origin (though, of course, the two might, *by chance*, correspond). So, for example, because it is "useful" if those around us are altruistic, the "English psychologists" infer that the utility of altruism explains the origin of the positive moral valence attached to it. Yet Nietzsche insists that we follow Darwin in recognizing that *current* function or value is one thing, while the function or value at the time of origin is another. Of course, there is no a priori reason to think that present function might not pick out the original cause (even if the inference from the former to the latter is fallacious); the reasons for disputing the coincidence are, as in Darwin, a posteriori.

> *The Origin of Moral Feelings* bears a handwritten inscription from the author as follows: "To the father of this book, with gratefulness from its mother."

4   This account sounds misleadingly like Nietzsche's own account of the origin of slave morality. The difference, however, is that Rée emphasizes the *phenomenology* of those who are the beneficiaries of altruistic acts: they are imagined to experience these as pleasant and useful. Nietzsche, by contrast, claims that slave morality is in the *interests* of slaves, whatever its phenomenology for them. Of course, the primary phenomenological aspect of the slave revolt, according to Nietzsche, is *ressentiment*, discussed below.

5   For discussion, see Thatcher (1989) and Clark and Swensen (1998: 129).

In the case of Rée's hypothesis about the origin of the morality of altruism, for example, Nietzsche rejects it because it is both "historically untenable" (GM I: 3) – about which more in a moment – and because it "suffers from an inner psychological contradiction" (GM I: 3), namely, that it is utterly implausible to think that anyone would have *forgotten* that altruism is useful: "this usefulness has been a permanent part of our everyday experience" (GM I: 3). But given that fact, Rée's explanation collapses: for if people cannot possibly have forgotten that altruism is useful, then they would realize that they only praise it because it is *useful to them*, i.e., because it is in their self-interest! That kind of stark moral hypocrisy would create an intolerable dissonance in our moral thinking and psychology, and thus it is implausible we could have forgotten such a self-interested origin of our valuation of altruism.

How, though, does Nietzsche know Rée's account of the origin of morality is "historically untenable" (as opposed to simply psychologically implausible)? Here is where philological expertise, of the kind Nietzsche has, plays an important role: "I was given a pointer in the *right* direction by the question as to what the terms for 'good,' as used in different languages, mean from the etymological point of view" (GM I: 4).[6] For what the etymology of the various words for "good"

---

6   Although Nietzsche lays the most emphasis on etymology as the clue to the *real* origins of morality, it is worth noting that he actually calls for *three* different methods of investigation in the First Essay: historical (GM I: 2); etymological (GM I: 4) and physiological (GM I: Note). Commentators typically conflate the first two – and ignore the third altogether. Yet each of these investigations contributes to the same critical project that we discussed in Chapter 4: that is, they illuminate the *types* of people for whom morality (MPS) is beneficial. For example, in the Note at the end of the First Essay, Nietzsche suggests that the physiological investigation of values would be needed to distinguish those values which "obviously had value with regard to the longest possible life-span of the race" as opposed to those which would contribute to "developing a stronger type" of human being. He adds: "The well-being of the majority and the well-being of the minority are conflicting evaluative viewpoints." All three inquiries suggested in the First Essay illuminate precisely this point – and, in particular, the correlation of moral values with the viewpoint of the former. Cf. D: 453: "it is from ['our sciences'] that the foundation stones of new ideals (if not the new ideals themselves) must come." Notice, of course, that science does not *create* new ideals, it just lays

(*gut*) reveals is that they start out as co-extensional with words for "spiritually noble," "aristocratic" and "spiritually privileged," while the words for "bad" (*schlecht*) express the concepts of "common," "plebeian," and "low" (GM I: 4; cf. p. 5).[7] He states the basic insight clearly in the work preceding the *Genealogy*: "The moral discrimination of values has originated either among a ruling group whose consciousness of its difference from the ruled group was accompanied by delight – or among the ruled, the slaves and dependents of every degree" (BGE: 260).

Nietzsche chooses the words "noble"/"master" and "slave" to describe the opposed "moral discrimination[s] of values" precisely because he thinks *actual* class differences were central to the origin of the moral concepts at issue.[8] In explaining the origin of master morality, Nietzsche appeals to "the continuing and predominant feeling of complete and fundamental superiority of a higher ruling kind in relation to a lower kind, to those 'below'" (GM I: 2). He says "that everywhere, 'noble,' 'aristocratic' in a social [or class] sense is the basic concept from which, necessarily, 'good' . . . developed" (GM I: 4).[9] And he remarks that "the concept of political superiority always resolves itself into the concept of psychological superiority" which is then expressed by the various moral concepts (GM I: 6); it is only the "democratic bias" (GM I: 4) of the modern age that has obscured this point. Finally, in recounting "the secret of how *ideals are fabricated on this earth*," Nietzsche imagines the slaves saying "that . . . they [are]

the "foundation"; the creation of new ideals is the work of philosophers-cum-legislators. See the discussion of German Materialism in Chapter 2.

7 The plausibility of Nietzsche's etymological claims receives interesting support from the discussion in Migotti (1998): 767–8.

8 In the *Genealogy*, Nietzsche does not in fact use the term "master morality" (*Herren-Moral*), a phrase that he only employs in his prior work, *Beyond Good and Evil* (260). In the *Genealogy*, Nietzsche draws the contrast rather with "noble" (*vornehm*) morality (e.g., GM I: 10), though he does once refer to "The Masters" (*Die Herren*) (GM I: 9). By contrast, Nietzsche does use the phrase *Sklaven-Moral* (slave morality) in both the *Genealogy* and *Beyond Good and Evil*.

9 Literally, Nietzsche speaks not of "in a social sense" but *im ständischen Sinne*, i.e., "in the sense of the estates."

better than the powerful, the masters of the world whose spittle they have to lick" (GM I: 14).

If class differences figure centrally in the explanation of the *origin* of the morality of good and evil, Nietzsche also plainly intends the terms "master" and "slave" to be understood in a *psychological* sense as well: i.e., as denoting certain distinctive psychological and moral attitudes such that a member of the ruling class in a socio-economic sense may nonetheless be "slavish" in his morality. (This turns out to be crucial for understanding the important section 13 of the First Essay, as we will see shortly.) Thus, once again, when introducing his insight into the origin of master morality, he says the concept of "good" here connoted "spiritually [*seelisch*] noble" (or "noble of soul"), "spiritually highminded" and "spiritually privileged" (GM I: 4). And although "good" may correlate with "superiority of power" or being "rich" or "propertied," what really matters is that the labels "also show a *typical character trait* [*Charakterzug*]" (GM I: 5). In other words, the concept of "good" in the hands of the masters connotes a distinctive psychological or characterological state, and not *simply* class position: "later 'good' and 'bad' develop in a direction which no longer refers to social standing" (GM I: 6). As a consequence, someone might have the distinctive psychological state, but not the class position. As Simon May usefully puts it: "'slave' and 'master' are intended to apply to *manners* of thought and being, exemplifiable across a broad range of human activities, rather than simply to historical individuals" (1999: 51)[10] – though, to reiterate, in the first instance, they *do* apply to "historical individuals" from different social classes. But the "manners of thought and being" survive the collapse of the class differences. What exactly those slavish and masterly psychological traits amount to are what we will turn to in the following two sections: first, by looking at the most important psychological trait of the "slavish," *ressentiment*, and second, by examining the resulting contrast between the "slave" morality of "good and evil" and the "master" morality of "good and bad" that the former displaces.

---

[10]   Cf. Richardson (1996): 52–8.

Ressentiment

"The beginning of the slaves' revolt in morality," writes Nietzsche, "occurs when *ressentiment* itself turns creative and gives birth to values: the *ressentiment* of those beings who, being denied the proper response of action, compensate for it only with imaginary revenge" (GM I: 10). *Ressentiment* is a distinctive psychological state that is the core of the First Essay's contribution to a naturalistic explanation of morality's origins. What, then, is *ressentiment* and how does it work?[11]

The psychological state Nietzsche calls *ressentiment* is often taken as a particular instance of a more general "psychological" *condition* – i.e., a person's whole way of being or mode of orientation towards the world – that Nietzsche calls "reactive," and that some commentators take to be central to Nietzsche's thinking.[12] The label of this more general condition is useful in calling our attention to the fact that *ressentiment* is a reactive state: it is a feeling that arises *in response* or *as a reaction* to some state of affairs. But not just any state of affairs suffices to produce *ressentiment*: it must be a state of affairs that is both *unpleasant* to the affected person and one which he is powerless to alter through physical action.[13] In the case of the slaves,

---

[11] Bittner (1994: 128) points out that, "The German word [*ressentiment*] . . . needs to be distinguished from the French word spelled and pronounced alike, which is also its source. The words need to be distinguished because they differ in sense. . . . [B]oth 'to resent' in English and '*ressentir*' in French suggest a more straightforward annoyance, less of a grudge than the German word does." Bittner's point is confirmed by the fact that in the German, Nietzsche does *not* italicize "ressentiment" except for occasional emphasis: Nietzsche treats the word like any other German word. This, of course, is lost in the English, where most translators continue to use Nietzsche's German word, thus italicizing it. I follow that convention.

[12] Deleuze (1962) and Richardson (1996) are the classic treatments, the latter considerably clearer than the former. May (1999: 42–50) offers a related discussion.

[13] Thus, Poellner (1995: 130–1, 253–4), in his otherwise highly illuminating treatment of *ressentiment*, is mistaken, I think, in limiting the emotion of *ressentiment* to "an 'other'" who is apprehended "as in some respect superior and as dislikeable or hateful at least partly for this reason" (p. 130), though that is plainly true of the *ressentiment* of the slave. But for Nietzsche,

ressentiment then expresses itself through a certain kind of *valuation*, rather than any other kind of action, though it is centrally a valuation that is a *response to* something external, rather than an expression of any inner certainty or self-satisfaction. Thus, Nietzsche writes:

> This reversal of the value-positing glance – this *need* to direct one's view outward instead of back to oneself – is a feature of *ressentiment*: in order to come about, slave morality first has to have an opposing, external world, it needs, physiologically speaking, external stimuli in order to act at all, – its action is basically a reaction.

(GM I: 10)

This, then, is the slave revolt in morals: slaves, unable to take physical action against the sources of their misery (their masters, their oppressors), are driven by their stewing hatred of their masters to do the only thing they can do, create new values, values that *devalue* the masters, that invert the masters' valuations: their valuations are, in effect, *projections* of these powerful reactive emotions.

It is important here to remember that *ressentiment* draws on the resources of more familiar emotions such as hatred and vengefulness. Men of *ressentiment* are, says Nietzsche, "cellar rats full of revenge and hatred" (GM I: 14). *Ressentiment* provides the slaves "an imaginary revenge" (GM I: 10)[14] and conceals "a whole, vibrating realm of subterranean revenge" (GM III: 14). The concept of "evil" (a creation

---

I take it, states of affairs can provoke *ressentiment* even when there is no question of perceived superiority: it is *powerlessness* in the face of an unpleasant external "something" that is key.

14 Bittner (1994: 133) objects that the slaves "cannot actually compensate themselves with a revenge they themselves consider imaginary," so it must be the case that the slaves do *not* consider it "imaginary." In that case, however, it cannot be the case they invented the values (the slave morality) that effects the revenge: for if they invented it, they would know it was imaginary. The paradox is cleverly sketched, but it ultimately depends on contentious assumptions introduced by Bittner, not Nietzsche. In particular, no reason is given for assuming that the *creation* of values must be *conscious*, or even *self-conscious* about itself as an act of creation. The *ressentiment* of slaves may lead them to create (i.e., cause to come into existence) values, without them realizing that this is an act of creation.

of the man of *ressentiment*) comes from "the cauldron of unassuaged hatred" (GM I: 11). His most striking actual example of a man of *ressentiment*, the Church Father Tertullian, is offered as an example of the "eternal *hate*" that informs Christianity (GM I: 15). *Ressentiment*, then, is Nietzsche's term of art for a special kind of festering hatred and vengefulness, one motivated by impotence in the face of unpleasant external stimuli, and that leads (at least among the impotent) to the creation of values that *devalue* (or at least make sense of) those unpleasant stimuli.[15] Note, of course, that the core elements of *ressentiment* – a negative, evaluative reaction to an external state of affairs that is unpleasant but which one cannot address through physical action – can afflict nobles as well: after all, even the most powerful may still come up against circumstances that are painful and beyond their immediate control. Indeed, Nietzsche observes that, "When *ressentiment* does occur in the noble man himself, it is consumed and exhausted in an immediate reaction, and therefore it does not *poison*" (GM I: 10). *Ressentiment* in the slavish type, however, *festers*, and it is out of this festering *ressentiment* that the slave revolt in morals is born.

Although *ressentiment* is most often associated with the First Essay, it makes appearances throughout the *Genealogy*: in the explanation of how a certain conception of justice arose (GM II: 11), and, most importantly, in the account of the origin of the ascetic ideal in the Third Essay, to which we will return at length in Chapter 8. Indeed, even in the First Essay, the role of *ressentiment* is not entirely negative.[16] As Nietzsche comments:

[15] The parenthetical will become important when we consider the role of *ressentiment* in the Third Essay.

[16] May (1999: 47) overstates the positive impact of *ressentiment*, largely by misconstruing the meaning of some of the passages he cites, e.g., GM I: 10, where Nietzsche calls men of *ressentiment* "cleverer" than more noble men. The German, of course, is *klüger*, which also has the connotation of "more prudent," in the sense of more cautious and calculating (a trait customarily attributed, pejoratively, to the Jews by nineteenth-century anti-semites). Nothing in this characterization is flattering, as the surrounding context should make clear: e.g., the man of *ressentiment* is said to have a "soul [that] *squints*; his mind loves dark corners, secret paths and back-doors, everything secretive appeals to him" (GM I: 10).

[O]ne would undoubtedly have to view all instinctive reaction and instinctive *ressentiment*, by means of which the noble races and their ideals were finally wrecked and overpowered, as the actual *instruments of culture*; which, however, is not to say that the *bearers* of these instincts were themselves representatives of the culture.

(GM I: 11)

The *original* nobles or masters – "Roman, Arabian, Germanic, Japanese nobility, Homeric heroes, Scandinavian Vikings" (GM I: 11) – "are not much better than uncaged beasts of prey in the world outside where the strange, the foreign, begin," says Nietzsche. With respect to the "other," Nietzsche explains, these masters:

compensate for the tension which is caused by being closed in and fenced in by the peace of the community for so long, they *return* to the innocent conscience of the wild beast, as exultant monsters, who perhaps go away having committed a hideous succession of murder, arson, rape and torture, in a mood of bravado and spiritual equilibrium as though they had simply played a student's prank, convinced that poets will now have something to sing about and celebrate for quite some time. At the center of all these noble races we cannot fail to see the blond beast of prey[17]. . . . It was the noble races which left the concept of "barbarian" in their traces wherever they went.

(GM I: 11)

The clearest example of such masters are, of course, the Athenians portrayed in Thucydides' *History* – Nietzsche mentions Pericles' Funeral Oration, which celebrates the Athenians' "shocking cheerfulness, and depth of delight in all destruction, in all the debauches of victory and cruelty" (GM I: 11) – and "the magnificent but at the same time so shockingly violent world of Homer" (GM I: 11). By helping defeat these barbaric nobles, *ressentiment* and the slave revolt bring

17 The "blond beast of prey" is plainly the lion, and not, as some have thought, a reference to Aryans. How could it be the latter, when a sentence later we are given as examples of these "blond beasts" the Arab, Japanese, and Roman nobility?

about social and material conditions in which certain kinds of cultural expression can flourish. In that sense, *ressentiment* proves itself an "instrument of culture," though the men of *ressentiment* are not themselves figures of cultural greatness.

Perhaps more important for Nietzsche is that through *ressentiment* "the human soul became *deep*" (GM I: 6); more precisely, Nietzsche attributes this accomplishment to the "priests," who are themselves in the grips of *ressentiment*, because they "are turned away from action and . . . are partly brooding and emotionally explosive" (GM I: 6): "Out of [their] powerlessness, their hates wells into something huge and uncanny to a most intellectual and poisonous level. . . . The history of mankind would be far too stupid a thing if it had not had the intellect of the powerless injected into it" (GM I: 7). At least some of those who can't act – namely, the priests – *think*: they plot revenge, cook up new evaluations, calculate, and scheme; as a result, "man first became an *interesting animal*" (GM I: 6).

Beyond good and evil

Ressentiment produces the slave revolt in morals, in which the "good" man of the master morality becomes the "evil" man of slave morality. Nietzsche says near the end of the First Essay that he equates the aim of the *Genealogy* with "the aim of that dangerous slogan . . . that is inscribed at the head of my last book '*Beyond Good and Evil*': . . . At least this does not mean 'Beyond Good and Bad'" (GM 1: 17). The "polemic" against morality in the *Genealogy* is not, then, a polemic against all values. As we saw in Chapters 3 and 4, Nietzsche's target is only "morality in the pejorative sense," i.e., morality as characterized by certain distinctive descriptive presuppositions and normative claims. The same theme recurs in the *Genealogy*, though now Nietzsche suggests that we can understand the contrast between the morality he rejects (MPS) and that system of valuation he does not in terms of the differences between the "good/bad" and "good/evil" axes of evaluation. Any morality, regardless of the class position of its adherent, will be "slavish" insofar as it is structurally similar to the morality of "good and evil" (and thus, in the terminology of the earlier chapters, would be an MPS). To understand, in turn, what it means to move "beyond good and evil" requires understanding the contrast with the "master" morality of "good and bad."[18]

To do justice to the *specific* discussion in the *Genealogy*, it will be useful to introduce two more refined categories, to distinguish between a "good–bad morality" (hereafter GBM) and a "good–evil morality" (hereafter GEM). Nietzsche's point, of course, in introducing the good/evil and good/bad distinctions is precisely to bring out general features of moralities, of which slave morality and master morality are just particular instances. Moreover, as Nietzsche emphasizes in *Beyond Good and Evil* (260), the interpenetration of the two moralities has eliminated their clear-cut ties to social class, so while the facts about

18 Nietzsche's slogan "beyond good and evil" has not gone unremarked upon by commentators. The most popular interpretive suggestion, offered in slightly different forms by both Walter Kaufmann (in his edition of BGE: 185 n. 21) and Alexander Nehamas (1985: 206 ff.), claims that Nietzsche uses the slogan "beyond good and evil" to emphasize "[t]he essential unity of what we commonly distinguish as good and evil" (Nehamas 1985: 209; see also pp. 206–7). Yet while it is true that the interdependence and interrelation of apparent opposites – truth and falsity, good and evil – is a recurring theme in Nietzsche, it is doubtful that he uses the phrase "beyond good and evil" to mark this idea. Consider, for example, Nehamas' treatment of the issue. On examination, it turns out that none of the three passages Nehamas cites in support of the "essential unity" reading even mention the distinctive slogan "beyond good and evil." Thus, Nehamas cites WP: 351 (1985: 209), where Nietzsche does discuss the relation between good and evil qualities, but without characterizing this as a matter of moving "beyond good and evil." Nehamas also cites BGE: 23 (p. 210) in which Nietzsche claims that "the affects of hatred, envy, covetousness, and the lust to rule" are "factors which, fundamentally and essentially, must be present in the general economy of life," but in which he says nothing in particular about the relation between good and evil, and nothing about what it means to move "beyond good and evil." Finally, Nehamas cites WP: 464 (p. 210) in which Nietzsche says only that his "new philosophers" will want "to develop both *the good and the bad* [*die guten und die schlimmen*] qualities [emphasis added] in man to their fullest extent" so that "each needs the other," but says nothing about "good and evil" [*gut und böse*] and nothing about "beyond good and evil." It would seem, then, that without some other textual evidence, we have no grounds for viewing this other genuine, but inapposite, Nietzschean theme as the core meaning of the slogan.

social class are important to the genealogy of the distinctions, they are no longer dispositive as to the character of any particular morality in the present. It is also important to keep in mind that Nietzsche only endorses GBM in the limited sense of endorsing the structure of good/bad values of which master morality is an instance, but master morality – which is, after all, originally "[a] morality of the ruling *group*" (BGE: 260; emphasis added) – also requires an embedding in particular communal practices and traditions anathema to the Nietzsche who assigns higher value to solitude and individual creation.[19] Finally, note that while GEMs will all be instances of MPS, the set of features that Nietzsche concentrates on in the First Essay is somewhat different (and narrower) than those associated with MPS in Chapters 3 and 4.

According to Nietzsche, the distinctions embraced by GBM and GEM differ along three dimensions: the "Genetic," the "Evaluative" and the "Metaphysical." Let us consider these accounts in turn:

Genetic differences

Two normative distinctions differ *genetically* insofar as they differ with respect to aspects of their origin. According to Nietzsche, the normative distinctions of GBM and GEM differ genetically in two respects: in terms of aspects of the *chronological* order in which the elements of the respective distinctions arose; and in terms of the *motives* that explain the genesis of the distinctions. First, for GBM, the term "good" (*gut*) is invented *first* as a spontaneous celebration of "the exalted proud states of the soul" (BGE: 260), while the term "bad" (*schlecht*) is an afterthought and designates all those who are not "good."[20] For GEM, by contrast, the term "evil" (*böse*) comes *first* (to designate "precisely the 'good man' of the other morality" (GM 1: 11)), while the term "good" (*gut*) comes second and simply designates all those

19 See the discussion of "higher" human beings in Chapter 3. Cf. Richardson (1996): 53–7, 68–70.

20 This point about chronology is clearly true of Nietzsche's paradigm cases – master and slave morality – but it is less clear that it is supposed to be (or needs to be) true of all later instances of GBM and GEM moralities.

who are not "evil" ("*'the Evil One'* ... *is* [the slave's] basic concept, from which he then evolves, as an afterthought and pendant, a 'good one' – himself" (GM 1: 10)).

Second, GBM and GEM have different motives. For GBM, the motive is self-affirmation and celebration of the "exalted, proud states of the soul." For GEM, Nietzsche describes the motive as reactive: "it involves wanting to *respond* to particular "external stimuli" by negating or devaluing them (GM 1: 10). Unlike GBM, then, the values of GEM arise first in response to something "outside" or "other" – in this case, a ruling, noble caste – rather than arising from an affirmation of self. Thus, Nietzsche says that GEM reflects the "poisonous eye of *ressentiment*" which is directed at the threatening actions of "the 'good' man of the other morality ... the noble, powerful, dominating man" (GM 1: 11). Thus, it is the *motivational* difference that explains the *chronological* difference: values that are reactive necessarily invent their positive terms *after* their negative ones because valuation is driven by a desire to negate something external; the opposite holds true for valuation motivated by self-affirmation.

Evaluative differences

Two normative distinctions differ *evaluatively* insofar as they differ with respect to i) the *subject-matter* of their valuations; and/or ii) what characteristics *substantive value* attaches to in their normative judgments. According to Nietzsche, the normative distinctions of GBM and GEM differ evaluatively in both respects. First, the subject-matter of the evaluative judgments of GBM is the *person* rather than particular actions of the person ("moral designations were everywhere first applied to human beings" (BGE: 260)). The subject-matter of the evaluative judgments of GEM, by contrast, is the individual *action*, for which the agent is held responsible (BGE: 260; GM I: 13). (We shall return to this important theme shortly.)

Second, the evaluative judgments of GBM attach substantive value to "the exalted, proud states of the soul" so that "the opposition of 'good' and 'bad' means approximately the same as 'noble' and 'contemptible'" (BGE: 260). By contrast, in GEM, substantive value attaches to "those qualities ... which serve to ease the existence for those who suffer," e.g., "pity ... patience, industry, humility and friendliness are honored"[21] (BGE: 260) with the final result that "a touch of disdain is associated ... with the 'good' of this morality ... the good human being [the one who performs 'good' acts] ... *is* good-natured, easy to deceive, a little stupid perhaps, *un bonhomme*" (BGE: 260). Conversely, GEM withholds substantive value from everything that "inspire[s] fear" (BGE: 260), from all that is "powerful and noble" (GM 1: 7). As one commentator aptly puts it:

> When the eye of *ressentiment* looks at the nobles, it does not see the tightly wound skein of power, wealth, courage, truthfulness and the like that the nobles themselves had perceived; it sees instead only cruelty, tyranny, lustfulness, insatiability, and godlessness (GM I: 7). Once the *ressentiment* of the weak has become creative and given birth to a new kind of morality, the slaves are able when they look at themselves no longer to see unrelenting, unredeemed misery and wretchedness, but rather a new kind of goodness, constituted by the [putatively] voluntary cultivation of patience, humility and justice.
>
> (Migotti 1998: 752)

Metaphysical differences

Two normative distinctions differ *metaphysically* insofar as they differ with respect to the "metaphysical" (or descriptive) conception of agency and the world presupposed by (or implicit in) the intelligible application of the norms to a given state of affairs. According to Nietzsche, GEM must presuppose that agents choose freely to do what they do, because GEM seeks to hold agents morally responsible for their actions. In GEM, says Nietzsche, one judges the actions of a "strong" man as though "there were an indifferent substratum behind the strong person, which had the *freedom* to manifest strength or not.

---

[21] In a related vein, Nietzsche remarks elsewhere that "higher beings" exist "beyond good and evil" in the sense that they are "beyond those values which cannot deny their origin in the sphere of suffering, the herd, and the majority" (WP: 1041).

But there is no such substratum" (GM 1: 13*)*. In contrast, GBM need *not* make any such assumption about a human capacity for free agency. First, the subject-matter of the judgments of GBM is the person, not particular actions to which responsibility might attach. Thus, GBM looks at persons, and views actions as expressive of persons, while GEM, because of its distinctive conception of persons as free agents, looks first at (what it takes to be free) actions.[22]

Second, the normative judgments of GBM assess the person (broadly speaking) in terms of his "nobility" (or lack thereof), and the judgment that a person is noble or contemptible is not one that depends on whether the agent acted freely. Even in a world in which agents did not act freely, "the cowardly, the anxious, the petty, those intent on narrow utility" (BGE: 260) would still be "bad" (*schlecht*) in the sense characteristic of GBM.

The contrast, then, between the characteristic normative distinctions of GBM and GEM breaks down as follows:

	Good and bad (GBM)	Good and evil (GEM)
Genetic		
Chronology	"Good" first	"Evil" first
	"Bad" as afterthought	"Good" second, as that which is not "evil"
Motive	Self-affirmative	Reactive/resentful
Evaluative		
Subject-matter	The person	Particular actions
Substantive value	Attaches to noble traits of "character"	Attaches to actions favorable to those that suffer
Metaphysical		
	No presumption that agents act freely	Presumption that agents act freely

[22] I am indebted here to Peter Railton.

So to move "beyond good and evil" is to abandon values with the genetic, evaluative and metaphysical properties of GEM (above). In the language of Chapter 3, it is to reject "morality in the pejorative sense," and embrace moral codes without the descriptive presuppositions and normative effects of this morality.

A useful illustration of the way Nietzsche employs this distinction in practice comes from his discussion of "noble" or "higher" human beings, which we first encountered in Chapter 4. Recall that GBM values are marked by the following evaluative property: they evaluate the "person" in terms of his "nobility" (broadly speaking), or lack thereof. In contrast, GEM values take as their evaluative subject-matter individual actions, for which agents are deemed responsible. Given this contrast, we should expect that discussions of what constitutes "nobility" (the substantive-value component of the evaluative property of GBM) should be couched in terms of what sort of "person" one is, as opposed to what sort of actions one performs. Now this, in fact, is what one finds in Nietzsche.

For example, Nietzsche remarks that "the 'higher nature' of the great man lies in being different, in incommunicability, in distance of rank, not in an effect of any kind – even if he made the whole globe tremble" (WP: 876). Similarly, Nietzsche suggests that what makes a person "noble" "is not actions . . . nor is it 'works;'" rather it is "the *faith* that is decisive here." In particular, Nietzsche claims that "*The noble soul has reverence for itself*" (BGE: 287).[23]

23 Nietzsche's language here is evocative of Kant's remarks about the "good will" in the *Metaphysical Foundations of Morals*. There he says: "A good will is good not because of what it performs or effects, nor by its aptness for attaining some proposed end, but simply by virtue of the volition; that is, it is good in itself and when considered by itself is to be esteemed much higher than all that it can bring about. . . . If with its greatest efforts this will should yet achieve nothing and there should remain only good will . . . then, like a jewel, good will would still shine by its own light as a thing having its whole value in itself" (First Section). No doubt Nietzsche intended the Kantian allusion, since he frequently voices his anti-Kantian views in Kantian-sounding terms. But the similarity is only superficial. For what marks the "good will" is its respect for the moral law: "The necessity of acting from pure respect for the practical law [of right action] is what constitutes duty, to which every other motive must yield, because it is the condition of a will being good *in itself,*

At first sight, one might worry that this is too thin a criterion of *nobility*: could not even the base man (the herd animal, the slave) *revere* himself (albeit without justification)? Nietzsche must presumably be prepared to deny this possibility on the grounds that self-reverence involves a certain primacy of self-regard foreign to the slave, whose sense of self is entirely derivative from a reaction to external stimuli. The distinction Nietzsche has in mind resonates – perhaps intentionally – with that drawn by Rousseau in the *Discourse on the Origin and Foundations of Inequality* (1755) between the "savage" and the "civilized" or "sociable" man: "[T]he savage lives within himself; the sociable man, always outside of himself, knows how to live only in the opinion of others; and it is, so to speak, from their judgment alone that he draws the sentiment of his own existence."

Analogously, central to slave morality is the "reversal of the value-positing glance – this *need* to direct one's view outward instead of back to oneself" (GM I: 10). But it is precisely this outward orientation that precludes reverence in Nietzsche's sense. For the reverence that marks the noble soul, Nietzsche tells us, involves "some fundamental certainty that a noble soul has about itself, something that cannot be sought, nor found, nor perhaps lost" (BGE: 287). The "inversion" of the value-positing glance, however, makes such certainty impossible. Any judgment about the value of the "self" must come after and depends upon the contrast with this first valuation. Thus, any assessment of the self by the slave, first, must be "sought" or "found" via an examination of what is external to the self and, second, is never "certain" for it always depends on what the external stimuli happen to be. The slave, then, cannot revere himself, though he *can* come to think himself "good" in the sense characteristic of GEM. Only the noble person, in whom values "grow spontaneously" (GM 1: 10), for whom morality is "self-glorification" (BGE: 260), is capable of genuine reverence for self.

These remarks about the defining criteria of nobility should not suggest, of course, that the "noble" man does not also act in certain

and the value of such a will exceeds everything" (ibid.). By contrast, what marks the noble soul is precisely its respect *for itself,* its "fundamental certainty ... about itself" (BGE: 287). In addition, of course, Nietzsche was highly critical of Kantian duty as a ground of action (e.g., A: 11).

distinctive ways.[24] The point, however, is that the locus of evaluation – the thing which distinguishes the "noble" man from the "contemptible" one – are certain aspects of his "character" (dispositions, personality traits, etc.) and not actions.[25] Given the attributes of character that distinguish the noble man from the ignoble, we may also be able to say in some general way what sort of actions will characterize the noble person; but these are neither necessary nor sufficient for nobility on Nietzsche's account. And this, of course, should be expected given the earlier account of the evaluative properties of GBM values.

As the preceding discussion illustrates, one claim in particular undergirds many of the differences between the competing normative worlds of GEM and GBM: namely, a difference about the metaphysics of agency.[26] This is clearest in what is perhaps the most famous and striking section of the First Essay, section 13. The precise topic of this section is the conceptualization of "good" and "evil" "by the man of *ressentiment*"; the explication proceeds via a parable. We are asked to consider how "lambs" would conceptualize the morality of what "birds of prey" do; by seeing what is absurd about such a moral valuation we will, at the same time, see what is absurd about slave morality (that is, about GEMs, or morality in the pejorative sense).

The difficulty is that while it is not "strange . . . that lambs bear a grudge towards large birds of prey" for eating lambs, there is some-

---

24 One should not conclude, either, that GEM values are unconcerned with character altogether. The point, however, is that GEM values *start* with a moral condemnation of what is other – e.g., the "masters" – and that this condemnation essentially involves judging *actions*.

25 Thus, I am not sure Migotti (1998: 749) is correct in saying that "[n]oble morality" involves "lives lived for the sake of the happiness inseparable from engaging in actions and activities deemed worthwhile in and of themselves, together with the honor consequent upon excelling at such actions and activities in the eyes of one's peers." Although Migotti's sensitive discussion does some justice to some of what Nietzsche says about the *original* nobles, Migotti's reading is hard to reconcile with Nietzsche's more general characterizations of nobility as a certain self-reverence, quite apart from particular actions.

26 Thus, the discussion in the First Essay puts more emphasis on the descriptive component of MPS (see Chapter 3) than Nietzsche does elsewhere.

thing "absurd" about imposing a moral interpretation on this state of affairs. But in our parable, this is exactly what lambs do when they express their anger at birds of prey by saying, "These birds of prey are evil; and whoever is least like a bird of prey and most like its opposite, a lamb – is good." In one sense, this is unobjectionable: *of course* lambs think this way, it's in their interest to believe this (indeed, Nietzsche calls it "cleverness" or "prudence" [*Klugheit*] for them to make such claims). But taken literally, it is quite absurd: birds of prey cannot help but eat little lambs, for that is just what birds of prey *essentially are*, i.e., predators of small animals. Birds of prey do not have free will; they have no internal locus of agency (no "doer") which deliberates about whether or not to eat little lambs ("the doing").

While this is uncontroversial enough with respect to birds of prey, it is important to remember that Nietzsche's real point is that it is equally "absurd" to presuppose a similar metaphysics of agency in the moral evaluation of what human beings do:

> [P]opular morality separates strength from the manifestations of strength, as though there were an indifferent substratum [i.e., a free will, an internal locus of agency] behind the strong person which had the *freedom* to manifest strength or not. But there is no such substratum; there is no "being" behind the deed, its effect and what becomes of it; "the doer" is invented as an after-thought, – the doing is everything.[27]

(GM I: 13)

This is of a piece with Nietzsche's doctrine of fatalism and his repudiation of free will discussed in Chapter 3: "the doing is everything" means there is no role in the explanation of action for an autonomous agent; each creature does what it must *essentially* do, what it is *fated* to do given the type-facts about it.

Why, then, do people believe otherwise? Nietzsche offers two explanations. First, a belief "in an unbiased 'subject' with freedom of choice" is *prudent*, it is a product of "an instinct of self-preservation

---

[27] This is compatible, of course, with thinking that *doing* is not criterial of being a "noble" person, as argued above. The point in this passage, after all, concerns not the nature of nobility, but the metaphysics of agency.

and self-affirmation": convince the strong that they have a choice, and one may actually change their behavior.[28] There is, however, a second explanation for belief in the metaphysics of free will hinted at by Nietzsche: "only the seduction of language (and the fundamental errors of reason petrified within it), which construes and misconstrues all actions as conditional upon an agency, a 'subject,' can make it appear" that the strong are free not to express their strength. What Nietzsche has in mind is the feature of Indo-Germanic languages that requires all action verbs that are not in the imperative or inquisitive moods to be accompanied by a grammatical subject. So, for example, "hits the ball" is not a grammatically correct sentence, but "He hits the ball" *is* grammatically correct. The difficulty comes when we assume grammar corresponds *to the way things really are*. The mistake is in thinking that because grammar dictates that one says, "I oppressed the weak," there must be something corresponding to this "I" – a doer – that makes a choice about whether or not to engage in acts of oppression. It is not language, per se, but syntax that "seduces" us into a meta-physics of agency.

Now, however, the reader must feel perplexed: can Nietzsche seriously be suggesting that a member of the elite of the late Roman empire has *no choice* but to whip his slaves, to keep them enslaved? How could a mere artifact of social and historical contingency – that someone was born in to an aristocratic family, rather than a slave family – constitute an *essential* trait of a person's nature, such that it dictates his conduct? Remember that Nietzsche speaks in this section of "the weakness of the weak" as "its *essence*, its effects, its whole unique, unavoidable, irredeemable reality." Wouldn't a second-century slave have done just fine as a slave owner but for an accident of birth?

There is no reason in the text, of course, to think Nietzsche is guilty of an implausible reification of contingent socio-economic facts; to the contrary, the *only* way to make sense of what he says here is

---

28 Of course, it can't be that the strong *choose* to change their behavior in response to this revaluation of their conduct; rather the claim must be that since values are among the causal mechanisms that affect developmental trajectories (see Chapter 4: 157–8), the behavior of the strong may, at some level, be caused (via some mechanism) to change when the normative universe they inhabit condemns their behavior.

to remember that while "master" and "slave" *begin* as class-specific terms, their ultimate significance is psychological for Nietzsche, not social. The claim, in other words, is that the distinctive traits of those who are slavish *in the psychological sense* are, indeed, part of their "essence" their "whole unique, unavoidable, irredeemable reality." Only then, on the assumption that "slavish" and "noble" are intended to have psychological or characterological connotations can we make sense of the crucial section 13 of the First Essay. A "slavish" psychology (or a "noble" one) is among the type-facts that can be constitutive of persons, of who one *essentially* is.

There remains, of course, a sense for Nietzsche in which slave owners have no "choice" as to whether to whip their slaves (or *not* to whip their slaves), since no one exercises autonomous choice about anything (Chapter 3). The crucial point, however, is that Nietzsche is not claiming that slave owners whip their slaves because of their class position (or because "noble" type-facts require them to do so); whatever the explanation for their actions, it is not one in which socio-economic class figures as an *essential* attribute of the actor, as a type-fact.

The triumph of slave morality

Slave morality is "victorious" (GM I: 7), though not absolutely: "there is still no lack of places where the battle" between slave and master morality "remains undecided" (GM I: 16). Indeed, a "distinguishing feature of the '*higher nature*,' the more spiritual nature," is "to be . . . really and truly a battle ground for these opposites" (GM I: 16; cf. BGE: 260). Yet the bottom line is clear: slave morality "has been dominant for a long time" (GM I: 16), so much so that its genesis must figure centrally in Nietzsche's genealogy of our morality.

But how could this happen? How could slave morality triumph in this way? Why would the masters have been seduced by a morality that requires such profound abnegation on their part? It is perhaps the oddest feature of the First Essay that Nietzsche never addresses this question explicitly, yet it must surely occur to every reader. So slaves suffer from *ressentiment* and invent new values: why should *that* have had any effect at all? Why would masters pay this any mind, why would they not view slave morality the way the birds of prey (GM I: 13) view the lambs' moral condemnation of them? Although Nietzsche avoids addressing the matter directly, we may piece together a partial answer from the First Essay.

Slaves (men of *ressentiment*) are repeatedly described by Nietzsche as *klug*, which is often rendered in English as "clever," though that may obscure the clear connotations of the German *klug*, which also can mean shrewd, prudent and cunning. Nobles, by contrast, are different in this regard, as Nietzsche explains:

> [T]he man of *ressentiment* ... knows all about keeping quiet, not forgetting, waiting, temporarily humbling and abasing himself. A race of such men of *ressentiment* will inevitably end up *cleverer* than any noble race, and will respect cleverness to a quite different degree as well: namely, as a condition of existence of the first rank, whilst the cleverness of noble men can easily have a subtle aftertaste of luxury and refinement about it: – precisely because in this area, it is nowhere near as important as the complete certainty of function of the governing *unconscious* instincts, nor indeed as important as a certain lack of cleverness [*Klugheit*], such as a daring charge at danger or at the enemy, or those frenzied sudden fits of anger, love, reverence, gratitude and revenge by which noble souls down the ages have recognized one another. ... To be unable to take his enemies, his misfortunes, and even his *misdeeds* seriously for long – that is the sign of strong, rounded natures with a superabundance of a power which is flexible, formative, healing and can make one forget.
>
> (GM I: 10)

The valence on these traits in this passage is plainly positive, but the inference they invite is also clear: lack of prudence, a tendency to forget and not to worry about one's enemies, makes the nobles easy targets for the clever, scheming, calculating men of *ressentiment*.

The nobles are, however, a special kind of target, and they must be conquered in a special way. As one commentator puts it: "masters lose their grip on their own morality by being made to feel guilty for being masters and adhering to master morality" (Migotti 1998:

754).[29] How exactly does *this* transformation occur? Nobles may not be especially prudent or shrewd, but why should they fall into the self-doubt slave morality demands?

A partial (but only partial) answer is suggested by sections 6 and 7 of the First Essay, which we have so far largely ignored. Nietzsche tells us that originally "the highest caste" typically included a "priestly" caste, whose commitment to "purity" quickly descends into a kind of asceticism:

> From the very beginning there has been something *unhealthy* about these priestly aristocracies and in the customs dominant there, which are turned away from action and which are partly brooding and partly emotionally explosive, resulting in the almost inevitable bowel complaints and neurasthenia which have plagued the clergy down the ages.

> (GM I: 6)

The values of the priestly caste then contrast markedly with that of the "warrior caste," who are the paradigmatic masters:

> The chivalric–aristocratic value-judgments [i.e., the morality of the masters] are based on a powerful physicality, a blossoming, rich, even effervescent good health which includes the things needed to maintain it, war, adventure, hunting, dancing, jousting and everything else that contains strong, free, happy action. The priestly-aristocratic method of valuation – as we have seen – has different criteria.

> (GM I: 7)

Indeed, says Nietzsche, it is "easy . . . for the priestly method of valuation to split off from the chivalric–aristocratic and then to develop further into the opposite of the latter" (GM I: 7). He proceeds to equate "the Jews" with the "priestly people," and says "*the slaves' revolt in morality* begins with" them (GM I: 7). For it is they,

> who, rejecting the aristocratic value equation (good = noble = powerful = beautiful = happy = blessed) ventured, with

---

[29] The discussion that follows is indebted to the illuminating treatment in Migotti (1998): 754–60, though I part company on certain issues.

awe-inspiring consistency, to bring about a reversal and held it in the teeth of their unfathomable hatred (the hatred of the powerless), saying, "Only those who suffer are good, only the poor, the powerless, the lowly are good; the suffering, the deprived, the sick, the ugly, are the only pious people, the only ones saved, salvation is for them alone, whereas you rich, you noble and powerful, you are eternally wicked, cruel, lustful, insatiate, godless, you will also be eternally wretched, cursed and damned!" . . . We know *who* became heir to this Jewish revaluation [i.e., Christianity].

(GM I: 7)

The slave revolt in morals, then, is here attributed not precisely to the slaves, but to the "priestly people," who at some point split off from the higher castes and then, out of *ressentiment* (their "priestly vengefulness" (GM I: 7)) invert the values of the masters, the chivalric–aristocratic values. The account here is so quick and elliptical that it is hard to know what Nietzsche is saying: is the slave revolt in morals really just the work of the priests, and not the slaves? If so, why does he refer to "the priestly people," and not simply the priestly caste? And why, then, call it a *slave* revolt in morals?

The character of the priest will return to center stage in the Third Essay of the *Genealogy*, and we shall have occasion, then, to consider more carefully his role in the genealogy of our morality. For now, though, we are still confronted with the issue of how the fact that a priestly caste might split off and turn against the paradigmatically noble parts of the higher caste explains the success of the slave revolt in morals. One commentator, remarking on these sections, says: "Nietzschean masters are rendered susceptible to the lure of slave morality by dint of their familiarity with the priestly form of nobility" (Migotti 1998: 756). Even this point, which is probably correct as far it goes, still underdetermines the outcome, namely the triumph of slave morality. Masters may not be shrewd or prudent, and they may already be somewhat familiar with slavish morality from their exposure to the priestly caste, but why do they *succumb* to slave morality in the way that they do?

In fact, I think the First Essay does not ultimately contain an adequate answer to this question. We will only be able to answer it when we appreciate the role of "bad conscience" (the subject of the Second Essay) and the "ascetic ideal" (the subject of the Third Essay) in human moral psychology. In particular, the powerful psychological mechanisms supporting the triumph of the ascetic ideal, together with the fact that slave morality is one expression of that ideal, will help close the explanatory gap between the hints the First Essay offers and the actual success of the slave revolt.

Yet there is one final question we should address here, since related issues will arise in the subsequent chapters as well. How can the *ressentiment* of slaves be proffered as a satisfying explanation of a momentous event like "the birth of Christianity" (EH III: GM)? Is a psychological explanation really enough to account for a transformation in human culture of this magnitude?

Of course, we must remember that the *Genealogy* is a polemic, whose ultimate aim is to free nascent higher human beings from their false consciousness about morality; Nietzsche's book is no academic treatise, aspiring to scholarly comprehensiveness. The moral psychology of "the birth of Christianity" may best serve Nietzsche's polemical ends, even if it does not exhaust the explanatory forces at work.

It is also useful to keep in mind the actual historical event to which Nietzsche is alluding most generally in the First Essay, namely, the triumph of Christianity in the Roman Empire. This, of course, did not occur by force of arms, as the outcome of some violent uprising or revolution. It was, instead, a profound and gradual change of consciousness that culminated with the conversion of the Emperor Constantine in 312 AD. Of course, a change in consciousness might admit of a materialistic explanation, of the Marxian or Braudelian variety, in which we appeal to economic, demographic, geographic, and/or climactic factors to explain a change in moral or religious ideas. At some level, Nietzsche himself respects the demand for materialistic explanation – recall that he speaks of "the actual physiological causation of *ressentiment*" (GM III: 15). But the focus of most of the argument in the *Genealogy* is at the psychological level: three fundamental psychological mechanisms – *ressentiment* (GM I), bad conscience (GM II), and the will to power (GM III) – that are native to creatures like us do all the explanatory work. Nietzsche needn't deny that other factors are at work; he has simply chosen to concentrate on those factors most proximate and most like the psychological phenomenon he's explaining: namely, the change in consciousness represented, in the First Essay, by the triumph of slave morality.

Chapter 7

A commentary on
the Second Essay

The *second* inquiry offers the psychology of the *conscience* – which is not, as people may believe, "the voice of God in man": it is the instinct of cruelty that turns back after it can no longer discharge itself externally. Cruelty is here exposed for the first time as one of the most ancient and basic substrata of culture that simply cannot be imagined away.

(EH III: GM)

Ressentiment, as we saw in the last chapter, was the fundamental psychological mechanism underlying the slave revolt in morals, but this revolt itself took place against the backdrop of another profound change in the human psyche: the development of *conscience* (*Gewissen*) and, in particular, *bad* conscience. As always, Nietzsche wants to find a naturalistic explanation for this change, one that would replace supernatural explanations like those which would explain conscience as "the voice of God in man." According to Nietzsche, creatures like us, once socialized by

civilization, have a capacity for internal self-assessment: we evaluate ourselves by normative standards and castigate ourselves for failure to live up to them. Any parent knows that small children lack this capacity – they respond only to fear (of punishment, of loss of love) – and Nietzsche claims that adult human beings, too, lacked it as well, until forced into civilized intercourse with their fellow humans. For human beings are *by nature* cruel and aggressive, but giving free rein to those natural impulses would obviously be incompatible with communal life. Thus, society forces the repression of these cruel instincts, which are not extirpated but internalized and directed against the actor himself: the capacity for *bad* conscience is an expression of cruelty toward oneself.

This much of the argument has been made famous by Freud in *Civilization and Its Discontents* which is, in large part, an extended defense of the same basic thesis that conscience or guilt arises from the internalization of aggressive or cruel instincts.[1] But Nietzsche's ultimate concern differs from Freud's. While Freud worries about the stability of civilization given the tension between the fundamental aggressive and erotic instincts and the demands of civilized society,[2] Nietzsche is interested exclusively in how bad conscience became "moralized," how a capacity for remembering one's debts became transformed into a feeling of guilt, a feeling of self-loathing and a capacity for self-flagellation – how, in other words, an awareness or consciousness of one's prior acts and debts became a capacity for a particular kind of *bad* (*schlecht*) conscience, namely, a *guilty* conscience.

The core argument of the Second Essay occurs in three parts. First, there is an explanation of how animals like us acquired a conscience, in the sense of an ability to remember our debts, that

---

[1] Freud takes internalized cruelty (intensified through the internalization of the threatening father-punisher figure) to *suffice* for an explanation of guilt (and moral conscience), whereas Nietzsche, as we will see, does not.

[2] According to the later Freud, of course, the aggressive instincts are themselves the externalization of a death instinct. No comparable claim is found in Nietzsche (though there is a brief allusion to a "will to death" in GS: 344), and in any case, this feature of Freud's view does not matter for the purposes of our discussion here.

expands upon earlier discussions (especially from *Daybreak*) about what Nietzsche called "the morality of custom" (GM II: 1–3). Second, there is a first inquiry into the real question, the origin of *bad* conscience, using once again an etymological clue: the fact that the German *Schuld* can mean both debt and guilt. The question is then framed as how the debtor–creditor relationship became *moralized*, such that one was not simply conscious of a debt, but felt *guilty* about owing it (GM II: 4–8). An actual answer to this question does not begin to appear, however, until the third part of the argument (GM II: 16–18), which introduces the basic thesis about bad conscience as the product of the internalization of cruelty. It turns out, however, that even this story is incomplete, for it does not yet explain "the actual moralization of" debt (*Schuld*)[3] (GM II: 21), which occupies sections 19–22. The origin of bad conscience is one thing; but not all bad conscience manifests itself as a *guilty* conscience, and it is this that Nietzsche really wants to explain. So the account of conscience, as reconstructed here, moves through three stages: an account of conscience, as the ability to remember debts; an account of *bad* conscience as the product of the internalization of cruelty ("animal 'bad conscience'" as Nietzsche calls it (GM III: 20); and finally, (the beginnings of) an account of how internalized cruelty turned into feelings of *guilt*.[4]

   This demarcation of the chapter obviously omits certain sections. GM II: 9–11, on the nature of justice, is actually irrelevant to the core argument of the Second Essay, though it is helpful for understanding *ressentiment* (see Chapter 6) and has been interpreted by some as suggesting a non-moral interpretation of the idea of a social contract (cf. Clark 1994: 27–9). GM II: 2–15, on the genealogy of punishment, has already been discussed in some detail in Chapter 5. Like the preceding sections, it is somewhat tangential to the argument of the

[3] Diethe translated the word as "guilt" in this section, but I am convinced by the argument in Risse (2001) that this is a significant mistake, for reasons that we will examine in detail below.

[4] In this organization of the argument, I am in basic agreement with Risse (2001: 57–8), who distinguishes the bad conscience that "arises through the internalization of instincts" from the later form of "bad conscience as a feeling of guilt."

Second Essay, though it does debunk the idea that punishment is the source of guilt (Risse 2001: 57), and, in the process, sheds light on Nietzsche's understanding of guilt, to which we return below.[5] It is, of course, also crucial for understanding the practice of genealogy, as discussed in Chapter 5, and it is useful in understanding the doctrine of will to power, to which we turn in the next chapter.[6]

GM II: 23–5, by contrast, is more central, in part because it sets the stage for the Third Essay. For what we learn in these concluding sections of the Second Essay is that there are ways "to keep 'bad conscience' at bay" (GM II: 23), so that while the Greeks were, like all members of civilized societies, possessors of such a conscience, its effect was rather different from that on the moral men of today. Indeed, the suggestion is made (GM II: 23–4) that the regulatory mechanisms of bad conscience (the internalized cruelty) might be enlisted in the service of very different normative ideals from those observed so far: internalized cruelty may be a brute fact about creatures like us, but internalized cruelty in the service of a *guilty* conscience is not. (This, of course, is why the Greeks can have a "bad conscience" and yet not suffer from guilt the way we moderns do.) What that means, in particular, is that the Second Essay has not *fully* explained why our "bad conscience" is bad in the particular way it is: only when we explain the power of the ascetic ideal in the Third Essay will we have a complete account of the role of bad conscience in the genealogy of our morality.

The morality of custom and the origin of conscience (1–3)

Nietzsche begins the inquiry with a characteristically naturalistic question: how can one "breed an animal" which is able to make and honor a promise? The assumptions underlying this are, of course, twofold: that human beings are certain kinds of animals, and that, as with other animals, one explains what they do (e.g., promise-making) not by appeal to their exercise of some autonomous capacity for choice but

---

[5]   Ridley (1998: 31–2) helped me appreciate this point.
[6]   Cf. also the earlier discussion of will to power in Chapter 4, esp. pp. 138–44.

in terms of the causal mechanisms acting upon them, e.g., breeding. Nietzsche soon identifies two preconditions for promise-making: *regularity* of behavior and a capacity for *memory*. Regularity is necessary because a promise-maker must be "answerable for his own *future*" (GM II: 1), since one can't be answerable for a future that is utterly unpredictable. Memory is essential for the obvious reason that only someone who can *remember* his promise can possibly honor it.

Two factors are singled out by Nietzsche as formative for the human animal in its development of regular behavior and a memory: the "morality of custom" and the role of pain in mnemonics. With "the help of the morality of custom and the social straitjacket, man was *made* truly predictable [*berechenbar*, or calculable]" (GM II: 2). Nietzsche here alludes to his own earlier discussion in *Daybreak* (esp. D: 9), which, drawing on the etymological connection between *Sittlichkeit* (morality) and *Sitte* (custom), advanced "the plausible hypothesis that customs constituted the first morality, that traditional ways of acting played the same role during early human life that 'rarefied and lofty' moral codes, rules, and principles play today: that is, they provided criteria for moral right and wrong" (Clark and Leiter 1997: xxix–xxx). In this earlier discussion, however, Nietzsche's goal was a certain naturalization of the (implausible) Kantian account of moral motivation as a matter of reverence for the moral law: Nietzsche proposes instead that it is "obedience to tradition" (and fear of the consequences of deviation from tradition) that really constitutes moral motivation – not some fictional "reverence" for a moral law (Clark and Leiter 1997: xxx).

By the time he writes the *Genealogy*, Nietzsche's point is different: although not repudiating the earlier claims, Nietzsche now lays the emphasis on the role of custom ("the social straitjacket") in making humans "truly predictable," i.e., regular in their behavior.[7] This development eventually yields the individual with a conscience, whom Nietzsche refers to as a "sovereign" or "autonomous" individual (GM II: 2). Of course, we know from the discussion in Chapter 3, that Nietzsche does not think human beings have a capacity for genuinely

---

[7] For a practice to be *customary*, patterns of behavior must, of course, be *regular*.

autonomous choice, so, as is often the case, Nietzsche is using familiar words in unfamiliar senses. For in the end, this "autonomous" individual, this fruit of the long tradition of the morality of custom, is distinguished by one overriding trait: he has "*the right to make a promise*" (GM II: 2) because he can actually pull it off, i.e., his behavior is sufficiently regular and predictable so that he can be "answerable for his own future" (GM II: 1), and he is able to remember what he has promised and honor that memory. But we know already from the opening lines of the Second Essay that this just means he is a certain kind of "animal" that has been bred the right way and nothing more.[8]

Indeed, should we be misled by the rhetoric of GM II: 2, Nietzsche soon reminds us of the real point when he asks in the very next section: "How do you give a memory to the *animal* man?" (GM II: 3, emphasis added). It might seem curious, of course, that Nietzsche thinks an explanation of the phenomenon of memory is even necessary: is it not simply an innate capacity of creatures like us? But Nietzsche thinks an explanation of memory is needed because of his anticipation of another central Freudian theme: the human capacity for repression. "Forgetfulness," says Nietzsche, "is . . . an active ability to suppress" aspects of experience one would otherwise remember, an ability which is necessary "like a doorkeeper or guardian of mental order, rest and etiquette: . . . there could be no happiness, cheerfulness, hope, pride, *immediacy*, without forgetfulness" (GM II: 1). As a result, the animal man needed the "technique of mnemonics," and indeed, says Nietzsche, "there is nothing more terrible and strange in man's pre-history than" these techniques, for they all depended on "blood, torments and sacrifices" (GM II: 3). Nietzsche reviews some of these techniques which he attributes to the Germans – "boiling of the criminal in oil or wine" and "the popular flaying" (!) are among his examples – and then concludes that:

> With the aid of such images and procedures, man was eventually able to retain five or six "I will nots" in his memory, in

[8]   Of course, not everyone is so successfully bred; there remain, e.g., "the febrile whippets who make a promise when they have no right to do so" (GM II: 2), i.e., they talk the language of promises, but they are not sufficiently regular in their behavior and/or they are not able to remember their commitments.

connection with which a *promise* had been made, in order to enjoy the advantages of society. . . . With the aid of this sort of memory, people finally came to "reason"!

(GM II: 3)

What bears emphasizing here is that we are discussing a phenomenon of pre-history: we are discussing what the animal man had to be like before regular civilized intercourse with his fellows ("the advantages of society") would even be possible. That means, of course, that the phenomenon we are discussing – the development of conscience, and, in particular, bad conscience – predates the events discussed in the First Essay of the *Genealogy*.

Bad conscience: debt and guilt (4–8)

If "conscience" – a capacity to remember one's promises – arises from the "social straitjacket" of the "morality of custom," together with the mnemonics of pain, this still does not explain "bad conscience," in particular, "the consciousness of guilt" (GM II: 4).[9] This question, of course, is distinctive to a genealogy of *morality*, since guilt is a distinctively moral emotion, the feeling produced by a perceived moral transgression of some kind. Once again, our first clue comes from etymology: "the main moral[10] concept '*Schuld*' ('guilt') descends from the very material concept of '*Schulden*' ('debts')" (GM II: 4). What, then, distinguishes a sense of debt (which, presumably, only requires a conscience, i.e., a memory of the debt) from a sense of

---

9 Nietzsche here writes as though the two ("bad conscience" and a "consciousness of guilt") are equivalent, but they cannot be for a variety of reasons: 1) the Greeks had bad conscience but did not suffer from guilt (the point noted above); 2) Nietzsche suggests (GM II: 23–4) "bad conscience" could be enlisted in the service of normative ideals that would not produce guilt; and 3) the internalization of cruelty is not by itself sufficient to explain guilt. We will revisit these issues later in the chapter. Risse (2001: 58) offers an even simpler explanation for this passage: the question Nietzsche is *really* interested in is how bad conscience qua guilty conscience arose, but en route to explaining that, he first explains how bad conscience, *simpliciter*, arose.

10 "Moral" in the sense of what we have been calling "morality in the pejorative sense," i.e., MPS.

guilt? This question will not actually be answered until later in the Second Essay, though the first suggestions are broached in the sections under consideration here.

We see a first distinction between "debt" and "guilt" when we notice how the punishment of debtors was conceptualized prior to the moralization of debt (i.e., the turning of debt into guilt). Nietzsche writes:

> Throughout most of human history, punishment has *not* been meted out *because* the miscreant was held responsible for his act, therefore it was *not* assumed that the guilty party alone should be punished: – but rather ... it was out of anger over some wrong which had been suffered, directed at the perpetrator, – but this anger was held in check and modified by the idea that every injury has its *equivalent* which can be paid in compensation, if only through the *pain* of the person who injures.
>
> (GM II: 4)

So this "equivalence between injury and pain" which emerged out of "the contractual relationship between *creditor* and *debtor*" did not depend on "any assumption about freedom or lack of freedom of the will" (GM II: 4). Being in debt, unlike being guilty, does not involve being *morally responsible*, in the sense of being an agent who is presumed to have the capacity for autonomous or free choice.[11] This, in any case, is the first distinguishing feature of guilt, of the moralization of the sense of indebtedness: debt can become moralized when the debtor is viewed as a free and *morally responsible* agent. We shall examine some of the other distinctive features of "guilt" shortly.

The sections that follow immediately in the Second Essay (5–11) are largely taken up with exploration of the non-moralized debtor/creditor relationship, and its various manifestations. There is, of course, the paradigmatic case of individual exchange (GM II: 5–6), but then there is also the case of the community and its members with those who violate communal norms being in the situation of debtors

---

[11] Being in debt does require, to be sure, that one have the traits of the one Nietzsche calls the "sovereign" individual who is sufficiently regular in his behavior and has a sufficiently good memory that he can honor his promises (GM II: 2).

(GM II: 9–11). Most strikingly, though, GM II: 5–7 emphasizes, at rather great length, the role of the infliction of pain in the earliest forms of debtor–creditor relationships. As Nietzsche writes:

> The equivalence [between a debt and an infliction of pain on the debtor] is provided by the fact that instead of an advantage directly making up for the wrong [to the creditor] (so, instead of compensation in money, land or possessions of any kind), a sort of *pleasure* is given to the creditor as repayment and compensation, – the pleasure of having the right to exercise power over the powerless without a thought . . . the enjoyment of violating. . . . [C]ompensation is made up of a warrant and entitlement to cruelty.

(GM II: 5)

But such compensation would not be satisfying except for the fact that, "To see somebody suffer is nice, to make somebody suffer even nicer – that is a hard proposition, but an ancient, powerful, human-all-too-human proposition" (GM II: 6).[12] The instinct for cruelty is, in other words, a fundamental human instinct, one whose satisfaction could easily compensate a creditor for debts owed. The centrality of this instinct to human life means that "when mankind felt no shame towards its cruelty, life on earth was more cheerful than it is today" now that "the animal 'man' is finally taught to be ashamed of all his instincts" (GM II: 7).

Why does Nietzsche spend so much time on the topic of human cruelty? There are three points worth noting. First, a fundamental human instinct for cruelty is a necessary presupposition of the account of the origin of bad conscience later in the Second Essay: bad conscience, after all, is said to arise from cruel instincts that had to be internalized. These early sections of the Second Essay set the stage, then, for the central claim of the chapter: they argue for the powerful

---

[12] Nietzsche continues: "No cruelty, no feast: that is what the oldest and longest period in human history teaches us – and punishment, too, has such very strong *festive* aspects!" (GM II: 6). This, of course, anticipates the discussion of punishment at GM II: 12–14, but the real significance of that discussion has already been dealt with in Chapter 5: namely, as an illustration and explicit methodological reflection on the practice of genealogy.

role of cruelty in human life. (As Nietzsche says in *Ecce Homo* (III: GM): "Cruelty is here [in the Second Essay] exposed as one of the most ancient and basic substrata of culture that simply cannot be imagined away.")

Second, Nietzsche suggests that our dominant moral attitudes are hostile to our basic human instincts (which would plainly be true if cruelty were one of those instincts); as such, our dominant moral standards necessarily cast a pall over existence: how can we affirm a world so firmly rooted in "immoral" instincts? This, as we have seen, is one reason for a revaluation of values: to thwart the pessimism about existence that flows from the existing "moral" evaluation of things.

Third, Nietzsche, for the first time, broaches the issue central to the Third Essay, namely the problem of suffering: for suffering is, of course, the most obvious (and objectionable) result of cruelty. While speculating that "pleasure in cruelty does not really need to have died out" (GM II: 7), Nietzsche makes a far more important observation: "What actually arouses indignation over suffering [hence over cruelty] is not the suffering itself but the senselessness of suffering" (GM II: 7). This is precisely the problem that the "ascetic ideal" of the Third Essay is introduced to solve, as we will see in Chapter 8. Humans are naturally cruel, and this cruelty produces suffering. But suffering is intolerable without some "meaning" attached to it: in the post-Christian era, at least, that meaning has been supplied by the ascetic ideal. This issue will occupy us centrally in the following chapter.

Bad conscience: internalized cruelty (16–18)

It contributes to the somewhat rambling feel of the Second Essay that the question first posed in GM II: 4 – "How . . . did . . . the consciousness of guilt . . . come into the world?" – only gets "a first, preliminary expression" (GM II: 16) twelve sections later! Emphasis must be laid, however, on Nietzsche's immediate cautionary note: what is coming in section 16 is, itself, a *first* and *preliminary* explanation of the phenomenon. The question of GM II: 4 will not *really* be answered until section 21, to which we return below.

Our "first, preliminary" answer addresses only the origin of "bad conscience" – not *guilty* conscience, but what Nietzsche later calls "animal 'bad conscience'" (GM III: 20) – and the answer is the same as the one popularized by Freud some forty years later in *Civilization and Its Discontents*. Nietzsche writes:

> All instincts which are not discharged outwardly *turn inwards* – this is what I call the *internalization* of man. . . . Those terrible bulwarks with which state [*staatliche*] organizations protected themselves . . . had the results that all those instincts of the wild, free, roving man were turned backwards, *against man himself*. Animosity, cruelty, the pleasure of pursuing, raiding, changing and destroying – all this was pitted against the person who had such instincts: *that* is the origin of "bad conscience."
>
> (GM II: 16)[13]

This development, Nietzsche emphasizes, "was not gradual and voluntary" (GM II: 17): it was "a forcible breach with [man's] animal past" (GM II: 16). But *who* forced it, one wonders? Nietzsche speaks, above, of "the state," but then clarifies what he really means in the next section:

> I used the word "state" [*Staat*]: it is obvious who is meant by this – some pack of blond beasts of prey, a conqueror and master race, which, organized on a war footing, and with the power to organize, unscrupulously lays its dreadful paws on a populace which, though it might be vastly greater in number, is still shapeless and shifting. In this way, the "state" began on earth: I think I have dispensed with the fantasy which has it begin with a "contract."
>
> (GM II: 17)

---

13 Freud (1930: 78–9) writes: "[Man's] aggressiveness is introjected, internalized; it is, in point of fact, sent back to where it came from – that is, it is directed towards his own ego. There it is taken over by a portion of the ego, which sets itself over against the rest of the ego as super-ego, and which now, in the form of 'conscience,' is ready to put into action against the ego the same harsh aggressiveness that the ego would have liked to satisfy upon other, extraneous individuals. The tension between the harsh super-ego and the ego that is subjected to it, is called by us the sense of guilt; it expresses itself as a need for punishment."

Nietzsche is being slightly unfair, since most social contract theorists (Locke is an exception) did not believe the state *really* began with actual contracting: rather, they argue that in *justifying* what it is states can do we should ask what it is people would have voluntarily *contracted* to permit. In any case, what Nietzsche wants to emphasize is that, while these beasts of prey "are not the ones in whom 'bad conscience' grew," they are the ones who cause it to grow in others, those dominated groups (GM II: 17).

Nietzsche's account, like Freud's, depends crucially on the premise that instinctual energy does not simply vanish: it must be continuously discharged somehow. When the instinct for cruelty of some people is denied external discharge as a result of their domination by "beasts of prey," the instinctual energy has no alternative but to find "internal" discharge: this it does in "bad conscience," which is now a form of cruelty towards oneself – hence we speak of the "pangs of conscience," of "suffering" from a "bad conscience," and the like. "Lacking external enemies and obstacles, and forced into the oppressive narrowness and conformity of custom," Nietzsche writes, "man impatiently ripped himself apart, persecuted himself, gnawed at himself, gave himself no peace and abused himself" (GM II: 16).

This dramatic development – which Nietzsche calls "a serious illness" and "a forcible breach with [man's] animal past" – was by no means, however, a purely negative development, one to be regretted. Most obviously, it made civilization and social intercourse possible, but more important for Nietzsche is that it gave man an "inner world," for man's "soul . . . gained depth, breadth and height in proportion to the degree that the external discharge of man's instincts was *obstructed*" (GM II: 16). Indeed, describing the turning of these instincts against "man himself, his whole animal old self," Nietzsche writes:

> This secret self-violation, this artist's cruelty, this desire to give form to oneself as a piece of difficult, resisting, suffering matter . . . this uncanny, terrible but joyous labor of a soul voluntarily split within itself, which makes itself suffer out of the pleasure of making suffer, this whole *active* 'bad conscience' has finally . . . as true womb of ideal and imaginative events, brought a

wealth of novel, disconcerting beauty and affirmation to light, and perhaps for the first time beauty itself.

(GM II: 18)

It must be noted, immediately, however that the "beauty" brought in to the world by this "active" bad conscience is not a work of art or other conventional object of aesthetic appreciation: rather, what bad conscience brings into being (it is this that gives man's soul "depth") are *ideals*: bad conscience explains how *"selflessness, self-denial, self-sacrifice"* could constitute "an ideal, something beautiful" (GM II: 18).[14] What is "beautiful" here, and what is a product of bad conscience, is the human capacity for setting up regulative ideals in the light of which human beings evaluate and reflect upon themselves. Bad conscience, as the product of internalized cruelty, also goes some distance – not the full distance, as we will learn in the Third Essay – toward explaining the attraction of a particular kind of ideal, namely *ascetic* ideals like those of "self-denial" and "self-sacrifice": such ideals produce the "pleasure [which] belongs to cruelty" (GM II: 18). "Only bad conscience," he adds, "only the will to self-violation provides the precondition [*Voraussetzung*] for the *value* of the un-egoistic" (GM II: 18). Bad conscience is a *precondition* because, given that creatures like us take pleasure in cruelty, we can take pleasure in cruelty to ourselves via an ideal of self-denial. Yet bad conscience is *only* a precondition because it underdetermines the acceptance of ascetic ideals, for a pleasure in cruelty could make itself felt through many kinds of ideals other than ascetic ones. If bad conscience is the precondition for the triumph of the ascetic ideal, the Third Essay will supply the additional factor that guarantees its success.

The moralization of conscience through religion (19–22)

Up to this point, Nietzsche has still not directly answered the question of GM II: 4: how did "the consciousness of guilt" "come into the world?" The internalization of cruelty is a major step in the direction

---

14 Here Diethe's rendering of *ein Ideal, eine Schönheit* seems to me more elegant than Clark and Swensen's more literal "an ideal, a beauty."

of an explanation, but it still underdetermines the phenomenon in question. After all, humans might have internalized cruelty not by feeling *guilty* but by being masochists of the coarsest kind (e.g., I could be cruel to myself simply by holding my hand in a fire, or sleeping on a bed of nails). And indeed, as we have just seen, the suggestion is that "bad conscience" *prior* to guilt still involved setting up regulative ideals on the basis of which one evaluated oneself. We see this, for example, in Sophocles' Oedipus, who upon discovering that he has killed his father and married his mother, gouges out his eyes at the same time remarking on "the flooding pain of memory, never to be gouged out." He then adds: "After exposing the rankness of my own shame, how could I look men frankly in the eyes?" Bad conscience in a Greek like Oedipus finds expression not in guilt or a sense of moral responsibility (Oedipus, after all, did not intentionally kill his father and marry his mother), but in overpowering feelings of shame at what has transpired. As Bernard Williams has powerfully argued, "it is a mistake to think that Homeric shame [and Greek shame more generally] involves merely adjustment to the prejudices of the community" (1993b: 81); rather shame is a response to internalized standards, in which the agent's act or omission (voluntary or not) "will lower the agent's self-respect and diminish him in his own eyes" (1993b: 90).

So what interests Nietzsche is how creatures like us moved beyond *this* kind of internal expression of cruelty – the pangs of conscience associated with shame – towards full-blown *guilt*. More precisely, the critical question is how a consciousness of *debts* turned into a feeling of *guilt* – keeping in mind, of course, that the same German word, *Schuld*, can mean both debt and guilt. What is involved in the *moralization* of debt? How does having a debt differ from feeling guilty?

"Guilt," says one commentator helpfully, "is an experience of reprehensible failure (not necessarily intentional) to respect ethical obligations which one recognizes as justified" (May 1999: 77). Guilt, then, does not require any *external* observer: one can feel guilty for transgressing norms, even if no one knows of the transgression.[15]

---

[15]   Although shame is often thought to *require* an external observer, Williams (1993b: 81–2) argues persuasively that this is not where the distinction between the two kinds of sentiments lies.

Moreover, to feel guilty is to feel that *one could have done otherwise* (one could have *not* transgressed the norms) and to feel that the transgression reflects a fundamental defect of character or personhood.[16] *Guilt* is a painful emotion, reflecting an awareness of deep inadequacy or deficiency: it entails self-laceration and self-loathing.

A consciousness of a debt can differ from guilt along all these dimensions: a debt can arise from conduct that is ethically permissible (I borrow money from a bank); a debt does not presuppose free agency underlying the events that give rise to the debt (I feel a debt to my father, though I *could not have done otherwise* than be his son); and a debt does not necessarily reflect a fundamental failure of character (I owe a large mortgage, but this does not make me a reprehensible person). Of course, debts can acquire some of the trappings of guilt, e.g., someone who runs up huge monetary debts may feel he or she is a reprehensible person for having done so. But once that happens, it is more natural to say that the person "feels guilty" about the debts, than to say only that he or she is in debt. The puzzle, to repeat, of the Second Essay is how a capacity to feel "in debt" turns into a capacity to "feel guilty." Sections 19–21 now set out an explanation.

Section 19 returns again to the non-moralized "relationship of a debtor to his creditor in civil law," which, says Nietzsche, actually has an analogue in "pre-history," namely "the relationship of the *present generation* to their *forebears*." "[P]eople recognize an *indebtedness* [*Schuld*], which continually increases because these ancestors continue to exist as mighty spirits, giving the tribe new advantages and lending it some of their power" (GM II: 19). "The ancestors of the most powerful tribes," says Nietzsche, eventually move into the "obscurity of divine mystery and transcendence," i.e., they become god-like or gods. It is out of this idea of "debts to gods" (GM II: 20) that Nietzsche proposes to find the origin of the guilty conscience.

Unfortunately, the Diethe translation of the *Genealogy* (like most others) obscures this line of argument by rendering the German *Schuld* as "guilt" in sections 20 and 21: "The feeling of guilt [*Schuldgefühl*]

---

16 Contrast GM II: 15, where Nietzsche notes that there is an *absence* of a guilty conscience when a wrongdoer feels "'something has gone unexpectedly wrong here,' *not* 'I ought not to have done that.'"

towards a deity continued to grow for several millennia" (GM II: 20) and, "So much for a brief and roughly preliminary outline of the connection between the concepts 'guilt' [*Schuld*] and 'duty' with religious precepts" (GM II: 21). As noted, the word itself admits both renderings; the question is which rendering makes most sense of the passages in question.[17] We can, in fact, make better sense of Nietzsche's argument by reading section 20 as concerning debt, not guilt.

Section 20 tells us that, "The feeling of debt towards a deity continued to grow for several millennia," and that "the Christian God as the maximal god yet achieved" produced "the greatest feeling of debt on earth." Given that section 20 is simply continuing the line of thought introduced in section 19, and given that section 19 (even on Diethe's rendering) concerned only "debt" (first to creditors, then to ancestors, then to ancestors-cum-gods), it makes more sense to treat Christianity as simply elevating the feeling of "debt" rather than "guilt," which he has not yet explained.

More significantly, though, this line of argument suggests precisely the conclusion that Nietzsche explicitly draws at the end of section 20: namely, that "the unstoppable decline in faith in the Christian God" should produce "a considerable decline in human consciousness of debt [*menschliches Schuldbewusstseins*]" such that "atheism" would involve a "*second innocence* [*Unschuld*]," i.e., an erasure of this feeling of indebtedness because humans would no longer believe in the creditor, namely, God. The use of *Unschuld* ("innocence") might suggest that the contrasting concept (*Schuld*) should be rendered as "guilt," rather than "debt," but one suspects Nietzsche puts *Unschuld* in italics in the German precisely to underline the ambiguity, which he quickly calls attention to at the beginning of section 21. Here Nietzsche tells us that the discussion of the concept "*Schuld*" and various "religious precepts" has so far been "preliminary" or "provisional" (*vorläufig*). Why? Because, says Nietzsche,

> I have so far intentionally set aside the actual moralization of these concepts . . . and at the conclusion of the last section I even spoke as though this moralization did not exist, conse-

---

[17]   I was led to appreciate this point by correspondence with Mathias Risse concerning Risse (2001).

quently, as though these concepts would necessarily come to an end once the basic premise no longer applied, the belief in our "creditor," in God.

(GM II: 21)

To "moralize" the concept of "debt" is precisely to turn it into "guilt": indeed, if that were not the case, then atheism *would* eliminate the "feeling of guilt." But atheism can only eliminate the feeling of "indebtedness" (*not* guilt) towards gods, because, in fact, the concept "debt" has been "moralized" in a way that makes it invulnerable to atheism. That is what section 20 had so far ignored in its discussion of the feeling of "debt" (not *guilt*). The question now is in what does the moralization of "debt" consist?

Nietzsche's official statement of the "moralization" comes in the parenthetical at the beginning of section 21. He defines the "actual moralization" of the "concepts 'debt' and 'duty'" as follows: "the way they are pushed back into conscience; more precisely, the entanglement [*Verwicklung*] of *bad* conscience with the concept of God." The crucial question, of course, is why atheism would not suffice to defeat this "entanglement" with the concept of God? After all, what distinguishes the argument of section 21 from section 20 is, on the reading proposed here, the claim that once debt is moralized, lack of belief in God no longer suffices to erase the (moralized) feeling of indebtedness. Why not?[18]

Nietzsche's answer, in a nutshell, is this: "this man of bad conscience has seized on the religious precept in order to provide his

---

[18]   The main difficulty in the useful Risse (2001) is that I do not see that he has a good answer to this question. Risse (2001) also emphasizes the distinctive role of *Christianity*, as distinct from "religious precepts" generally, in Nietzsche's answer. There is no doubt that most of the rhetoric and concepts Nietzsche alludes to in GM II: 21–2 are recognizably Christian ones; however, as we will see more clearly in Chapter 8, what *really* turns bad conscience into guilt is the attachment of bad conscience to the ascetic ideal. And that latter ideal, it turns out, is manifestly *not* a purely Christian phenomenon: ours is "the ascetic planet *par excellence*" (GM III: 11) and the teacher of the ascetic ideal, the ascetic priest appears "regularly and universally . . . in almost any age; he does not belong to any race in particular; he thrives everywhere; he comes from every social class" (GM III: 11).

self-torture with its most horrific hardness and sharpness. Guilt towards *God*: this thought becomes an instrument of torture" (GM II: 22). In short, man's internalized cruelty (his "bad" but not yet "guilty" conscience) disposes him to seize upon instruments like the concept of debt to God and to turn it into *guilt* before God in order to enhance his ability to torture himself. Nietzsche's implicit suggestion is that this drive towards self-torture is too powerful a psychic force for a mere cognitive proposition, like the denial of God's existence, to have any force.

How exactly do the religious precepts make possible this exceptional "self-torture"? According to Nietzsche, religions (at least the ascetic religions with which Nietzsche is most often concerned, like Christianity and Buddhism[19]) take the concept of a "debt" (towards God, as in Christianity, though not in Buddhism) and transform it into the idea of a debt that can *never* be discharged (at least not in this world): "a once-and-for-all payment *is to be* foreclosed" (GM II: 21), for example via ideas like "original sin" in Christianity (GM II: 21) or the idea "of existence in general . . . as inherently worthless" and thus unredeemable, as in Buddhism (GM II: 21). This is now "guilt" severed from any *particular* transgression and turned into a general state of being for the actors so afflicted. Of course, Nietzsche finds Christianity's "stroke of genius" on this score the most "horrifying," namely the Christian idea of "the creditor sacrificing himself for his debtor, out of love . . . out of *love* for the debtor" (GM II: 21). In other words, the creditor (God) who sacrifices his son (Jesus) for the "debts" (sins) of mankind "out of love" for this debtor (sinner) has, through the very same gesture, simply amplified mankind's feeling

[19] Elsewhere, Nietzsche calls Buddhism and Christianity "nihilistic religions . . . religions of decadence," but denies that Buddhism teaches "asceticism" (A: 20). But this is because, according to Nietzsche, Buddhism embraces "no categorical imperative, no *compulsion* whatever" since this "would merely increase the excessive sensitivity" which is the source of suffering and which Buddhism seeks to alleviate (A: 20). That there is no "categorical imperative" towards asceticism (or anything else) does not mean, of course, that Buddhism does not involve a hypothetical imperative: namely, *if* you want to relieve your suffering, *then* take the following measures, most of which are basically ascetic in character (after all, the cessation of desire is one of the prime objectives of Buddhism).

of indebtedness to wholly new levels: one has not only the original debt, but now the even greater debt resulting from the creditor's astonishing sacrifice! The internalized cruelty associated with "bad conscience" can now "seize" upon this religious tenet "in order to provide his self-torture with its most horrific hardness and sharpness" (GM II: 22). Nietzsche writes:

> We have here a sort of madness of the will showing itself in mental cruelty which is absolutely unparalleled: man's *will* to find himself guilty and condemned without hope of reprieve, his *will* to think of himself as punished, without the punishment ever measuring up to the crime, his *will* to infect and poison the fundamentals of things with the problem of punishment and guilt in order to cut himself off, once and for all, from the way out of this labyrinth of "fixed ideas," this *will* to set up an ideal – that of a "holy God" – in order to be palpably convinced of his own absolute worthlessness in the face of this ideal. . . . What ideas he has, what perversity, what hysterical nonsense, what *bestiality of thought* immediately erupts, the moment he is prevented, if only gently, from being a *beast in deed*!
>
> (GM II: 22)

The reason, then, that atheism cannot defeat the moralized concept of "debt" is because the reasons for that moralization – the drive to self-torture that grows out of the bad conscience as internalized cruelty – are so powerful in the psyche that they make real atheism impossible. Indeed, the suggestion appears to be that belief in God has become an epiphenomenon of the will to self-torture; giving up belief in God, by itself, would simply not affect the deep, underlying structure of internalized aggression that originally gave rise to that belief.

There is something, though, curious about this explanation. Bad conscience is a product of internalized cruelty. But guilty conscience is a product of bad conscience *in conjunction with* the moralization of the concept of debt. The concept of debt is moralized through its association with religious precepts, that elevate the feeling of indebtedness to new, painful extremes, i.e., the feeling of debts that can never be discharged, debts that reflect badly on one's personhood, debts for which one is eternally responsible. But then the explanation for why debts are moralized in this way appears, once again, to be that we have a bad conscience, i.e., we take pleasure in cruelty to ourselves. So it looks, then, like the internalization of cruelty is the *whole* explanation for the rise of guilty conscience: it explains our capacity for internal self-assessment (we relish being cruel to ourselves), *and* it explains why debt becomes moralized and turns in to guilt.

If that were right, we would be left with a puzzle. Since the internalization of cruelty is an event of pre-history (a necessary precondition for civilization), this means that even Nietzsche's Greeks and Romans – his paradigms of adherents of "master morality" from the First Essay – have a bad conscience. But there is nothing to suggest that they have a *guilty* conscience, for they have no concept of "God-the judge" or "God-the-Hangman" (GM II: 22), and no concept of "original sin" (GM II: 21). Yet if internalized cruelty *really* explained everything, then they too should have a guilty conscience. Something, then, is still missing from the explanation.

Bad conscience and the ascetic ideal (23–5)

The next section, in fact, calls attention to this puzzle, for now Nietzsche tells us immediately "that there are *nobler* ways of making use of the invention of gods than man's self-crucifixion and self-abuse," and this was true in particular of "the *Greek gods*, these reflections of noble and proud men in whom the *animal* in man felt deified" (GM II: 23). These Greeks, Nietzsche says, "used their gods expressly to keep 'bad conscience' at bay" (GM II: 23).[20] The Greeks

20 The German here is: "*Diese Griechen haben sich . . . ihrer Götter bedient, gerade um sich das 'schlechte Gewissen' vom Leibe zu halten*" The crucial expression here – *vom Leibe zu halten* – is rendered by Diethe as "at bay," by Clark and Swensen as "at arm's length," and, least literally, by Kaufmann as "to ward off." Mathias Risse points out to me that the connotation of the expression in German is that whatever is kept "at arm's length" is something I have never had interaction with, which is less obviously the connotation of the English "at bay." The fact remains, however, that the logic of the whole argument of GM II entails that the Greeks must have had "bad conscience" – as members of civilization, they had internalized their cruelty, after all – but they did not have *guilt*. They did not have *guilt* because they had different kinds of gods; but the question still remains *why* those gods and "religious

did this by inventing gods that *deflected* feelings of guilt, rather than causing them. Attributing human misconduct to "foolishness" and "mental disturbance" – "*not* sin! you understand?" – the Greeks, in turn, laid the blame for such disturbances on the gods:

> "A god must have confused him [the human wrongdoer]," [the Greek] said to himself at last, shaking his head. . . . In this way, the gods served to justify man to a certain degree, even if he [the Greek] was in the wrong they [the gods] served as causes of evil – they did not, at that time, take the punishment on themselves, but rather, as is *nobler*, the guilt.

(GM II: 23)

Here we have explicit confirmation that one can have "bad conscience" and at the same time not have it expressed via the self-torture associated with Christian guilt. The Greeks have bad conscience – as we saw earlier, Greeks like Oedipus can suffer from the throes of internal self-assessment (e.g., by reference to shame norms) – but deflect its expression in guilt in part through the creation of very different gods. What, then, explains why the Greeks created different gods from we moderns? More precisely, what else explains the moralization of debt beyond simply the fact of internalized cruelty – something the Greeks had without having guilt?

The key is that the Greek gods expressed a particular kind of *ideal*, an ideal of "noble and proud men in whom the *animal* in man felt deified" (GM II: 23). And this, Nietzsche tells us, is rather different from "we moderns": "For too long, man [i.e., modern man] has viewed his natural inclinations with an 'evil eye,' so that they finally came to be intertwined with 'bad conscience' in him" (GM II: 24). "All the ideals . . . up to now," he adds, "have been hostile to life and have defamed the world," i.e., they have been "ascetic" ideals – he mentions "all those other-worldly aspirations, alien to the senses, the instincts, to nature, to animals" (GM II: 24). He concludes by suggesting that a different kind of spirit – "spirits which are strengthened by wars and victories, for which conquest, adventure, danger and even pain have

precepts" rather than the kind that yield guilty conscience? GM II never quite resolves this question but, so we will argue, GM III does.

actually become a necessity" – would be needed to "redeem us . . . from the ideal held up till now" (GM II: 24). Such a spirit he dubs an "Antichrist and anti-nihilist" (GM II: 24) and equates him with "*Zarathustra the Godless*" (GM II: 25).

What Nietzsche deftly does in these final sections is set the stage for the Third Essay, which introduces and examines the phenomenon of "the ascetic ideal," which is precisely an ideal that is "hostile to life" and to "the instincts, to nature" (GM II: 24). All the major modern religions embody this kind of ideal, whereas Nietzsche's Zarathustra preaches a contrary ideal. Zarathustra is, of course, a parody of the Christ-figure in The New Testament, delivering an anti-Christian message, i.e., he advocates a different ideal than that which has been "held up till now."

The reason the internalized cruelty of the Greeks did not produce a guilty conscience, and the reason the Greeks produced gods that kept "'bad conscience' at bay," is because they were *not* adherents of the ascetic ideal. That is the crucial difference between us and the Greeks, and the basic reason that they do not have guilt, whereas we do. Thus, a full explanation of the rise of *guilty* conscience needs not only the fact of internalized cruelty *but also* an account of why human beings adopted the ascetic ideal, the ideal which, *conjoined with* bad conscience, gives moderns the guilty conscience that the Greeks lacked (or held "at bay"). It is the task of the Third Essay to answer this crucial question, how "the priestly reinterpretation of the animal 'bad conscience' (cruelty turned back on itself)" produced "guilt" in its developed form (GM III: 20).

Bad conscience is necessary for guilt, which, in turn, is necessary for "morality" in Nietzsche's pejorative sense, i.e., MPS. But bad conscience alone gives us only "guilt in its raw state" (GM III: 20); real guilt requires bad conscience to be put in the service of the ascetic ideal, and it is only the Third Essay that will explain why that should come to pass.

Chapter 8

A commentary on the Third Essay

> The *third* inquiry offers the answer to the question whence the ascetic ideal, the priests' ideal, derives its tremendous *power* although it is the *harmful* ideal *par excellence*, a will to the end, an ideal of decadence. Answer: not, as people may believe, because God is at work behind the priests but *faute de mieux* [lacking something better] – because it was the only ideal so far, because it had no rival. "For man would rather will even nothingness than *not* will." – Above all, a *counterideal* was lacking – *until Zarathustra*.
>
> (EH III: GM)

As a result of being forced into civilized intercourse with our fellows, creatures like us had to internalize our instinctive cruelty, and thus acquired an "animal 'bad conscience' (cruelty turned back on itself)" (GM III: 20). Under the influence of ascetic religions like Christianity and Buddhism, this internalized cruelty turned into a searing and unrelenting sense of *guilt*, a feeling of fundamental inadequacy and reprehensibility,

a state of despair about the human condition and nihilism. But why did the ascetic religions have this tremendous influence? Why did the Greek way of handling "bad conscience" not persist? The Second Essay presents no real answer.

Within civilization itself, meanwhile, some creatures, "the slaves," came to suffer from a different kind of psychological malady, *ressentiment*, an emotion so powerful that it finally found expression in a first revaluation of values, the subject of the First Essay. But why did the "masters" of antiquity succumb to this revaluation? Why did slave morality triumph? The First Essay provides no satisfactory answer.

The Third Essay of the *Genealogy* is naturally read as supplying answers to the two open questions from the earlier essays. "What do ascetic ideals mean?" Nietzsche asks at the start of the chapter. But the more immediate question for the reader is: what *are* ascetic ideals? "[T]he three great pomp words of the ascetic ideal," Nietzsche says later, "are: poverty, humility, chastity" (GM III: 8). Ascetic ideals are those norms that valorize poverty, humility, and chastity – more generally, norms which valorize *all* states of self-denial in which we forgo satisfaction of desires, not only the rapacious and sensual desires – the desires for wealth, fame, domination, sexual gratification, and so forth suggested by the "three great pomp words" – but also ordinary desires, whose cessation is the object, for example, of Schopenhauer's Buddhism-inspired doctrines.[1] Explaining the success of ascetic ideals – "the earth [is now] the ascetic planet *par excellence*" (GM III: 11) – will, at the same time, explain the transformation of bad conscience into *guilt* and the triumph of slave morality. It will also, of course, complete the genealogy of morality.

Section 1 of the Third Essay gives us an outline of some (but not all) of the argument to follow.[2] The question "what do ascetic

[1] More precisely, the goal is the cessation of *self-directed* desires like a desire for one's own sexual pleasure, a desire for one's own material satisfactions, and so on.

[2] Thus when Nietzsche says in the Preface that the Third Essay "is a commentary on the aphorism that precedes it" (GM Pref: 8), he plainly means the Third Essay is an interpretation of GM III: 1, and *not* the rather obscure two-line epigram from Zarathustra. See Wilcox (1997) and Janaway (1997). As to that

ideals mean?" (GM III: 1) can be read as equivalent to the question, "What explains the attraction of ascetic ideals?", where the relevant kind of explanation will appeal to the particular *meaning* that ideal has for different kinds of people. The Third Essay is concerned primarily with four kinds of people: artists (GM III: 2–5); philosophers (GM III: 5–10); priests (GM III: 10–13, 15); and, most importantly, the "majority of mortals," whom Nietzsche tells us in section 1 are "physiological casualties and the disgruntled" (GM III: 13–22).[3] In each case, the explanation for the attraction of the ascetic ideal will avoid the supernatural – it's not that "God is at work" (EH III: GM) – and will instead rely on the explanatory principle first introduced in the discussion of philosophers and the ascetic ideal:

> Every animal, including the *bête philosophe*, instinctively strives for an optimum of favourable conditions in which fully to release his power and achieve his maximum feeling of power [*Machtgefühl*]; every animal abhors equally instinctively, with an acute sense of smell which is "higher than all reason," any kind of disturbance and hindrance which blocks or could block his path to the optimum.

(GM III: 7)

If every animal manifests this instinctive drive towards maximum feelings of power, then an explanation of the appeal of ascetic ideals will have to explain how those ideals, too, satisfy that drive. "Will to power" now comes center stage in the argument of the Third Essay, for while the connection between, e.g., the will to power of philosophers and the ascetic ideal will be fairly straightforward, it will seem, at least initially, paradoxical that an ideal of self-denial could

---

quote (from Z I: "On Reading and Writing") – "Carefree, mocking, violent – this is how wisdom wants *us*: she is a woman, all she ever loves is a warrior" – one plausible hypothesis is that he is here describing an attitude towards knowledge and truth quite different from the dominant ascetic attitude that he critiques in GM III: 23 ff. (On this point, I am indebted to Neil Sinhababu.)

3   An additional case alluded to in GM III: 1, women, is not in fact discussed in the essay, except for a superficial reference in GM III: 14. "Saints" are also mentioned in GM III: 1, and are discussed, arguably, in GM III: 17. See Janaway (1997: 256–7).

really constitute the will to power of the vast majority of mortals, as Nietzsche contends.

Although section 1 of the Third Essay anticipates much of the argument, it still omits mention of two important themes: first, the famous discussion of perspectivism that occurs in GM III: 12; and second, the crucial discussion of the ascetic ideal and the will to truth (GM III: 23–7).[4] Although the discussion of perspectivism occurs as part of the treatment of the "priest," it will make more sense, conceptually, to consider the issue of perspectivism in connection with Nietzsche's discussion of science, truth, and the ascetic ideal that concludes the essay.

Artists, philosophers, and the will to power

The substantive argument of the Third Essay begins with what is, ostensibly, an investigation of the meaning of ascetic ideals for artists. Nietzsche takes as a case study Richard Wagner's late-in-life turn to Christian sentimentality in the opera *Parsifal*: his "homage to chastity" (GM III: 2) and embrace of "sickly Christian and obscurantist ideals" (e.g., Parsifal's discovery of "compassion" for all living things) (GM III: 3). In truth, however, GM III: 2–5 is merely a prelude to the discussion of philosophers and the ascetic ideal. For the real conclusion of the first discussion is that, for artists, ascetic ideals mean *"nothing at all"* (GM III: 5) since artists, considered as a class, "never stand independently" but are, rather, "the valets of a morality or philosophy or religion" (GM III: 5). In other words, there is nothing distinctive of artists qua artists that we can seize upon to explain their

---

4   Janaway (1997: 257) claims that GM III: 23 begins the exposition of the meaning of the ascetic ideal for "scholars" [*Gelehrte*], another "type" alluded to in GM III: 1. Of course, in GM III: 1, Nietzsche treats "philosophers and scholars" as a unit, rather than separating out "scholars" as he does priests, women, and so forth. Janaway (1997: 266 n. 10) objects, however, that Schopenhauer, whom Nietzsche discusses at GM III: 5–6, is "a genuine philosopher" for Nietzsche, not a mere scholar, and therefore that discussion could not do justice to "scholars" as well. That *might* be correct, though Schopenhauer is not the only figure discussed in these sections. In any case, little turns on this dispute: if Janaway is correct, then, in fact, GM III: 23 ff. is, in fact, anticipated in GM III: 1, albeit rather obliquely!

attraction to ascetic ideals; we must look to the moral, philosophical or religious precepts which the artist embodies or embraces to understand his attraction to asceticism. Thus, says Nietzsche, Wagner "took the philosopher Schopenhauer as his front man," and so we arrive at "the more serious question: what does it mean if a genuine *philosopher* [like Schopenhauer] pays homage to the ascetic ideal" (GM III: 5). And with that the discussion of artists and ascetic ideals is at an end.[5]

With philosophers, then, we enter the real argument of the Third Essay. Attraction to the ascetic ideal belongs to "the type" philosopher (GM III: 7), and it is at this point that Nietzsche appeals to the explanatory principle of will to power quoted above. But how does asceticism permit a philosopher to "release his power and achieve his maximum feeling of power" (GM III: 7)? According to Nietzsche, "asceticism, a hard and hearty renunciation with a good will, belongs among the most favourable conditions for the highest spirituality" (GM III: 9). Asceticism is conducive to the optimal conditions for the philosophical way of life in two respects, one spiritual or intellectual, the other a matter of external practicality.

Gratification of the sensual and rapacious desires, Nietzsche argues, distracts one from the cultivation of the intellectual or spiritual life (Nietzsche uses the term *Geistigkeit* (spirituality, intellectuality) in this context): the philosopher needs "reins on an unbridled and irritable pride or a willful sensuality or . . . an inclination to luxury and to the most exquisite things" (GM III: 8).

---

[5]   As is often the case in Nietzsche, there remains much of interest in these opening sections, even independent of their role in the argument of the Third Essay – which, as noted in the text, is minimal. For example, Nietzsche's observation that,

> it is certainly better if we separate an artist sufficiently far from his work as not immediately to take the man as seriously as his work. After all, he is merely the pre-condition for the work, the womb, the soil, sometimes the manure and fertilizer on which it grows, – and as such he is something we have to forget about in most cases if we want to enjoy the work.
>
> (GM III: 4)

has been often invoked, with some justice, in consideration of Nietzsche's own work.

Such conditions of restraint, Nietzsche says, are "the most proper and natural prerequisites for [the philosopher's] *best* existence and *finest* productivity" (GM III: 7).

Schopenhauer represents, for Nietzsche, a paradigmatic example of embrace of the ascetic ideal as a defense against sensual and rapacious desires. The route to that conclusion, however, may strike the reader as a bit circuitous, since it starts with a discussion of Schopenhauer's aesthetics. Schopenhauer, according to Nietzsche, ostensibly adopts Kant's view that genuine aesthetic appreciation is *disinterested*, i.e., "without interest," such that the standpoint of aesthetic appreciation reflects, like the moral point of view, "the glory of . . . impersonality and universality" (GM III: 6). Indeed, Schopenhauer appears to extend the Kantian line of thought by claiming that aesthetic appreciation even "counteracts *sexual* 'interestedness'" (GM III: 6) and produces a "calming of the will" (GM III: 6), i.e., it produces an ascetic state in the observer of the beautiful. But the initial impression of Schopenhauer's aesthetics is misleading, Nietzsche argues, for, in fact, "beauty pleased [Schopenhauer] too, out of 'interest,' in fact, out of the strongest, most personal interest possible: that of the tortured person to escape from torture" (GM III: 6). Schopenhauer, in other words, was tortured by his own powerful desires – hence he treated "sexuality as a personal enemy" (GM III: 7) and spoke of "the base craving of the will" and "the penal servitude of volition" (GM III: 6) – and had an *interest* in finding relief from their demands: this he found, in part, in the appreciation of beauty; aesthetic enjoyment provided relief from other, painful desires.

Thus, for Schopenhauer, we explain the appeal of the ascetic ideal (in the form of the doctrine promoting aesthetic appreciation "without interest") in terms of its providing "*an escape from torture*" (GM III: 6), i.e., the "torture" of all-too-powerful sensual desires.[6] In fact, this same style of explanation – the ascetic ideal as an escape from a kind of torture – will recur later when the time comes to explain the appeal of the ascetic ideal to the "majority of mortals."

[6] Indeed, despite his famed pessimism, Schopenhauer, the man, was, in fact, a *bon vivant* who enjoyed drink, women, and the nightlife. He *clearly* felt the strong attraction of sensual desires.

There are also practical obstacles put up by the external world to the philosopher's life, for "his drive[s] . . . to doubt . . . deny . . . research, investigate, dare . . . his will to neutrality and objectivity" all put him at odds with "the primary demands of morality and conscience" (GM III: 9). Indeed, extrapolating from earlier treatments of these themes (D: 42), Nietzsche says that the first "contemplative men" – the first to be, like philosophers, "inactive, brooding and unwarlike" – were "widely despised when they were not feared" (GM III: 10). But by making themselves fearful – especially through various forms of severe asceticism, i.e., "cruelty towards themselves, imaginative forms of self-mortification" (GM III: 10) – these first contemplative men created space in which their form of life would be permitted to persist. And thus we have the practical value of ascetic ideals for philosophers:

> [T]he philosophic spirit has always had to disguise and cocoon itself among *previously established* types of contemplative man, as a priest, magician, soothsayer, religious man in general, in order for its existence *to be possible* at all: *the ascetic ideal* served the philosopher for a long time as outward appearance, as a pre-condition of existence, – he had to *play* that part in order to be a philosopher. . . . The peculiarly withdrawn attitude of the philosophers, denying the world, hating life, doubting the senses, desensualized, which has been maintained until quite recently to the point where it almost counted for the *philosophical attitude as such*, – this is primarily a result of the desperate conditions under which philosophy evolved and exists at all: that is, philosophy would have been *absolutely impossible* for most of the time on earth without an ascetic mask and suit of clothes, without an ascetic *misconception* [emphasis added] of itself.
>
> (GM III: 10)

Contemplative types, like the "priests," defended their way of life through an embrace of the ascetic ideal: such an ideal both valorized *their* way of living and, in certain circumstances, made them fearful to others, who were frightened by the capacity of these ascetics for self-denial and self-torture. Philosophers, in turn, had to cast themselves in the role of existing ascetic types in order to have the

251

opportunity to pursue philosophy. Thus, by embracing the ascetic ideal, the philosopher achieves "the optimum of favourable conditions in which fully to release his power," i.e., to be a philosopher.

Notice that the doctrine of will to power that is at play in this argument is precisely the one that we argued in Chapter 4 (pp. 138–44) was really paramount for Nietzsche: namely, will to power as a psychological hypothesis about the best explanation for human action in most, if not all, cases. Thus, in the Third Essay, will to power is presented as an "instinctiv[e] striv[ing]" for conditions in which the agent achieves "his maximum feeling of power [*Machtgefühl*]" (GM III: 7). The talk here is of "instincts" and "strivings" and "feelings," all familiar psychological categories, and all consistent with Nietzsche's later characterization of the *Genealogy* as "studies by a psychologist" (EH III: GM). This way of reading the doctrine of will to power also saves it, happily, from the ludicrous extremes to which Nietzsche sometimes takes it in *Nachlass* material, where he experiments with the idea of will to power as a property of *all* organic life, and even of inorganic nature itself.[7] Returned to its rightful role as a psychological hypothesis, the famous doctrine of the will to power not only ceases to be a piece of crackpot metaphysical speculation, but also becomes a plausible competitor to psychological hedonism, the doctrine that people instinctively strive for pleasure.[8] For like pleasure, what produces a "feeling of power" is context-sensitive, depending, for example, on the person's condition or status, the opportunities available, and the prevailing norms. As Nietzsche notes, there is a "subtlety of the feeling of power" (D: 245), which makes it available for a wide range of explanatory work. Of course, all the examples Nietzsche offers feed upon notions of *domination, control, status*, and

---

[7] Even the illuminating account of will to power as a claim about "the essence of life" in Richardson (1996) ends up acknowledging that, while will to power may first-and-foremost be a property of drives, Nietzsche's "interest is mainly in persons" which are amalgamations of drives (1996: 44): and with persons, of course, psychological categories leap to the fore in explanation. On the other hand, the appeal to "power" in GM III: 7 is, *contra* Richardson (1996: 19–20), most naturally construed by analogy to psychological hedonism.

[8] More precisely, Nietzsche must claim that feelings of pleasure are simply epiphenomena of the feeling of power, such that one could have the latter without the former, but not vice versa.

growth, and thus are extensions of ordinary paradigms of power, e.g., political domination of a group of people, physical control of a prisoner, superior status in an organization (e.g., the chief executive), growth of an empire. But it is always the psychological resonance and analogues of these cases that interest Nietzsche. So, for example, the ascetic is said to enjoy the "triumph over oneself" and thus "revel[s] in an extremity of power" (D: 113). Similarly, the Brahmins (who also reappear in GM III: 10) are "those who can control themselves and who are thereby accustomed to a feeling of power" (D: 65). A more subtle case is discussed in a section titled "*On the doctrine of the feeling of power*. – Benefiting and hurting others are ways of exercising one's power upon others; that is all one desires in such cases" (GS: 13). To be in a position to benefit others is to have a status – "a consciousness of difference" which itself gives "a feeling of power" (WP: 688) – over and above the beneficiary; so too with hurting, though here as well there is a kind of domination and control that is made tangible through the ability to hurt. This leads, conversely, to the explanation for "praise": "A sort of restoration of balance in respect of benefits received, a giving in return, a demonstration of *our* power [i.e., status] ... [one] claims the right of being *able* to affirm, of being *able* to dispense honors" (WP: 775).

Indeed, once one appreciates the explanatory nuances of Nietzsche's conception of will to power, it is easy to see how the explanatory principle of GM III: 7 is, in fact, at work in the earlier essays of the *Genealogy*, albeit less explicitly.[9] Thus, Nietzsche describes one of the "*disguised* forms of the will to power" as involving "the imaginary consolation of outranking those who actually possess power; the recognition of an order of rank that permits judgments even of the more powerful; ... the invention of new tables of value" (WP: 774). Surely we recognize, here, the slaves of the First Essay, who by undertaking the first revaluation of values – the "slave revolt in morals" (which is "the invention of new tables of value") – have the "imaginary consolation of outranking [in terms of ethical standing, and ultimate reward in the afterlife] those who actually

---

[9]   I am grateful to Christopher Janaway for pressing this line of interpretation on me.

possess power" and who establish a new "order of rank that permits judgment even of the more powerful."

In the same passage (WP: 774), Nietzsche also describes "the sense of duty, conscience . . . self-condemnation" as being "disguised forms" of will to power as well, in the sense, presumably, that they involve *control* and *domination* of the self, as well as hurting the self. Perhaps most importantly for the argument yet to come in the Third Essay, this same *Nachlass* passage describes "disguised" will to power in its "lowest form" as follows: "will to exist at all, 'the drive to self-preservation'" (WP: 774; cf. BGE: 13: "self-preservation is only one of the indirect and most frequent *results*" of will to power). As he puts the point elsewhere, it is "individuals in conditions of distress" who seek self-preservation, rather than "*the expansion of power*" (GS: 349). For some, at least, the maximum "feeling of power" consists in survival itself. We shall return to this important point shortly.

Priests, humanity, *ressentiment,* and the ascetic ideal

Philosophers first found their place in the world by emulating ascetic priests – but what then was the meaning of the ascetic ideal for priests? That is the question to which Nietzsche now turns, and at least part of the answer is, of course, already apparent from GM III: 10: the ascetic ideal made the life of the priest possible amidst an early "chivalric–aristocracy" that valued "war, adventure, hunting, dancing, jousting and everything else that contains strong, free, happy action" (GM I: 7), precisely the kind of life priests did *not* lead. The "priests" Nietzsche speaks of throughout the Third Essay are, at least in the first instance, presumably some amalgamation of New Testament figures like Paul and Peter of the first century AD (the New Testament being the object of the polemic in GM III: 22), as well as the early "Church Fathers" of the second and third centuries AD (cf. GM III: 22), figures like Tertullian (whose rancorous tirade about the punishments that will befall the Roman oppressors is quoted at length in GM I: 15).[10] For

[10] This is the allusion Nietzsche presumably intends given the specific references noted in the text, as well as given the fact that the doctrines promoted by these priests are often recognizably Christian ones.

these early Christian proselytizers, their "*right* to exist stands and falls with [the ascetic] ideal" (GM III: 11), i.e., it is essential to achieving the "favourable conditions in which fully to release [their] power and achieve [their] maximum feeling of power" (GM III: 7). But if, in the first instance, ascetic priests are particular historical actors during the final centuries of the Roman Empire, Nietzsche is quite clear that the "type" of the ascetic priest occurs throughout history: "he does not belong to any race in particular, he thrives everywhere; he comes from every social class" (GM III: 11). After all, the "monstrous method of valuation" characteristic of ascetic priests "is not inscribed in human history as an exception and curiosity: it is one of the most wide-spread and long-lived facts there are" (GM III: 11). What all ascetic priests have in common is that they are a) *advocates* and *teachers* of the ascetic ideal, and b) the ascetic ideal is the pre-condition for achieving their "maximum feeling of power." But why, exactly, is b) true?

Part of the answer is obvious: the ascetic ideal valorizes the *kind* of life ascetic priests lead – one of "poverty, humility, chastity" (GM III: 8). But more than that is at stake, since Nietzsche tells us that through this ideal, the priest "place[s] himself at [the] head [of the 'herd,' i.e., the majority of mortals] as their shepherd" (GM III: 13), that the ascetic ideal is his "best instrument of power" (GM III: 1). The ascetic priest *comes to power* through his teaching of the ideal, he becomes the "shepherd" of the "herd," the leader, in effect, of the "majority of mortals" (GM III: 1), he is responsible for making "the earth . . . the ascetic planet *par excellence*" (GM III: 11). That means, of course, that the *power* of the ascetic priest can only be fully explained if we can explain the attraction and meaning of the ascetic ideal for those he leads, i.e., humanity at large.

Initially, at least, the appeal of the ascetic ideal seems paradoxical, and certainly hard to square with the thesis that, "Every animal . . . instinctively strives for an optimum of favourable conditions in which fully to release his power and achieve his maximum feeling of power" (GM III: 7). As an ideal demanding self-denial and self-flagellation, this appears to be the opposite of an ideal maximizing "power"! "The ascetic treats life as a wrong path" (GM III: 11), "a deep instinct forbids him to procreate" (GM III: 11), and yet still we find the ascetic priest throughout history! Nietzsche repeatedly underlines the paradoxical nature of this phenomenon: "It must be a necessity of the first rank which makes this species [the ascetic priest] continually grow and prosper when it is *hostile to life*, – *life itself must have an interest* in preserving such a self-contradictory type" (GM III: 11). Or similarly: "A self-contradiction such as that which seems to occur in the ascetic, 'life *against* life,' is – so much is obvious – seen from the physiological, not just the psychological standpoint, simply nonsense" (GM III: 13).

Yet just as Darwinian adaptationists assume that every biological phenomenon must be explained in terms of natural selection (no matter how unconducive to reproductive fitness it may appear on the surface),[11] so too Nietzsche assumes that whatever explains "life" must also explain these particular instances of life which *appear* hostile to it. "'Life against life,'" Nietzsche says is a "self-contradiction" that "can only be *apparent*; it has to be a sort of provisional expression, an explanation, formula, adjustment, a psychological misunderstanding of something, the real nature of which was far from being understood" (GM III: 13). "Life," of course, is rather vague, but we have already seen the explanatory constraint at issue: the doctrine of will to power of GM III: 7. If, in fact, "every animal" strives to maximize the feelings of power, then even those "animals," like ascetic priests or the majority of mortals who embrace the ideal taught by the ascetic priest, must fit within the same explanatory scheme. But how and why?

The crux of the argument involves three claims.

1   Suffering is a central fact of the human condition.
2   Meaningless suffering is unbearable and leads to "suicidal nihilism" (GM III: 28).
3   The ascetic ideal gives meaning to suffering, thereby seducing the majority of humans back to life, i.e., it maximizes their feeling of power within the constraints of their existential situation.

This, in schematic form, is the central argument of the Third Essay, most (but not all) of which is laid out in the crucial sections 13–21. Let us consider each claim in turn.

---

11   Many evolutionary biologists are not, to be sure, adaptationists in this sense, since they think non-selectionist forces at work in evolution play a larger role than adaptationists allow.

1   *Suffering is a central fact of the human condition.* Nietzsche takes over this theme from Schopenhauer,[12] though his account of the causes of this suffering are multifarious, even in the *Genealogy*: sometimes he attributes suffering to brute facts of physiology, other times to psychological and social factors. So, for example, as we saw in Chapter 7, the human instinct towards cruelty (GM II) yields suffering. So, too, internalizing cruelty via bad conscience (GM II) causes suffering – think of Oedipus's psychological suffering after he discovers that he has killed his father and married his mother. The slaves suffer, obviously enough, at the hands of the masters (GM I). But "the *majority* of mortals" are also said to suffer since they are "physiological casualties and . . . disgruntled" (GM III: 1) (cf. GM III: 13, where he again refers to "the whole herd of failures, the disgruntled, the under-privileged, the unfortunate, and all who suffer from themselves"). Nietzsche also invokes a more characteristically Schopenhauerian explanation for suffering, when he appeals to the fact that humans are endlessly striving and so are "unsatisfied and insatiable" (GM III: 13). Indeed, at the very end of the Third Essay, even a kind of existential *angst* is said to be a source of suffering: man "*suffered* from the problem of what he meant," the problem of the "justification or explanation or affirmation" of his existence (GM III: 28).

Thus, physiology, psychology, and society all conspire to produce a basic truth about the human situation: for the vast majority, *suffering* is the basic, continuing fact about their lives.

2   *Meaningless suffering is unbearable and leads to "suicidal nihilism"* (GM III: 28). The fundamental problem is not, Nietzsche thinks, suffering per se – although he only makes this point explicitly in the last section of the Third Essay. "[S]uffering itself was *not* [man's] problem," Nietzsche says. The problem was the persistent question: "Suffering for *what*?" (GM III: 28).[13] Indeed, we can go further: "Man, the bravest animal and most prone to suffer, does *not* deny suffering as such: he *wills* it, he even seeks it out, provided he

---

12   See Chapter 2: 55–6.

13   This theme actually makes its first brief appearance in the Second Essay: "What actually arouses indignation over suffering is not the suffering itself, but the senselessness of suffering" (GM II: 7).

is shown a *meaning* for it, a *purpose* of suffering. The meaningless-ness of suffering, *not* the suffering, was the curse which has so far blanketed mankind" (GM III: 28).

This crucial theme is, in fact, already anticipated earlier in the Third Essay when *ressentiment* returns to center stage in the argument. Although in the First Essay, *ressentiment* – the festering hatred and vengefulness of the impotent in response to unpleasant external stimuli – was attributed to the slaves (and the "slavish" psyche), we now learn in the Third Essay that this psychological state is widespread. "[W]orm-eaten physiological casualties," Nietzsche says, "are all men of *ressentiment*, a whole, vibrating realm of subterranean revenge, inexhaustible and insatiable in its eruptions against the happy" (GM III: 14). Since "the *majority* of mortals" are "physiological casualties" (GM III: 1), it follows that most people suffer from *ressentiment*.

But why would suffering itself (for physiological or other reasons) give rise to *ressentiment*? Because, says Nietzsche:

> [E]very sufferer instinctively looks for a cause for its distress; more exactly, for a culprit, even more precisely for a *guilty* culprit who is receptive to distress, – in short, for a living being upon whom he can release his emotions, actually or in effigy, on some pretext or other: because the release of emotions is the greatest attempt at relief, or should I say, at *anaesthetizing* on the part of the sufferer, his involuntarily longed-for narcotic against pain of any kind.

(GM III: 15)

Sufferers *instinctively* look for someone to blame because, more funda-mentally (and more obviously), they *instinctively* want to relieve their suffering:[14] the *discharge* of their *ressentiment* would numb their suffering, but *ressentiment* can only be discharged when it has an object. So the psychological logic of this phenomenon has two stages and one premise. The two stages are: sufferers want relief from their suffering, hence, sufferers seek someone to blame for their suffering, someone (or thing) upon whom to vent their *ressentiment*. The premise

[14] That, too, is presumably an instinct to achieve the maximum feeling of power, i.e., through the cessation of suffering.

is: the discharge of strong emotions deadens suffering. Nietzsche asserts the premise at several points. "*Excess of feeling*," he says, is "the most effective anesthetic for dull, crippling, long-drawn-out pain" (GM III: 19). All powerful emotions – Nietzsche names "anger, fear, voluptuousness, revenge, hope, triumph, despair, cruelty" (GM III: 20) – "throw the human soul out of joint, plunging it into terror, frosts, fires and raptures to such an extent that it rids itself of all small and petty forms of lethargy, apathy and depression, as though hit by lightning" (GM III: 20).

The discussion here is of a piece with Nietzsche's very first characterization of *ressentiment* as providing an "imaginary revenge" (GM I: 10) against unpleasant stimuli. In the case of the actual slaves, to be sure, the stimuli were *really* external (i.e., the masters, their oppressors) and the discharge was, in effect, the creation of new values that denounced the masters, i.e., the slave revolt. But whatever the cause of suffering, it always calls forth, Nietzsche thinks, the feeling of *ressentiment*, this desire for revenge – imaginary or real – this desire "for a *guilty* culprit who is receptive to distress . . . upon whom [the sufferer] can release his emotions" (GM III: 15). "'Someone or other must be to blame [*muss schuld daran sein*] that I feel ill' – this kind of conclusion is peculiar to all sick people, and in fact becomes more insistent, the more they remain in ignorance of the true reason" (GM III: 15).[15] Until he finds such a cause for his suffering, however, "that most dangerous and explosive material, *ressentiment*, continually piles up" (GM III: 15).

Now we see why Nietzsche says (in GM III: 28) that it is *meaningless* suffering that is the real problem for humankind: for only with a meaning attached can the sufferer discharge his emotions properly and deaden the pain, for it is the *meaning* that gives direction to the discharge of *ressentiment*, by identifying whom to blame.[16] In cases of meaningless suffering, by contrast, "*ressentiment* . . . piles up"

[15] As Ridley (1998: 54) points out, the very fact that the conceptual apparatus of *blame* is in play here indicates that these events must post-date the basic facts of the slave revolt discussed in the First Essay.

[16] There might, of course, be other ways to give meaning to suffering, but for the mass of humanity this is the primary way. (I am grateful to Sebastian Gardner for clarification on this issue.)

because the sufferer can find no "*guilty* culprit who is receptive to distress ... upon whom [the sufferer] can release his emotions" (GM III: 15). The ultimate consequence of such unrelieved suffering would be "suicidal nihilism" (GM III: 28). The question, in turn, is how "to detonate this explosive material [*ressentiment*] without blowing up" the sufferer (GM III: 15).

3   *The ascetic ideal gives meaning to suffering, thereby seducing the majority of humans back to life.* The "genius" of the ascetic priest, says Nietzsche, is "the *alleviation* of suffering" (GM III: 17), though the means he employs are quite various. There are, first of all, the "innocent" means for relieving suffering that Nietzsche discusses at GM III: 18, and which he summarizes as follows:

> [T]he total dampening of the awareness of life, mechanical activity, the small pleasure, above all the pleasure of "loving one's neighbour," herd-organization, the awakening of the communal feeling of power, the consequence of which is that the individual's dissatisfaction with himself is overriden by his delight at the prosperity of the community.
>
> (GM III: 19)

The priest's primary instrument, however, is not so "innocent," since it makes use of *guilt* itself. More precisely, the priest uses the ascetic ideal to give a meaning to suffering, and in so doing, prevents *ressentiment* from piling up to dangerous levels. Thus, Nietzsche says the priest is the "*direction-changer* of *ressentiment*" (GM III: 15) in the following sense. Every sufferer, as we have seen, cries out for a culprit. The innovation of the ascetic priest is to provide an accessible "culprit," the sufferer himself! So the priest says: "'Quite right, my sheep! Somebody must be to blame [for your suffering]: you yourself are this somebody, you yourself alone are to blame for it, *you yourself alone are to blame for yourself*'" (GM III: 15). In short, the sufferer *himself* is to be the object of his own *ressentiment*, since he is taught that he *himself* is the cause of his own suffering. As a result, the sufferer now has "a living being upon whom he can release his emotions" (GM III: 15), namely, himself. He discharges his emotions against himself, in turn, by lacerating himself with feelings of guilt.

Although the latter is, itself, a cause of additional suffering, this is now suffering *with a meaning*, hence bearable.

To see why this suffering is meaningful (hence bearable), we need to make *explicit*, in a way Nietzsche does not, the role of the ascetic ideal in this process. Such an ideal, recall, valorizes self-denial, and stigmatizes satisfaction of the rapacious and sensual desires. Yet human beings are fundamentally creatures of desire, who are "unsatisfied and insatiable" (GM III: 13), who lust after power, cruelty, sexual gratification, and so forth.[17] This means, of course, that humans stand almost continuously in violation of the ascetic ideal: all their basic instincts and inclinations are fundamentally anti-ascetic! The ascetic priest seizes upon this fact in order to provide a meaning for human suffering: in a nutshell, one suffers, according to the priest, as *punishment* for failure to live up to the ascetic ideal. As Nietzsche puts it:

> Man, suffering from himself in some way, at all events physio-logically, rather like an animal imprisoned in a cage, unclear as to why? what for? and yearning for reasons – reasons bring relief –, yearning for cures and narcotics as well, finally consults someone who knows hidden things too – and lo and behold! from this magician, the ascetic priest, he receives the *first* tip as to the "cause" of his suffering: he should look for it within *himself*, in *guilt*, in a piece of the past, he should understand his suffering itself as a *condition of punishment*.
>
> (GM III: 20)

By setting up the asceticism *as an ideal* by which most humans fall short, the priest can then reinterpret the basic existential fact of human suffering as "feelings of guilt, fear, punishment" (GM III: 20): you suffer because you are guilty for betraying the (ascetic) command-ments of your god, you suffer as punishment for your transgressions against this ideal, you suffer because *you* are a sinner, one who trans-gresses against the (ascetic) values laid down. This is why Nietzsche

17 See, e.g., GM I: 15 ("These weaklings – in fact *they*, too, want to be the pow-erful one day; this is beyond doubt"); D: 204 ("The means employed by the lust for power have changed, but the same volcano continues to glow").

says that "the main contrivance" used by the ascetic priest is "the *feeling of guilt*": he took the "animal-psychology" of bad conscience ("guilt in its raw state") and gave it a "priestly reinterpretation" and turned it into what we now recognize as "guilt" and "sin" (GM III: 20). The reinterpretation involves attaching the internalized cruelty (i.e., bad conscience before it is fully moralized) to an ascetic ideal, so that it is transmuted into the searing feelings of guilt discussed at the end of the Second Essay: the ascetic ideal "brought all suffering within the perspective of *guilt*," and thus gave it a meaning (GM III: 28). Priestly concepts like "guilt" and "sin" and "damnation" "make the sick *harmless* to a certain degree" by "giv[ing] their *ressentiment* a backwards direction [towards themselves] . . . and in this way . . . *exploit*[s] the bad instincts of all sufferers [to find someone to blame for their suffering] for the purpose of self-discipline, self-surveillance and self-overcoming" (GM III: 16).

Remember that the crucial premise here is that the discharge of strong emotions has an anesthetic effect. Nietzsche says that the "guilty" methods (GM III: 19–20) for alleviating suffering all rely upon "*excess of feeling* . . . as the most effective anesthetic for dull, crippling, long-drawn-out pain" (GM III: 19) (cf. GM III: 20: "*The ascetic ideal utilized to produce excess of feelings*"). Or similarly: "the release of emotions is the greatest attempt at relief, or should I say, at *anaesthetizing* on the part of the sufferer, his involuntarily longed-for narcotic against pain of any kind" (GM III: 15). Thus, by allowing the sufferer to discharge his *ressentiment* against himself in powerful feelings of *guilt* (for his transgressions against the ascetic ideal), the priest thereby anesthetizes the original suffering.[18] This isn't, to be sure, "a real *cure* in the physiological sense" (GM III: 16), since the priest treats "only suffering itself, the discomfort of the sufferer [and] *not* its cause" (GM III: 17) (the real cause, of course, has nothing to do with violating the ascetic ideal). But – and this is the critical point – it does allow the bulk of suffering humans to "retain their hold on life" (GM III: 13) by making their suffering intelligible. Thus,

[18] Remember: the *new* suffering, attendant upon the feelings of guilt, is bearable because meaningful: one suffers from guilt *because* one has transgressed the ascetic ideal (one is a sinner, etc.).

Nietzsche repeatedly emphasizes that "the ascetic ideal is a trick [*Kunstgriff*] for the *preservation* of life" (GM III: 13) and that since "*the ascetic ideal offered man a meaning* . . . the door was [thereby] shut on all suicidal nihilism" (GM III: 28).

In sum, the ascetic priest exploits a fact about our existential situation – namely, that most humans suffer[19] – by concocting a fictional explanation for this suffering: we suffer because we violate the ascetic ideal. Now our suffering has a meaning, and the suicidal nihilism which would result from meaningless suffering and undischargeable *ressentiment* is thwarted, since this *ressentiment* is now discharged against the agent himself in the form of powerful feelings of guilt, which then deaden the pain associated with the original suffering. Of course, by producing feelings of guilt, the priest's story about the ascetic ideal "brought new suffering with it, deeper, more internal, more poisonous suffering, suffering that gnawed away more intensely at life" (GM III: 28). "But in spite of all that," Nietzsche quickly adds, "man was *saved*, he had a *meaning*" (GM III: 28). And thus "from now on he could *will* something . . . the *will itself was saved*" (GM III: 28), i.e., it was still possible for humans to retain their hold on life, to *will* to do things, since their suffering, at last, had a meaning.

We can now see, too, why Nietzsche thinks the ascetic ideal is part of the "favourable conditions in which [the majority of mortals can] fully . . . release [their] power and achieve [their] maximum feeling of power" (GM III: 7). It is precisely because "*the ascetic ideal springs from the protective and healing instincts of a degenerating life* which uses every means to maintain itself and struggles for its existence" (GM III: 13). The ascetic ideal makes it possible for the majority of suffering mortals to escape "suicidal nihilism" and remain attached to life. And as Nietzsche tells us elsewhere, "will to exist at all, 'the drive to self-preservation'" is one of the "disguised" forms of the will to power, albeit its "lowest form" (WP: 774). The maximum feeling of power available to most people is only this: not to despair so much that they give up on life altogether.

---

[19] Nietzsche, to be sure, does *not* distinguish between the genuinely existential causes of suffering – e.g., desire, physiological malady, bad conscience – and the contingent, social causes.

Truth, science, and perspectivism

By the time we have reached GM III: 23, we have, in fact, answered the crucial question about the meaning of the ascetic ideal. We have explained "the *monstrosity* of its power" (GM III: 23). The ascetic ideal, as taught by the priests, exploits an existential fact about our situation – namely, that we suffer – by giving this fact a meaning, and thwarting the "suicidal nihilism" which would otherwise have resulted. The ascetic ideal allows the bulk of humanity to maintain its grip on life at the same time that it brings the priests to power as leaders of humanity. This ideal, then, "expresses one will" (GM III: 23), a "will [to] nothingness" to be sure (GM III: 1), since this is an ideal of self-denial and self-abnegation.[20] But at least this ideal makes possible an interpretation of our situation, one that gives direction to *ressentiment* and permits some relief from the suffering that characterizes that situation. The ascetic ideal "believes there is nothing on earth of any power which does not first have to receive a meaning, a right to existence, a value from it, as a tool to *its* work, as a way and means to *its* goal" (GM III: 23).

It seems the book might have intelligibly ended here (or skipped right to GM III: 28), except for the claim emphasized by Nietzsche in *Ecce Homo* which is quoted in the epigraph to this chapter: namely, that the ascetic ideal triumphed "because it was the only ideal so far, because it had no rival" (EH III: GM). This consideration has, thus far, played no role in our interpretation. Yet if Nietzsche really thinks the absence of rivals is important to explaining the success of the ascetic ideal, then it is incumbent upon him to consider what rivals there might be. Thus, in GM III: 23, Nietzsche introduces an entirely new question: "Where is the *counterpart* to [the ascetic ideal's] closed system of will, goal and interpretation?" The answer Nietzsche considers – the possible "rival" – is this: "modern *science*" is the "counterpart" to the ascetic ideal, since it "has hitherto got by well enough

---

[20] On the idea of "willing nothingness," and its relationship to Schopenhauer, see Janaway (1998b: 31–2). At GM III: 28, Nietzsche equates "willing nothingness" with willing in accordance with the "ascetic ideal," which, in turn, is equated with "hatred of the human," as well as "the material," and "the senses," as well as "fear of happiness and beauty, this longing to get away from appearance, transience, growth, death, wishing, longing itself."

without God, the beyond and the virtues of denial," i.e., all the accoutrements of the ascetic ideal (GM III: 23). Most of the rest of the book (GM III: 23–7) is devoted to debunking this idea by showing that "science today . . . is not the opposite of the ascetic ideal but rather the latter's own *most recent and noble manifestation*" (GM III: 23).

There are two aspects of science that make it fundamentally ascetic in Nietzsche's view: the typical character of scientific practice, which like philosophy (as discussed in GM III: 5–10), thrives on self-denial and ascetic traits; and, more significantly, the "unconditional will to truth" (GM III: 24) which Nietzsche takes to be part of science. It is important to emphasize at the start, however, the precise focus of Nietzsche's attack here, for he is neither "against" science, nor against "truth." He says of "science" that "there [is] so much useful work to be done" and he says, "I delight in [scientists'] work" (GM III: 23). Moreover, as we will see shortly, he nowhere attacks the existence or objectivity of truth in the Third Essay, only the excessive *valuation* of truth characteristic of the scientific outlook. The *asceticism* of science and its "will to truth" are his targets. There is no skepticism levelled here against the epistemic standing of scientific truths and thus nothing of the postmodern skepticism that recent, anachronistic readings have claimed to find in Nietzsche.

What is the connection between science and asceticism? "Science," says Nietzsche, "rests on the same base as the ascetic ideal: the precondition of both the one and the other is a certain *impoverishment of life*, – the emotions cooled, the tempo slackened, dialectics in place of instinct, *solemnity* stamped on faces and gestures" (GM III: 25). On this account, scientific practice, like the activity of philosophy, demands a kind of asceticism from its practitioner. This is, however, only a minor theme in Nietzsche's discussion, and his target quickly reaches beyond science proper to all so-called "free spirits," all "these hard, strict, abstinent, heroic minds who make up the glory of our time, all these pale atheists, Antichrists, immoralists, nihilists, these sceptics, ephectics"[21] (GM III: 24) – a group that must, in fact,

---

[21] The method of ancient skepticism, as described by Sextus Empiricus, is "ephectic" because it involves a suspension of judgment and belief, a holding back and reserve.

include Nietzsche himself, as the labels "Antichrist" and "immoralist" would suggest![22] The whole intellectual outlook of all these different thinkers and seekers after truth is simply the "most intellectualized product" of the ascetic ideal (GM III: 24). But in what sense, exactly, does the intellectual posture of scientists and "free spirits" give expression to the ascetic ideal?

Nietzsche's basic answer is simple: scientists (at least "science today" [GM III: 23]) and free spirits "overestimate truth" (GM III: 25), i.e., they overestimate the *value* of truth: "[U]nconditional [*unbedingte*] will to truth is *faith in the ascetic ideal itself*" (GM III: 24). "[P]recisely in their faith in truth [free spirits] are more rigid and more absolute than anyone else." (GM III: 24). This *faith* in truth is the "faith that truth can *not* be assessed or criticized" (GM III: 25): truth is taken to be the *highest* value, an unquestioned good, and thus the will to that truth is "unconditional," i.e., no other value could override the pursuit of truth. Thus Nietzsche also calls it the "faith of the Christians, which was also Plato's faith, that God is truth, that truth is *divine*" (GM III: 24). Scientists, atheists, and even Antichrists and immoralists like Nietzsche all give expression to this faith: it is precisely because they all pursue "'truth at any price'" (GS Pref: 4) that they are able to tear down God, religions, and morality, as well as plumb the depths of reality itself in pursuit of scientific knowledge.[23] So, e.g., Nietzsche says, "Unconditional, honest atheism ... is ... *not* opposed to the ascetic ideal as it appears to be; instead, it is only one of the ideal's last phases of development ... – it is the awe-inspiring *catastrophe* of a two-thousand-year discipline in truth-telling, which finally forbids itself the *lie entailed in the belief in God*" (GM III: 27).[24]

So far, however, this account simply pushes the original question back a level. If science, and the whole outlook of skeptical "free

---

[22] Though there are also important (ancient) skeptical (or ephectic) themes in Nietzsche as well, as I have learned from unpublished work by Jessica Berry.

[23] As Nietzsche says in GM III: 27: "All great things bring about their own demise through an act of self-sublimation: that is the law of life, the law of *necessary* 'self-overcoming' in the essence of life."

[24] Conversely, then, the true opponent of the ascetic ideal is art, because in art "*lying* sanctifies itself and the *will to deception* has good conscience on its side" (GM III: 25).

spirits," gives expression to the ascetic ideal in virtue of expressing an overestimation of the value of truth and an unrelenting pursuit of it, then the question simply becomes: why is an unconditional will to truth essentially *ascetic*? What, in other words, does the ascetic ideal have to do with the will to truth?[25] Why does treating the value of truth as *beyond question* give expression to a kind of asceticism?

One possibility is suggested by a theme we first considered in Chapter 2, when we originally encountered Nietzsche's concern with the overestimation of the value of truth and knowledge (most vivid, perhaps, in Nietzsche's attack on Socratic optimism in *The Birth of Tragedy*). Recall Nietzsche's enthusiasm for Presocratic thinkers like Thales, a "man of wisdom," who rejected the "man of science" who pursued knowledge "at any cost" (PTAG: 3).[26] Thales, for Nietzsche, is the first to appreciate that, "Science ... first needs a value-ideal ... science itself never creates values" (GM III: 25), and that it is the task of "*genuine philosophers*" to legislate such values (BGE: 211), i.e., not to take for granted, as science does, that truth "at any price" is the highest value. Indeed, Nietzsche thinks the Greeks, at least before Socrates, understood that "truth at any price" is a bit of "youthful madness," since the truth – e.g., about "the irrationality and suffering of human existence" (PT: 136) – can be terrible, a threat to life, an invitation to "suicidal nihilism." Insofar as some truths are terrible, the pursuit of truth "at any price" is necessarily hostile to life, i.e., ascetic. (That means, of course, that science can be done in a "non-ascetic" way insofar as it does not pursue truth "at any price" – a proposal being developed, without reference to Nietzsche to be sure, by some contemporary philosophers of science, notably Kitcher (1997).) As Nietzsche puts the point in a *Nachlass* passage: "it would be possible

25 Note that at one point, Nietzsche actually misstates the general problem. In GM III: 25, he writes, "Both of them, science and the ascetic ideal, are still on the same foundation – that is to say, both overestimate truth. . . ." In fact, I think this was simply sloppiness on Nietzsche's part here, for everywhere else in this discussion the claim is *not* that the ascetic ideal rests on the unconditional will to truth, but the opposite. So what he really should have said here is that both science and the will to truth rest on the same foundation: the ascetic ideal.
26 See Chapter 2: 41–3.

that the true constitution of things was so hostile to the presuppositions of life, so opposed to them, that we needed appearance in order to be able to live" (WP: 583). In that case, of course, the will to the *truth*, to move beyond appearance, would be truly life-denying because it would threaten the "presuppositions of life" (namely, appearance).

This is plainly a major part of the explanation of the essentially ascetic nature of an unconditional will to truth. But, in fact, there is another consideration at work here, pertaining to the way we understand truth itself. Nietzsche provides a clue when he gives as a reason for rejecting the "*metaphysical* value" of truth the following: "Strictly speaking, there is no 'presuppositionless' knowledge, the thought of such a thing is unthinkable . . . a philosophy, a 'faith' always has to be there first, for knowledge to win from it a direction, a meaning, a limit, a method, a *right* to exist" (GM III: 24). So the overestimation of truth also involves an error about the nature of the truths we can actually know: it supposes, falsely, that our knowledge could be "presuppositionless." More precisely, the will to truth is a will to *non-perspectival* truth, to truth as known from no particular perspective at all (what philosophers now often call "the view from nowhere" or a "God's eye point of view," and what Nietzsche designates as the object of "presuppositionless knowledge"). This, of course, is precisely the topic first broached by Nietzsche at GM III: 12, the most famous treatment of Nietzsche's doctrine of "perspectivism" in the corpus.[27] If we understand the sense in which knowledge is necessarily perspectival, we will also then understand why the will to a non-perspectival truth gives expression to an ascetic ideal.

Remember the context of GM III: 12. Nietzsche is still in the process of introducing the figure of the ascetic priest, whose very existence, as we saw, Nietzsche deems paradoxical: "It must be a necessity of the first rank," he says, "which makes this species continually grow and prosper when it is *hostile to life*" (GM III: 11). The beginning of GM III: 12 continues on this theme, noting the *epistemic* peculiarities of the ascetic priest, the way he "will look for *error* precisely where the actual instinct of life most unconditionally judges there to be

[27] For general treatments of perspectivism, see especially Leiter (1994) and Poellner (2001). I borrow, a bit, from Leiter (1994) in the discussion that follows.

truth."[28] The ascetic is said to "deny" his "own 'reality'" by denying not just "the senses" but also denying "*reason*" itself. Here Nietzsche quite explicitly is thinking of Kant as a denier of "reason," as a philosopher who also expresses the ascetic ideal with his doctrine of transcendental idealism, the doctrine that the only knowable world is the world as we humans experience it (the phenomenal world), as distinct from the way the world really is in-itself, i.e., the noumenal world. Nietzsche paraphrases this "ascetic self-contempt and self-ridicule of reason" as follows: "'*there is* a realm of truth and being [i.e., the noumenal world], but reason is firmly *excluded* from it!'" (GM III: 12). Nietzsche is, to be sure, embracing one kind of critical reaction to transcendental idealism according to which Kant, far from vindicating knowledge, actually undermined it by putting the *real* "realm of truth and being" out of bounds.

It is here that we enter the famed discussion of perspectivism, which is presented as a post-Kantian way of understanding the "'objectivity'" of knowledge. The Kantian way, of course, entails that the *really* objective world, the noumenal world, is unknown to us humans, but within the phenomenal world – the world as we experience it – objectivity is possible insofar as this world conforms to categories that the human mind necessarily imposes upon experience. (Nietzsche, remember, is supposing, in keeping with his critical view of transcendental idealism, that genuinely objective knowledge would involve knowledge of the noumenal world.) The alternative view, "perspectivism," Nietzsche characterizes in terms of its view of "objectivity" (a term Nietzsche here puts in quotes), which is

> understood not as "intuition [*Anschauung*][29] without interest" (which is, as such, a non-concept and an absurdity), but as

---

[28] It should be worrisome to postmodern readers of Nietzsche that among the doctrines the ascetic priest calls an "error" (which are, in fact, truths) is "the whole conceptual antithesis 'subject' and 'object'" (GM III: 12). Nietzsche – like common sense and most of the philosophical tradition – views the distinction between "subject" and "object" as quite intelligible, rather than an untenable dualism to be overcome, as postmodernists would have it.

[29] Diethe renders this "contemplation," which is not helpful, philosophically, since it obscures Nietzsche's disagreement with Schopenhauer's NeoKantian view. See the discussion below in the text.

having in our power our "pros" and "cons": so as to be able to engage and disengage them so that we can use the *difference* in perspectives and affective interpretations for knowledge. From now on, my philosophical colleagues, let us be more wary of the dangerous old conceptual fairy-tale which has set up a "pure, will-less, painless, timeless, subject of knowledge" . . . – here we are asked to think of an eye which cannot be thought at all, an eye turned in no direction at all, an eye where the active and interpretative powers are to be suppressed, absent, but through which seeing still becomes a seeing-something, so it is an absurdity and non-concept of the eye that is demanded. There is *only* a perspective seeing, *only* a perspective "knowing"; the *more* affects we allow to speak about a thing, the *more* eyes, various eyes, we are able to use for the same thing, the more complete will be our "concept" of the thing, our "objectivity." But to eliminate the will completely and turn off all the affects[30] without exception, assuming we could: well? would that not mean to *castrate* the intellect?

(GM III: 12)

Notice, to start, that the focus of this passage is *knowledge* (more precisely, the nature of knowing) and not *truth* per se (i.e., what actually is the case). Knowing could be perspectival in the sense described here, but truth might not be. Philosophically, this is an important distinction, but, unfortunately, Nietzsche is not always attentive to it. Some commentators (e.g., Poellner 2001) suggest that, for Nietzsche, truth itself is also perspectival. I shall develop a somewhat different reading here.

Initially, there are two striking features of this passage: it casts itself in opposition to a certain picture, the picture of a "pure, will-less, painless, timeless, subject of knowledge"; and it invokes an analogy between knowing and seeing. Both reflect an implicit dialogue with Schopenhauer, for, in the first instance, Nietzsche is quoting "Schopenhauer's exact formula for the subject in aesthetic

---

[30] Oddly, Diethe translates "*die Affekte*" as "emotions," though she earlier in this passage renders the same term "affect." I have, for consistency, stuck with "affect" and "affective."

experience, the subject whose will is blissfully suspended and who remains as a passive 'mirror' of objective reality" (Janaway 1998b: 27). As Christopher Janaway explains:

> In this [Schopenhauerian] account the subject of aesthetic experience allegedly leaves behind empirical particulars and survives as the receptor for the eternal [Platonic] Ideas which are the "adequate objectification" of the thing in itself. . . . At the same time the subject of aesthetic experience loses the sense of himself or herself as an individual and becomes, in Schopenhauer's words, "the *single* world-eye that looks out from every cognizing being."
>
> (Janaway 1998b: 27–8; quoting
> Schopenhauer 1818: 198)

So the Schopenhauerian knower – that "pure, will-less, painless, timeless, subject of knowledge" – is precisely one who achieves knowledge of the noumenal world,[31] and whose knowing is analogous to that of seeing from no *particular* perspective, since what it "sees" (knows) is what every "cognizing being" would see or know.

Nietzsche's doctrine of perspectivism, then, involves a repudiation of both parts of Schopenhauer's (quasi-Kantian) picture: there is no knowledge of the noumenal world, because knowledge is necessarily perspectival;[32] and while knowing *is* like seeing, seeing (so Nietzsche argues) is – *contra* Schopenhauer – *necessarily* perspectival as well. Let us consider these points in reverse order.

Nietzsche takes seriously, in a way Schopenhauer does not, the analogy between seeing and knowing, in the sense that Nietzsche thinks knowing is like *actual* seeing. For in the case of our visual grasp of an object, the following four claims are clearly true:

1   Necessarily, we see an object from a particular perspective: for example, from a certain angle, from a certain distance, under certain conditions.

---

[31]   It is only in the context of art, in particular music, according to Schopenhauer, that we make contact with the noumenal world.

[32]   Kant, of course, also denies that there is *knowledge* of the noumenal world. It is in this regard, among others, that Schopenhauer's view is only "quasi-" Kantian.

2　　The more perspectives we enjoy – for example, the more angles we see the object from – the better will be our conception of what the object is actually like.

3　　We can never exhaust all possible perspectives on the object of vision.

4　　There are identifiable factors that would distort our perspective on the object: for instance, we are too far away or the background conditions are poor.

Now Nietzsche thinks knowledge is the same, in the sense that:

1'　　Necessarily, we know an object from particular perspective: that is, from the standpoint of particular interests and "affects."

2'　　The more perspectives we enjoy, the better will be our conception of what the object is actually like.

3'　　We can never exhaust all possible perspectives on the object of knowledge (there are infinite interpretative interests).

4'　　There are identifiable factors that would distort our perspective on the object: that is, certain interpretative interests will distort the nature of the object.

On Nietzsche's rendering of the analogy, the analogue of optical perspective is "interest" or "affect": thus, in GM III: 12, he equates "*more* affects" with "*more* eyes"; he says to "turn off all the affects" would "castrate the intellect"; and he says "intuition without interest" is "an absurdity." Now knowing is perspectival, i.e., interest-dependent, in at least two senses, one genetic, the other constitutive. First, Nietzsche takes it to be an a posteriori truth about creatures like us that our pursuit of knowledge always is motivated by some "affect" or "drive" or "interest." So Nietzsche observes that "anyone who considers the basic drives of man . . . will find that all of them have done philosophy at some time – and that every single one of them would like only too well to represent just *itself* as the ultimate purpose of existence and the legitimate *master* of all the other drives" (BGE: 6). Of course, Nietzsche does not completely deny that there is ever an "interest" in knowledge for the sake of knowledge; rather he says that,

> among scholars who are really scientific men . . . you may really find something like a drive for knowledge, some small,

independent clockwork that, once well wound, works on vigorously *without* any essential participation from all the other drives of the scholar. The real "interests" of the scholar therefore lie usually somewhere else – say, in his family, or in making money, or in politics. Indeed, it is almost a matter of total indifference whether his little machine is placed at this or that spot in science.

(BGE: 6)

But this case is plainly the exception, and it gives only "something like" a drive to knowledge. In general, both "reason" and "conscience" "bow" "[t]o our strongest drive, the tyrant in us," whatever that should happen to be (BGE: 158).

That the "affects" play a causal role in the genesis of knowing would not, by itself, be sufficient for perspectivism, however. What is necessary is that the affects also play a constitutive role in knowledge. What Nietzsche says of philosophers – "most of the conscious thinking of a philosopher is secretly guided and forced into certain channels by his instincts" (BGE: 3) – applies quite generally to knowing: knowers and inquirers are moved by their desires, their passions, their affections, to ask certain kinds of questions, look into certain kinds of topics, pursue certain directions of research. So just as seeing an object from a certain angle plays a constitutive role in what is seen (you see the *front* of the door, but not the back, because you are standing outside), so too interests or affects play a constitutive role in knowledge: you come to *know* about the aspects of the phenomena in question that answer to your particular interests and desires.

Consider a useful analogy (first broached in Chapter 1). If we wanted to get knowledge of a particular geographic area by making a map of it, the kind of map we make would necessarily be determined by our interests. As automobile drivers, we would want to create a road map; as geologists, a topographical map; as tourists, our interest would be in a map with entertaining attractions. Each "affective interpretation" would tell us something about the region; and if we tried to "turn off all the affects" we wouldn't make any map at all, since the idea of a map that captured *nothing* or *everything* is nonsensical. Instead, the map corresponding to each set of interests would give us genuine knowledge of the area, and the more interests embodied in maps, the more we would know about the area: "the more complete will be . . . our 'objectivity'" (GM III: 12).

In emphasizing the infinite plurality of possible perspectives from which knowledge might be had, Nietzsche's perspectivism is already at odds with a view widespread in science, and one nicely captured in the title of a book by the eminent physicist Steven Weinberg: *Dreams of a Final Theory* (1991). Perspectivism is revisionary of ordinary views in denying that there can be such a thing as a "final" theory, even in physics. There might be a theory that is "final" relative to a very particular set of interests; but there are always additional interests which might turn the "cognizing" eye in new directions, and so in that sense there is no "final" theory of the whole.

At the same time, perspectivism, as reconstructed so far, is not radically revisionary in the manner of postmodern skepticism, since the picture is compatible with the idea of "maps" that give us no knowledge whatsoever: an interest in knowing the location of all the leprechauns would not yield a map that gave any actual knowledge of the geographic region in question (unless, of course, the map showed there to be none!). (So, too, for Nietzsche, the "Christian" map of the world gives us no knowledge either – it has not "a single point of contact with reality" (A: 15).) It bears emphasizing that there is *nothing* in the optical analogue Nietzsche invokes, and nothing in his opposition to the Kantian/Schopenhauerian view, that requires him to deny the existence or possibility of objective knowledge: after all, GM III: 12 is, itself, a passage about the right way to think of both "knowing" and "objectivity," not a repudiation of either.

It is true, to be sure, that the characterization of our epistemic situation that arises from Nietzsche's perspectivism alters the sense in which knowledge is objective and the sense in which we can say some other perspective is "false" to the way things are. Indeed, the doctrine of perspectivism has much in common with the famous image of "Neurath's boat," that the American philosopher Quine helped popularize. According to the logical positivist Otto Neurath, our epistemological situation is analogous to that of sailors who must rebuild their ship while at sea. Since they cannot rebuild the whole ship at once – they can not step outside the ship, as it were, and rebuild it from scratch – they must choose to stand firm on certain planks in the boat (those that are in the "best" shape, i.e., those that "work") while reconstructing others. Of course, at a later date, the sailors may choose to rebuild the planks they stood on previously, and in so doing they will choose to stand firm on other planks that meet their practical needs (typically, reliable prediction of the future) at that time.

For Neurath and for Quine, our epistemological situation is the same: we necessarily stand firm on certain "planks" in our theoretical conception of the world (e.g., certain hypotheses, empirical claims, epistemic norms, etc.), while evaluating or "rebuilding" others. In epistemological matters, we simply have no other way to proceed: we are "at sea" within a particular theory of the world, and we can not climb out of that theory and rebuild the whole thing at once. But this hardly precludes us from engaging in the epistemic evaluation of claims. As Quine writes in a well-known passage:

> Have we ... so far lowered our sights as to settle for a relativistic doctrine of truth – rating the statements of each theory as true for that theory, and brooking no higher criticism? Not so. The saving consideration is that we continue to take seriously ... our own particular world-theory or loose total fabric of quasi-theories, whatever it may be. Unlike Descartes, we own and use our beliefs of the moment, even in the midst of philosophising. ... Within our own total evolving doctrine, we can judge truth as earnestly and absolutely as can be; subject to correction, but that goes without saying.
>
> (1960: 24–5)

So, too, on Nietzsche's perspectivist picture, we are also "at sea" within the background of extant "affective interpretations" of the world, but it is precisely that background that gives us our epistemic bearings. We can't appeal to the "facts" as seen from no perspective at all – that's Neurath's point as well – but we can surely appeal to the facts as interpreted within our best-going theories of the world, i.e., those that are the product of various and sundry "affective interpretations."

Of course, Quine, in the quoted passage, speaks of "truth," not simply knowledge. And so far we have examined perspectivism as a doctrine about knowledge, i.e., an epistemological doctrine, and *not* as a semantic doctrine about truth or a metaphysical doctrine about how things really are. If, as a metaphysical matter, there is a way things really are as seen from no perspective at all – if there is, in other words, a noumenal realm – then epistemic perspectivism has skeptical implications, in the same way that Kant's transcendental idealism does: it suggests that the world we know – the phenomenal world for Kant, or the world as constituted by the extant "affective interpretations" for Nietzsche – is not the *real* world, but a kind of illusion.

There are three possible responses to this problem of how to reconcile perspectivism as a purportedly non-skeptical doctrine about knowledge with the idea of a noumenal world: we can extend perspectivism to the metaphysical domain as well; we can deny the *intelligibility* of the idea of a noumenal world; or we can deny the *relevance* of the noumenal world. Poellner (2001: 88–98) adopts the first strategy, arguing that Nietzsche's doctrine of perspectivism is also a kind of *metaphysical* thesis to the effect that not only *knowing* but reality itself is necessarily perspectival. In that event, of course, perspectival knowing is fully adequate to reality, since reality itself is perspectival. Clark (1990) takes the second approach, arguing that Nietzsche rejects the very *intelligibility* of the noumenal world, and, as a consequence, "all basis is lost for regarding the empirical world or the results of empirical investigation [the 'phenomenal' world] as illusory" (Clark 1990: 114).[33] In other words, if there is no noumenal world, then there is nothing above and beyond the world as we know it (perspectivally). Poellner and Clark give nuanced and philosophically robust defenses of these readings, either of which would suffice to deflect the worry that perspectivism entails skepticism. Remember, of course, that our real concern here is with the connection between a will to non-perspectival

---

[33] I also defended a version of this view in Leiter (1994). The claim about *unintelligibility* will, however, collapse into the first approach if the only argument against the intelligibility of the noumenal world depends on the truth of perspectivism as a metaphysical thesis. This is how we first broached the topic in Chapter 1, where we used arguments from Poellner (1995: 79–111) to make sense of Clark's claim about unintelligibility. While those may be the *best* arguments for the unintelligibility of the noumenal world, they are not the only ones: see Clark (1990: 46–50, 95–125).

truth and asceticism, so a fully adequate discussion of the Poellner and Clark readings would take us far afield of our central concerns in the *Genealogy*. Instead, let me elaborate on the third possibility, which allows us to remain, as it were, agnostic on some of the more difficult metaphysical questions.[34]

In the section of *Twilight of the Idols* on "How the 'True World' Finally Became a Fable," Nietzsche gives a six-part account of the history of the "error" of our belief in a noumenal realm (to use Kant's terminology). In this history, the crucial moments come in Nietzsche's stages 4 and 5:

4   The true world – unattainable? At any rate, unattained. And being unattained, also *unknown*. Consequently, not consoling, redeeming, or obligating: how could something unknown obligate us?

5   The "true" world – an idea which is no longer useful for anything, not even obligating – an idea which has become useless and superfluous – *consequently*, a refuted idea: let us abolish it!

Notice that the *grounds* for "abolishing" the idea of the noumenal world given here are not, e.g., that it is unintelligible, or that reality is necessarily perspectival, but rather that the idea of such a world is not "useful." We can, then, call this third response to our problem the "pragmatic" response. *Perhaps*, the pragmatic response says, there is a way things really are as seen from no perspective at all; but the possibility of such a world makes no difference to us, since we can know nothing about it. Practically speaking, what Kant calls the "phenomenal" world is all that matters. In a seminal contemporary discussion, Mark Johnston helpfully articulates this kind of pragmatic attitude as follows:

> [Pragmatism] nowhere needs to claim that metaphysical statements [e.g., about the noumenal world] are devoid of truth-value. It is enough that interest in such unconstrained claims is just idle. . . . The practical element in Pragmatism is best presented

---

34   Poellner (2001: 111–19) explores a similar possibility as well, under the heading "metaphysical indifferentism."

as a normative claim, the claim that our interest in truth should always be a practically constrained interest, an interest restricted in principle to accessible truth. . . .

[I]f you are interested in getting at the truth don't waste your time with truth which you can't in principle recognize as such.

(1993: 112–13)

Only knowable truths matter, on this pragmatic picture, and so the possible existence of unknowable truths simply should not concern us. This certainly seems to be Nietzsche's posture in the famous passage from *Twilight* noted above, and it is at least consistent with the epistemic emphasis of GM III: 12, which, like the view described here, is officially agnostic about the (metaphysical) question of the existence of the noumenal world. So on this reading, the will to non-perspectival truth is really the will to *know* truths that can never be known by creatures like us.

How, then, is such a will ascetic, or life-denying? Nietzsche's answer is that such a will implicitly, perhaps even explicitly, denigrates the actual truths available to us in the world we really inhabit. As he puts it in the *Nachlass*: "It is of cardinal importance that one should abolish the *true* [i.e., noumenal] world. It is the great inspirer of doubt and devaluator in respect of the world *we are*: it has been our most dangerous attempt yet to assassinate life" (WP: 583).[35] He makes the same point even more systematically in a series of four "propositions" from *Twilight of the Idols* written around the same time as the *Nachlass* passage; I quote only the two most relevant ones:

> *Second proposition.* The criteria which have been bestowed on the "true being" of things are the criteria of non-being, of *naught*; the "true world" has been constructed out of contradiction to the actual world. . . .
>
> *Third proposition.* To invent fables about a world "other" than this one has no meaning at all, unless an instinct of slander, detraction, and suspicion against life has gained the upper hand

---

[35] Poellner (2001: 115) called this passage to my attention. Cf. his discussion at pp. 115–19.

in us: in that case, we avenge ourselves against life with a phantasmagoria of "another," a "better" life.

(TI III: 6)

So the will to non-perspectival knowledge of truth is ascetic or life-denying because it demeans the actual world as mere "appearance"; it sets up as "real" all the characteristics that "contradict" our actual life; and it may even (per the "third proposition") reflect a motive that is hostile to life. These charges are, to be sure, both somewhat speculative and somewhat metaphorical in nature; but they are plainly part of the grounds on which Nietzsche deems the will to truth to be ascetic, and they also make clear the link between the earlier discussion of perspectivism (GM III: 12) and the concluding sections of the Third Essay.

Two final puzzles about the Third Essay

A reader of the Third Essay, especially in the context of the overall account of Nietzsche in this book, must surely be struck by two interpretive puzzles that, as of yet, have not been fully explored. Both pertain to the final discussion of science and the will to truth that were reviewed in the prior section. While we have seen that Nietzsche's critique is not directed at either the epistemic status of science or the possibility of truth, it still sits uneasily at points with other aspects of both the *Genealogy* and Nietzsche's general philosophical practice.

First, there is the perhaps surprising fact that Nietzsche seems to indict himself in his attack on the ascetic ideal! For recall that it is not only scientists, but also all those "hard, strict, abstinent, heroic minds who make up the glory of our time, all these pale atheists, Antichrists, immoralists, nihilists, these sceptics, ephectics" (GM III: 24) who overvalue truth. Given how closely Nietzsche identifies himself throughout his mature work with the labels "Antichrist" and "immoralist," it seems that the charge he levels here must apply to himself as well. All these thinkers are said to possess "faith" in truth as a precondition of their critical work: they are able to tear down God, religions, and morality – not to mention plumb the depths of reality itself in science – precisely because they pursue the truth relent-lessly, since, for them, truth is the highest value. Recall that Nietzsche calls atheism that "awe-inspiring *catastrophe* of a two-thousand-year discipline in truth-telling, which finally forbids itself the *lie entailed in the belief in God*" (GM III: 27). He describes his own critical work – "I am no man, I am dynamite," he says (EH IV: 1) – in similar terms:

> [T]he truth speaks out of me. – But my truth is *terrible*; for so far one has called *lies* truth.
>
> [W]hen truth enters into a fight with the lies of millennia, we shall have upheavals, a convulsion of earthquakes, a moving of mountains and valleys, the like of which has never been dreamed of.
>
> I am by far the most terrible human being that has existed so far; this does not preclude the possibility that I shall be the most beneficial. I know the pleasure in destroying to a degree that accords with my powers to destroy. ... I am the first immoralist: that makes me the annihilator *par excellence*.
>
> (EH IV: 1–2)

He goes on to describe the critique of morality itself as, "The self-overcoming of morality, out of truthfulness" (EH IV: 3), and credits himself with being the first to have "*uncovered* Christian morality" (EH IV: 7).

Does all this mean that Nietzsche is as much a servant of the ascetic ideal as scientists and "free spirits"? That conclusion is not yet warranted, for we must keep in mind that what makes the will to truth hostile to life is when the truths it uncovers are, in fact, dangerous to life. But as we have seen in earlier chapters (especially 3 and 4), Nietzsche thinks the "truths" he is pursuing about morality are, in fact, advantageous for life, since, of course, he equates "life" in this regard with the flourishing of the highest human beings.[36] To "uncover" morality is to free nascent higher human beings from their false consciousness about morality, and thus make it possible for them to flourish. In doing so, Nietzsche thereby "serves life" (to employ his

---

[36] See the discussion in Chapter 4 at pp. 125–6.

metaphorical way of talking) rather than damages it. And, of course, it is important to keep in mind that Nietzsche wants to circumscribe his audience precisely because he views himself as the purveyor of "terrible truths" that would, indeed, be dangerous for the wrong kind of reader. "Our highest insights," he says, "must – and should – sound like follies and sometimes crimes when they are heard without permission by those who are not predisposed and predestined for them" (BGE: 30). As a result, "All those of noble spirit and taste select their audience when they wish to communicate; and choosing that, one at the same time erects barriers against 'the others'" (GS: 381).

A second, and related, puzzle raised by the concluding sections of the Third Essay is its compatibility with Nietzsche's naturalism, a central theme we first introduced in Chapter 1, and which we have seen at work in the *Genealogy*, as each essay has appealed to a psychological mechanism in creatures like us – *ressentiment*, bad conscience, will to power – that helps explain the genesis of morality. Contrast, now, this naturalistic approach with what looks like a sustained polemic against naturalism as a form of asceticism in GM III: 25:

> Has not man's self-deprecation ... been unstoppably on the increase since Copernicus? Gone, alas, is his faith in his dignity, uniqueness, irreplaceableness in the rank-ordering of beings, – he has become animal, literally, unqualifiedly and unreservedly an animal, man who in his earlier faiths was almost God. ... All science ... is seeking to talk man out of his former self as though this were nothing but a bizarre piece of self-conceit. ... Does this really *work against* the ascetic ideal?

How is this lament about turning man into an "animal" to be reconciled with Nietzsche's call for us "to translate man back into nature," to become "deaf to the siren songs of old metaphysical bird catchers who have been piping ... 'you are more, you are higher, you are of a different origin!'" (BGE: 230)? Or what of the Nietzsche who writes the following?

> We no longer derive man from "the spirit" or "the deity"; we have placed him back among the animals. We consider him the strongest animal because he is the most cunning: his spirituality

is a consequence of this. On the other hand, we oppose the vanity that would raise its head again here too – as if man had been the great hidden purpose of the evolution of the animals. And even this is saying too much: relatively speaking, man is the most bungled of all the animals, the sickliest, and not one has strayed more dangerously from its instincts. But for all that, he is of course the most *interesting*.

As regards the animals, Descartes was the first to have dared, with admirable boldness, to understand the animal as *machina*: the whole of our physiology endeavors to prove this claim. And we are consistent enough not to except man, as Descartes still did: our knowledge of man today goes just as far as we understand him mechanistically. Formerly man was given a "free will" as his dowry from a higher order: today we have taken his will away altogether. . . .

Formerly, the proof of man's higher origin, of his divinity, was found in his consciousness, in his "spirit." To become *perfect*, he was advised to draw in his senses, turtle fashion, to cease all intercourse with earthly things, to shed his mortal shroud: then his essence would remain, the "pure spirit". . . . [But] the "pure spirit" is a pure stupidity: if we subtract the nervous system and the senses – the "mortal shroud" – *then we miscalculate* – that is all!

(A: 14)

Even if the level of contradictoriness in Nietzsche is exaggerated by superficial readers, this may seem a case where the charge seems warranted: he, on the one hand, appears to vilify the naturalistic impulse – to understand humans as just like other animals – as an expression of the ascetic ideal, and yet, elsewhere, seems to call repeatedly for precisely such a naturalization. Strictly speaking, of course, this is not contradictory unless we also take him to be saying in the concluding sections of the Third Essay that we should give up all those activities that give expression to the ascetic ideal. But that, of course, is not quite what he says; he does not call, for example, for us to abandon science – "there being so much useful work to be done" here (GM III: 23) – but rather for science to be informed by a different, non-ascetic ideal: "science today has absolutely *no* faith . . . in an ideal *above* it, – and where it is still passion, love, fire, *suffering*, it is not the opposite of the ascetic ideal but rather the latter's own *most recent and noble manifestation*" (GM III: 23). (Note, of course, that it is a *noble* expression of asceticism!) The naturalization project can, then, be one worth pursuing if enlisted in the service of a different ideal.

But that, of course, is exactly how Nietzsche approaches the naturalistic project. We have emphasized since the very first chapter that Nietzsche's naturalistic approach is merely an instrument in the service of the revaluation of values, i.e., the revaluation of the "ascetic" values that have come to predominate as morality. By looking at our ascetic morality as just another natural phenomenon, Nietzsche removes it from the realm of divine commandment or the eternal, unchanging order of things; he shows morality to be another phenomenon of nature, with a history and particular causes.[37] Naturalization, for Nietzsche, is fundamentally non-ascetic, because it is ultimately in the service of an anti-ascetic end: to free nascent higher human beings from their false consciousness about MPS (itself an expression of asceticism), and thus permit them to flourish.

Unifying the three essays

One of the difficulties confronting the reader of the *Genealogy* is that Nietzsche fails to instruct the reader as to the connection between the three essays. His summary of the book in *Ecce Homo* hardly helps matters; he describes the essays as each bringing forth "a *new* truth" without explaining their connection to one another, and concludes by labeling the volume, "Three decisive preliminary studies by a psychologist for a revaluation of all values" (EH III: GM).

Nietzsche's own summation, however, understates the links between the three essays. We saw, for example, at the end of the last chapter that while the Second Essay tells us that it is the combination of bad conscience (internalized cruelty) and ascetic religions that gives

---

[37]   He also, of course, tries to gain rhetorical advantage from showing that moral-
       ity presupposes a picture of persons that can not be squared with the most
       robust naturalistic understanding of human agency and nature (cf. Chapter 3).

us *guilt*, there was no explanation for why bad conscience should have been put in the service of the ascetic ideal, rather than some other: the Greeks, recall, managed "to keep 'bad conscience' at bay" via gods that reflected a non-ascetic ideal (GM II: 23). By explaining, as he does in the Third Essay, the triumph of the ascetic ideal – by explaining "the *monstrosity* of its power" (GM III: 23) – it would seem that he has explained why bad conscience became attached to the ascetic ideal: for only such a use of *guilt* could relieve the suffering of the "majority of mortals" who could not, otherwise, bear their senseless suffering. Remember that Nietzsche argues that it is the ascetic priest who took the "animal-psychology" of bad conscience ("guilt in its raw state") and gave it a "priestly reinterpretation" and turned it into what we now recognize as "guilt" and "sin" (GM III: 20). The reinterpretation involved attaching bad conscience (qua internalized cruelty) to an ascetic ideal, so that it was transformed into the searing feelings of guilt discussed at the end of the Second Essay: the ascetic ideal "brought all suffering within the perspective of *guilt*," and thus gave it a meaning (GM III: 28).

This plainly goes some distance towards closing the explanatory gap we found at the end of the Second Essay. But it does not go far enough yet, in a way that bears on the connection between the Third and the First Essays as well. For somehow the Greeks whose bad conscience did not turn in to guilt (because they did not embrace the ascetic ideal in their religion) also did not succumb to the "suicidal nihilism" that would be the consequence of "meaningless suffering" (GM III: 28). But how did they avoid it? After all, the dilemma to which the ascetic ideal is an answer – "the meaninglessness of suffering" – reflects a brute existential reality about the *human* situation. Here the rhetoric of the concluding section of the book (GM III: 28) becomes enormously significant:

> Except for the ascetic ideal: man, the *animal* man, had no meaning up to now. His existence on earth had no purpose; "What is man for actually?" – was a question without an answer; there was no *will* for man and earth; behind every great human destiny sounded the even louder refrain "in vain!" *This* is what the ascetic ideal meant: something was *missing*, there was an

immense *lacuna* around man, – he himself could think of no justification or explanation or affirmation, he *suffered* from the problem of what he meant. Other things made him suffer too, in the main he was a *sickly* animal: but suffering itself was *not* his problem, but the fact that there was no answer to the question he screamed, "Suffering for *what*?" . . . The meaninglessness of suffering, *not* the suffering, was the curse which has so far blanketed mankind, – and *the ascetic ideal offered man a meaning*!

Note that there is no distinction drawn here between the era of the Homeric Greeks, or the Romans, and the "Christian" era, i.e., the ascetic era which encompasses the modern world as well. *Until* the ascetic ideal, Nietzsche tells us, "man . . . had no meaning" and even suffered from that fact. So, too, then must the Greeks and the Romans have suffered from that fact; so, too, then must they themselves have been at risk of the "suicidal nihilism" which is the consequence of meaningless suffering. Nietzsche's later summary of the Third Essay in *Ecce Homo* may seem, at first, somewhat peculiar: the ascetic ideal triumphs, he says, "because it was the only ideal so far, because it had no rival." Of course, that elliptical explanation makes more sense in light of our exposition of the Third Essay: the triumph of the ascetic ideal is the product of the *conjunction* of 1) the absence of alternative ideals that render suffering meaningful and 2) *the imperative (on pain of suicidal nihilism) to render meaningful the suffering that characterizes the human situation*. Nietzsche's heroic Greeks, who held bad conscience at bay, nonetheless suffered: and according to GM III: 28, they, too, lacked an answer to the fundamental, existential question of, "Suffering for *what*?" They, too, then had to succumb, *eventually*, to the attractions of the ascetic ideal, for that was the only device available *so far* for giving a meaning to suffering and thus blocking "suicidal nihilism."[38]

[38] This, perhaps surprising, hypothesis is less so if we keep in mind that even in *The Birth of Tragedy*, Nietzsche was arguing that the Greeks were in decline – though there, of course, the symptom of decline was the rise of Socratic rationalism. The language of the new 1886 preface – the "Attempt at a Self-Criticism" – is relevant here: "might not this very Socratism," Nietzsche asks,

And now we can see, as well, the link with the explanatory puzzle of the First Essay: namely, why did slave morality triumph, why did the masters – the elite of the late Roman Empire – adopt such a morality? As we argued at the end of Chapter 6, Nietzsche gives no satisfactory explanation of that remarkable transformation (though he identifies some factors that might contribute to the success of slave morality, like the status and cunning of the priestly caste even within noble societies). But if we keep in mind that slave morality is, of course, ascetic in character – it is especially life-denying for the masters, whose whole way of life it condemns – we now have an explanation: what ultimately explains the triumph of slave morality is the same thing that explains the triumph of the ascetic ideal, namely, its ability to give a meaning to suffering, the basic *existential* problem for "man," both slave and master. In sum: because the ascetic ideal was the *only* ideal so far, and because it was able to satisfy the imperative to make suffering meaningful, the Third Essay also explains why the Roman masters of the First Essay and the heroic Greeks of the Second ultimately succumbed to the modern moral world view. The *ressentiment* of "slaves" and the internalized cruelty of civilized humans may have laid the foundation for morality, but it was the ability of asceticism to resolve the existential dilemma that ultimately accounted for the success of the slave revolt and the transformation of bad conscience into guilt.

Can the ascetic ideal really bear the immense explanatory weight Nietzsche assigns it here? Speculative, historical moral psychology of the kind Nietzsche is practicing here is not, it is fair to say, a developed field. What would count as empirical evidence here is not entirely obvious. Whether, then, Nietzsche's reconstruction of the genealogy of our morality is really plausible, it should, nonetheless, be clear that the three essays of the *Genealogy* are connected,

"be a sign of decline, of weariness, of infection, of the anarchical dissolution of the instincts?" (BT Pref: 1). Or similarly: "The question of the Greek's relation to pain [or suffering, one might add], his degree of sensitivity, is basic: did this relation remain constant? Or did it change radically?" (BT Pref: 4). Nietzsche, of course, thinks it changed radically, and that the Socratic turn in Greek culture was a symptom of this, a "symptom of a decline of strength, of impending old age, and of physiological weariness" (BT Pref: 4).

with the Third Essay addressing the phenomenon – the triumph of the ascetic ideal – that proves essential to understanding everything else. If empirical moral psychology wanted a research agenda, the *Genealogy* sets a profound one.

One final point is worth noting here. For the way Nietzsche has now structured the explanation for the triumph of the ascetic ideal – hence the triumph of MPS quite generally – it turns out that enormous significance would attach to the creation of an alternative ideal, something we have not had, he says in *Ecce Homo*, "until Zarathustra," i.e., until Nietzsche himself created such an ideal! Such an alternative ideal must be able to bear the burden of answering the question, "Suffering for *what*?" and thus blocking "suicidal nihilism," for that is the existential task the ascetic ideal discharges. But what is that alternative ideal?

In *Ecce Homo*, Nietzsche says that, "the fundamental conception of [*Thus Spoke Zarathustra*]" is "eternal recurrence, this highest formula of affirmation that is at all attainable" (EH III: Z-1).[39] To be able to affirm the eternal repetition of one's life would, of course, mean that one was no longer at risk of "suicidal nihilism": the suicidal nihilist wants to end his life, not repeat it eternally. So the teaching of the eternal recurrence is presumably the alternative ideal Nietzsche has in mind, since it is the ideal taught by Zarathustra, for whom, "Pain is *not* considered an objection to life" (EH III: Z-1) and who "says Yes to the point of justifying, of redeeming even all of the past" (EH III: Z-8). Indeed, elsewhere, as we first saw in Chapter 4, Nietzsche calls eternal recurrence "the ideal of the most high-spirited, alive, and world-affirming human being who has not only come to terms and learned to get along with whatever was and is [including suffering], but who wants to have *what was and is* repeated into all eternity" (BGE: 56).

But what is the *meaning* that this alternative ideal, the eternal recurrence, provides for the existential fact of suffering? Here, perhaps, is Nietzsche's greatest affinity with the twentieth-century

[39] Zarathustra says that, "Human existence is uncanny and still without meaning. . . . I will teach men the meaning of their existence – the overman" (Z Pref: 7), where the overman, of course, is the one who is able to affirm the eternal return.

existentialists, especially Camus. For the "meaning" embodied in affirmation of the eternal return is precisely that *there is no meaning or justification for suffering*: "[T]he basic fact of the human will," says Nietzsche is that, "*it needs an aim* – , and it prefers to will *nothingness* [i.e., the ascetic ideal] than *not* will" (GM III: 1). The eternal return does not so much provide a "meaning" for suffering – to affirm the doctrine of eternal return is to recognize that there is no such meaning – as it provides an *aim* for the will other than the ascetic ideal: namely, to will the repetition of everything through eternity. To admit that there is no meaning or justification for suffering is, indeed, an "abysmal thought" (e.g., Z III: 13), which is why Nietzsche says, "If this thought gained possession of you, it would change you as you are or perhaps crush you" (GS: 341). This is the attitude of existential commitment, through brute force of will, to carry on in the absence of such a meaning or vindication, to give up, in effect, asking "Suffering for *what*?" Of course, as we saw in Chapter 4, it is only the highest human beings who can embrace the doctrine of eternal return; in that sense, the ascetic ideal will remain essential for the rest of humanity. But Nietzsche thinks it is at least possible for some – those higher human beings, presumably, who are Nietzsche's recurring concern – to avoid both suicidal nihilism and asceticism. The one who embraces this alternative ideal would endorse Nietzsche's "formula for greatness in a human being," namely, "*amor fati*" (love of fate): "that one wants nothing to be different, not forward, not backward, not in all eternity. Not merely bear what is necessary, still less conceal it . . . but *love* it" (EH II: 10).

Nietzsche since 1900

Critical questions

Prof. Nietzsche was one of the most prominent of modern German philosophers, and he is considered the apostle of extreme modern rationalism and one of the founders of the socialistic school.

(from an obituary in *The New York Times*, August 26, 1900, p. 7, col. 4)

Misreadings of Nietzsche are legion, though most mistaken interpretations are not as transparently wrongheaded as the obituary accorded Nietzsche by *The New York Times*.[1] The dominant misreadings of the past fifty years go wrong more subtly, by ignoring or down-playing Nietzsche's moral philosophy, for

---

[1] The obituary also describes Nietzsche as "largely influenced by the pessimism of Schopenhauer," without noting that the "influence" was primarily in the form of defining a position against which he reacted. It also tells the reader, falsely, that Nietzsche was "of Slavonic ancestry" and that "he lost his parents early in life." It describes his field of study as "Oriental languages," and attributes his death to "apoplexy" and his early retirement to "an affection of the brain and eyes" brought on by "overwork."

example, or by treating him as a proto-postmodernist or by erasing his naturalism.

When the Danish critic Georg Brandes (1842–1927) first introduced a wider European audience to Nietzsche's ideas during public lectures in 1888, he concentrated, quite properly, on Nietzsche's vitriolic campaign against morality and what Brandes dubbed (with Nietzsche's subsequent approval) Nietzsche's "aristocratic radicalism." This reading, of course, underlined precisely the general themes that have occupied us here. Nietzsche was *primarily* concerned with questions of value and culture (especially the value of morality and its effect on culture), and his philosophical standpoint is a deeply *illiberal* one: what matters are *great* human beings, not the "herd." The egalitarian premise of all contemporary moral and political theory – the premise, in one form or another, of the equal worth or dignity of each person[2] – is simply absent in Nietzsche's work. It is not, of course, that contemporaries have discovered "facts" or "arguments" for the egalitarian premise that Nietzsche missed; it is rather that the *Weltanschauung* has changed in fundamental ways in the century since Nietzsche wrote. This may be an uncomfortable fact about Nietzsche, but it is a fact nonetheless. Of course, if he were merely an outdated nineteenth-century elitist, we would not read him today; he transcends his time by severing the elitism from class and ethnicity, and by embedding it in an ambitious and novel moral psychology, which we have seen in the *Genealogy*.

Since World War II, the "ethical" dimension of Nietzsche's thought – his attack on morality and revaluation of values, of which the *Genealogy* is a key part – has received far less attention than Brandes accorded it. The immediate cause of this transformation in Nietzsche studies is plain enough. By the time the Nazis came to power in the 1930s, Nietzsche dominated the intellectual and cultural landscape in Germany, so much so, that *every* political ideology, from the fascistic to the anarchic, tried to claim his authority to enhance its own legitimacy. The Nazi misreadings of Nietzsche[3] acquired the advantage, needless to say, of the success of their political movement.

---

[2]   Utilitarian theories respect the egalitarian premise by giving the same weight to each person's utility or well-being; Kantian theories respect it by emphasizing the constraints that the dignity of the individual places upon the pursuit of social goals.

[See facing page for n. 3.]

By the end of the Second World War, Nietzsche's association in popular consciousness with the Nazis made it hard enough to discuss his philosophy in polite academic circles, even without delving into his illiberal and disturbing "ethical" views. To rescue Nietzsche for scholarly study, it was necessary either to whitewash his ethical views (as Walter Kaufmann did in his famous 1950 study, where Nietzsche becomes a benign secular humanist),[4] or to locate Nietzsche's primary philosophical concerns outside of ethics: for example, as a metaphysical philosopher, concerned fundamentally with questions of ontology (as in Heidegger's famous misreading (1961)); or as a certain sort of philosophical skeptic about truth, knowledge, and meaning (an approach favored both by French writers like Jacques Derrida and Anglophone philosophers like Arthur Danto). This latter approach, which dominated Nietzsche studies from the 1960s until quite recently, received its most sophisticated articulation in Alexander Nehamas' 1985 study, *Nietzsche: Life as Literature*. The price of this approach, however, has been to give us a "Nietzsche" that, one suspects, Georg Brandes would not have recognized.

More recently, there has been a growing backlash to both the Kaufmannesque whitewash and the "French" trivialization of Nietzsche. Clark (1990) put to rest the proto-deconstructionist Nietzsche, though that caricature of his thought remains popular outside academic philosophy. Others, including the present author, have argued for the role of naturalism in Nietzsche's philosophy (cf. Chapter 1). Questions of value have returned to center stage in scholarly discussion of Nietzsche,[5] and Nietzsche is now the subject of respectful and even appreciative attention by mainstream moral philosophers like Christine Korsgaard, Thomas Nagel, and Bernard Williams.[6]

---

[3] The misuse of Nietzsche's work by the Nazis, with the help of Nietzsche's sister, is well-documented in Kaufmann (1974: 3–18, 42–6, 284–306).

[4] The obscurity which soon befell Morgan (1941) is attributable almost entirely to its bad timing. The less textually sound Kaufmann (1974; 1st edn, 1950) achieved greater fame in large part by tackling the Nazi misreadings directly.

[5] See, e.g., Clark (1994), Clark and Leiter (1997), Detwiler (1990), Geuss (1997), Hunt (1991), Leiter (1993, 1995, 1997), May (1999).

[6] For critical discussion, however, of the use of Nietzsche by recent Anglo-American morality "critics" like Williams, see Leiter (1997).

Yet the return of value theory to center stage in Nietzsche studies has also given new life to the troubling questions that arise in light of Nietzsche's indifference to the egalitarian premise. Many of these questions have surely occurred to the reader of this volume. Does Nietzsche really favor the abolition of a morality of altruism and compassion, and if so, in favor of what? (If our morality is really in the interests of the oppressed, so much the better for it!) Is Nietzsche so naive as to think that the prevalence of altruism and equality are the primary problems of the modern world? What politics would Nietzsche recommend to us in light of his repudiation of the egalitarian premise? We will conclude by addressing squarely some of these natural worries about the Nietzsche we have encountered throughout this study.

Perhaps the most striking feature of the reception of Nietzsche in the last decade is the large literature that has developed on Nietzsche's purported "political" philosophy (Detwiler (1990) is representative). Even the casual reader knows, of course, that Nietzsche has intense opinions about *everything*, from German cuisine to the unparalleled brilliance (in Nietzsche's estimation) of Bizet's operas, not to mention various and sundry "political" matters. The interpretive question, however, is whether scattered remarks and parenthetical outbursts add up to *systematic* views on questions of philosophical significance. Unfortunately, scholarly caution has not been the hallmark of the "revival" of interest in Nietzsche's political philosophy.[7]

[7] Lack of "scholarly caution" would be a charitable characterization of the work of those intent on excoriating Nietzsche's alleged "political thought." So, e.g., Nussbaum (1997) begins her hatchet job on Nietzsche by declaring that, "Nietzsche claimed to be a political thinker, indeed an important political thinker" (p. 1), though she can produce, of course, no explicit textual evidence showing Nietzsche to claim any such thing. Instead of real evidence, she claims that, "In *Ecce Homo* he announced that he was 'a bringer of glad tidings like no one before me,' and that those glad tidings are political" (p. 1). In fact, Nietzsche does *not* say the "tidings" are political; indeed, as has been argued at length in this book, the "tidings" are directed only at select readers, nascent higher human beings, for whom morality is harmful. That this section from *Ecce Homo* (IV: 1) concludes with the hyperbolic claim that only with Nietzsche does "the earth [first] know *great politics*" does as little to establish that he has a political philosophy as the claim, *in the very same*

A handful of passages – notably sections 56–7 of *The Antichrist* – are the slender evidence on which elaborate views about the ideal forms of social and political organization are attributed to Nietzsche.[8] In particular, Nietzsche is said to endorse (in A: 56–7) the caste-based society associated with the Hindu Laws of Manu as his political ideal:

> The *order* of castes, the supreme, the dominant law, is merely the sanction of a *natural order*, a natural lawfulness of the first

passage, that Nietzsche's "glad tidings" will cause "upheavals, a convulsion of earthquakes, a moving of mountains and valleys" does to establish that he has a geological theory! Nussbaum goes on to suggest that "serious political thought" (p. 2) – by which she means, "serious" academic *liberal* political theory – must address seven precise topics (e.g., "procedural justification" ("procedures . . . that legitimate and/or justify the resulting proposals" for "political structure,"), "gender and the family," and "justice between nations") – most of which, of course, Nietzsche does not address. (Marx does not address most of them either, though Nussbaum politely avoids comment on this point, since it might suggest that "serious political thought" in her sense did not exist before the rise of a large class of bourgeois academics after World War II.) Instead of drawing the obvious conclusion – Nietzsche was not interested in questions of political philosophy – she decries his "baneful influence" in political philosophy (p. 12). Although Bertrand Russell's irresponsible polemics against Nietzsche in *A History of Western Philosophy* (1945) – e.g., "King Lear on the verge of madness, says: 'I will do such things – what they are yet I know not – but they shall be the terror of the earth.' This is Nietzsche's philosophy in a nutshell" – are now routinely held up for ridicule by Nietzsche scholars (cf. Schacht 1983: x), Nussbaum (1997) should remind us how readily Nietzsche inspires scholarly recklessness in the service of moral indignation.

8 Even the more balanced discussion in Detwiler (1990) ends up relying heavily on an essay the 27-year-old Nietzsche never published (pp. 39–41, 63)! As to passages in the "mature" corpus, Detwiler adduces ones that "appear to have explicit political implications" (p. 43; cf. p. 44), or that "strongly suggest . . . political consequences" (pp. 45–6), or that "raise the issue of troubling political implications of Nietzschean immoralism" (p. 49). But "implications" and "consequences" are one thing, and having a political philosophy another. The canon of political philosophers is composed of thinkers (like Hobbes, Locke, and Rousseau) who have philosophical views about political questions – the state, liberty, law, justice, etc. – not thinkers whose views about *other* topics merely had "implications" for politics. As the conscientious Detwiler admits: "[t]he political implications of Nietzsche's revaluation of values are never center stage for long" (p. 58).

rank, over which no arbitrariness, no "modern idea" has any power ... Nature, not Manu, distinguishes the pre-eminently spiritual ones, those who are pre-eminently strong in muscle and temperament, and those, the third type, who excel neither in one respect nor in the other, the mediocre ones – the last as the great majority, the first as the elite.

(A: 57)

This reading, however, cannot withstand much scrutiny, as Thomas Brobjer (1998) has shown decisively. As Brobjer notes, the only other published discussion of the laws of Manu, in *Twilight of the Idols*, is highly critical, not laudatory (pp. 304–5); Nietzsche's discussions of comparable caste-based societies are all critical (pp. 308–9); and Nietzsche's unpublished notebooks contain numerous entries on the theme "a critique of the Laws of Manu" (pp. 310–12). The passage from *The Antichrist* only *seems* laudatory when read out of context; as Brobjer remarks:

[Nietzsche's] purpose [in these passages in *The Antichrist*] is to make the contrast with Christianity as strong as possible, to provoke the reader, to make the reader "realize" that even the laws of Manu ... is higher and more humane than Christianity. Whereas Christianity destroys, the intention at least of the laws of Manu was to save and protect.

(1998: 312–13)

In other words, the *rhetorical context* of the passage is crucial, though it is completely ignored by all those commentators bent on inventing a Nietzschean political philosophy. Indeed, the passage quoted above from A: 57 is specifically introduced to illustrate the use of the "holy lie" (the lie being, in this case, the claim that "nature, not Manu" distinguishes the castes). And as even the title of the book would suggest, Nietzsche's target is Christianity, and the laws of Manu are invoked simply to drive home that point. Thus, although Manu and Christianity both depend on lies, *at least* the Manu lies, according to Nietzsche, are not put in the service of Christian ends, i.e., "poisoning, slander, negation of life, contempt for the body, the degradation and self-violation of man through the concept of sin" (A: 56). Similarly,

Nietzsche goes out of his way to show that Christian views of female sexuality compare unfavorably with Manu views (A: 56).

Yet surely, the reader will protest, Nietzsche's attack on morality has political *implications*! When Nietzsche commends the laws of Manu for "mak[ing] possible the higher and the highest types" (A: 57), does this not resonate, all too obviously, with Nietzsche's central concern that morality is harmful to the highest types of human beings? The "resonance" is, of course, undeniable, but that hardly shows Nietzsche *endorses* the laws of Manu: most obviously, the "higher types" protected by the laws of Manu – essentially a priestly caste – have nothing in common with the nascent Goethes that concern Nietzsche. Nietzsche's worry for these potential higher types is, as we have emphasized throughout, that they suffer from *false consciousness*, i.e., the false belief that "morality in the pejorative sense," i.e., MPS, is good for them. MPS is a threat to the flourishing of nascent Goethes, and it is this flourishing that interests Nietzsche above all. It would suffice for Nietzsche's purposes that nascent Goethes give up their faith in MPS – in other words, it is individual attitudes not political structures that are Nietzsche's primary object ("The ideas of the herd should rule in the herd," says Nietzsche, "and not reach out beyond it" (WP: 287)). That should hardly be surprising if we recall Nietzsche's sustained hostility to politics throughout his career.

Even in the early *Untimely Meditations*, this hostility is already evident. So, for example, Nietzsche comments:

> Every philosophy which believes that the problem of existence is touched on, not to say solved, by a political event is a joke- and pseudo-philosophy. Many states have been founded since the world began; that is an old story. How should a political innovation suffice to turn men once and for all into contented inhabitants of the earth? [That people think the answer to existential questions might come from politics shows] that we are experiencing the consequences of the doctrine ... that the state is the highest goal of mankind and that a man has no higher duty than to serve the state: in which doctrine I recognize a relapse not into paganism but into stupidity. It may be that a man who sees his highest duty in serving the state really knows

no higher duties; but there are men and duties existing beyond this – and one of the duties that seems, at least to me, to be higher than serving the state demands that one destroys stupidity in every form, and therefore in this form too. That is why I am concerned with a species of man whose teleology extends somewhat beyond the welfare of a state ... , and with [this kind of man] only in relation to a world which is again fairly independent of the welfare of a state, that of culture.

(U III: 4)

The same, almost anarchistic attitude is apparent in *Thus Spoke Zarathustra*, where Nietzsche calls the "state ... the coldest of all cold monsters" and remarks, aptly enough, that "the state ... whatever it says it lies ... Everything about it is false" (Z I: 11). "Only where the state ends, there begins the human being who is not superfluous" (Z I: 11). Of course, it is only the latter individual that *really* interests Nietzsche. And who is that individual? The next section (Z I: 12) tells us: he is the one who values his "solitude," which is precisely what the "marketplace" of politics violates, with its "showmen and actors of great things." "Far from the market place and from fame happens all that is great" (Z I: 12): in other words, great things (and great people) are to be found far from the realms of politics and economics.

Nietzsche, then, has no political philosophy, in the conventional sense of a theory of the state and its legitimacy. He occasionally expresses views about political matters, but, read in context, they do not add up to a theoretical account of any of the questions of political philosophy. He is more accurately read, in the end, as a kind of *esoteric moralist*, i.e., someone who has views about human flourishing, views he wants to communicate at least to a select few. "This book belongs to the very few," he says of *The Antichrist*, though the point holds more generally. Indeed, Nietzsche is clearly describing his own work when he writes in an earlier book:

It is not by any means necessarily an objection to a book when anyone finds it impossible to understand: perhaps that was part of the author's intention – he did not want to be understood by just "anybody." All the nobler spirits and tastes select their audience when they wish to communicate; and choosing that, one at the same time erects barriers against "the others." All the more subtle laws of any style have their origin at this point: they at the same time keep away, create a distance, forbid "entrance," understanding, as said above – while they open the ears of those whose ears are related to ours.

(GS: 381)

Or similarly: "Our highest insights must – and should – sound like follies and sometimes like crimes when they are heard without permission by those who are not predisposed and predestined for them" (BGE: 30). Nietzsche, the esoteric moralist, wants to reach only select individuals – those nascent higher human beings who are "predisposed and predestined" for his ideas – and alter their consciousness about morality. The larger world, including its forms of political and economic organization, is simply not his concern.

Even without a political philosophy, however, there still remain disturbing questions about Nietzsche's critique of morality and its political *implications*. Let us consider these in turn.

1   When Nietzsche objects centrally that morality is an obstacle to "the highest power and splendor possible" to man, one is tempted to dismiss this as hyperbole: for surely if there is a culture of mediocrity and banality in ascendance – a culture of Zarathustra's "last men" – it is not primarily the work of morality, but, more likely, of economics – for example, the free market, the leveling effects of which have been described by sociologists, historians, and philosophers. Indeed, the right model for culture critique, one might want to say, is not the "idealistic" sounding Nietzsche we have encountered here, but rather the Marxist and materialist Theodor Adorno (1903–69) who traces cultural mediocrity to its capitalist roots.

Now while the early Nietzsche – especially in "Schopenhauer as Educator" (1874) – did worry about the effects of capitalism, militaristic nationalism, and proto-fascism on the cultural conditions for the production of genius, the later Nietzsche seems all-too-ready to lay the blame for all cultural decline at the doorstep of morality, i.e.,

MPS.[9] Nietzsche's challenge may be a novel and important one, but anyone who reads his repeated denunciations of morality can not escape the feeling that he suffered from a certain explanatory tunnel-vision, with the result that, in some measure, his case against morality seems overstated.

2   On further reflection, however, one might want to say something much stronger: Nietzsche's point is not just hyperbolic, but perversely backwards. For surely it is the *lack* of morality in social policy and public institutions – a lack which permits widespread poverty and despair to persist generation upon generation; that allows daily economic struggle and uncertainty to define the basic character of most people's lives – that is most responsible for a lack of human flourishing. Surely, in a more moral society, with a genuine commitment to social justice and human equality, there would be far more Goethes, far more creativity and admirable human achievement. As Philippa Foot has sharply put it: "How could one see the present dangers that the world is in as showing that there is too much pity and too little egoism around?" (1973: 168).

Here, though, we must be careful in how we construe the Nietzschean point.[10] Consider the Nietzsche who asks: "Where has the last feeling of decency and self-respect gone when even our statesmen, an otherwise quite unembarrassed type of man, anti-Christians through and through in their deeds, still call themselves Christians today and attend communion?" (A: 38). Clearly this Nietzsche is under no illusions about the extent to which public actors do not act morally. Indeed, Nietzsche continues in even more explicit terms: "Every practice of every moment, every instinct, every valuation that is translated into *action* is today anti-Christian: what a *miscarriage of falseness* must modern man be, that he is *not ashamed* to be called a Christian in spite of all this!" (A: 38). What, then, is going on here? If Nietzsche is not, contrary to Foot's suggestion, embracing the absurd view that

---

[9]   To be sure, Nietzsche often blames "Christianity" for cultural decline, but remember that, for Nietzsche, Christianity was simply "the most prodigal elaboration of the moral theme to which humanity has ever been subjected" (BT Pref: 5).

[10]   We first broached this topic in Chapters 4 and 5: see pp. 132–4, 184–7.

there is too much pity and altruism in the world, what exactly is his critical point?

Recall Nietzsche's paradigmatic worry: that a nascent creative genius will come to take the norms of MPS so seriously that he will fail to realize his genius. Rather than tolerate (even welcome) suffering, he will seek relief from hardship and devote himself to the pursuit of pleasure; rather than practice what Nietzsche calls "severe self-love", and attend to himself in the ways requisite for productive creative work, he will embrace the ideology of altruism, and reject "self-love" as improper, and so forth. As we emphasized in Chapter 5, it is not that Nietzsche thinks people *practice* too much altruism – after all, Nietzsche tells us that egoistic actions "have hitherto been by far the most frequent actions" (D: 148) – but rather that they *believe* too much in the value of altruism, equality, happiness and the other norms of MPS. Even though there is neither much altruism nor equality in the world, there is almost universal endorsement of the *value* of altruism and equality – even, notoriously (and as Nietzsche seemed well aware), by those who are its worst enemies in practice. So Nietzsche's critique is that a culture in the grips of MPS, even without acting on MPS, poses the real obstacle to flourishing, because it teaches potential higher types to disvalue what would be most conducive to their creativity and value what is irrelevant or perhaps even hostile to it.

We documented in Chapter 5 the many passages supporting this interpretation of Nietzsche's critique.[11] Here is a typical one, from *Twilight of the Idols*, where Nietzsche describes the man "improved" by MPS as,

> a caricature of man, like a miscarriage: he had become a "sinner," he was stuck in a cage, *imprisoned among all sorts of terrible concepts* [*schreckliche Begriffe*]. And there he lay, sick, miserable, malevolent against himself: full of hatred against the springs of life, full of suspicion against all that was still strong and happy.
>
> (TI VII: 2, emphasis added)

---

[11]   See especially pp. 184–7.

So, contrary to Foot, Nietzsche is not claiming that people are *actually* too altruistic and too egalitarian in their practice; he is worried that (as a consequence of the slave revolt in morals, etc.) they are now "imprisoned among ... concepts" of equality and altruism, and that this conceptual vocabulary of value is itself the obstacle to the realization of certain forms of human excellence. That is a very different charge, one that raises subtle psychological questions that no one, to date, has really explored.

3   One might want to respond on Foot's behalf, however, and insist that there is still something perverse about the Nietzschean attack on morality. Granted Nietzsche does not believe that most people are *actually* too altruistic and society *in practice* is too egalitarian; granted that Nietzsche's real worry is that we, as a moral culture, pay so much lip-service to the value of altruism, egalitarianism, and the rest that the result is deleterious for the self-conception and development of nascent Goethes. Yet surely it is still the case that if our society *really* were more altruistic and egalitarian, more individuals would have the chance to flourish and do creative work. This is the core of the charge of perversity, and nothing said so far has exonerated Nietzsche from it.

Now, in fact, it seems that it is precisely this moral optimism common, for example, to utilitarians and Marxists – this belief that a more moral society would produce more opportunity for more people to do creative work – that Nietzsche does, indeed, want to question. Nietzsche's illiberal attitudes in this regard are apparent; he says – to take but one example – that, "We simply do not consider it desirable that a realm of justice and harmony [*Eintracht*] should be established on earth" (GS: 377). It is bad enough for Nietzsche that MPS values have so far succeeded in saying, "stubbornly and inexorably, 'I am morality itself, and nothing besides is morality'" (BGE: 202); it could only be worse on his view if more and more of our actions were really brought into accord with these values. For Nietzsche wants to urge – contrary to the moral optimists – that in a way largely unappreciated, and (perhaps) unintended a thoroughly *moral* culture undermines the conditions under which the most splendid human creativity is possible, and generates instead a society of Zarathustra's "last men" (Z Pref: 5):

"What is love? What is creation? What is longing? What is a star?" thus asks the last man, and he blinks.

The earth has become small, and on it hops the last man, who makes everything small. His race is as ineradicable as the flea-beetle; the last man lives longest.

"We have invented happiness," say the last men, and they blink.

If we are trained always to think of happiness and comfort and safety and the needs of others, we shall cut ourselves off from the preconditions for creative excellence on the Nietzschean picture: suffering, hardship, danger, self-concern, and the rest.

Consider a particularly powerful statement of this view. Speaking of those "eloquent and profoundly scribbling slaves of the democratic taste and its 'modern ideas'" who seek to promote "the universal green-pasture happiness of the herd" and who take "suffering itself . . . for something that must be abolished" (BGE: 44), Nietzsche retorts that when we look at

> how the plant "man" has so far grown most vigorously to a height – we think that this has happened every time under the opposite conditions, that to this end the dangerousness of his situation must first grow to the point of enormity, his power of invention and simulation (his "spirit") had to develop under prolonged pressure and constraint into refinement and audacity. . . . We think that . . . everything evil, terrible, tyrannical in man, everything in him that is kin to beasts of prey and serpents, serves the enhancement of the species "man" as much as its opposite does. Indeed, we do not even say enough when we say only that much.
>
> (BGE: 44)

Note that, at the end of this passage, Nietzsche hints at a role for morality as well – it is just that what morality opposes is equally important. He, of course, qualifies this by suggesting that even to concede their equal importance may "not even say enough": that is, perhaps there will not be much role for morality at all in the conditions under which "the plant 'man'" will grow to its greatest heights. But notice that, even in this passage, what is called for is not a *political* transformation, but an *individual* one, that of the nascent higher human being: it is "*his* situation" that "must first grow to the point of enormity" and it is "*his* power of invention and simulation" that "had to develop under prolonged pressure and constraint into refinement and audacity." As he writes in a *Nachlass* note of 1887, regarding those "human beings who are of any concern to me": "I wish [them] suffering, desolation, sickness, ill-treatment, indignities – I wish that they should not remain unfamiliar with profound self-contempt, the torture of self-mistrust, the wretchedness of the vanquished" (WP: 910). This is not the outline of a political program, but rather a severe regimen for the realization of individual potential – at least for the select few.

Moral philosophy in the last hundred years has been largely indifferent to the facts about human psychology.[12] Yet Nietzsche's approach to moral philosophy is one that depends crucially on psychological claims about moral motivation, about the effect of moral beliefs, about the structure of our whole moral psychology (conscience, guilt, reasons for acting, and so on). Nietzsche was plainly not an academic social scientist in the twentieth-century mold – though the latter's results have been sufficiently paltry that it is hard to hold that deficiency against him. Rather, through a combination of wide-ranging cultural and historical learning, heightened sensitivity, and a remarkable capacity for penetrating introspection, Nietzsche produced a set of claims about morality and its psychological sources that continue to command the attention of novelists, poets, philosophers, and even the occasional psychologist more than a century later. Why *are* moralities of renunciation (sexual and otherwise) so prevalent among human beings? What *would* a culture suffused with morality (more precisely, MPS) actually look like, and would it be one that we would admire? Can a Beethoven or a Goethe *really* take moral demands seriously? Does commitment to morality preclude the cultivation of certain traits and talents? Is moral conscience severable from the pleasure in cruelty? Is the psychology of "love of truth" the same as the psychology of self-denial? Are human excellence and moral

[12]   This is beginning to change; see, e.g., Doris (2002).

commitment in fundamental tension? How, in fact, can human beings be reconciled with the fact of suffering? What *are* the alternatives to the ascetic ideal, and *for whom* will they work?

Nietzsche sets a profound task for the moral psychology of the future; it remains a challenge to the philosophers and psychologists of that future, including the readers of this book, to complete it.

Bibliography

Works by Nietzsche

The Antichrist, in *The Portable Nietzsche* (1954).

Beyond Good and Evil, translated by W. Kaufmann, New York: Vintage, 1966.

The Birth of Tragedy, translated by W. Kaufmann, New York: Vintage, 1966.

The Case of Wagner, translated by W. Kaufmann, New York: Vintage, 1966.

Daybreak: Thoughts on the Prejudices of Morality, translated by R. J. Hollingdale, edited by M. Clark and B. Leiter, Cambridge: Cambridge University Press, 1997.

Ecce Homo, translated by W. Kaufmann, New York: Vintage, 1967.

The Gay Science, translated by W. Kaufmann, New York: Vintage, 1974.

Human, All-too-Human, translated by R. J. Hollingdale, Cambridge: Cambridge University Press, 1986.

Nietzsche contra Wagner, in *The Portable Nietzsche* (1954).

Philosophy in the Tragic Age of the Greeks, translated by M. Cowan, Washington, DC: Regnery Gateway, 1962.

Philosophy and Truth: Selections from Nietzsche's Notebooks of the Early 1870s, edited and translated by D. Breazeale, Atlantic Highlands, NJ: Humanities Press, 1979.

The Portable Nietzsche, edited and translated by W. Kaufmann, New York: Viking, 1954.

Sämtliche Werke: Kritische Studienausgabe in 15 Bänden, edited by G. Colli and M. Montinari, Berlin: de Gruyter, 1980.

Thus Spoke Zarathustra, in *The Portable Nietzsche* (1954).

Twilight of the Idols, in *The Portable Nietzsche* (1954).

Untimely Meditations, translated by R. J. Hollingdale, Cambridge: Cambridge University Press, 1983.

The Will to Power, translated by W. Kaufmann and R. J. Hollingdale, New York: Vintage, 1968.

Other works

Anderson, Lorin (1980), "Freud, Nietzsche," *Salmagundi* 47–8: 3–29.

Anderson, R. Lanier (1996), "Overcoming Charity: The Case of Maudemarie Clark's *Nietzsche on Truth and Philosophy*," *Nietzsche-Studien* 25: 307–41.

Barnes, Jonathan (1986), "Nietzsche and Diogenes Laertius," *Nietzsche-Studien* 15: 16–40.

Beam, Craig (1996), "Hume and Nietzsche: Naturalists, Ethicists, Anti-Christians," *Hume Studies* 22: 299–324.

Bergmann, Frithjof (1988), "Nietzsche's Critique of Morality," in R. Solomon and K. Higgins (eds) (1988).

Bett, Richard (1989), "The Sophists and Relativism," *Phronesis* 34: 139–69.

Bittner, Rüdiger (1994), "*Ressentiment*," in Schacht (1994).

Brobjer, Thomas H. (1995), *Nietzsche's Ethics of Character: A Study of Nietzsche's Ethics and Its Place in the History of Moral Thinking*, Uppsala: Department of History of Science and Ideas, Uppsala University.

—— (1998), "The Absence of Political Ideals in Nietzsche's Writings: The Case of the Laws of Manu and the Associated Caste-Society," *Nietzsche-Studien* 27: 300–18.

—— (2001), "Nietzsche's Disinterest and Ambivalence towards the Greek Sophists," *International Studies in Philosophy* 23: 5–23.

—— (forthcoming), *Nietzsche's Knowledge of Philosophy: A Study and Survey of the Philosophical Influences on Nietzsche*.

Büchner, Ludwig (1870), *Force and Matter*, translated by J. G. Collingwood, London: Trubner.

Burnyeat, Myles (1990), *The Theaetetus of Plato*, Indianapolis: Hackett.

Clark, Maudemarie (1990), *Nietzsche on Truth and Philosophy*, Cambridge: Cambridge University Press.

—— (1994), "Nietzsche's Immoralism and the Concept of Morality," in R. Schacht (ed.) (1994).

—— (1998a), "Introduction: Nietzsche's Path to the End of the Twentieth Century," in Clark and Swensen (eds) (1998).

—— (1998b), "On Knowledge, Truth, and Value: Nietzsche's Debt to Schopenhauer and the Development of His Empiricism," in Janaway (ed.) (1998a).

Clark, Maudemarie and Leiter, Brian (1997), "Introduction," in Friedrich Nietzsche, *Daybreak: Thoughts on the Prejudices of Morality*, translated by R. J. Hollingdale, Cambridge: Cambridge University Press.

Clark, Maudemarie and Swensen, Alan (eds and trans.) (1998), *On the Genealogy of Morality*, Indianapolis: Hackett.

Craig, Gordon (1991), *The Germans*, New York: Penguin/Meridian.

Danto, Arthur ([1965] 1980), *Nietzsche as Philosopher*, New York: Columbia University Press.

Deleuze, Gilles (1962), *Nietzsche and Philosophy*, translated by H. Tomlinson, New York: Columbia University Press, 1983.

DeMan, Paul (1979), *Allegories of Reading*, New Haven: Yale University Press.

Dennett, Daniel (1984), "Foreword," in Ruth Garrett Millikan, *Language, Thought and Other Biological Categories*, Cambridge, Mass.: MIT Press.

—— (1995), *Darwin's Dangerous Idea: Evolution and the Meaning of Life*, New York: Simon & Schuster.

Detwiler, Bruce (1990), *Nietzsche and the Politics of Aristocratic Radicalism*, Chicago: University of Chicago Press.

Doris, John (2002), *Lack of Character: Personality and Moral Behavior*, Cambridge: Cambridge University Press.

Dreyfus, Hubert and Rabinow, Paul (1983), *Michel Foucault: Beyond Structuralism and Hermeneutics*, 2nd edn, Chicago: University of Chicago Press.

Foot, Philippa (1973), "Nietzsche: The Revaluation of Values," in Solomon (ed.) (1973a). Also reprinted in Richardson and Leiter (eds) (2001).

—— (1994), "Nietzsche's Immoralism," in Schacht (ed.) (1994).

Foucault, Michel ([1966] 1970), *The Order of Things*, translated by A. Sheridan, New York: Random House.

—— (1971), "Nietzsche, Genealogy, History," in P. Rabinow (ed.) (1984) *The Foucault Reader*, New York: Pantheon. Also reprinted in Richardson and Leiter (eds) (2001).

Frankfurt, Harry (1988), *The Importance of What We Care About*, Cambridge: Cambridge University Press.

Freud, Sigmund (1930), *Civilization and Its Discontents*, edited and translated by J. Strachey, New York: W. W. Norton & Co., 1961.

—— (1957), *The Standard Edition of the Complete Psychological Works of Sigmund Freud*, edited and translated by J. Strachey, London: The Hogarth Press.

Gardner, Sebastian (1999), "Schopenhauer, Will, and the Unconscious," in Christopher Janaway (ed.), *The Cambridge Companion to Schopenhauer*, Cambridge: Cambridge University Press.

Gay, Peter (1988), *Freud: A Life for Our Time*, New Haven: Yale University Press.

Gemes, Ken (1992), "Nietzsche's Critique of Truth," *Philosophy & Phenomenological Research* 52: 47–65. Also reprinted in Richardson and Leiter (eds) (2001).

Geuss, Raymond (1981), *The Idea of a Critical Theory: Habermas and the Frankfurt School*, Cambridge: Cambridge University Press.

—— (1994), "Nietzsche and Genealogy," *European Journal of Philosophy* 2: 275–92. Also reprinted in Richardson and Leiter (eds) (2001).

—— (1997), "Nietzsche and Morality," *European Journal of Philosophy* 5: 1–20.

Gossman, Lionel (2000), *Basel in the Age of Burckhardt: A Study in Unseasonable Ideas*, Chicago: University of Chicago Press.

Gregory, Frederick (1977) *Scientific Materialism in Nineteenth-Century Germany*, Dordrecht: D. Reidel.

Guthrie, W. K. C. (1962), *A History of Greek Philosophy, Volume 1: The Earlier Presocratics and the Pythagoreans*, Cambridge: Cambridge University Press.

—— (1971), *The Sophists*, Cambridge: Cambridge University Press.

Hayman, Ronald (1980) *Nietzsche: A Critical Life*, New York: Penguin.

Heidegger, Martin (1961), *Nietzsche*, edited D. F. Krell, 4 volumes, San Francisco: Harper & Row, 1979–1982.

Hollingdale, R. J. (1985), *Nietzsche: The Man and His Philosophy*, London: Ark Paperbacks.

Hunt, Lester (1991), *Nietzsche and the Origin of Virtue*, London: Routledge.

Janaway, Christopher (1994), *Schopenhauer*, Oxford: Oxford University Press.

—— (1997), "Nietzsche's Illustration of the Art of Exegesis," *European Journal of Philosophy* 5: 251–68.

—— (ed.) (1998a), *Willing and Nothingness: Schopenhauer as Nietzsche's Educator*, Oxford: Oxford University Press.

—— (1998b), "Schopenhauer as Nietzsche's Educator," in Janaway (ed.) (1998a).

Janz, Curt P. (1978), *Friedrich Nietzsche: Biographie*, 3 volumes, Munich: Hanser. [An English translation is in preparation.]

Jaspers, Karl (1965), *Nietzsche: An Introduction to the Understanding of His Philosophical Activity*, translated by C. Wallraff and F. Schmitz, Chicago: Regnery.

Johnston, Mark (1993), "Objectivity Refigured: Pragmatism Without Verificationism," in J. Haldane and C. Wright (eds), *Reality, Representation, and Projection*, Oxford: Oxford University Press.

Jones, Ernest (1955), *The Life and Work of Sigmund Freud, Volume 2*, New York: Basic Books.

Kane, Robert (1996), *The Significance of Free Will*, New York: Oxford University Press.

Kaufmann, Walter (1959), "How Nietzsche Revolutionalized Ethics," in *From Shakespeare to Existentialism*, Princeton: Princeton University Press.

—— (1974), *Nietzsche: Philosopher, Psychologist, Antichrist*, 4th edn, Princeton: Princeton University Press.

Kirk, G. S., Raven, J. E. and Schofield, Malcolm (eds) (1983), *The Presocratic Philosophers*, 2nd edn, Cambridge: Cambridge University Press.

Kitcher, Philip (1997), "An Argument about Free Inquiry," *Noûs* 31: 279–306.

Lange, Friedrich ([1865] 1950), *History of Materialism*, 2nd book, translated by E. C. Thomas, New York: Humanities Press.

Leiter, Brian (1992), "Nietzsche and Aestheticism," *Journal of the History of Philosophy* 30: 275–90.

—— (1993), "Beyond Good and Evil," *History of Philosophy Quarterly* 10: 261–70.

—— (1994), "Perspectivism in Nietzsche's *Genealogy of Morals*," in Schacht (ed.) (1994).

—— (1995), "Morality in the Pejorative Sense: On the Logic of Nietzsche's Critique of Morality," *British Journal for the History of Philosophy* 3: 113–45.

—— (1996), Review of Peter Berkowitz, *Nietzsche: The Ethics of an Immoralist*, *Mind* 105: 487–91.

—— (1997), "Nietzsche and the Morality Critics," *Ethics* 107: 250–85. Also reprinted in Richardson and Leiter (ed.) (2001).

—— (1998a), "The Paradox of Fatalism and Self-Creation in Nietzsche," in Janaway (ed.) (1998a). Also reprinted in part in Richardson and Leiter (ed.) (2001).

—— (1998b), "Naturalism and Naturalized Jurisprudence," in B. Bix (ed.), *Analyzing Law: New Essays in Legal Theory*, Oxford: Oxford University Press.

—— (2000), "Nietzsche's Metaethics: Against the Privilege Readings," *European Journal of Philosophy* 8: 277–97.

—— (2001a), "Moral Facts and Best Explanations," *Social Philosophy & Policy* 18: 79–101.

—— (2001b), "Classical Realism," *Philosophical Issues* 11: 244–67.

MacIntyre, Alasdair (1990), *Three Rival Versions of Moral Enquiry: Encyclopedia, Genealogy, and Tradition*, South Bend: University of Notre Dame Press.

Magnus, Bernd (1978), *Nietzsche's Existential Imperative*, Bloomington: Indiana University Press.

—— (1988), "The Use and Abuse of *The Will to Power*," in Solomon and Higgins (eds) (1988).

Mann, Joel (2000), "Nietzsche's Interest in and Enthusiasm for the Greek Sophists," unpublished manuscript, Austin, TX.

May, Simon (1999), *Nietzsche's Ethics and his 'War on Morality'*, Oxford: Clarendon Press.

Migotti, Mark (1998), "Slave Morality, Socrates, and the Bushmen: A Reading of the First Essay of *On the Genealogy of Morals*," *Philosophy & Phenomenological Research* 58: 745–79.

Moleschott, Jacob (1853), *Lehre der Nahrungsmittel: Für das Volk*, 2nd edn, Erlangen: Ferdinand Enfe.

—— (1859), *Physiologie der Nahrungsmittel: Ein Hanbuch der Diatetik*, 2nd edn, Giessen: Emil Roth.

Morgan, George (1941), *What Nietzsche Means*, Cambridge, Mass.: Harvard University Press.

Mottinari, Mazzino (1982), *Nietzsche Lesen*, Berlin: de Gruyter.

Mourelatos, A. P. D. (1987), "Gorgias on the Function of Language," *Philosophical Topics* 15: 135–70.

Nagel, Thomas (1986), *The View from Nowhere*, New York: Oxford University Press.

Nehamas, Alexander (1985), *Nietzsche: Life as Literature*, Cambridge, Mass.: Harvard University Press.

Nussbaum, Martha (1997), "Is Nietzsche a Political Thinker?" *International Journal of Philosophical Studies* 5: 1–13.

Pizer, John (1990), "The Use and Abuse of '*Ursprung*': On Foucault's Reading of Nietzsche," *Nietzsche-Studien* 19: 462–78.

Poellner, Peter (1995), *Nietzsche and Metaphysics*, Oxford: Oxford University Press.

—— (2001), "Perspectival Truth," in Richardson and Leiter (eds) (2001).

Quine, W. V. O. (1960), *Word and Object*, Cambridge, Mass.: MIT Press.

—— (1961), *From a Logical Point of View*, 2nd edn, Cambridge, Mass.: Harvard University Press.

—— (1969), *Ontological Relativity and Other Essays*, New York: Columbia University Press.

—— (1981), *Theories and Things*, Cambridge, Mass.: Harvard University Press.

Railton, Peter (1986a), "Facts and Values," *Philosophical Topics* 14: 5–31.

—— (1986b), "Moral Realism," *Philosophical Review* 95: 163–207.

—— (1990), "Naturalism and Prescriptivity," in E. F. Paul, J. Paul and F. Miller Jr (eds) *Foundations of Moral and Political Philosophy*, Oxford: Blackwell.

Richardson, John (1996), *Nietzsche's System*, Oxford: Oxford University Press.

Richardson, John and Leiter, Brian (eds) (2001), *Nietzsche*, Oxford: Oxford University Press.

Ridley, Aaron (1998), *Nietzsche's Conscience: Six Character Studies from the Genealogy*, Ithaca: Cornell University Press.

Risse, Mathias (2001), "The Second Treatise in *On the Genealogy of Morality*: Nietzsche on the Origin of the Bad Conscience," *European Journal of Philosophy* 9: 55–81.

Rorty, Richard (1989), *Contingency, Irony and Solidarity*, Cambridge: Cambridge University Press.

Rousseau, Jean-Jacques ([1755] 1964), "Discourse on the Origin and Foundations of Inequality," in R. Masters (ed.), *The First and Second Discourses*, New York: St. Martin's Press.

Salaquarda, Jörg (1978), "Nietzsche und Lange," *Nietzsche-Studien* 7: 236–53.

Schaberg, William (1995), *The Nietzsche Canon: A Publication History and Bibliography*, Chicago: University of Chicago Press.

Schacht, Richard (1983), *Nietzsche*, London: Routledge.

—— (ed.) (1994), *Nietzsche, Genealogy, Morality: Essays on Nietzsche's* Genealogy of Morals, Berkeley: University of California Press.

Schnädelbach, Herbert (1983), *Philosophy in Germany: 1831–1933*, translated by E. Matthews, Cambridge: Cambridge University Press.

Schopenhauer, Arthur ([1818] 1969), *The World as Will and Representation, Vol. 1*, translated by E. F. J. Payne, New York: Dover.

—— ([1841a] 1965), *On the Basis of Morality*, translated by E. F. J. Payne, Indianapolis: Bobbs-Merrill.

—— ([1841b] 1985), *On the Freedom of the Will*, translated by K. Kolenda, Oxford: Oxford University Press.

—— ([1844] 1969), *The World as Will and Representation, Vol. 2*, translated by E. F. J. Payne, New York: Dover.

Schutte, Ofelia (1984), *Beyond Nihilism: Nietzsche Without Masks*, Chicago: University of Chicago Press.

Silk, M. S. and Stern, J. P. (1981), *Nietzsche on Tragedy*, Cambridge: Cambridge University Press.

Smart, J. J. C. (1984), "'Ought,' 'Can,' Free Will and Responsibility," in *Ethics, Persuasion and Truth*, London: Routledge.

Solomon, Maynard (1977), *Beethoven*, New York: Schirmer Books.

Solomon, Robert C. (ed.) (1973a), *Nietzsche: A Collection of Critical Essays*, Notre Dame: University of Notre Dame Press.

—— (1973b), "Nietzsche, Nihilism, and Morality," in Solomon (ed.) (1973a).

Solomon, Robert C. and Higgins, Kathleen (eds.) (1988), *Reading Nietzsche*, New York: Oxford University Press.

Stack, George (1983), *Lange and Nietzsche*, Berlin: de Gruyter.

Stegmaier, Werner (1994), *Nietzsches "Genealogie der Moral,"* Darmstadt: Wissenschaftliche Buchgesellschaft.

Strawson, Galen (1994), "The Impossibility of Moral Responsibility," *Philosophical Studies* 75: 5–24.

Stroud, Barry (1977), *Hume*, London: Routledge.

—— (1996), "The Charm of Naturalism," *Proceedings and Addresses of the American Philosophical Association* 70: 43–55.

Thatcher, David S. (1989), "*Zur Genealogie der Moral*: Some Textual Annotations," *Nietzsche-Studien* 18: 587–99.

Velleman, J. David (1992), "What Happens When Someone Acts?" *Mind* 101: 461–81.

Vitzthum, Richard C. (1995), *Materialism: An Affirmative History and Definition*, Amherst, NY: Prometheus Books.

Watson, Gary (1987), "Free Action and Free Will," *Mind* 96: 145–72.

Westphal, Kenneth (1984a), "Was Nietzsche a Cognitivist?" *Journal of the History of Philosophy* 22: 343–63.

—— (1984b), "Nietzsche's Sting and the Possibility of Good Philology," *International Studies in Philosophy* 16: 71–90.

Whitman, James (1986), "Nietzsche in the Magisterial Tradition of German Classical Philology," *Journal of the History of Ideas* 47: 453–68.

Wilcox, John T. (1974), *Truth and Value in Nietzsche: A Study of His Metaethics and Epistemology*, Ann Arbor: University of Michigan Press.

—— (1997), "*Genealogy* III Is an Exegesis – of What?" *Journal of the History of Philosophy* 35: 593–610.

Williams, Bernard (1985), *Ethics and the Limits of Philosophy*, Cambridge, Mass.: Harvard University Press.

—— (1993a), "Nietzsche's Minimalist Moral Psychology," *European Journal of Philosophy* 1: 4–14. Also reprinted in Schacht (ed.) (1994).

—— (1993b), *Shame and Necessity*, Berkeley: University of California Press.

Williamson, D. G. (1986), *Bismarck and Germany, 1862–1890*, London: Longman.

Woodruff, Paul (1993), *Thucydides on Justice, Power and Human Nature*, Indianapolis: Hackett.

—— (1999), "Rhetoric and Relativism: Protagoras and Gorgias," in A. A. Long (ed.), *The Cambridge Companion to Early Greek Philosophy*, Cambridge: Cambridge University Press.

Index

action, agency 58–63, 76, 78–9, 147n, 161, 209–11, 214–17, 283n; Nietzsche's theory of 91–104, 112, 157–9; *see also* free will
Adorno, Theodor 297
AEP *see* Anthropocentric Evaluative Practice
aesthetic, aesthetics 32, 35, 41, 144–5, 250, 270–1
affects 20, 91, 99n, 142, 270, 272–3, 275; *see also* drive(s); instincts; interests
agency *see* action
altruism (unegoistic) 57–8, 128–9, 134–5, 154, 184, 187–8, 194–5, 198–9, 235, 292, 299–300; *see also* selflessness
amor fati 85–6, 120, 288
Anaximenes 40
Anderson, Lanier 17–18n

Anderson, Lorin 2n
Anthropocentric Evaluative Practice 171–2; *see also* genealogy
anti-realism *see* value(s), anti-realism about
anti-semitism 34
Antiphon 47
appearance *see* phenomenal world
aristocracy, aristocratic 219, 254, 290
Aristotle 121n
art, artists 33, 56, 122–3, 132, 135, 182, 234, 247–9, 271n
ascetic ideal, ascetic morality 189, 190–1, 204, 221, 226, 232, 235, 239n, 243–4, Ch. 8 *passim*, 302–3
atheism 238–42, 265–6, 279
Autonomy Condition 87, 96–9; *see also* free will

bad *see* good and bad
bad conscience 58, 190, 221, 223–6,
    229–44, 245–6, 257, 262, 263n,
    281, 283–6; and man's "inner
    world" 234–5; moralization of *see*
    guilt
Barnes, Jonathan xiv, 36
Beam, Craig 2n, 10
becoming what one is 83–6
Beethoven 25, 115, 116n, 122–3,
    302
Bentham, Jeremy 130n, 133n, 198
Bergmann, Frithjof 76, 180n, 187–9
Berry, Jessica 266n
Bett, Richard 45–7
Bismarck, Otto von 34
Bittner, Rüdiger 202n, 203n
Bizet 292
blond beast 205n, 233
body 69–71, 84n, 128
Brahmins 253
Brandes, Georg 33, 290–1
Braudel, Fernand 221
breeding 226–7
Brobjer, Thomas 47–8n, 50n, 54n,
    65n, 67, 116n, 181n, 197–8n, 294
Brochard, Victor 50n
Büchner, Ludwig 7, 64–7, 68n,
    69–70
Buddhism 189, 240, 245–6
Burckhardt, Jacob 39n
Burnyeat, Myles 108–9n

Caesar, Julius 116
Callicles, Calliclean 47, 51–3, 124,
    145–6, 177
Camus, Albert 288
capitalism 1, 34, 297
causa sui 94, 98; *see also* free will
Causal Essentialism 82–3, 98; *see
    also* Types, Doctrine of
causation, cause 10–11, 22–3
character 58–63, 82, 89, 201, 214,
    237; "acquired character" 62;
    giving style to 97n, 117–18

chemistry 65–6, 69
Chisholm, Roderick 90n
Christ *see* Jesus
Christianity, Christian(s) 12–13, 16,
    74, 79, 132, 172–3, 184, 186,
    189, 191, 193–7, 204, 220–1,
    238–40, 243, 245, 248, 254n, 255,
    260, 274, 294, 298
Churchlands, Patricia and Paul 63
Clark, Maudemarie xin, xii, xiii,
    xv–xvi, xvii, 2n, 13n, 14–17,
    17–18n, 22, 23, 33, 35n, 57, 76n,
    77n, 139–40, 142, 168–70, 172n,
    181n, 182, 183–4, 187–8, 198n,
    225, 227, 235n, 242n, 276–7,
    291
Classical Determinism *see*
    determinism
Classical Fatalism 82–3
classical philology xiv, 31–2, 35–9,
    66, 71–2, 197, 199–200
Classical Realism 39, 47–53, 71,
    105, 177, 184, 187
compassion (*Mitleid,* pity) 55, 56–8,
    75, 128–9, 187–8, 194, 210, 248,
    292, 298–9
compatibilism 88, 93–4
conscience 173, 223–9, 239, 251,
    254, 273, 302; *see also* bad
    conscience
consciousness 87, 91–3, 95, 100,
    103
Constantine, Emperor 195, 221
Copernicus 281
Cornaro 156–7
Craig, Gordon 34–5
creation, creativity 96–101, 122,
    133, 208, 298–300
cruelty 173, 182, 190, 220, 223–6,
    229n, 231–6, 240–2, 244, 245,
    251, 257, 259, 261–2, 283, 286,
    302; *see also* bad conscience
culture 27–8, 32–3, 35, 129, 132–4,
    185, 205–6, 223, 290, 297,
    299–300, 302

custom, morality of 183n, 225–9
Czolbe, Heinrich 66

Danto, Arthur xiii, 2n, 72, 75, 76n, 147n, 291
Darwin, Charles (Darwinian) 168, 198, 256
debt(s), debtor(s) 224–5, 229–31; contrasted with guilt 237; moralization of 230, 236–42, 243; *see also* bad conscience
decadence 158–9, 191
deconstruction, deconstructionism 1, 14, 38, 43, 291
Deleuze, Gilles 54n, 76n, 202n
DeMan, Paul 14, 38, 71–2, 96
democracy 136, 140, 301
Democritus 39n, 48, 51, 63
Dennett, Daniel 7, 168, 190n
Derrida, Jacques xiv, 1, 2, 38, 291
Descartes, René 67, 275, 282
determinism, deterministic 5, 56, 59, 82–3, 88, 95, 97–8; Classical Determinism defined 82
Detwiler, Bruce 291n, 292, 293n
Diethe, Carol xv–xvi, 235n, 237–8, 242n, 269n, 270n
Dionysian, Dionysus 119–20, 132
Dreyfus, Hubert 2, 167
drive(s) 91, 95, 99–100, 102–3, 155, 187, 251, 252n, 272; *see also* affects; instincts; interests
Dühring 67n
Dummett, Michael 137n

egalitarianism *see* equality
egoism, egoistic 57–8, 183–6, 298; *see also* selfishness
Eleatics 15n, 39n, 44–5
elitism 1, 290
Empedocles 40, 51
empiricism 14, 17n, 39, 43–7, 71–2
Epicurus 63

epiphenomenal, epiphenomenalism 87, 91–3, 95; Kind-Epiphenomenalism 91–2; Token-Epiphenomenalism 92
equality (egalitarianism) 28, 75, 128–9, 135–6, 185, 194, 290, 292, 298–300
error, necessity of 160–1
esoteric moralist: Nietzsche as 296–7
essence, essentialism 2, 8, 12, 25–6, 82–3, 141, 166–7, 170, 215–17
eternal recurrence/return xvii, 119–20, 132, 287–8
evil *see* good and evil
existentialism 1, 287–8

false consciousness 28, 176–7, 181, 221, 280, 283, 295; *see also* morality, in the pejorative sense, normative component of, critique of
falsification thesis 17n
fascism 297
fatalism, fate 52, 60–3, 71–2, 81–8, 98, 101, 157–9, 215; Nietzsche's fatalism defined 81–3; *see also* Causal Essentialism
Feuerbach, Ludwig 64, 65n, 66, 69
food (nutrition) 64, 69–71, 106–7, 111
Foot, Philippa 75, 76n, 77, 138, 144–6, 174n, 298, 300
Förster-Nietzsche, Elizabeth 33
Foucault, Michel 2, 5n, 72, 165–7, 172n
Frankfurt, Harry 93–4
free spirits 116, 130, 265–7
free will, freedom of the will 56, 59–61, 69, 71–2, 78, 80, 210–11, 215–17, 227–8, 230; critique of 87–101 (*Causa Sui* Argument 88–91; Naturalistic Argument 88–9, 91–101); Free Will Thesis 80, 112, 163; and seduction of

language 216; *see also* Autonomy
Condition; compatibilism;
fatalism; will
Freud, Sigmund 2, 5, 7, 11–12, 12n,
95, 224, 228, 233–4

Gardner, Sebastian 12–13n, 259n
Gay, Peter 2
GBM (good/bad morality) *see* good
and bad
GEM (good/evil morality) *see* good
and evil
Gemes, Ken 2n, 159, 161, 171n
genealogy 165–79; and critique
173–9; differences from study of
family pedigree 167–8, 171n; as
fiction? 180–1; and history 165–7,
180; of morality 167–8, 171–2,
182–3, 286; and naturalism
172–3, 182, 188; of punishment
169–72, 225–6; *see also*
Anthropocentric Evaluative
Practice; genetic fallacy
genetic fallacy 173–9; *see also*
morality, Nietzsche's critique of
German Materialism *see*
Materialism, German
Germans, Germany 34–5
Geuss, Raymond xvi, 76n, 77n, 79n,
80n, 113, 125, 165, 167, 172n,
174n, 175n, 291n
Glaucon 51, 53n
God 5, 60, 172–3, 183, 193, 223,
238–42, 245, 247, 261, 265–6,
268, 279, 281; Greek conception
of god(s) 242–4, 284
Goethe 115–17, 120, 122, 132, 151,
295, 298, 300, 302
good and bad 193–4, 199–201,
206–17
good and evil 193–4, 195, 201,
206–17
goodness 46; absolute goodness 107;
objectivity of 108–11, 146–7,
150–5; prudential goodness

106–7, 110, 124–5; *see also*
interests; relationalism
Gorgias 47, 51
Gregory, Frederick 65, 67, 69–70
Grote, George 50
guilt 76, 190, 218, 224–6, 229–30,
232, 233n, 235–44, 260–3, 284,
286, 302; contrasted with debt
237; distinguished from shame
236; *see also* bad conscience
Guthrie, W. K. C. 40–1, 45, 47, 49,
51, 52n, 107–8, 176

happiness 27–8, 128, 129–34, 139,
299, 301
Harm Puzzle 132–4
Hayman, Ronald 67
health 85, 118–19, 123, 131, 158–9,
219
hedonism 52n, 121, 130, 252
Hegel 53–4
Heidegger, Martin xiv, xvi, 291
Helmholtz, Hermann von 44n, 66
Heraclitus 39n, 40–1, 51–2, 63,
106–8
higher men/human beings 74, 78,
79n, 105, 113–14, 115–27, 133,
145–6, 150–3, 157–9, 161–2, 176,
181, 185–7, 212–14, 221, 280,
283, 288, 290, 295, 297, 299,
302; *see also* human
excellence/greatness
Hippocrates 48, 51
Hitler, Adolf 151
Hobbes, Thomas 293n
Holbach, Baron d' 63–4
Hollingdale, R. J. xvi–xvii, 143n
Homer(ic) 205, 236, 285
human excellence/greatness 26–8,
35, 86, 114, 126, 129, 132–4,
136, 161–2, 185, 288, 290, 296,
300, 302; *see also* higher
men/human beings
human nature 2–5, 25–6, 47; *see*
also naturalism

Humboldt, Wilhelm von 35
Hume 2, 4–5, 10, 11–12, 13n, 73, 88, 93, 198
Hunt, Lester xii, xiii, 45n, 138n, 147n, 291n
Hutcheson, Francis 198

idealism, idealist 15, 44, 53–4, 66, 269
illiberal(ism) 290–1, 300
instincts 75, 127–8, 158, 190, 225n, 231–4, 244, 252; see also affects; drives; interests
interests 20, 79, 105–12, 177, 272–4; objective 109–10; see also affects; drive(s); goodness; instincts
internal critique see morality, Nietzsche's critique of
interpretation 37–8
Islam 189

Janaway, Christopher 55–6, 246n, 247n, 248n, 253n, 264n, 271
Janz, Curt 35n, 65, 67
Jaspers, Karl 142
Jesus 240, 244
Jews, Judaism 50, 189, 195–6, 219–20
Johnston, Mark 277–8
Jones, Ernest 2

Kane, Robert 88n
Kant, Kantian 10, 12–13n, 15–7, 18n, 20, 23, 54, 57, 65, 73, 79, 80n, 84n, 101, 102n, 129, 161–3, 212n, 250, 269, 271, 274, 276–7, 290n
Kaufmann, Walter xiii, xv, 35n, 75–6, 85n, 121n, 135n, 138n, 142, 174n, 181, 197n, 207n, 242n, 291
Kitcher, Philip 267
knowledge 13–22, 66, 71, 247n, 268–79, 291; limitations on (value of) 41–3, 160–1; see also perspectivism; truth

Koons, Robert C. 82n
Korsgaard, Christine 291

Laertius, Diogenes 36
La Mettrie 63, 67
Lange, Friedrich 15, 21, 23, 54, 65–6, 68n, 70
LaRochefoucauld 12n, 183
"last man"/last men 27–8, 130, 297, 300–1
Lecky, W. E. H. 198
Leiter, Brian xii, xvii, 2n, 3n, 8, 13–14, 33, 38, 48, 52n, 57, 76n, 116n, 138n, 139, 148n, 154, 183, 227, 268n, 276n, 291n
Leucippus 63
life 256; affirmation of 119–20, 287–8; value of 57–8; see also morality; value(s)
Locke, John 293n
Lucretius 63

Machiavelli 49
MacIntyre, Alasdair 146, 165
Magnus, Bernd xviin, 75n, 143n
Mann, Joel 48n
Manu 293–5
Marx, Karl (Marxian) 5, 28, 64n, 221, 293n, 300
master morality 171–2, 197, 200n, 201, 206–8, 218
masters see nobility
materialism 6, 11, 23–5, 63, 65, 68
Materialism, German 7, 35, 51–2, 54, 63–71, 72, 200n
May, Simon xin, 101n, 125n, 180n, 201, 202n, 204n, 236, 291n
Migotti, Mark 181n, 200n, 214n, 218–19
Mill, John Stuart 130, 139, 198
Millikan, Ruth 7
M-Naturalism see naturalism
Moleschott, Jacob 64, 66, 69–70
Montinari, Mazzino xvii, 139–40, 143n

moral facts 147n, 148
moral psychology 189, 221, 286–7, 290, 302–3
morality: of custom 183n, 225–9; as harmful to higher human beings *see* in the pejorative sense, normative component of, critique of; as harmful to life 125–7; as matter of taste 147, 147–8n, 153; naturalized account of 3, 6, 8–9, 11, 182–4, 188, 194, 202, 227; Nietzsche's critique of 26–8, 56, Ch. 3 *passim*, Ch. 4 *passim*, 173–9, 280 (Catalogue Approach to 74–5, 77; internal critique 76–7, 174–5; Origins Approach to 75–7; Presuppositions Approach to 76–7; summarized 161–2; Universality Approach to 76–7); origin of 28, 53, 75, 173–9, 182–8, 198–9, 281; in the pejorative sense (MPS) (and bad conscience 244; causal powers of 177–9; defined 74, 78–9, 161–3, 212; descriptive component of 78–81 (critique of 81–112, 159–161); normative component of 78–9, 127–9 (critique of 113–15, 127–36, 150, 155, 157–9, 161, 179, 185–9, 221, 280, 283, 295, 297–302)); as projection 149, 203; rational foundation for 10; Schopenhauer's view of 57–8; scope of (Scope Problem) 74–7, 161; as symptom 9; universal applicability of 75–7, 80–1, 104–12, 113–14; *see also* Callicles, Calliclean; genealogy; master morality; slave morality; value(s)
Morgan, George 138n, 291n
motive(s) 80, 92, 101–4, 174–5, 183–5, 187–8, 208–9; Kant's view of 102n; *see also* action; free will

Mourelatos, A. P. D. 176
MPS *see* morality, in the pejorative sense

Nachlass xvi–xviii, 18, 65n, 138–9, 143–4, 252
Nagel, Thomas 68, 291
Napoleon 116
nationalism 297
naturalism, naturalist 2–3, 26, 45, 63–4, 71, 226, 291; methodological naturalism (M-Naturalism) 3–7, 21, 25, 39–41, 43, 63, 68, 71–2; Nietzsche's naturalism 6–11, 23, 26, 28, 35, 38, 43, 78, 148–9, 155–9, 172–3, 182–3, 191, 281–3, 290; substantive naturalism (S-Naturalism) 3, 5–6, 11, 24–5, 63 (*see also* human nature; materialism; morality, naturalized account of; will to power)
nature, human *see* human nature
Nazism 290–1
Nehamas, Alexander xvi, 2n, 38, 52n, 71–2, 76, 83–4n, 96–7, 113, 115–16n, 166n, 207n, 291
Neurath, Otto 274–5
Newton, Newtonian 4
nihilism 55–6, 58, 246, 250n, 256, 263–4, 265, 267, 279, 284–5, 287–8
nobility, noble(s) (masters) 120–2, 150, 190, 193–5, 200–1, 203–4, 209–14, 217, 219, 242, 246, 257, 259, 281, 286
noumenal world/objects (things-in-themselves) 15–21, 23, 38n, 54–5, 57–8, 66, 269, 271, 276–8
Nussbaum, Martha 292–3n
nutrition *see* food

Odysseus 7
Oedipus 7, 236, 243, 257

Overbeck, Franz 190n
overman 287n

Parmenides 39n
Pascal 70
Pericles 48, 205
perspectivism 12–21, 248, 268–79;
    Skeptical Reading of 13–14, 20,
    45; *see also* knowledge; truth
pessimism *see* nihilism
phenomenal world/objects (world as
    it appears) 21, 23, 38n, 54–5,
    57–60, 66, 269, 276–7, 279
phenomenalism 18n, 45
philology *see* classical philology
philosophy 67–8, 249–52, 265, 273;
    see also naturalism; value(s),
    creating/legislating
physicalism *see* materialism
physiology xvii, 8–9, 24, 64–72,
    88–9, 95–6, 140, 203, 221, 256–8,
    262
pity (*Mitleid*) *see* compassion
Pizer, John 166n
Plato, Platonic xiii, 15–16, 39, 44,
    46, 48, 50–1, 166, 266, 271
Poellner, Peter xiii, xvi, 17n, 18–20,
    90n, 202n, 268n, 270, 276–7,
    277n
polemic 180–1, 206, 221
political philosophy: Nietzsche's
    292–7
politics 292, 295–7, 302
postmodern, postmodernism 2, 14,
    38n, 43, 182n, 265, 269n, 274, 290
power *see* will to power
practical reason 10
pragmatism 1, 277–9
predestination 60; *see also* fatalism
Presocratics 15n, 35, 39–53, 71–2,
    267
Price, Huw 5n
priest(s), priestly 119n, 191, 206,
    219–20, 245, 247, 251, 254–5,
    260–4, 268, 284, 286, 295

promises, promise-making 226–8
Protagoras, Protagorean 45–7, 106–8
psychoanalysis 1, 89
psychologist, psychology 172–3,
    252, 283; *see also* naturalism
psycho-physical facts 8–9, 91, 95,
    105, 148, 157; *see also* type-facts
punishment 169–72, 225–6, 230,
    261; *see also* genealogy

Quine, W. V. O. 3, 26, 63, 274–5

Rabinow, Paul 2, 167
Railton, Peter 3n, 6, 45, 106–12,
    211n
rationalism 32, 43, 285–6n, 289
reactive 202, 209, 211; *see also*
    ressentiment
realism *see* Classical Realism;
    value(s), realism about
Rée, Paul 197, 198n, 199
relationalism 45–6, 106–8, 111, 147;
    see also goodness
relativism 44–7, 107, 275
religion 221, 235, 238–42, 283–4;
    see also ascetic ideal; Buddhism;
    Christianity; God; guilt; Islam;
    Jews
repression 228
ressentiment 9, 75, 119n, 173–4,
    182, 189, 193–4, 196, 201–6,
    210, 214, 217–18, 221, 223,
    225, 246, 258–60, 262–4, 281,
    286
revaluation of values *see* value(s)
reverence *see* self
rhetoric 47, 154–5, 161, 176, 181,
    283n, 294
Richardson, John xii, xiii, xvi, 201n,
    202n, 208n, 252n
Ridley, Aaron xin, 129n, 226n, 259n
Risse, Mathias 190n, 225n, 226,
    229n, 238, 239n, 242n
Ritschl, Friedrich 31, 31–2n, 36,
    38

Romans, Roman Empire, Rome
189–90, 194, 196, 205, 216, 221,
242, 254–5, 285–6
Rorty, Richard 1, 2n, 11, 21–2, 83n
Rousseau, Jean-Jacques 213, 293n
Russell, Bertrand 293n

Salaquarda, Jörg 65n
Schaberg, William 33n
Schacht, Richard xvi, 2n, 13n, 56,
74–5, 76n, 101n, 125–6, 138–9,
144, 146, 293n
Schnädelbach, Herbert 44n, 54, 64,
66n, 67, 71
Schopenhauer 10, 12n, 15, 17n, 35,
40, 51–2, 53–63, 65–6, 68n, 69n,
72, 81, 83, 86n, 90, 98, 101,
116n, 249–50, 257, 264n, 269n,
270–1, 274, 289n, 297
Schutte, Ofelia 75, 76n
science 6–7, 11, 14, 16, 21–2, 33,
36, 41, 44, 51, 65–8, 71, 96–7,
143n, 248, 264–7, 272, 274,
279–83
scope problem see morality
self 58, 84n, 103, 254; affirmation
of 209, 211, 216; creation of
96–101; love of 127–8, 134–5,
185, 299 (see also egoism;
selfishness); mastery of 99–101;
overcoming of 116n, 262;
preservation of 254, 263;
reverence for 120–1, 149, 212–13;
transparency of 78, 80, 101–4,
112, 163 (see also morality, in the
pejorative sense, descriptive
component of, critique of); see
also action; character
selfishness (self-interest) 126, 183,
199; see also egoism
selflessness 75, 128, 134–5, 175n,
235; see also altruism
sex, sexuality 55–6, 127, 195, 246,
250, 261, 302
Sextus Empiricus 265n

shame 236
Sher, Itai 171n
Silk, M. S. 33, 36–7
Similarity Thesis 80, 104–12, 163;
see also morality, in the
pejorative sense, descriptive
component of, critique of
Sinhababu, Neil 247n
Skeptical Reading see perspectivism
skeptics, skepticism 265–6, 274,
276, 279, 291
slaves, slave revolt in morals, slave
morality 75, 124, 152, 171–2,
174, 181, 189–91, 194–5, 197,
200–6, 209, 213, 216–22, 223,
246, 253, 257–9, 286
Smart, J. J. C. 63, 79n
S-Naturalism see naturalism
Socrates, Socratic 39, 43, 50–1, 267,
285–6n; see also rationalism
Solomon, Maynard 122–3
Solomon, Robert 76n
Sophists, Sophistic 10, 35, 39–53,
71, 105, 107–8, 176
Sophocles 48
Spencer, Herbert 121
Spinoza 4, 7, 41, 51–2, 63, 116n
Stack, George 65n, 66
Stegmaier, Werner xin
Stern, J. P. 33, 36–7
Stoics 140–1
Strawson, Galen 89–90, 94n, 98
Stroud, Barry 5
style see character
suffering 56, 72, 128–34, 185, 220,
232, 234, 256–63, 267, 284–8,
299, 301, 303
supernatural, supernaturalism 5, 11,
25, 172–3, 247
Swensen, Alan xin, xv–xvi, 181n,
182, 198n, 235n, 242n

Taylor, Charles 68
Tertullian 204, 254
Thales 39n, 40–1, 267

Thatcher, David xin, 181n, 198n
thing-in-itself/things-in-themselves
see noumenal world
Thrasymachus 47, 51
Thucydides 12n, 39n, 47–51, 184, 205
Transparency of the Self Thesis *see* self, transparency of
truth 13–22, 154–5, 247n, 265–70, 275–81, 291; value of 42–3, 159, 266–8, 278–80; *see also* knowledge; perspectivism; will to truth
type-facts 8–10, 71–2, 78, 91–2, 94–8, 100, 102, 105–6, 112, 148–9, 155, 157–8, 217
Types, Doctrine of 8, 68, 91, 157; *see also* Causal Essentialism

unconscious (non-conscious) 89, 91–3, 95, 103, 155
unegoistic *see* altruism
utilitarian, utilitarianism 74, 79n, 129–30, 133n, 139, 290n, 300

value(s): anti-realism about 137–8, 146–55, 159–61; creating/ legislating 6n, 11, 41–2, 68, 97–8, 122, 143n, 195, 204, 267; epistemic 13–14, 154–5, 160 and life 125–7; moral 28, 74, 106, 147–55 (*see also* morality); non-moral (prudential) *see* goodness, prudential; realism about 136–46, 155; revaluation of 3, 26–9, 43, 56, 74, 76, 86, 118, 136, 150, 155, 179, 181, 188, 191, 194–7, 202–3, 232, 253, 283, 293n; role in causing action 96–8

Velleman, J. David 90, 92, 94, 100
Vitzthum, Richard 64–5
Vogt, Karl 64n, 65
Voltaire 116n

Wagner, Richard 32–3, 55, 248–9
Watson, Gary 88, 90n, 94
Weber, Max 1, 146
Weinberg, Steven 274
welfare *see* goodness, prudential
Westphal, Kenneth 13n, 38
Whitman, James 32n, 36n, 37, 38n
Wilcox, John 13n, 14, 138n, 143n, 153, 246n
will 69, 80, 88, 92–3, 263–4, 288; freedom of *see* free will; for Schopenhauer 55–6, 58–9, 59n, 63, 250
will to power xvii, 8, 50, 79, 105, 124, 126, 138–44, 173, 177–81, 191, 221, 226, 247–55, 258n, 261, 263, 281
will to truth 42, 248, 265, 267–8, 278–9, 302; *see also* truth, value of
Williams, Bernard 1, 76n, 79n, 236, 291
Wissenschaft 35–7, 39, 41; contrasted with wisdom (*Weisheit*) 41–3, 267; *see also* science
Wittgenstein, Ludwig 170
Woodruff, Paul 45, 47, 50, 176

Zarathustra 27–8, 53n, 84n, 115n, 130, 147, 150, 244, 245, 287, 300–1